John Thrupp

The Anglo-Saxon home

A history of the domestic institutions and customs of England

John Thrupp

The Anglo-Saxon home
A history of the domestic institutions and customs of England

ISBN/EAN: 9783337204174

Printed in Europe, USA, Canada, Australia, Japan

Cover: Foto ©Andreas Hilbeck / pixelio.de

More available books at **www.hansebooks.com**

THE
ANGLO-SAXON HOME.

THE

ANGLO-SAXON HOME:

A

HISTORY OF THE DOMESTIC INSTITUTIONS

AND CUSTOMS OF ENGLAND,

FROM THE FIFTH TO THE

ELEVENTH CENTURY.

By JOHN THRUPP.

———

LONDON:

LONGMAN, GREEN, LONGMAN, & ROBERTS,

14, LUDGATE HILL.

———

M.DCCC.LXII.

LONDON: T. RICHARDS, 37, GREAT QUEEN STREET.

PREFACE.

THE materials which exist for a history of the social life of our Anglo-Saxon forefathers would not be abundant, even if they were all trustworthy; but unhappily a large proportion of them cannot be so considered. We have a very valuable collection of laws, the bulk of which are of undoubted authenticity; and we have an immense number of charters, of which a considerable proportion are *known* to be forgeries, and a still greater number are regarded with suspicion. We also possess numerous chronicles and histories which were written at a very early period; but the majority of them have been more or less discredited by modern criticism. They nevertheless afford a great amount of valuable information, though the numerous errors they contain, particularly as to names and dates, prove that they cannot always be implicitly relied upon. These inaccuracies, however, are of more importance to the historian and biographer than to the student of social history. This may be explained by an illustration. Let us suppose that we find in the legislation of a particular century numerous laws punishing the crime of stabbing men when drinking, and that we find in the chronicles of the same period three or four accounts of kings or princes who were stabbed when drinking by a step-mother, brother, or courtier, at times and places which are mentioned. In each of these stories a critic might possibly point out an error as to a date, place, or person. This would much inconvenience a writer of biography; but to the student of the history of society, who values the story solely as a confirmation of what he had already learnt from other sources, viz., that a particular vice was remarkably prevalent in a particular century, the errors of detail are of minor consequence. The chronicles may therefore often be used as evidence of general customs, when they cannot be relied on to prove particular facts. In those instances in which the chronicler lived at the period of which he wrote, and was generally believed and respected by his cotemporaries and immediate successors (as was the case with Bede), it is comparatively immaterial, for *the purpose of forming an opinion as to the manners of the time*, whether his anecdotes are true or false. It is enough that they were so consistent with what was *then* deemed probable, that no one *at that time* doubted their truth.

We also possess some Anglo-Saxon poetry. One poem, that of Beowulf, throws light on the customs of an almost pre-historic period ; and some of the shorter poems (published in the *Codex Exoniensis*), such as *The Scop's Tale*, and *The Fortunes of Men*, are useful to the student of social history.

The illustrations of MSS. have proved of great service to writers on domestic manners, architecture, furniture, costume, and sports and pastimes ; and a very important

amount of information has been derived from the numerous collections of antiquities which have been formed in
various places ; but where, as in these pages, the main
object of the writer is to trace the history of domestic
civilisation, laws and legal documents are by far the
most trustworthy and valuable evidence.

The work most frequently referred to in such of the
following chapters as discuss the relative position of husband and wife, parent and child, master and servant, differences of rank, and vices and virtues, is *The Ancient
Laws and Institutes of England*, published by the Record
Commissioners. Next in value, I am inclined to place
The Codex Diplomaticus Anglo-Saxonum, edited by the
late Mr. Kemble. *The Ancient Laws and Institutes of
Wales*, also published by the Record Commissioners, is
a work of great value.

These works relate exclusively to England, and they
furnish us with a more valuable amount of knowledge
than can be derived from any other source. They do
not, however, contain a full exposition of the laws and
customs of England. They are merely fragments, and
on many important matters their teaching is scanty and
obscure. I have occasionally endeavoured to supply
from the laws of the Northmen (or Danes), and from
those of the Angles, Saxons, Jutes, and Frisians of the
continent, some of the information which is not contained in our own ; but I have only done so in those
cases in which our own and continental customs were
substantially the same.

It was by the Danes that the eastern and northern

parts of this country were conquered, and permanently occupied, and Danish monarchs for many years sat on the throne of England. The Danish settlers preserved and most jealously defended their native laws and customs, and were governed by the Dane-lagh, and not by the English law, down to, if not after, the time of the Norman Conquest.

The other tribes named, though the laws of all were substantially the same, retained their local customs in the different districts in which they settled; and through many centuries we read of the laws of Wessex, Kent, Northumbria, and Mercia, as distinguished from one another. When, therefore, our knowledge of the customs of the Danish and Teutonic colonists who settled here is scanty or obscure, we may fairly endeavour to supply the deficiency by a reference to the institutions of the countries whence they came.

In addition to the codes of the tribes already named, we possess the laws of several cognate nations, including those who formed the empire of Charlemagne, of the Franks, the Lombards, the Wisigoths, and others. All these codes are curiously alike, though they differ in matters of detail, and occasionally, though very rarely, in matters of great importance.[1]

I will add but one other observation on this subject. The whole of the ancient laws of all these nations and tribes, though usually enacted by the kings and public

[1] I think that the most important differences are the laws of the Salian Franks restricting the inheritance of women, and the laws of the Lombards and others relating to the judicial combat. Neither of these laws ever prevailed in Anglo-Saxon England.

assemblies, were reduced into writing by the clergy, who in so doing modified them very considerably; and this they always did with a view to reduce them to accordance with the civil law of Rome, and the canon law of the church. They also borrowed their legal phraseology from these sources.

As the ecclesiastical regulations introduced into this country by the Christian clergy were all based on the teaching of the catholic church, no apology is necessary for a reference to foreign councils as evidence of their meaning.

To the chapters devoted to the main topic of this work, viz., the history of domestic civilisation, I have added a few others to complete the picture of domestic life in England from the fifth to the eleventh century. I should have added a chapter on domestic manners and architecture, but this subject has been lately treated at length by my friend Mr. Thomas Wright.[1] I avail myself of the opportunity which a preface affords, to express my obligations to him for his careful perusal of the following pages prior to their publication, for many valuable suggestions, and for the assistance he has afforded me in passing them through the press.

I have in the appendix given a glossary of the few technical terms with which I have been unable to dispense.

J. T.

7, Warwick Square, S.W.
    April 21, 1862.

---

[1] *History of Domestic Manners and Sentiments of England during the Middle Ages*, by Thomas Wright, F.S.A.

CONTENTS.

b

CONTENTS. ix

THE ANGLO-SAXON HOME.

INTRODUCTION.

It is the object of the following pages to give a true picture of the domestic life of our Anglo-Saxon fore-fathers, and in so doing to trace the gradual development among them of the domestic affections and of the morals and manners of private life.

There are numerous works by distinguished writers on the history of the Anglo-Saxon Church, and on its theological opinions. There are also many, by scholars of no less eminence, exclusively devoted to the political state of our ancient commonwealth. The literature of the period has been examined and illustrated with the greatest learning and ability; and its civil and military annals have been traced and criticised in all the most famous histories of England. There is not, however, to the best of my belief, any work devoted to the history of the Anglo-Saxon HOME.

It is true that, in most of the standard histories of the Anglo-Saxons, a chapter will be found giving an account of their "manners and customs"; but as this is merely accessory to the main object of the work, it is naturally very brief and generally very scanty. There is usually some account of what is called the social condition of the

B

Anglo-Saxons, but no attempt has been made to point out the different eras of civilization through which the morals and manners of the people passed. There is, in fact, no history of their social development; yet there was as much difference between the morals and manners of the time of Hengist and Horsa and those of the reign of Edward the Confessor, as between the customs of England under Henry VII and those of the present day. To describe them generally, without reference to any particular period, is to pourtray a social state, which, existing partly in one age and partly in another, had as a whole no existence at all.

Some slight perception of this difficulty appears to have occurred to the mind of the anonymous author of a deservedly popular history; as he states, in effect, that it is unnecessary to attempt to trace the social advance of the Anglo-Saxon people, seeing that they never made any such advance worthy of notice. If, however, we bear in mind that they passed from a state of society in which women were bought by their husbands, and had no legal protection of life or limb, to one in which the sex occupied a position of freedom and security, not inferior to that which it enjoys at the present day; from an age when infanticide was lawful and children might be legally sold, to one in which they were nearly as carefully tended as they are now; from a state of barbarism in which domestic servants could be slain at pleasure, and when every man had a right to wage private war on whom he pleased, to a period when the lives and property even of slaves were duly protected, and when law and morality had put an end to what was at first a state of incessant bloodshed: it is difficult to comprehend how it can be said that there was no social progress. And if to these considerations we add, that we can follow the religious history of the Anglo-Saxon from the time of his being an ignorant and bloodthirsty heathen to his state of demi-conversion, and thence until he became an enlightened Christian, there can be no doubt of the fact that an immense advance in civilization, morality, and religion, took place during the six centuries which elapsed between the arrival of Hengist the Saxon and that of William the Norman.[1]

In tracing the social progress made during this long period, it may be convenient to divide it into three eras, and briefly to point out the characteristics which distinguished each of them. It must be admitted that we cannot fix the exact limit when any of them commenced or ended, yet their duration may be easily explained in general terms. The first may be called the early Saxon, the second the Saxon-Danish, and the third the Saxon-Norman period.

The first of these periods would occupy the time when the colonists from the mouth of the Elbe were arriving in ever increasing numbers on the southern and eastern coasts, and were gradually reducing the natives under their subjection. This period would extend from the arrival of Hengist and Horsa in the middle of the fifth century to the youth of king Egbert or the end of the eighth. The second era would embrace the years that elapsed between the habitual invasions of the Danes and their final and peaceful settlement in the country, or from A.D. 787 to the reign of Cnut. The third or Norman period of Anglo-Saxon history would be that comprised between the time of Cnut's death and the Norman conquest.

---

[1] "'Saxons' is another vague word, which has probably concealed as much ignorance as any word except Druids. It generally means confusedly all Englishmen who lived between 445 and 1066—that is, during a space as long as that which separates us from Henry III. Most people seem to believe that 'all the Saxons,' like 'all the ancients,' lived at once, and that Hengist and Harold may have been most intimate friends."—*Saturday Review*, April 27, 1861.

These three eras were marked by decided differences in manners and morals, and by equally marked distinctions in laws and language.

The exact period at which the inhabitants of Northern Germany and the islands at the mouth of the Elbe first began to colonise this country is not known; but it is certain that long before the famous migration under the leadership of Hengist and Horsa, the Teutonic peoples had formed settlements on the northern and eastern coasts of England and in the northern parts of France. It is probable that their visits first took place at least three or four hundred years prior to this era, and that at their earliest coming they arrived either in single families or in small numbers.

There is no reason for supposing that they were then otherwise than welcome guests. There were in the south and east of England hundreds of miles of uncleared forest, there were boundless marshes which any one might usefully drain, and broad and fertile plains which no one occupied. To these the stranger was welcome, for in taking them he deprived no man of anything; and his labours in clearing and cultivating the soil tended to the good of the community. He might also have been welcome in the Roman towns, where the number of Roman colonists was rapidly decreasing, and in need of recruits from abroad. At that time the arrival of the Saxon was rather a benefit than a disadvantage, and there can be no doubt that the Anglo-Roman and Anglo-Saxon races at first intermingled in a friendly spirit.[1] But the number of the emigrants constantly and rapidly increased, and they came in larger companies, while the quantity of

[1] At Canterbury, Colchester, Rochester, and other places, we find Roman and Saxon interments in the same cemetery; and in an extensive burial ground at Osengal in the Isle of Thanet, a Roman interment in a leaden coffin was met with. Wright's *Celt, Roman, and Saxon*, p. 392.

unoccupied land as rapidly diminished; and visits, that were at first innocuous, soon became not only unwelcome, but aggressive. The Saxon came hither to settle, peaceably if he could; but if not, still to settle. It was absolutely necessary that he should possess land, and if he could not obtain it by amicable means, he must take it by force. The necessities of this position immediately placed him in a state of antagonism to the previous inhabitants, and in one of open warfare with their Roman governors.[1] It is, therefore, not surprising to find that long before the abandonment of this country by the Romans, these immigrants had given the Imperial Government so much trouble, that a military officer of high rank had been specially appointed, with the title of "count of the Saxon shore" in Britain, for the protection of the eastern and southern coasts and the control of the Saxon system of forcible colonization.

The period during which this system was carried on is, however, for the purposes of social history, almost prehistoric; for we have no materials for a description of the social life of the inhabitants of these realms prior to the middle of the fifth century. At that time vast numbers of persons migrated from the coasts of the German ocean, from the mouths of the Elbe, the Eider, and the Rhine, and from Holstein, Holland, Zealand, Westphalia, Saxony, and countries even further north, to these shores. All these, though composed of different tribes, were of cognate origin; and after their arrival received the general designation of Anglo-Saxons.[2]

The three most powerful bodies, of which they were composed, were the old Saxons, who inhabited the southern parts of Holstein; the Angles from the Baltic

---

[1] *Zosimus*, lib. vi, c. 6.
[2] They are said, by some writers, to have been called Saxons from *sax*, *saex*, *sœx*, *saks*, a sort of long knife or sword, which they always carried on their persons.

shores of the same duchy ; and the Jutes from Jutland.
It is sometimes pretended that these tribes were distinguished by many and marked differences of laws and
customs, but the instances quoted are rather diversities of
language or dialect than of political or social institutions.[1]
On their settlement in this country the Angles are supposed to have taken possession of the northern and
eastern counties, the Jutes to have settled in Kent and
the Isle of Wight, and the Saxons to have selected the
southern and south-western shores ; but of whatever
tribes they were, and in whatever part they settled, they
systematically paved the way for the arrival of more
numerous and powerful bodies of their race.

When the followers of Hengist and Horsa landed in
Kent they found a Teutonic population ready to receive
them, and had no difficulty in founding in that country
the first of the kingdoms of the Octarchy.   Hengist (for
Horsa was killed soon after his arrival)[2] became king of
Kent in A.D. 473, and about twenty years afterwards,
according to the traditions handed down to us by the
Anglo-Saxon annalists, Ella founded the Saxon kingdom
of Sussex.

The tide of invasion seems to have swept along the
southern coast ; and the next kingdom in order of date
was Wessex, destined to be the division of the conquered
territory which, through Cerdic, and his descendants,
Ecgbert, Alfred the Great, and Athelstan, gave to the

---

[1] The fact so much insisted on, that Kent is divided into "lathes" while other English shires were divided into "hundreds" or wapentakes, does not seem to me very material, as they were all originally divisions for military purposes. The existence of the Jutish law of gavelkind in Kent, whereby the land descends to all the sons equally, in lieu of to the eldest son, and whereby the heir becomes of age at fifteen instead of at twenty-one, is instanced by Dr. Lappenberg : and this would have been important evidence had it not been the universal law of England prior to the Conquest.   Selden, *Analect.*, l. ii, c. 7.

[2] Nennii *Historia Britannorum*, c. xlvi.

whole of England a series of kings, from whom the reigning monarch of this country derives her title to the British crown.

Having, according to these same traditions, occupied nearly the whole of the southern coasts, the invaders attacked the eastern shores, where they also found large bodies of their fellow countrymen. In Norfolk, Suffolk, Cambridge, and Ely, was founded the kingdom of East Anglia; and about the same time that of the East Saxons in Middlesex, Essex, and Hertfordshire. A few years afterwards the Angles possessed themselves of the eastern coast between Newcastle and Edinburgh, and formed the kingdom of Bernicia; and immediately afterwards that of Deira in Yorkshire and part of Lancashire. These two subsequently formed the kingdom of Northumbria.

It was not till about a hundred and forty years after their acquisition of Kent, that the Angles spread themselves over the centre of England, and founded (A.D. 586) the kingdom of Mercia, which was for many years the most prosperous and powerful of the Anglo-Saxon states.

It is not to be supposed that the previous inhabitants tamely surrendered their country to the invader. For fifty years they bravely defended themselves, under leaders whose fame has been shadowed in romance and poetry, under such names as Aurelius, Uther Pendragon, and Arthur. The struggle was hardly ended till the beginning of the eighth century, when the Britons had either become amalgamated with the invaders, reduced to serfdom, or driven into the fastnesses of Wales and Cornwall.[1]

---

[1] *Archæology of Wales*, vol. i, 4, 13, and 57. The Britons for many centuries disbelieved in the death of king Arthur, or at least expected him to return alive and deliver them from Saxon domination. — William of Newb., *Hist. proem*, p. 13; Will. Malmesb., *De Gestis Reg. Angliæ*, lib. i, c. 1; Johannes de Fordun, *Scott. Chron.*, l. iii, c. 25; Nennii *Historia Britannorum*, cc. lxii et lxiii.

It was but a few years after the establishment of the
kingdom of Mercia that the most important event in the
annals of the Saxons occurred.

In A.D. 595, St. Augustine, sent hither by pope Gregory
the Great, converted Ethelbert king of Kent to the
Christian faith; and his conversion was rapidly followed
by that of his subjects.   After this period the whole country became gradually converted to a species of Christianity.
It is not possible to give to the religion at first adopted
by the Saxons a higher title, because it did not put an
end to the public worship of idols, or restrain the erecting
in the same church of an altar to our Lord and Saviour
and of another to Woden or Friga; nor did it prevent the
offering up of the Eucharist and a sacrifice to devils in
the same edifice, almost at the same time, and through
the agency of the same ministers.[1]

Gregory the Great had desired that the heathen temples
should not be pulled down, but purified and applied to
Christian purposes; and that the new converts should
not be required to abandon their savage modes of worship, but to change the object of them.   They were to be
induced gradually to modify their heathen practices, so
that by degrees their evil tendencies might evaporate, and
their ceremonies, without being destroyed, become imbued
with a Christian feeling.[2]   The result of this teaching, or
of an injudicious application of it, was an era in which
the nation professed and practised a curious combination
of improved heathendom and debased Christianity.

The fifty or sixty years which succeeded the arrival of
Saint Augustine in England are sometimes spoken of in
these pages as the era of Saint Augustine, and form a
second subdivision of the first Saxon era.

[1] Henr. Huntind., l. iii; Bede, *Hist.
Eccles.*, l. ii, c. 15.
[2] The authorities for this statement are Bede, *Hist. Eccles.*, l. i, c.
29 ; Opera Gregorii Papæ, iv, 387 ;
and Henr. Huntind., l. iii.

The period that immediately followed it was one of the most brilliant in Anglo-Saxon annals. It was adorned by men of the highest character for learning and ability, and had reason to be proud of archbishops Theodore and Ecgbert, of the venerable Bede, of Aldhelm, Wilfrid, St. Boniface, and many others, whose names are illustrious even at the present day. During this period not only the canon but the civil law of Rome was extensively taught in England; schools were established and numerously attended, in which classical literature was successfully cultivated; libraries were formed, and a constant communication maintained with the learned of France, Germany, and Italy. Written codes of law were compiled and promulgated, and justice systematically administered. Very numerous and extensive monasteries were built, and monastic discipline was adopted and strictly observed by a very large and energetic body of men. Of this period I shall sometimes speak as the era of archbishop Theodore. If it be taken (as it may be) as extending from his time to the death of Ecgbert archbishop of York (A.D. 766), it witnessed not only the success of monastic institutions in England, but the beginning of their corruption and decay. The terrible results to England of their too great extension, and the abandonment within their walls of all that really constituted monasticism, while they were crowded with unwarlike kings and idle nobles, will be dwelt on fully hereafter.

It was but a few years after the death of the great archbishop of York, that an event occurred which was second in its national importance to none in Anglo-Saxon history save the conversion of the nation to the Christian faith. In the middle of the eighth century, according to the Anglo-Saxon chronicle, but probably at an earlier date, the systematic invasion of this country by the Danes

commenced. At first the Danes were merely pirates, who
came in the summer to plunder, burn, and slaughter, and
departed at the approach of winter, laden with booty and
slaves ; but the transitory character of their visits was
not destined to be of long duration.

At the time of their first appearance king Ecgbert was
a young man, but during his lifetime the character of
their forays rapidly changed. Year after year the frequency of their inroads and the strength of their fleets
increased; and unhappily for the Saxons the duration
of their stay increased also. In the year 851 they for
the first time wintered in the Isle of Thanet, the dearest
territory of the men of Kent, and from that time to their
final amalgamation with the Saxon, the country was subjected to the horrors of constant foreign invasion and
civil war. During the whole of the ninth century the
Danish fleets surrounded England "as with a net," and
the most energetic monarchs were unable to hurry from
north to south, and from east to west, with sufficient
rapidity to repulse the innumerable hordes that poured
like a deluge from all sides and involved the country in
universal ruin.

The result of such a state of misery soon became evident
in the social condition of the people. The numerous
monasteries which Theodore and others had erected or
endowed were plundered and burnt, their libraries were
destroyed, their scholars were dispersed, and the clergy
and the monks were put to the sword. Learning, piety,
and morality disappeared, and the nation became ignorant, unjust, cruel, and rapacious; and yet when peace
was partially restored, at the conclusion of the reign of
Alfred, some benefits were found to have arisen from the
fiery trials to which the country had been subjected. The
centuries of warfare which had passed had dealt the death

blow to all that remained of the patriarchal system of the primitive Anglo-Saxon. In such a time neither individuals nor families could stand alone, and a far more close and extensive military and political organisation became necessary. The responsibilities and independence of families were rapidly lost in those of tythings, hundreds, or "weapon-takes," and the rights of these were soon merged in the more important combinations of counties; while the counties themselves were formed into divisions under one executive authority. Numerous petty kingdoms altogether disappeared from the scene, and the larger kingdoms of the Heptarchy, after absorbing all minor powers, were themselves blended together, and shortly afterwards, under king Athelstan, became England.

The same necessities which controlled political society coerced individuals. Humble freemen and small landowners could no longer protect themselves, and the Anglo-Saxon churl or yeoman was glad to surrender his allodial land to some powerful earl who could afford him protection, and to receive it back again from him as a tenant for life or years, paying rent or doing suit and service. At the later part of this era he could, if he preferred it, surrender his land to some rich abbey or monastery, the ability of which was often more ample both for war and peace than that of any but the most powerful nobles. His only other resource was to fly to a large town, and endeavour to obtain the protection of the burghers, who in many cases were collectively powerful enough to set at defiance nobles, bishops, and even kings. These wars also laid the foundation of something like the feudal system, and gave rise to a military aristocracy, totally different from that of the patriarchal nobles of royal or divine descent.

Towards the conclusion of the reign of king Alfred,

there came a short lull in the hitherto unceasing storm
of war. The greatest military event in the reign of the
hero-king was probably the battle of Ethandun, the first
of a series of victories over the Danish invaders; but the
most important in a social point of view was his treaty
of peace with Guthrum, whereby the rights of both Saxons
and Danes were clearly fixed, and the foundations laid
for the subsequent amalgamation of the two races.

The few years of peace enjoyed by Alfred in his later
days were employed in labours for the civilization of his
people. He rebuilt monasteries, and endeavoured to
people them with scholars. He brought over from the
continent whatever men of merit he could induce to
attend his court, and he personally set an example of
literary industry. He collected the ancient laws, re-
modelled and improved them, and laboured to perfect the
administrative organization. He established and developed a system for the relief of the poor ; and he administered justice personally, heard appeals from his judges,
and constantly watched over their proceedings with a
view to correct ignorance or corruption. He taught his
subjects the art of ship building, and laid the foundations
of the far-famed navy of England; and he introduced a
military organization which gave the country an army,
instead of the disunited bands on which it had hitherto
depended.

During the forty years that elapsed between the death
of Alfred the Great and that of Athelstan, the northmen
continued the invasion of this country, and sometimes
received the assistance which, in breach of all good faith,
their countrymen, who were already settled here, were
ready to give them. But this aid was by no means
certain, and the Danish settlers gradually learnt to look
on the new arrivals from their own land with in-

creasing coolness. The Danish pirates had also the misfortune to find in Edward and Athelstan monarchs who were not unworthy to wear the crown of the great Alfred.

This period was remarkable for the rapidity with which the country passed out of its tribal state, or from a collection of petty kings and chiefs into a great and united country. The development of the system of "guilds," which will be spoken of hereafter, the growing authority of the crown, and the increasing unity and power of the great towns, prove that the necessities of the age had taught our ancestors the advantage of executive authority, and the value of systematic combination on a large scale. Before this era had passed away, they had abandoned the character of a large number of independent and loosely confederated towns and counties, and had become a nation. The same result occurred at the same time to their three great antagonists. Under the energetic governments of Gorm the old, Harold-fairhair, and Eric, Denmark, Norway, and Sweden became national unities.

It was not the destiny of Alfred, Edward, and Athelstan to be succeeded by monarchs equal to themselves. The country which had been governed by men not inferior in energy, ability, or will, to Edward I, Henry VIII, or queen Elizabeth, was to be ruled by kings who possessed no one of their great gifts, and the power of the sceptre which had been wielded by giants was to pass into the hands of sybarites, and be delegated to ministers.

The statesmen to whose hands the government of England was entrusted during the half century that followed the death of Athelstan were almost all ecclesiastics. Several of them were men of most distinguished ability, as the chancellor Thurkytel (abbot of Croyland), and Odo archbishop of York; but by far the greatest of all was the celebrated Dunstan, archbishop of Canterbury.

Shortly after the death of Athelstan a struggle for political power commenced between the laity and clergy, which at the time of Dunstan ended in the complete subjugation of the former. Under the reign of this celebrated churchman, an ecclesiastic who had robbed or beaten a layman could not be punished by the civil law, though he might be tried before ecclesiastical tribunals at the instance of his brother clergymen. But the jurisdiction which the church exercised over its members was, so far as the laity were concerned, a delusion and a snare. No layman was permitted to bring an accusation or give evidence against a priest for murder, rape, or any other injury. Nor was the property of a layman more respectfully considered than his person. A priest who held land of a layman subject to rent and services, was not compelled to pay or perform them ; for to pay the rent was to impoverish the church ; and to perform the services was to subject the children of God to the children of men.[1]

The church also took charge of " the health of souls," and consequently considered it her right and duty to compel the observance of sound morality. Under this pretence, it controlled all contracts, in order that they might be equitable ; established a standard of weights and measures, that they might be uniform ; overlooked the pre-

---

[1] Theod. *Pœnit.*, xxi, 26, Thorpe, ii, 25 ; *Capit. et Frag.* Theodori. " Quod testibus clerici devinci debeant." Thorpe, ii, 73; *Concil. Romanorum sub Silvest.*, c. 3 ; Ecgb. *Excerpt.*, cxliv, " Ut nullus laicus clerico crimen audeat inferre." Thorpe, ii, 121; Ecgb.*Excerpt.*, cxliv; *Capit. Car. Magni et Ludov.*, lib. i, tit. 1, c. 30. " Laicus non sit testis contra clericos." Wilkins, *Concilia*, i, 110 and 753. A priest guilty of murder to be judged by the bishop only. *Laws of Edward and Guthrum*, c. 4, Thorpe, ii, 169. See also *Ll. Longobard.*, lib. iii, tit. 1, s. 11 ; *Capit. Karoli Magni et Ludov.*, lib. v, c. 225, 287, lib. vi, c. 154 and 155, lib. vii, c. 208; *Additamm. Ludov. Pii*, iv, tit. 33, 44, 61].

paration and registration of all deeds, that they might be recorded in monasteries ; took charge of the property of all who died, that it might be applied for the good of their souls ; laid fanciful restrictions on the contract and dissolution of marriage, that pseudo-incests might be avoided ; and levied forfeitures on all guilty of witchcraft, fornication, or immorality, that satisfaction being made to the church, the national conscience might be soothed. Of the validity of all accusations on these subjects, and of the nature of the punishments to be inflicted, the clergy were to be the sole judges, a right they exercised with a constant view to their own interests. By far the most common punishments were building a monastery, endowing a church, or making over lands or goods to the clergy.

This mode of dealing with a freeman's rights would not have been quietly endured by the most effeminate of nations, and was intolerable to the independent and self-reliant race whose offspring we have the honour to be. Hence arose an era of conflict between the temporal and spiritual powers, which was waged through several centuries with various success.

Happily for the persecuted layman, the priesthood at this time quarrelled among themselves. The great majority of the parochial clergy and a very large proportion of the canons were married men, and had ties and interests in the welfare of the nation inconsistent with a total devotion to a foreign power. They were cold, and perhaps more than cold, in aiding Dunstan in his great work of establishing a theocratic or hierarchical government ; and their lukewarmness was more irritating to the vehement archbishop than an opposition he naturally expected, and which, when overcome, he appears to have treated with a forgiving temper.

The archbishop desired to compel the whole of the clergy to take monastic vows, and to recognise the duty of obedience to the rule of St. Benedict. The married clergy were naturally unwilling to put away their wives, and not less so to part with their preferments. Hence arose a conflict which partially diverted the archbishop from his attacks upon the laity, and which continued to agitate the clergy long after the conclusion of the Anglo-Saxon era.

However indignant we may be at the tyranny of the sainted Dunstan, it is impossible to deny that his was an age of great social improvement, in which the doctrines of Christianity were made to tell on the morals and manners of the nation, and in which the prosperity of the country was ensured by a wise and vigorous administration. Among Dunstan's prime objects were the unity of the Church and the centralization of ecclesiastical power. In seeking the oneness of the Church, the archbishop unintentionally contributed to the concentration of civil power and the unity of the state.

After the death of Dunstan, no character appears on the stage of Anglo-Saxon history worthy to be compared with him in point of dignity or influence, till the accession of Cnut the Great. To this monarch we are indebted for a wise appreciation of his era, and for a vast number of useful laws, marking a higher order of social development than any that had preceded them. The large number of kingdoms over which he ruled, compelled this monarch to entrust various divisions of England to the government of a few military nobles, who thereby acquired a power and wealth that enabled them to set his successors at defiance. Under him the Danes and the Saxons may be said to have become one people, though the Danish element preponderated in the north and east, and the

Anglo-Saxon in the southern and western districts. With the reign of Cnut ended the Saxon-Danish era. Were it possible to exclude it from an age of which it was the end and perfection, the Norman-Saxon period might be considered as having commenced prior to his death.

If a great political and social change must be imputed to the leading influence of some one person, the Norman conquest might be ascribed to Emma, the daughter of Richard duke of Normandy, whom her countrymen loved to call "the gem of the Normans," and of whom the Saxons spoke as "the fairy's gift." She married first, Ethelred II, and secondly, on his death, Cnut the Great. By the former she had two sons, Alfred, and Edward the Confessor, whom she caused to be educated in Normandy; and by the latter, Harthacnut, a most unworthy son of a great father. It was through her influence that numerous Norman prelates and knights received endowments in England at the hands of her husband and children, and that the sons of the Anglo-Saxon nobility were sent for education to the court of Normandy.

It was in the reign of her son Edward that the seed she had sown bore fruit. Under him England became rapidly Norman. Norman bishops filled almost every see, Norman counts were made earls of English provinces, Norman knights built castles in the most commanding situations, and on Norman followers were lavished all the offices and benefits the crown had to bestow. The king, though by birth a Saxon, could not speak his own language, and his nobles, magistrates, and courtiers universally adopted the language, dress, and manners of the Norman court. The imbecility of the king compelled him to rely for protection and direction on a few great and able earls, whose power (already too great) he farther augmented, whose ambition he inflamed,

C

and among whom he created rivalries and dissensions destined to prove the ruin of his country. On his death, he left England an easy prey to the nation he loved better than his own.

It is not proposed in these pages to consider the result of the Norman Conquest. It is enough to say of it, that it has not been exceeded in violence, in cruelty, or in consequent desolation and misery, by the most terrible catastrophes recorded in European history. He who desires "to sup full with horrors" will find a truthful description of this reign of terror in the eloquent pages of Augustin Thierry.

CHAPTER I.

THE WIFE.

SECTION I.—SENTIMENT.

IN considering the domestic life of a people, the relative position of husband and wife is indubitably the most important topic. Other relationships influence, but this dominates, the home. It controls the relation of parent and child, influences the conditions of domestic servitude, and suggests the amusements of the leisure hour.

The home is the wife's kingdom; and on her rights, character, and conduct, its happiness or misery, barbarity or civilization, almost entirely depend. But where the people are barbarous, the rank of the female sex is humble, and it is not until a nation has made great progress in civilization that woman attains the position due to her natural dignity, and necessary to the exercise of her legitimate influence.

It has been repeatedly asserted, that, while the founders of Rome treated women as household goods, and the accomplished children of the caliphs looked on them as mere instruments of pleasure—while the polished Athenian valued them as domestic drudges, "who should lay out money with economy"—the barbarous Anglo-Saxon loved and reverenced the sex, and nourished those sentiments of affection and deference, which have raised women to their present rank, and invested them with the power to make domestic life not only a blessing in itself but a school of civilization.

For this view of the Anglo-Saxon character there is no lack of authority among modern writers; and as no one of them is more generally popular than Sharon Turner, his words may be fairly quoted as the exponent of this opinion. Speaking of the Anglo-Saxon women, he says, " their persons, their safety, and their property, were protected by express laws, and they possessed all that sweet influence, which, while the human heart is responsive to the touch of love, they will ever retain in those countries which have the wisdom and urbanity to treat them as equal, intelligent, and independent beings."[1]

Sharon Turner's views on this subject have been so generally accepted, that it appears like a heresy to dissent from them, though they are supported by no very great amount of evidence. Certain passages are quoted from Tacitus, in which he speaks of the Germans as looking upon women as enveloped in a kind of sanctity; of their reverencing sibyls, who claimed the power of prophecy ; and of their fearing witches who practised incantations. And to this it is added, that their princesses exercised supreme powers of government, and commanded armies.

[1] Turner, *Hist. Anglo-Sax.*, vol. iii, c. viii ; Kemble's *Saxons in England*, vol. i, p. 232 ; Tacitus, *De Mor. Germ.*, c. viii. That on several occasions the German women preferred death to dishonour, shews that their virtue and courage merited the position which they afterwards enjoyed, but it does not shew that they possessed it. Tacitus, *De Mor. Germ.*, c. vii and viii. The Marcomanni are said to have sent a prophetess as ambassadress to Domitian. The Cimbri and Sistones are said to have been governed by prophetesses ; but the former were Scandinavians, and the latter Norwegians. The song of Regnar Lodbrog (commonly quoted as evidence on this topic) is a Scandinavian song, and was probably not written prior to the twelfth century. The ode of Harold the Valiant in the Knigtlinga Saga, is also Scandinavian. All these authorities, which are quoted to show that we inherited the spirit of chivalry from the Saxons, support the opinion that we are indebted for it to the Northmen.

The last allegation, however, is supported by a very limited number of examples, and some of them, few as they are, are of very doubtful authenticity.

In contradiction to the generally received opinion, it may be said, that the Anglo-Saxon women were, at one time, sold by their fathers and always beaten by their husbands ; that they were menial servants even when of royal rank; that they were habitually subject to coarse personal insult; and that they were never addressed, even in poetry, in the language of passion or respect.

The feeling entertained for them by the male sex may be estimated by their general social position; and their social position may be ascertained by considering the motives which at different times induced men to seek them as wives; by the mode of their wooing; the impediments to, and conditions of, marriage; the ceremonies that attended it; the rights it conferred; the disabilities it induced; and the grounds and modes of its dissolution.

SECTION II.—THE MODE OF SEEKING AND OBTAINING A WIFE.

In those ancient times, which the French love to call the heroic, women were in no respect their own mistresses, but were entirely at the disposal of others. The youthful anxieties and pleasures of courtship were unknown; for no man sued a woman for a consent that she was not permitted to give and had no power to withhold. Thence it was that a great source of female power was lost. Maidens were never in a position to command the tender and sedulous attention which a man must pay to the woman he wooes, and the memory of which must have an influence over both so long as they live together.

The most ancient mode of wooing (if wooing it can be

called) had at least the merit of simplicity; it consisted
in carrying off the desired object by physical force. All
the numerous nations who lived by hunting and war, or
by fishing and piracy, adopted this course; and many of
the most famous wars known to the early history, or
still more ancient fables, of Greece, Rome, and Scandinavia, arose from it. In all countries the mode of proceeding was the same. The young men of a tribe, who were
in want of female companions, invaded the territory of
some neighbouring tribe blest with a stock of marriage-
able daughters. They chose a time when the men were
engaged in war, piracy, or some distant occupation, and
seized by force the fair ones they desired, and carried
them off. If the parents returned before the prey had been
secured, the captors were of course followed, and, when
overtaken, a battle was fought with a view to recapture
the booty; and, even if the parents were too late to
rescue their daughters, a sanguinary war often ensued.

This species of marriage was universal among the
Scandinavian and Teutonic nations. Nothing among
them was deemed more honourable than to acquire a
wife by forcibly carrying off the sister, daughter, or even
wife, of a public enemy or private foe. To do so was
" to be famous in history, and to be the theme of the
song of the scalds."[1]

The law recognised and approved this system, for the
law was merely established custom; but the more eminent chieftains saw the mischief it engendered, and endeavoured to regulate it so as to diminish the evil. With

[1] *Saxo Gram., Histor. Dan.*, lib. i,
p. 34. There are traces of it in all
Scandinavian nations, and it is said
to have existed in Ireland. *Gent.'s
Magazine*, March, 1767. The higher
the rank of the lady carried off, and
the greater the danger of the enterprise, the more honourable it was.
Weland and his two brothers, who
exceeded all their cotemporaries in
heroism, wrested from supernatural
powers three elf-maidens, whom
they compelled to become their
wives.

this view they insisted that before recourse was had to violence, the lady should be *demanded* of her father. If he refused to surrender her, it was then lawful to break open his house, beat all who resisted, and take the lady away by force. If any one, attacking or defending, was slain on the occasion, no penalty was incurred or revenge permitted. The lady was said, in the rhyming laws our fathers loved, to be

> " Legitime capta,
> Non vi rapta."

This form of marriage, when our chroniclers affected to be classical, was called the " *mos Laconum maritandi*," or " the Spartan form of marriage."[1]

The bloodshed which resulted from it suggested a modification. It sometimes happened, on the occasions referred to, that the rough captors managed to make themselves agreeable to their fair captives—that the young women had not an insuperable objection to marriage—and that the barbarous fathers, though they did not altogether like being robbed of their children, were not unwilling to see them satisfactorily settled. When, therefore, the parents overtook the fugitive lovers, they found two courses open to them ; one was to fight a desperate, and possibly unsatisfactory, battle ; and the other, to come to an amicable arrangement. The latter was so obviously preferable for both parties, that it soon

---

[1] *Steirnhook, De jure Suevorum,* p. 152; Worsaae, *Danes and Norwegians in Britain,* pp. 8 and 29. There can be no reasonable doubt that it was in use in England. Centuries later, public complaints were heard that " Welshmen and other villains" thus obtained wives in the western counties; and there are traces of the custom in a game or ceremony still occasionally practised on the marriage of a Welsh peasant. After the wedding, the bridegroom mounts on horseback and takes his bride behind him. A certain amount of law (as it is termed in coursing) is given them, and then the guests mount and pursue them. It is matter of courtesy not to overtake the young people, but, whether overtaken or not, they return with their pursuers to the wedding feast. Brand's *Popular Antiquities,* vol. ii, p.155 (edit. 1849). *Notes and Queries,* vol. xi, N.S., p. 415. The Tartars are said to have had a similar custom. Clarke's *Travels,* p. 333.

became generally adopted, and led to a recognised form of marriage.

It became customary for the fugitive lovers to conduct their flight very leisurely, and, when the parents came up, to open a parley. Thanks to the extent of paternal authority, and to the enterprise of the slave trader, every woman had in those times her recognised price. The lover tendered the market value of the lady in money or cattle ; and the father, after exacting a general promise that the self-elected bridegroom would treat his wife well, accepted the money and parted with his daughter.

This mode of proceeding was perfectly in keeping with the earliest Anglo-Saxon notions. It was half-robbery and half-purchase—half-piracy and half-trading, and was thoroughly characteristic of the age. By a very simple transition it passed into a third and better known form of marriage, more suitable to an age in which law and order were beginning to acquire power. To carry off a woman by violence, fight a battle in order to retain her, and after all *to buy* her, was clearly superfluous, if her relatives would sell her without compulsion. It was better to offer her father her price, than to have the labour and danger of a foray, and pay for her in the end.

But there were sentimental difficulties to be dealt with. To *sell* a daughter for money is even to the most sordid a distasteful idea; though to fail to recapture her, particularly when she does not wish it, and to accept a compensation for the insult of carrying her off, may be a proceeding not inconsistent with dignity. Public opinion, however, demands the long continuance of a state of transition, in order that the ideas of commercial benefit may gradually drown those of military honour.[1]

[1] Traces of this feeling seem to have remained till a comparatively late period in Ireland. Brand's *Popular Antiq.*, vol. ii, p. 139.

It was in this state of transition that St. Augustine found our Anglo-Saxon fathers, as is rendered clear by some of their earliest laws. " If a man carry off a maid by force," says Ethelbert, (A.D. 600), "let him pay fifty shillings *to her owner*, and afterwards *buy her* from him." Again he says, if a man carry off a freeman's wife, let him *procure him another with his own money*, and deliver her to him."[1]

In these laws we have a partial recognition of the lawfulness of force—at least to the extent of a non-obligation on the marauder to return the stolen lady, be she maid or wife.

From a mixed system of marriage, half-robbery, half-purchase, it is a natural gradation to that of purchase " *pur et simple*." This took place among the Anglo-Saxons, at a very early period;[2] and if the Danes (as it is the fashion to call the Northmen) had then formed settlements in the north-eastern districts, it was probably the same with them. In their native land the Northmen had at first married by force, then by a mixed process such as we have described, and afterwards, in obedience to the laws of Frotho III, by purchase only.[3]

Between the fifth and the tenth century English women gradually obtained the right of disposing of themselves in marriage. At first both state and church required the daughter to accept without question or comment whomsoever her father pleased.[4] She obtained, however, at a very early period in England (and also in Rome and on the continent) the right of making an objection to a

[1] *Ll. Ethelberti*, s. 31 and 82, Thorpe, i, 11 and 25; Marculfi *Formulæ*, for. 82 and 83; *Pœnit. Ecgb.*, lib. iv, 13, Thorpe, ii, 209.

[2] *Codex Exoniensis*, p. 338 ; Dasent's *Burnt Njal*, pref. p. xxv.

[3] Saxo Gram., l. viii, p. 408; l. v, p. 235; *Ll. Æthelberti*, s. 77, Thorpe, i, 23; Grimm, *Deutsche Rechtsalter-* *thümer*, p. 421.

[4] Tertull. *ad Uxor.*, lib. ii, c. ix (Paris, 1664, p. 172) ; *Cod. Theod.*, lib. iii, c. vii; *Justin. Cod.*, lib. v, 4, 18, and 20; *Synod. Sti. Patri.*, c. 22; Wilkins's *Concil.*, i, 4 ; *Ll. Wisigoth.*, lib. iii, tit. 1, s. 2; *Ll. Burgund. Add.*, i, tit. 13, s. 4.

suitor for some grave and specific cause, as insanity, leprosy, or crime; but of the validity of this objection her father was sole judge.[2] The church and the state, however, insisted with a constantly increasing earnestness that it was a father's duty to weigh these objections fairly; and after an early period if he did not do so the right of judging passed from him to his family or the public tribunals.[1] In the latest era the lady, though still required to assign a reason for a refusal, obtained the privilege of deciding on its sufficiency, and thereby became her own mistress. This right probably was not fully established in England prior to the middle of the tenth century.[2]

A system of marriage by purchase is not without its inconvenience; particularly when managed by men remarkable for sharpness in bargaining, and with very undeveloped ideas as to the obligations of honesty. The sale of a daughter afforded an admirable field, both to match-making mammas and cash-loving papas, for a display of auctioneering talent. It was their interest to puff the young lady's charms, and they did this with so much success that the law came to the assistance of over-persuaded bachelors. It was declared, that if a man bought a maiden, with cattle, and the father had deceitfully misrepresented his daughter's attractions, the husband should be at liberty to return her, and receive back his money.

Within what time after marriage, *at the earliest period* of Anglo-Saxon history, a dissatisfied husband was bound to return an unacceptable spouse does not appear; but in

[1] *Ulpian. Fr.*, xii, s. 1; *Justin. Cod.*, v, 4, 20; *Pandec.*, xxiii, 1, 12; *Nestor.*, apud Levesque, tom. ii, p. 112.

[2] *Lex. Pap. Poppæa, Heinecius Juris Rom.*, i, 5; G. L. Böhmer, *Prin. Juris Canon.*, s. 369; *Synod. Sti. Patric.*, iii, c. xxvii; Wilkins'

Concil., i, 6.

[3] *Edict. Clotaire* (A.D. 560); *Edic. Clotaire*, ii, (A.D. 615); Michelet, *Origine du droit français*, ii, 98; *Ll. Longob.*, (A.D. 712), ii, tit. 11, c. 4; *Ll. Cnuti*, s. 85, Thorpe, i, 417.

the Danish-Saxon era he was required to do so before she had acquired a right to braid her hair and consider herself a matron.

When the Anglo-Saxons were sufficiently civilized to appreciate the bad taste of selling their daughters, they desired to represent it to others, and to express it even to themselves, in a form and in language which veiled its native ugliness. The money paid by the lover for the purchase of the lady was no longer called her *price*. In England it was called the "foster-lean," and on the continent the "bride-keep." In both it was supposed to represent the expense which the parent had incurred in rearing the bride, and which, if he had to transfer his property in her to another, it was reasonable that he should be repaid.

Although the heathen Anglo-Saxons probably understood their system of marriage by purchase, no complete or intelligible account of it, prior to their conversion to Christianity, has been recorded for the instruction of modern times. It was not till the eighth and ninth centuries that their marriage customs appeared to have been reduced into a well-defined institution with fixed laws, ceremonies, and consequent rights. For this advance in jurisprudence they were indebted to the Christian clergy; and for the form it took, to the teachings of the Mosaic law, to the civil law of Rome, and to the canons of the church.

There were then, as there have been ever since, two ideas of marriage. One regarded it only as a civil contract to be determined by the law of the land, free from the interference of ecclesiastical authority; while the other represented it as a sacramental or religious rite, over which, as to its conditions, ceremonies, and dissolution, the Christian Church (or the clergy who repre-

sented it) had *exclusive* jurisdiction. These two anta-
gonistic ideas have warred against each other from the
time of the Anglo-Saxons to the present day ; and, while
the latter has been ever energetically maintained by the
great bulk of the priesthood, the former has been successfully defended, through many centuries, by our most
eminent lawyers, patriots, and statesmen. Public opinion,
then as now, adopted neither of the extreme views ; but,
while it boldly asserted the right of the citizen to marry,
subject to no limitation but the law of the land, it recognised marriage as one of those civil contracts, upon which
even the most thoughtless would desire and earnestly
supplicate a spiritual blessing.

The contest between these ideas renders it very difficult to trace accurately the history of marriage among
the Anglo-Saxons. We know but little of it save through
the clergy, and we know that they were most zealously
intent upon introducing a mass of Jewish and Roman
laws, against which the laity stubbornly struggled.

The only account that we can give of our marriage
customs, is rather a history of what the clergy wished
them to be, than of what they were.[1]

SECTION III.—RESTRICTIONS ON MARRIAGE.

Among all nations who have made any progress towards civilization, the marriage of persons very nearly
connected by blood has been prohibited by law. These
restrictions have varied according to the climate, religion,
and social state of the country in which they have been
enacted. In a semi-barbarous, patriarchal state, where a
few families are scattered over a very thinly populated

---

[1] It is also to be observed that they varied in different districts, according to the extent of clerical in-fluence, being more numerous in the Anglo-Saxon than in the Anglo-Danish districts.

territory, these laws are either almost unknown, or almost entirely disregarded. Where the members of a family only know one another, they must, as at the time of Abraham (who married his half-sister), marry one another, or neglect the institution altogether. It was in this state that Cæsar found the inhabitants of the country when he visited our shores. Ten or twelve members of one family lived together in one hut, having, as Cæsar alleges, their wives in common; and they who were so living were generally brothers with brothers, and parents with children. Many persons have been inclined to doubt the accuracy of Cæsar's statement, but it is supported by the testimonies of Dion Cassius and St. Jerome, and, when compared with the habits of other nations in a similar state of barbarism, has not any inherent improbability.[1]

What the customs of the Germans on this point were at the time of Tacitus does not appear; but they seem to have permitted polygamy in their chiefs, though the mass of the nation abstained from the practice, and the chiefs adopted it rather from political than from personal motives. It is, therefore, probable, that they did not attach so much importance to the laws regulating the inception of marriage, as might have been anticipated from a nation so severe in enforcing fidelity in the performance of its duties.[2]

Morality must, however, have improved rapidly; for on the arrival of St. Augustine, he found the Saxons reasonably attentive to the fundamental laws prohibiting marriage between very near blood relations, though with-

---

[1] Cæsar de Bello Gallico, lib. v, c. 14. See, as to the Garamantes, Solinus, *Polyhistor*, c. 33, as to the Tuscans, *Athenæus*, xiii, 3, and as to the Heliopolitans, *Socrates*, lib. i, c. 13, Νομον ειναι φησι παρα τοις Τυρρηνοις, κοινας υπαρχειν τας γυναικας — τρεφειν δε τους Τυρρηνους παντα τα γινομενα παιδια, ουκ ειδοται ότου πατρος εστιν εκαστον. As to the intercourse between the sexes among the Picts and Scots, see Palgrave's *Anglo-Saxon Commonwealth*, vol. i, c. xvi..

[2] Tacitus *de Mor. Germ.* c. xviii.

out attaching any great importance to them. The only marriages forbidden by the Church of Rome on the ground of consanguinity, which the Saxons generally practised, were those of first cousins. These St. Gregory interdicted, affirming that, though they were permitted by a certain worldly law of the Roman republic, yet it had been found by experience that no offspring could come of such wedlock. He had, however, a merciful "regard for our national customs," and forbad the clergy to enforce the ecclesiastic laws which prohibited marriage with all collateral relations within the seven degrees of consanguinity. The bishops in the seventh century were as liberal as the pope, and did not impose capricious restrictions on marriage, but, as their power increased, their liberality diminished ; and, in the eighth century, they forbad the marriage of first cousins, and, in the eleventh, that of second cousins.[1]

Prior to their conversion to Christianity, neither the Anglo-Saxons nor the cognate nations of the continent recognised any restrictions on the freedom of marriage save those which arose from consanguinity. Restrictions on the ground of either matrimonial or spiritual affinity were unknown, or disregarded by them. This is proved by the revolting custom of marrying a stepmother, or father's widow, which was common both on the continent and in England.[2]

In the sixth century, Ermengist, the king of the Varni, when at the point of death, required his son Radiger to

---

[1] Bede, *Eccl. Hist.*, l. ii, c. xxvii. The worldly law referred to is probably that of Justinian, *Instit. Justiniani*, lib i, c. x, s. 4. The words of St. Gregory are "Sobolem ex tali conjugio non posse succrescere." These words are usually translated as in the text, but another translation has been suggested which the words will bear, viz., "the offspring of such a match cannot thrive."

[2] In reference to one of these marriages it was said, "multi sunt in Anglorum gente, qui, dum adhuc in infidelitate essent, huic nefando conjugio dicuntur admixti." Gregorii Magni *Opera*, ii, 1155.

marry his stepmother, "even as our national custom requires."[1] As the stepmother was a daughter of the Frankish king Theudebert, the command might possibly have been given from political motives; but let them have been what they may, the son obeyed under circumstances peculiarly painful and dangerous. At the time when Radiger married his stepmother, he was enamoured and beloved of an Anglo-Saxon lady, the sister of a king of the East Angles, who no sooner heard of his infidelity than she determined to punish it. With the assistance of her brother, she is said to have raised an Anglo-Saxon army, and, passing over to the continent, invaded the territory of her faithless lover. The king marched against her, but was defeated in battle, and, in his flight, was captured by the conquerors, bound, and brought before his offended mistress with a view to execution. She covered him with reproaches for his breach of faith, but offered to spare his life, on condition that he would immediately repudiate his stepmother and marry her. It is unnecessary to add that the young king preferred this arrangement to any one of the numerous modes of execution at that time prevalent; that the elder lady disappears from the scene; and that the young couple were duly married, and lived happily ever afterwards.[2]

Nor was the custom of marrying a stepmother confined to the continent. Ethelbert, king of Kent, who was the first bret-walda or great king converted to Christianity, "having most gloriously governed his temporal kingdom for fifty-six years, in A.D. 616, entered into the eternal joys of the kingdom of heaven." Upon his death he was suc-

---

[1] Procopius, *De Bello Gothico*, l. iv, c. 20.

[2] Bede, *Eccl. Hist.*, l. ii, c. 5. *Anglo-Sax. Chron.*, A.D. 616. Flor. Wigorn, A.D. 616. It has been said that at this time Eadbald was married to Emma, the daughter of a king of France. (Sim. Dunelm., p. 645.—*Genealogies of Kentish Kings*, p. 635). But polygamy was permitted to Teutonic princes. (Tacitus, *De Mor. Germ.*, c. 18).

ceeded as king of Kent by his son Eadbald, who immediately *renounced Christianity,* and married his father's
widow. So powerful was his opposition to the Christian
cause, that Justus and Mellitus, the most distinguished of
the bishops, abandoned the island in despair, and Lauren-
tius, archbishop of Canterbury, (the successor of St. Augustine) prepared to follow their example. On the night prior
to his departure, the archbishop lay down to rest in the
church he was about to leave for ever. Weary with sorrow
and prayer, he at last fell asleep, and then the chief of the
apostles descending from heaven visited him, reproached
him bitterly for his faintheartedness, and scourged him
with apostolical severity. Next morning the archbishop
repaired to the king and showed him his bleeding wounds.
Eadbald inquired who had dared to scourge a man of so
much consequence; and on hearing that the wounds had
been inflicted by the apostle of Christ for his (the king's)
salvation, he became alarmed at so great a miracle, abjured the worship of idols, *renounced his unlawful marriage,* and embraced the faith of Christ.[1]

The miracle, however, did not put an end to the custom
of marrying a step-mother; for two centuries and a half
afterwards the offence was again committed by a king of
England. Ethelwulf (the successor of Egbert) married in
his old age Judith the daughter of the king of France,
who at the time of her marriage was about twelve years
old.[2] Some two years afterwards he died, and was succeeded by his eldest son, Ethelbald, the offspring of a

---

[1] Bede, *Eccl. Hist.,* lib. ii. c. 5;
Ang. Sax. Chron., A.D. 616; *Hist.
Monast. Sancti August.,* p. 144-146.
[2] According to Sharon Turner,
Osberga, Ethelwulf's first wife, who
was the mother of Alfred the Great,
died A.D. 856 (*Anglo-Sax. Hist.,* vol.
i. p. 431). According to Sir F. Palgrave (*History of Normandy and
England,* vol. i, p. 528), and Dr.
Lappenberg (*Anglo-Saxon Kings,*
vol. ii. p. 25), Ethelwulf repudiated
Osburga prior to his second marriage.
Mr. St. John (*Four Conquests of
England,* vol. i, p. 233), states that
she was neither dead nor divorced at
the date of Ethelwulf's second marriage.

former marriage, who immediately espoused Judith, his step-mother.[1]

As it was the custom of our ancestors to marry their stepmothers, it follows, as of course, that they had no hesitation in marrying their wives' sisters, or their nephews' or uncles' widows.[2]

All these marriages were contrary to the law of the Catholic church, and were consequently forbidden by the clergy, who rather sought to increase than diminish the impediments to marriage. In addition to prohibitions based on matrimonial affinity, they endeavoured to introduce numerous others founded on spiritual relationships. These were of the most absurd character; and the arguments used in their support were absolutely fantastic.

It was argued that, as a man ought not to marry his natural mother through whom he had become a member of the temporal world, à fortiori he ought not to marry his spiritual mother or god-parent, through whom he had been made a member of Christ. Both sexes were therefore prohibited from marrying a god-parent, and as a woman might not marry her father in the flesh, it was decreed that she might not marry the spiritual father who baptized her, and through whom she entered the kingdom

---

[1] It is stated in the *Annals of Winchester*, that, on the admonition of St. Swithun, Ethelbald repented of this marriage, repudiated Judith, and sent her back to France. The date of her return to France has been matter of controversy, but it must have been prior to A.D. 863. In this year she married her father's forester, whom he afterwards made earl of Flanders. Asser; Ingulph; Prudens Trecens., A.D. 858; Hincmar, A.D. 862; none of whom mention her divorce. It rests solely on the authority of Matthew of Westminster and Thomas Rudborn. Mr. Kemble says,

"to him (Baldwin, earl of Flanders) she bore Matilda, William the Conqueror's wife," and the same statement occurs in a note to Dr. Giles's translation of William of Malmesbury. This is a mistake, as Judith would have been nearly 200 years old at the time of Matilda's birth. Will. Malmes., lib. ii, s. 117; Asser, *vita Alfredi*, p. 858; Kemble's *Saxons in England*, vol. ii. p. 408; Pauli's *Alfred the Great* (by Thorpe), c. 2; *Annales Bertiniani*, Bouquet, vii, 77.

[2] Gildas, *De Excid. Brit.*, ss. 27, 32, and 35.

D

of God.[1] These prohibitions were afterwards extended; and a man was forbidden to marry the mother of his god-daughter,[2] because they had already a spiritual child and must be assumed to be already married. Nor might a man or woman marry a god-sib or gossip; because, being the joint god-parents of a child, or one the god-parent of the other's child, they were considered to be already joined in spiritual wedlock. These prohibitions were at last carried to the extent of forbidding a man to marry all those to whom he was *spiritually* related within the prohibited degrees of carnal consanguinity.[3]

These restrictions were not only tyrannical and absurd in the eyes of the laity, but utterly unintelligible to some of the most eminent of the Anglo-Saxon clergy. St. Boniface, in writing to Nothhelm (archbishop of Canterbury, A.D. 735) says, " I should like also very much to have your opinion with reference to a matter in which I have through indiscretion committed an offence. Without sufficient consideration I gave my sanction to a marriage under the following circumstances:—A man stood god-father to a child, and on the death of the child's father married the mother; now this the authorities of Rome declare to be a deadly sin; they rule that in all such cases there shall be a divorce, and that in a Christian land *capital punishment* or perpetual banishment must be insisted on. If in any of the writings of the Catholic fathers, or in any canon or in any decree of the church, you find this to be regarded as so great a crime, have the kindness to point it out carefully, in order that I may know on what authority to act in forming my judgment

---

[1] Theodor. *Pœnit.*, xx, 2, 18; Ecgb. *Excerpt.*, 131 and 134; Justiniani *Codex*, lib. 5, let. 4; *De Nuptiis*, l. 26.

[2] *Sex. Decret.*, lib. 4, let. 3, *De Cognat. Spirit.*, c. 2; *Council of*

Trullo, c. 53, apud Labb., vi, 1167; Roger de Wendover, A.D. 615.

[3] *Concil. Eanham*, c. 8; and compare also Bracton, lib. 4, 298; Coke's *Instit.*, v. 2 (1 & 2 Philip & Mary, c. 8).

on this affair. I cannot myself understand why this spiritual relationship should render such a marriage so great an offence, when we are all of us, through baptism, sons and daughters of our Lord, and in this, brothers and sisters."[1]

Upon the absurd system of creating capricious restrictions on the freedom of marriage, the general law which prohibited a man from marrying another man's wife was extended so as to prohibit an union with one who, by taking religious vows, had become (figuratively) the spouse of Christ.[2] And this prohibition was illogically stretched, so as to include even those who had been placed in religious foundations for education, and had not taken vows.

King Edgar, when on a visit to the convent of Wilton, had become enamoured of a young lady of the name of Wulfrith, who had not taken the veil, but was a pupil of the nuns. The king carried her off from the convent, and married her. When this came to the knowledge of St. Dunstan, he reproached the king with his offence, imposed on him a penance, and required him to restore the lady to her guardians. It is matter of controversy whether the king did so or not; but if he did, it is certain that her restoration did not take place until he had had by her a daughter named Editha. It is probable that, being of vagrant affections, he grew tired of the fair Wulfrith, and in obedience to the church and his own inclinations, ultimately permitted her to return to her convent.[3] This was

---

[1] St. Bonifac., *Epist.* 15.

[2] Theodor. *Pœnit.*, xxi ; Ecgb. *Excerp.*, 131 & 134 ; *Ll. Æthel.*, v. 1, c. 12 ; *Ll. Cnuti Eccl.*, c. 7. This prohibition was but little attended to by the laity. The instances of royal marriages with nuns are by no means rare. Ethelwald, nephew of Alfred the Great, married a nun whom he carried off from Winburne, and thereby involved himself in a quarrel with the bishop of Winchester. But they were oftener taken as mistresses than as wives. Roger de Wendover, A.D. 901 ; *Chronica de Mailros*, 1. 146.

[3] Eadmer, *Vita St. Dunstani, Anglia Sacra*, ii, 218 ; Wm. Malmes., 1.

exactly the course pursued a few years later by Swegn, the brother of Harold II, who was refused permission to marry Editha, abbess of Leominster. He carried her off, retained her as long as his passion lasted, and then, being refused permission to marry her, sent her back to her cloister.[1] In these cases, the restrictions on marriage did not promote either morality or happiness.

The clergy did not positively prohibit second marriages, though they disapproved of them.[2] They appear to have been more anxious to prevent the marriage of widows than of widowers. With this view they sometimes prevailed on brides, at the time of their marriage, and sometimes on widows, *immediately on the death of their husband,* to take " vows of widowhood," whereby they bound themselves to marry once only. Widows, who made these vows in the first intensity of grief, often repented of them; Cnut, therefore, forbad the making of such vows " with unbecoming haste," which appears to have meant, within a year of the husband's death. On a widow taking this vow, all her property passed to the monastery, of which she became an inhabitant. Here she wore a ring and russet gown as a mark of her profession, but was free from the restrictions imposed on other female inmates. Among those who are mentioned as having taken these vows, are the sister-in-law of Cuneglas, and Adelfleda, the widow of duke Athelstan.[3]

The only restriction on second marriages which the clergy succeeded in enforcing, was a prohibition to a widow to marry within a year of her husband's death; and even this she might do if she were willing to sacrifice

ii, c. 8 ; Wm. Malmes., *De Pontif.,* l. ii, fo. 143 ; Hume's *Hist. of England,* c. ii, p. 86 ; Lingard's *Anglo-Saxon Church,* vol. ii, p. 283.

[1] Flor. Wigorn. A.D. 1049.

[2] Ælfrici *Past. Epist.,* 43, Thorpe, ii, 383.

[3] Du Cange, *V. Vidua;* Matthew Paris, 398, 707, 960 ; *Ll. Cnuti* Sec., s. 74 ; Thorpe, i, 417 ; *Ll. Longobar.,* ii, tit. 6 ; *Addimenta Ludov.,* ii, tit. 11 ; *Hist. Eliensis,* c. 8.

her dower. At first, the land she so forfeited passed to her husband's next of kin, but in the Saxon-Norman era the church appears to have regarded her second marriage within the year as a purely ecclesiastical offence, and her lands were therefore seized by the bishop for his own benefit.[1]

Marriages with a divorced woman, a prostitute, two sisters, or a first cousin, were disapproved; and the parties to them were declared guilty of bigamy, and incapable of holding priestly office. No priest was permitted to be present at their celebration, to bestow upon them a spiritual benediction, or even to partake of the wedding feast.[2] The parties to such marriages were also liable to ecclesiastical censure and penance; but the marriages (in Theodore's opinion) were valid, and the married pair were not allowed to separate.[3]

It was also on religious grounds that a Christian woman was forbidden to marry a Jew. At first, the crime involved no penalty, save ecclesiastical censure; but at a later period the influence of the clergy sufficiently prevailed to cause the punishment of death to be attached to the offence. In the latest Anglo-Saxon era the unfortunate offender was burnt to death; and in the Anglo-Norman period, buried alive.[4]

These innumerable impediments to marriage were not only restraints on personal liberty, but outrages on natural affection. It is not, therefore, to be wondered at, if the feeling of the laity on the subject varied from indifference to contempt, and from hatred to defiance. Alfric, arch-

---

[1] *Ll. Æthel,* v, 21; vi, 2; *Ll. Cnut. Sec.,* s. 74; *Ll. Hen. Primi,* xi, 13, xii, 3; Coke's 1 *Inst.,* 8; *Concil. Laod.,* can. 80; *Codex Theod.,* lib. iii, tit. 8, "De secundis nuptiis"; *Domesday Book,* t. ii, fo. 199.

[2] *Concil. Neocæsar.,*c. 7, ap. Labbe, vi, 1556; Alfric's *Pastoral,* s. 43, Thorpe, ii, 383; Ælfrici *Colloq.* 9; *Inst. of Polity,* 22; Thorpe, ii, 333; Theod. *Pænit.,* xvii, 9; Ecgb., *Excerp.* 91.

[3] Theod. *Pænit.,* xix, s. 15 and 18; Ecgb., *Pænit., Add.* i; Thorpe, ii, 18, and 233.

[4] Coke, 8 *Inst.,* 89; Fleta, 54.

bishop of York, was asked to translate the Pentateuch into Anglo-Saxon for the benefit of his converts, but he declined the task, stating that if they ever discovered that the Jewish patriarchs disregarded the orthodox prohibitions on marriage, it would be impossible afterwards to satisfy his flock that they might not do likewise.[1]

It was not till the tenth century that the clergy possessed a leader with sufficient energy and ability to enforce these prohibitions and trample down all opposition. An Anglo-Saxon earl had, in defiance of the clergy, married his cousin. Dunstan, who was then in the zenith of his power, annulled the marriage and forbad all intimacy between the two offenders. The earl troubled himself as little about the priestly prohibition as his forefathers would have done; but he failed to appreciate his antagonist, who immediately excommunicated him, and excommunication, in Dunstan's time, practically involved outlawry. The earl appealed to the court of Rome, and by the application of those golden arguments to which the successors of St. Peter then usually listened, obtained an order for his pardon. But Dunstan, who cared no more for his spiritual sovereign than for the prince of darkness whose nose he is reported to have pulled, or for his temporal sovereign whom he had personally chastised, refused compliance with the papal mandate. He said truly that the earl was no penitent; that he gloried in his sin, and mocked at the church; and that, in obedience to no power, human or divine, would he pardon an insolent and impenitent sinner. The whole power of England, ecclesiastical, civil,

[1] Alfric's *Præf. Genesis Anglice* (Thwaites), p. 1; Flodoard, *History of Rheims*, lib. iv, c. 5, p. 612, and the epistle of pope Formosus (Wilkins, *Concilia*, p. 200). This epistle *may* be genuine, but it contains an inexplicable confusion of dates and names; but, if every ancient document which presents confusion in this respect is to be treated as spurious, the number of recognized authorities will be terribly reduced.

and military, was in the hands of Dunstan, and he employed it so effectually, that ere long he compelled the stout-hearted earl to fall at his feet, an attrite, if not a contrite penitent. Dunstan, who was ferocious to all who resisted him, but not vindictive when victorious, at once pardoned the offender and received him into his good graces.[1]

The conduct of the earl, whether right or wrong, expressed the feelings of a nation who detested a tyranny which sought to limit the freedom and happiness of married life. The baneful interference of this tyranny extended from the cottage to the palace, and one of the earliest victims of its cruelty was of royal rank.

In the year 955, king Edwy, then a youth of seventeen, succeeded his uncle Edred on the throne. He was married to a young and beautiful bride of about his own age, named Elgiva, who is said to have been related to him within the prohibited degrees of consanguinity. His coronation naturally followed his succession, and at this ceremony, as was usual, several days were devoted to feasting and intoxication. On one of these, the king, weary of the revelling, retired to the apartment of his bride, and amused himself in toying with her in the presence of her mother. Dunstan, who was a guest at the dinner-table, enraged at the withdrawal of the king, forced his way into the royal apartments, loaded the queen with reproaches, and with the aid of the prelate Kinsey compelled the unwilling monarch by personal violence to return to the festive board. This proceeding not unnaturally offended the queen, made her the mortal enemy of her husband's powerful minister, and ultimately provoked her to become a leader of that party among the

[1] The authorities for this anecdote are Baronii *Annal. Eccles.*, tom. xvi, p. 308; Eadmer, *Vita Dunstani*, *Anglia Sacra*, ii, 215.

nobles who resisted the encroachments of the ecclesiastical power. The unfortunate lady paid dearly for her enmity. About two years afterwards she was seized by the emissaries of archbishop Odo, and, on the ground of the objections to her marriage, was separated from the king. To destroy her influence with him and the fascination of her beauty, her lips were burnt, her cheeks scored with red-hot irons, and herself driven into exile. She fled to Ireland, and there remained until her wounds were healed and her beauty had revived. She then returned to England to rejoin her husband; but, in the neighbourhood of Gloucester, she was captured by "the servants of God," who cut the muscles of her thighs, and mutilated her in so cruel a manner that she died a few days afterwards. Such were the means by which "Saint" Dunstan and "Odo the Good" punished a disregard of ecclesiastical prohibitions in a queen. If they could deal so cruelly with their young and lovely sovereign, it is not probable that they were very tender with. more humble opponents.[1]

But the relative power of clergy and laity was not destined to remain what it was in the time of St. Dunstan. At a later period, A.D. 1085, Malgar, archbishop of Rouen,

---

[1] As St. Dunstan is the hero of the Catholic and high church party, and the *bête-noire* of their antagonists, there is no incident connected with his conduct in this matter that has not been zealously contested. It has been alleged that there were two ladies of the name of Elgiva, or of some similar name—for even the name is disputed; by some that the mother was the king's mistress; and by others, that she was not his mistress, but a near relation. Some writers state that both mother and daughter were the king's mistresses, and that Edwy was a married man at the time. Many allege that Elgiva was not his queen; and some say that the event occurred at his coronation, while others assert that it happened at a witenagemot. It has also been stated that he was not toying with his queen, but indulging in conduct, both with mother and daughter, of the grossest description. It is sometimes alleged that the retainers of the archbishop, who murdered her, acted without express orders, and, sometimes, that they acted by the orders of Odo, but without the sanction of Dunstan. Others state that archbishop Odo was dead at the time, and that the servants were Dunstan's. Bridferth, *Vita S. Dunst., Acta SS.*

attempted to enforce the ecclesiastical laws of consanguinity against William the Conqueror, who was too
nearly related to his wife Matilda. The archbishop required him to put her away; and, on his refusal, excommunicated him. The Conqueror, instead of yielding,
expelled the archbishop from his see and drove him into
exile.[1] He also disgraced and banished Lanfranc, a Lombard monk, who had violently espoused the cause of the
archbishop. The latter, during his exile, changed his
opinion, and by obtaining the sanction of the pope to the
marriage he had previously denounced, became a favourite
with the Conqueror, and ultimately archbishop of Canterbury.[2]

The amount of tyranny practised by unscrupulous
prelates, under colour of their right to annul any marriage which they were pleased to call incestuous, cannot
be exaggerated. Of it, a most distinguished Anglo-Saxon
scholar says, " Amidst the striking cases on record, the
cases of kings and nobles, we look in vain for a true measure of the misery which these prohibitions must have
entailed upon the humbler members of society, who possessed neither the influence to compel, nor the wealth to
purchase, dispensations from an arbitrary and oppressive
rule. The sense and feeling of mankind at once revolt
against restrictions for which neither the law of God
nor the dictates of nature supply excuse, and which
resting upon a complicated calculation of affinity, were

Bened., Sæc. V, p. 654. Osbern, *De Vita Odonis*, ap. Wharton, lib. i, 84; Malmesbury, *De Pontif.*, lib. i; Malmesbury, *Reg. Ang.*, lib. ii, c. 7; *Hist. Rames.*, i, c. 7; John of Wallingford, p. 543; Flor. Wigorn., A.D. 958, 959; Hume's *History of England*, vol. i; Hook's *Lives of Arch. Canter.*, vol. i, p. 379; Dr. Lingard's *Anglo-Saxon Church*, vol. ii, p. 274 and 445; Wright's *Biographia Brit. Lit.*, vol. i, p. 431; Sharon Turner, vol. ii, p. 251; Kemble's *Saxons in England*, vol. ii, p. 410; Soames's *Anglo-Saxon Church*, p. 184, and the authorities there referred to. Charters recently published leave no room for doubt that she was the king's wife. See *Cod. Dipl.*, 1201.

[1] Will. Malmesb., lib. iii, s. 267.

[2] *Vita Lanfranci, Script. Rer. Galliæ et Franc.*, xiv, 31.

often the means of betraying the innocent and ignorant into a condition of endless wretchedness. But they were invaluable engines of extortion and instruments of malice; they led to the intervention of the priest with the family in the most intolerable form, and they furnished weapons which could be used with almost irresistible effect against those whom nothing could reach, but the tears and perhaps broken heart of a beloved companion."[1]

Nor were these the only or possibly the least evils of the tyrannical interference of the clergy in this matter. It rendered mankind impatient of reasonable restrictions on the freedom of marriage. The laws which they knew and felt most were palpably cruel and absurd, and they naturally, though erroneously, judged the whole by a part. A just contempt for a prohibition to marry a godmother's niece, or a second cousin, is unfortunately apt to be extended not only to all similar restrictions, but to the authors of them.[2]

SECTION IV.—MARRIAGE CEREMONIES.

At the period when women were married by force, there could have been no matrimonial rites; and when they were acquired by purchase, the marriage ceremony was exceedingly simple. The earliest form of marriage in this, and many other countries, consisted only of the process of handfasting. The contracting parties took one another by the hand, and publicly consented to be husband and wife. The lady's friends were present, received

---

[1] Kemble's *Saxons in Engl.*, ii,412.

[2] At the council of Trent the clergy appear to have appreciated the mischief which they had done. "Docet experientia, propter multitudinem prohibitionum, multoties in casibus prohibitis ignoranter contrahi matrimonia, in quibus vel non sine magno peccato perseveratur, vel ea *non sine magno scandalo dirimuntur.*" *Concil. Trident.*, Sess. xxiv, De Reformat. Matrimon., c. 2.

the purchase-money, or foster-lean, and publicly gave her to her husband. The *form* of giving away is still retained; but it is not so demonstrative as it was in Anglo-Saxon times, when delivery of the thing transferred was necessary to the validity of a contract. The bride's guardian took her by the *neck and shoulders*, and placed her in the bridegroom's arms.[1]

When our ancestors invented the formula on which our present marriage service is based, they endeavoured to express the idea that marriage is a legal transfer of a woman to a husband; and they imitated the alliterative cadence and phraseology of deeds conveying land or other property.

In a very ancient marriage-service, which is clearly of Anglo-Saxon origin, the bride's contract is as follows : " I take thee, John, to be my wedded husband, to have and to hold, from this day forward, for better for worse, for richer and poorer, in sickness and health, to be bonny and buxom, in bed and at board, till death do us part, and thereto I plight thee my troth." At a later period, the words, " If Holy Church do so ordain," were added. According to the form in use in Northumbria, the bridegroom's promise was as follows : " I take thee, Alice, to be my wedded wife, to have and to hold, at bed and at board, for fairer for fouler, for better for worse, in sickness, in health, till death us do part." Other formulæ differ but little from these. In all of them, the bride promises to be " buxom and bonny, at bed and at board"; but, further than these words extend, does *not* promise

---

[1] "Dextra data acceptaque invicem, Persæ et Assyrii fœdus matrimonii ineunt." Alex. ab. Alexandro, lib. ii, c. 5. Ihre's *Glossar. Suedo-Goth.*, vol. i, p. 435, 781; Palsgrave's *Esclaircissement de la Langue Française*, b. iii, fo. 12; Layamon's *Brut*, vol. i, p. 95, and vol. iii, p. 312. This custom long continued in Scotland. See *The Christian State of Matrimony* (1543), p. 43; Sir John Sinclair's *Acc. of Scotland*, xii, 615; Colquhoun's *Roman Civil Law*, vol. i, p. 480.

either to honour or to obey.[1]   In the eastern counties, in
which the Danes retained their own laws and customs,
the form of contract was more advantageous to the
woman.

The Danish form of marriage originally consisted of
handfasting, and words of mutual consent pronounced at
a public meeting, the delivery of the bride by her father
to the husband, and her being publicly taken to his home
by him.   At a later period, the hands of the young people
were joined together by the bride's father, who said, " I
join this woman to you in honour to be your wife, with a
right to half of your bed and keys, and to a third of your
goods acquired or to be acquired, according to the law of
the land and of St. Eric.   In the name of the Father,
and of the Son, and of the Holy Ghost."[2]

The binding force which the northmen, in general,
ascribed to their legal formulæ is very curious.   It was
quite sufficient that they were *said* ; whether the parties
who said them, understood or intended to say them, was
immaterial.   Gunlang, " with the serpent's tongue," desiring to become learned in the law, sought instruction
from Thorstein the wise.   He passed a year in listening
to the teaching of the great master, and relieved the
tedium of his legal studies by contemplating the charms
of the fair Helga, the wise man's daughter.   One day,
when seated at table, Gunlang said to Thorstein, " One
law-form yet remains which thou hast not taught me,
nor do I yet know how a maiden is to be wedded."
Thorstein answered that few words were needed, and
he recited the form of espousal.   Gunlang then craved

---

[1] *Liber Pontif. Exon.*, p. 260; Spelman, *Uxor Ebraica*, lib. ii, c. 27;
Mashall's *Monumenta Ritualia*, vol.
i, p. 46; Palgrave's *Anglo-Sax. Commonwealth*, vol. ii, p. 136.

[2] Steirnhook, *De Jure Suevorum*,

p. 160. The Roman woman who was
married by the ceremony called *con-
farreatio*, received the keys from her
husband at the time of the marriage.
Colquhoun's *Roman Civil Law*, 1.
471.

leave to repeat his lesson to Helga, a proposal to which
the father assented, slightly hinting that the sport was
idle. The lover, however, persisted, pronounced the wedding words with audible precision and solemnity, and
named his witnesses. All that were present laughed at
the child's play; but, in after times, Gunlang insisted on
the validity of the marriage, claimed his bride, and successfully vindicated his right in bloodshed and death.[1]

SECTION V.—ESPOUSALS.

These matrimonial ceremonies were in use prior to the
conversion of the nation to Christianity ; but, after this
event, the clergy claimed to exercise exclusive authority
over all matters relating to marriage. It was probably
about the tenth century that they succeeded in substitut-
ing among the higher classes in the south of England the
Roman system of espousals for the "engagements" of
the earlier Anglo-Saxon times.

Espousals were contracts to marry at a future time,
entered into subject to known conditions, by fixed forms,
created present rights and duties, and involved ascertained legal consequences. The first thing necessary to
their validity, was the *free* consent of both parties ; and
therefore their establishment tended to confirm the right
of the sex to select their own husbands.[2] But, notwithstanding the necessity of free consent, children might be
espoused by their parents at seven years of age. If either
of them, on arriving at the age of ten, wished to terminate the engagement, they were at liberty to do so,
without exposing themselves or their parents to any
penalty. If they did so between the ages of ten and

---

[1] Palgrave's *Ang. Sax. Commonwealth*, ii, 138.

[2] *Cod. Justiniani*, l. i, tit. 1; *Cod.
Theod.*, lib. iii, tit. 1.

twelve, the parents, and not the child, were liable to penalties; but if, after the age of twelve years, the child declined to fulfil its engagement, both the child and its parents were liable to punishment. It was absolutely necessary that espousals should be made publicly, and that the friends of both parties should be present as witnesses.[1]

In England, the ceremony commenced with a statement by the man, woman, and woman's friends, that they were all consenting parties to the engagement. The bridegroom then formally promised to *treat his betrothed well,* "according to God's law, and the custom of society."[2] But this vague promise, which had habitually been made from the earliest times, was not now deemed sufficient; and the bridegroom was required to give a "wed," or "security," that he would duly perform his promise. From this "wed," the ceremony was called a wedding, a name which it has retained to the present time. The persons to whom the "wed" was given were called "for-speakers," and answered to our trustees, or guardians.[3]

The next step was for the bridegroom to state what he proposed to give for the bride's foster-lean. At first the foster-lean was paid *at the time of the espousals;* but this part of the Roman system was not suited to the acuteness of Anglo-Saxon dealings, as very soon became evident. A father, who possessed an attractive daughter,

---

[1] As to the "frequentia et fides amicorum," vide *Cod. Theod.*, lib. iii, tit. 7.

[2] There is no conclusive evidence as to what amounted "to treating a wife well." The guardian of a female ward was placed *verbatim et literatim* under the same engagement, and the Lombard laws explain negatively what this meant. They define ill-treatment to consist in killing her either by hunger or thirst, or in not supplying her with clothes and shoes suited to her rank and fortune; in attempting her virtue, or marrying her to a serf; or in beating her foully, unless she was under age, and it was for the purpose of discipline, amendment of morals, or the inculcation of female duties. *Ll. Longobar.*, l. ii, tit. ii, l. 4.

[3] *Ll. Edmundi*, s. 2, Thorpe, p. 255.

espoused her to an amorous youth, and obtained the
foster-lean; he then immediately espoused her to another,
and obtained a second payment; and, after the second
espousals, he engaged her to a third, with the same satisfactory result : and all this without parting with her.[1]
On each of these occasions two or three lovers were
cheated out of their affections and their cash; and their
furious, but not unnatural, indignation, threatened to be
fatal to the ecclesiastical, but by no means popular, institution of matrimonial pre-contracts. Archbishop Theodore, with a view to avert its destruction, forbade parents
to give an espoused girl to another ; but if she was altogether opposed to the first espousals, she was to retire to
a convent. This mild measure proved altogether inefficient, and it was ultimately arranged, that the bridegroom should not pay the foster-lean at espousals, but
should give security for its payment on completion of the
marriage.[2]

The next stipulation related to the morning-gift, which
will be more conveniently considered hereafter. The
bridegroom had next to state what provision he would
make for his wife in case she survived him. It was inti-
mated, that to give her half his property in case there
were no children, and all, if there were, was not unreasonable, subject to the wife's giving up a portion in the
event of her second marriage.[3]

The preliminaries of espousals being satisfactorily disposed of, the ceremony took place. It consisted, first, in
the ancient system of hand-fasting, and next, in the interchange of something " to bind the bargain." The article
given by the bridegroom was called " arrha," or " earnest,"
and might consist of an ox, a saddled horse, arms, a ring,

---

[1] *Ll. Boior.*, tit. vii, c. 17. *Confess.*, 20; Ecgb., *Pœnit.*, ii, 12.
[2] Theod., *Pœnit.*, xvi, 29; Ecgb., [3] *Ll. Edmundi*, Thorpe, i, 255.

or merely a kiss. In the sixth century, when St. Leotard was persuaded to marry, he presented to his *fiancée*, on his espousals, a ring, a kiss, and a pair of shoes, each of which had a typical signification. But, from an early period, rings and coins were preferred to everything else as presents between lovers.[1]

In the ceremony of espousals, the man placed a ring on the woman's right hand, to be *so* worn so long as she was bound to remain a maid.[2] After the hand-fasting, the bridegroom and bride exchanged a solemn kiss, as shewing that having, by the joining together of hands, been united in the body, they were, by the interchange of a kiss, joined together in the breath, or Holy Spirit. On the continent, if, after the bestowal of the kiss, the bridegroom died prior to marriage, his property was equally

---

[1] "Et dicuntur arrhæ, annuli, vel pecuniæ, vel aliæ res dandæ sponsæ per sponsum, quæ datio subarrhatio dicitur, præcipue tum quando fit per annuli dationem." *Sarum Ritual.* Maskell's *Mon. Rit.*, vol. i, p. 44.

[2] Rings had been used as outward signs of contract by the Jews and Romans at the coronation of kings and the ordination of bishops; were in use among the Anglo-Saxons; and were in accordance with the law of Rome and the canons of the Church. Selden's *Uxor Hebraica*, l. ii, c. 14; *Cod. Theod.*, l. iii, tit. 3; *De Sponsalibus,* leg. 5. The ring was placed on the right hand in imitation of the ceremony adopted on the consecration of bishops, when the vow of continence was taken. The following occurs in a matrimonial benediction given by Martene in reference to the transfer of the ring from the right hand to the left: "Et eum deinceps in sinistra ferat, ad differentiam gradus episcopalis, ubi annulus in signaculum integræ et plenæ castitatis in dextra manu publice est portandus." Wheatley gives the following reasons for the use of the ring. "The reasons," he says, "why a ring was pitched upon for the pledge rather than anything else, was, because anciently the ring was a seal, by which all orders were signed, and things of value secured (Gen. xxxviii, 18; Esther iii, 10-12; 1 Maccab. vi, 15); and therefore the delivery of it was a sign that the person to whom it was given was admitted into the highest friendship and trust (Gen. xii, 42). For which reason it was adopted as a ceremony in marriage to denote that the wife, in consideration of her being espoused to the man, was admitted as a sharer in her husband's counsels, and a joint partner in his honour and estate: and therefore we find that not only the ring, but the keys also, were in former times delivered to her at the marriage. That the ring was in use among the old Romans, we have several undoubted testimonies. (Juvenal, *Sat.* vi, ver. 26, 27; Plin., *Hist. Nat.*, lib. iii, c. 1; Tertull. *Apol.*, c. vi, p. 7 A.) Pliny, indeed, tells us that, in his time, the Romans used an iron ring without any jewel; but Tertullian hints that in the former ages it was a ring of gold." *Rational Illustration of the Common Prayer*, p. 390, edit. 1759.

divided between his spouse and his family; but, if he had omitted it, the whole of his property passed to his heirs. As the clergy regarded this as part of their system, they probably attempted to introduce it here; but there is no evidence that they did so, although the kiss was by no means an idle ceremony.[1]

After the interchange of presents, the bridegroom gave security for the performance of the promises he had made, and his friends guaranteed it. On the part of the lady, her friends gave security to the husband, that they would make good any liability she might incur during her married life; for it was not her husband, but her family, who were responsible for her behaviour.[2] At the conclusion of the espousals, a mass-priest was required to pronounce on them a religious benediction, and with this the ceremony concluded.

It was not necessary that the marriage should immediately follow the espousals; and the church seems to have favoured an interval between them. The delay, however, involved many dangers, and sound sense dictated that it should be as short as possible.

When we consider the early age at which children were betrothed, it cannot excite our surprise that in very many cases, one or both parties were reluctant to complete their engagements. For these occurrences the law provided. If the man neglected or refused to complete the espousals by matrimony within two years, he forfeited the amount of the foster-lean.[3] And if the lady refused

---

[1] *Cod. Theodosii*, lib. iii, tit. 5; De Sponsalibus; Tertullian, *De Velandis Virginibus*, c. xi; Strutt's *Manners and Customs*, vol. iii, 153.

[2] *Ll. Edmundi*, s. 7, Thorpe, i, 257.

[3] *Ll. Inæ*, 31, Thorpe, ii, 464; Theod., *Pœnit.*, vi, 29, Thorpe, ii, 11. By the Salic law a man who was guilty of a breach of promise was fined sixty-two shillings (*Ll. Salic.*, l. 70); and by the Bavarian, twenty-three shillings, and was required to swear, with twelve compurgators, that he did not do it through the ill-will of his relations, or on account of her faults, but solely from a preference for some other lady. (*Ll. Baio.*, l. xiv.)

E

to do so, she was bound not only to return the foster-lean, but an early *ecclesiastical* law required her to repay it fourfold, and a later, twofold. The state, however, was not so severe as the church; for by common law she escaped by returning the money, with an addition of one-third. She was also compelled by law to return all presents made to her during courtship.

SECTION VI.—THE MARRIAGE CONTRACT.

From the ceremonies that attended the pre-matrimonial contract, we pass to the contract of marriage itself; with the single observation that during no period of the Anglo-Saxon era were espousals a *necessary* preliminary to marriage. The marriage ceremony differed very little from that of espousals, which had, in fact, been based upon it. The most important act was the hand-fasting, and the consent to be man and wife publicly expressed. The ring, if the parties had been previously espoused, was transferred from the bride's right hand to her left, as a sign that she abandoned her vow of virginity and accepted a position of obedience. If no espousals had taken place, a wedding-ring was placed on the *left* hand of the bride, with words of matrimonial contract in the *present* tense. In this ceremony the bridegroom held the ring on the *first* finger of the bride's left hand, saying, " In the name of the Father ;" he then held it on the second, saying, " In the name of the Son ;" and then on the third, saying, " In the name of the Holy Ghost ;" and lastly, he placed it on the fourth finger, and left it there, saying, " Amen."[1]

There was one curious observance attending marriage which is worthy of observation. By an ancient Anglo-

[1] See the *Liber Pontif. Exon.*, p. 260. The first finger was considered to typify the first person in the Trinity; the second, the second person; the third, the third; and the fourth, finality.

Saxon custom, an unmarried girl was required to wear her hair long and loose, for flowing locks were typical of freedom and chastity. After a certain time she was permitted to plait it, with a view to cleanliness, but never to bind or braid it round her head. For these reasons it was, that on her wedding day she always undid the plaits and wore it wildly dishevelled on her shoulders. The longer it was, the more clearly it expressed virginity and noble birth; and the more loose and scattered, the better it typified freedom from previous obligation.

At the earliest period of Anglo-Saxon history, the damsel's hair was, on her marriage (or entering a convent), cut short like that of a slave, to shew that she had accepted a position of servitude.[1] When, however, Anglo-Saxon wives rose in dignity, they freed themselves from this disfiguring ceremony, and though they were never permitted to wear their, hair loose like free unmarried girls, they obtained permission to bind it in folds round their heads. These volutes, which, in their origin, were badges of servitude, were afterwards looked upon as crowns of honour, which no single woman was permitted to wear.

Upon marriage, the authority or "mund" of the father over the daughter was transferred to the husband, and for this a fee was paid by the latter. In the time of St. Augustine, the sum paid for mund on the marriage of an earl's widow was fifty shillings; on that of a gentleman's twenty shillings; of a person's of the third class, twelve shillings; and of the fourth, six shillings.[2] As no *physical* transfer of the "mund" could take place, a figurative one was necessary; and in accordance with the customs of the Arabs, Jews, Goths, and Anglo-Saxons, a shoe was used as a type or sign. The father delivered the bride's shoe

[1] Optatus, *De Schismat. Donat.*, lib. vi, Paris, 1702, p. 95; Hieron. Epist. xlviii ad Sabusian., c. iii (Ve- net., 1766); Bened., vol. i, p. 1089. [2] *Ll. Æthelbert.*, s. 75 and 72, Thorpe, i, 21 (see note).

E 2

to the bridegroom, who struck or touched her on the head with it.[1] This typified his assumption of marital authority, and probably had its origin in the custom of placing the foot on the neck of a prisoner or slave. When the young couple retired to rest, the shoe was placed at the head of the bed on the husband's side, as a sign of the authority he had just acquired.[2] If the wife was suspected of being a strong-minded woman, it was thought facetious to steal into the room, and slyly transfer the shoe from the husband's side to the wife's, as a quiet hint that she would probably rule the roast.

At the conclusion of the ceremony, the young people were presented by their parents or for-speakers to the priest for benediction.[3] In the benediction, they were enjoined to pass the first, and sometimes the second and third, nights of married life in virginity and prayer. If the injunction had been duly observed, the newly-married couple were permitted, on the fourth day, to be present at the celebration of the sacrament, though not to communicate.[4]

The nuptial benediction was pronounced under a veil, or *care-cloth*, held at each corner, by a tall man, over the bride and bridegroom.[5] If the bride was single, and of good character, she was also presented by the priest with a wreath of victory, as a sign that she had conquered the temptations of celibacy, and entered gloriously into that

---

[1] *Boulster Lecture*, 1640, p. 290; Brande's *Pop. Antiq.*, ii, 169. It is worthy of remark that it is stated in a recent publication that, at a Jewish wedding at Rabat, it is still customary for the bridegroom to strike the bride with a shoe in token of authority and supremacy. *Pillars of Hercules*, vol. i, p. 305.

[2] Michelet's *Life of Luther*, l. iv, c. i; *Origines du Droit français*, t. i, p. 45.

[3] *Ll. Edmundi*, s. 8, Thorpe, i, 257; *Concil. Carthag.*, iv, c. 13 (Labb. ii, 1201).

[4] Selden's *Uxor Ebraica*, lib. ii, c. 28; Ecgb. *Excerp.*, 8, Thorpe, ii, 110; Ecgb. *Pœnit.*, l. ii, s. 21, Thorpe, ii, 191; *Concil. Carthag.*, iv, c. 13; *Concil. Valen.*, c. 110; Stratford's *Constit.*, A.D. 1243; Martene, t. ii, p. 126.

[5] Brande's *Popular Antiquities*, vol. ii, p. 141.

state which is typical of the triumphant union of the church with her Lord and Saviour.[1] The bridal wreath was composed of myrtle or olive leaves, intermixed with purple flowers, and fastened together with white silk, or of olive leaves wreathed together with purple and white flowers. The white was symbolical of virgin purity, and the purple of the blood of our Lord.[2]

A widow, on her marriage, had neither wreath nor veil, as neither could be worn twice. She was also required to have her hands covered, while those of a single girl were to be uncovered.[3]

There are still traces of these customs in the veil and wreath worn by single girls when they marry, which are not usually worn by widows ; and in the occasional practice of throwing an old shoe after a bride when she leaves the paternal roof. Although a religious ceremony was strongly recommended, and usually adopted, it was not absolutely necessary to the validity of a marriage.[4] At certain marriages (as in those of widows), admitted to be

---

[1] St. Chrysost. *Hom.* 9, *in Tem.*, p. 1567; Wernsley's *Trigurine Liturgy*, p. 152 ; Seldeni *Uxor Ebraica*, vol. iii, pp. 653 and 661 ; *Capit.* Ottonis Episc. Verselensis, c. 94.

[2] Martene, vol. ii, p. 121 ; Bingham's *Christian Antiq.*, v. iii, c. 22 ; Leland's *Collect.*, v. 322.

[3] *Ordo ad faciendum sponsalia, Salisbury Manual.*

[4] " Digamus tamen unum annum . . . . abstineat se a carnibus ; non dimittat tamen uxorem. Trigamus, ut superius, ... abstineat se a carnibus, tamen non separentur." Theod. *Liber. Pœnit.*, xix, 15, 16. In the Decretal of Alexander III (who was pope from A.D. 1159 to 1181) to the bishop of Norwich is the following—" Ex tuis litteris intelleximus virum quemdam et mulierem sese invicem recepisse, nullo sacerdote præsente, nec adhibita solemnitate quam solet Anglicana eccle-

sia exhibere, et aliam prædictam mulierem ante carnalem commixtionem solemnitur duxisse et cognovisse ; tuæ prudentiæ duximus respondendum quod, si prius vir et mulier ipsa de præsenti se receperint, dicendo unus alteri, ego te recipio in meam, et ego te recipio in meum : etiamsi non intervenerit illa solemnitas, nec vir mulierum carnaliter cognoverit, mulier ipsa primo debet restitui, quum nec potuerit nec debuerit post talem consensum alii nubere." Martene, vol. ii, c. 9, art. 3 ; Viner's *Abridg. title Marriage, F.* Reeve's *History of English Law*, vol. iv, p. 52-55 ; Swinburne's *Treatise of Sponsals*, s. 14, pt. i, p. 193. As to what the law of England may have been on this point from the " time of legal memory " until the 26 George II, has been a matter on which the most eminent judges have differed. A most elaborate account

valid by both church and state, no priest was permitted to be present. Nor is it probable that, in that part of the country which was mainly inhabited by Danes, any religious ceremony would have been acceptable. For more than two hundred years after their conversion to Christianity, the Scandinavians jealously maintained their ancient form of marriage; and, as has been already stated, at their simple rites, it was not the priest, but the bride's father, who officiated.

The clergy struggled hard to induce the Danes and Normans to admit the *necessity* of some religious ceremony on these occasions, but without success. Rollo, duke of Normandy, at the taking of Paris, captured Popa, the daughter of count Beranger, whom he married " after the custom of his country" (*more Danico*), without any religious ceremony; and his son, Guillaume Longue-espée, when he espoused the fair Espriota, followed his example.

> " Icele ama moult e tout chere,
> Mais *à la Danishe manere*
> La volt avoir, non autrement;
> Ce dist l'estoire, qui ne ment."

It was in this manner that the Danes, when they settled in the eastern counties, married the daughters of the Anglo-Saxon nobility whom they partially conquered. The Norman clergy did not hesitate to call the women so married, concubines; but this was unjust, as in that and the following century, both forms of marriage, the ecclesiastical and the civil, were legal.[1]

Anglo-Saxon marriages took place at the house of the

of it will be found in the "Opinion of the Judges" in Beamish *v.* Beamish (in error) ordered to be printed by the House of Lords, 21st Feb., 1861.

[1] Sir F. Palsgrave's *History of Normandy*, vol. ii. p. 107. It was not until after the Anglo-Saxon era that the handfasting, giving away, the espousals by words of the future, the contract in the words of the present, the symbolic delivery of the ring, and the spiritual benediction, were all blended into one ceremony, and a full marriage service thus constituted out of them.

parents either of the bride or of the bridegroom. It was not till the Anglo-Norman era, or possibly even later, that marriages were celebrated in the church porch, and the benediction pronounced in the chancel. And it was not till the year 1199 that marriages were celebrated in churches.[1]

When the wedding was over, the bride, accompanied by her bridesmaids and her friends, was conducted in procession to her future home. This ceremony afforded to facetious youths an opportunity for a very boisterous and cruel specimen of fun. They collected a quantity of foul water in tubs, or stoops, and a heap of filth of any description they could find; with this they waylaid the bridal procession, soused the bride with the dirty water, and pelted her with the rubbish. The bride was of course insulted, frightened, probably hurt, and her bridal dress certainly spoiled. As, in those days of scanty wardrobes, the bridal costume formed no small portion of a lady's *trousseau*, the proceeding was doubly vexatious to the

The distinction between the Anglo-Saxon benediction and a marriage service is very clear, though it has not always been borne in mind. The benediction was a blessing on a marriage already contracted, and which would have been valid without it; while a marriage service is a religious rite by which a marriage is constituted. Although a marriage benediction was occasionally in use in England from the seventh century, yet there was no marriage service, properly so called, until the end of the twelfth. Dr. Lingard, *Ang. Sax. Church*, vol. ii, p. 10, on the authority of Martene, vol. ii, p. 51, gives a sketch of an Anglo-Saxon marriage service; but I have not been able to find this or any other Anglo-Saxon marriage service in Martene. There is one rather like it in Selden's *Uxor Ebraica*, lib. ii, c. 27.

[1] Dr. Lingard says, " There is no trace of any form of marriage contract in ancient sacramentals previously to the close of the twelfth century ; and the *earliest* mention of it occurs in the constitutions of two English prelates, Richard Poere, bishop of Sarum, and Richard de Marisco, bishop of Durham, who ordered the parish priests to teach the bridegroom this form.—' I take thee, N, for my wife ;' and the bride a similar form, ' I take thee, M, for my husband,' Wilkins, *Con.*, i, 582." Lingard's *Ang. Sax. Church*, vol. ii, p. 10. I would, however, refer to the benediction pronounced on the marriage and coronation of king Ethelwulf and Judith, the daughter of king Charles of France, which is given at full length in Bosquet's *Script. Rerum Gallicarum*, vol. ii, p. 621.

fair bride, and consequently doubly entertaining to the
gentlemen, "who enjoyed the joke." Among this number we must not include the bridegroom and his friends,
who had preceded her home. They were expecting a
bride all smiles and elegance, they received one all tears
and dirt ; and as the pugnacious Anglo-Saxons always
rejoiced in any decent excuse for fighting, it was not to
be expected that they would peaceably endure so gross a
provocation. The bridegroom and his friends usually
sallied out upon the jokers ; and, as in those days all
freemen carried arms, bloodshed was the natural result.
This system of joking was subsequently repressed by legal
enactments.[1]

The notion that there was something facetious in annoy-
ing brides by covering them with filth, continued during
several centuries.

When in the romance Robert the Devil was condemned
by way of penance to act the fool for a certain time,
we find him performing a series of facetiæ for the amusement of the emperor's court. After having thrust a dog's
tail into a Jew's mouth, thrown a live cat into the beef-
cauldron, and performed one or two other tricks equally
amusing (?), we read—

> " Robert saw a bride that should be marryed,
>   And soone he toke her by the hande,
>   So into a foul dung-mixen he her caryed,
>   And in the myre he let her stande."

On which

> " Lords and barons laughe that they could not stande,
>   To see him make myrthe *withouten harme* ;
>   They sayd, he was the meryest in all that lande."[2]

On her marriage, the father presented his daughter

[1] *Ll. Longobard.* lib. i, tit. xvi,
s. 8.

[2] *Robert the Devyll*, a metrical romance, p. 37, etc.

with a wedding gift proportioned to his means, and this was called the Fader-fiod, or father's fee. It was the separate property of the wife during marriage, and remained hers if she survived her husband.[1] In the Anglo-Danish districts, all the relations of the bride and bridegroom were *bound* to make them presents proportioned to the nearness of their relationship.

The lady, on her marriage (or at the previous espousals), received numerous presents from her intended, and these were often of great magnificence. A sister of king Athelstan was engaged to, and ultimately married, Hugh Capet, count of Paris. On her espousals, he sent her a multitude of handsome presents, some of which were hardly suited to a lady's taste. To horses and trappings, oriental spices, perfumes, jewels, and holy relics, which are generally agreeable to the sex, he added the sword of Constantine the Great, the spear of Charlemagne, and the banner of St. Maurice.[2] We must not, however, infer from the splendour of the engaged presents, that the delicacy of a *fiancée's* feelings were very tenderly respected. Nothing could exceed the splendour of the gifts which king Otho sent to Eadgyth (the sister of Athelstan) when he proposed to her. The lady accepted both the offer and the gifts, and was sent with great magnificence and attendance to the court of the German emperor. With her was sent her younger sister Adiva, that, if the emperor were disappointed with his betrothed, whom he had not then seen, *he might marry her sister if he liked !* Otho preferred his intended, but considerately provided Adiva with a husband in the person of an Alpine prince who formed one of his court.[3]

[1] From a comparison of our own with continental laws, we may infer that this custom was of Saxon origin. *Ll. Ethelberti*, lxxxi, Thorpe, vol. i, p. 25 ; *Ll. Saxonum*, tit. viii, art. 2.
[2] William of Malmesbury, l. ii, c. 6 ; Ingulphus, A.D. 938.
[3] Roswitha *De Gestis Odonis*, p.

Royal weddings were in those times celebrated with
incredible magnificence ; but none ever equalled in splendour that of Gunhilda, the sister of Harthacnut, with the
emperor Henry III. Never had there been previously
seen in England such a display of gold, silver, and gems,
garments of rich magnificence, and servants and horses,
as on this occasion.

A marriage would have been a miserable thing in the
opinion of our forefathers, if it had not concluded with a
feast. No sooner was an Anglo-Saxon engaged, than he
hastened to invite all his friends and neighbours to his
wedding. In the Danish districts a man was obliged to
ask all his own and all his wife's relations within the
third degree, either by blood or marriage, and to them
he generally added all the influential people he knew,
particularly those who attended the court or parliament.[1]

The clergyman who had pronounced the benediction
came, as a matter of course, and was accompanied by as
many of his clerical brethren as he chose to invite. And
even if the marriage had been "after the Danish manner,"
in which no religious ceremony had been used, or one
within the prohibited degrees, the inferior clergy were
nothing loth to attend. Their attendance on occasion of
such weddings was again and again forbidden by their
ecclesiastical superiors, who pointed out how inconsistent it was that they should one day drink toasts
to the health and happiness of a bride, on whom, on
the following day, they would impose the penances
which the church awarded for a clandestine marriage.
But the humbler Anglo-Saxon clergy loved a jovial
entertainment better than church discipline, and to

166 ; Will. Malmes., l. ii, c. 6 ; In-   [1] Steirnhook, *De Jure Suevor*, p.
gulphus, A.D. 938.   155.

the entertainment they went, in defiance of their superiors.[1]

The wedding feast lasted, as was usual with feasts on
solemn occasions, three days at least, and was conducted
with the greatest profusion, gluttony, and drunkenness.

On the first day, when the guests had, for the time,
eaten sufficiently, the clergy rose and sang a psalm or
spiritual song suited to the occasion, and then the general
company sang as pleased them. At last the singing was
taken up by the wandering gleemen, who always made
their appearance wherever there was entertainment to be
had. The songs of these roystering harpers were, at
the best, of a very worldly character; and as the merriment increased, they grew more and more reckless of
propriety; till, when everybody was nearly or quite
intoxicated, they often accompanied "their immodest
ribaldry with pantomime of the grossest character."[2]
The bride and bridegroom, however, were not obliged to
remain until the close of the night's revelry. When the
evening of the first day appeared to the more sober portion of the guests to be fairly spent, a procession was
formed, headed by the clergy, and the bride was conducted, with musical honours, to the nuptial couch.[3]
The bed was then formally blessed by the priest, and the
marriage-cup drunk by the bride and bridegroom; after
which, those who formed the procession returned to their
feasting, and drank as long and as hard as the supply
of liquor and their constitutions permitted.

At the marriage of Alfred the Great, wise and temperate as he was, he was compelled to indulge in such excesses, that he never altogether recovered from an illness

---

[1] Theod. *Pœnit.* xvii, 10; Ecgb.
Excerp., 91; *Institute of Polity*, s.
22, Thorpe, ii, 333.
[2] Bingham's *Christ. Antiq.*, b. 22,
c. 4; Colquhoun's *Civil Law*, vol. i,
p. 471.
[3] Bingham's *Christ. Antiq.*, vol.
vii, b. 22, c. 4; *Historia Eliensis*, l.

which they brought on.[1]   About a century afterwards, a marriage feast took place, which was followed by still more disastrous consequences.   In the reign of Hartha-cnut, one of his nobles, named Osgod Clapha, who re-sided near Lambeth, on his estate still called after him Clapa-ham, or Clapham, gave a feast to celebrate the marriage of his daughter.   The king honoured it with his presence, and, after feasting most profusely, staggered to his legs late at night to propose a toast.   He fell down intoxicated, was removed into an adjoining apartment, and died in a few minutes.[2]

At the earliest period of Anglo-Saxon history, a wed-ding was not completely binding on the husband till the following day.   On the morning after the wedding, the husband was at liberty to present his wife with a morning gift.   By so doing, he admitted that the representation of her charms was not exaggerated, nor the sum he had paid for her excessive.   On its receipt, the wife immediately rose, dressed her dishevelled air, and braided or bound it in full volutes around her head.   This ceremony being once performed, her liability to be returned to her parents ceased, and she acquired the full rights of a married woman.   At first the morning gift was altogether op-tional; the husband gave anything or nothing as he pleased.   But as women grew in influence, (and at some time prior to the period of king Alfred), it was always expressly agreed that the husband should bestow upon his wife a morning gift, as he thereby relinquished his right to return her; but its value was allowed for a con-siderable time to depend entirely on his generosity and goodwill.[3]

i, c. 4; *De Gestis Herewardi Sax-onis*, p. 58.
[1] Pauli's *Life of Alfred*, c. 3, A.D. 868.

[2] *Anglo-Sax. Chron.*, A.D. 1042; Flor. Wigorn., A.D. 1042, 8th June.
[3] Du Cange v. Morgen-gifu; *Ll. Ethelb.*, c. 81; *Ll. Cnuti*, sec. 74;

At first, it was commonly a trivial present ; but in the course of time it rose from a trifling pledge of affection to a magnificent dotation, and often included horses, slaves, churches, and even large estates. Elfleda tells us in her will, that she received an estate called Pettendun as her morning gift : and Elfhelm informs us that he gave his wife as a morning gift " Beadwan, and Burge-sted, and Strætford, and three hides at Heonhealem."[1] And Eadgyth, the sister of Athelstan, received from her husband Otto, emperor of Germany, the city of Magdeburg as her " morning gift."[2]

At the latest period of Anglo-Saxon history, the *amount* of the morning gift was always a matter of stipulation prior to the marriage. It became after marriage absolutely the property of the wife, and in the event of her becoming a widow she disposed of it as she pleased.

One of the consequences of marriage insisted on by the clergy was the legitimation of illegitimate children by the subsequent marriage of their parents. When the bride and bridegroom had already a family, the children knelt between them at the marriage service under the care-cloth, and were supposed thereby to obtain the benefit of the nuptial benediction.[3] This practice was continued by the peasantry in some villages in England to a comparatively late period, with the exception that the wife's apron was substituted for the Anglo-Saxon care-cloth.

Turner's *Hist. of Anglo-Saxons*, b. 7, c. 8.

[1] Turner's *Hist. of Anglo-Saxons*, vol. iii, b. 7, c. 8 ; Lye, *Sax. Dict. v. Morgen-gifu.*

[2] Lappenberg, *Anglo-Sax. Kings*, vol. ii, p. 110. It is stated by Dr. Henry, on the authority of Muratori, that in every country in Europe there were laws restraining the amount of the morning gift, but I am not aware that there was ever any such law in England. Among the Lombards it was not permitted to exceed one-fourth of the husband's fortune. Du Cange, v. *Donum Matutinale.* It was also limited by the laws of the Visigoths. *Ll. Wisigoth.*, lib. iii, c. 5. The sneer in which Gibbon indulges at the expense of the ladies who stipulated for morning gifts is founded on a misapprehension, as it did not arise from any consciousness of demerit. *Decline and Fall*, c. xxxi.

[3] *Opuscula* R. Grostesti Episcop. Linc., p. 321.

SECTION VII.—DIVORCE.

Having treated of the mode and circumstances attending the contract of marriage, we will proceed to notice the customs attending its dissolution. There are three modes (other than death) by which a marriage may be dissolved, the use of which marks different eras in the history of the social position of women. The first is repudiation; the second, separation; and the third, divorce. The first is the act of one party only without the consent of the other; the second is by mutual consent; and the third is the act of the law either at the instance of one or of both the parties, or acting spontaneously. The first affords every facility for cruelty towards the wife; in the second, her will is consulted; and in the third, the law, in the interests of morality, exercises an active control over the dissolution of marriage.

It has been already stated that, at the earliest period, a dissatisfied husband was at liberty to return his wife, and thereby terminate the marriage; and there is no doubt that at that time the power of repudiation on the part of the husband was almost, if not altogether, unlimited. But pride and self-respect, as they very often do, supplied the place of morals, and though repudiation was not objected to on the score of immorality, it was nevertheless resented as an affront to the lady and her family. Gwendoline and her friends, according to the romance of Brut, not only levied war on king Locrine for repudiating her and marrying the beautiful Estrild, but put both offenders to death. Penda, the king of the Mercians, declared war against Coenwalch, king of the West Saxons, for putting away his sister. And at a much later period, Athelstan resented a similar insult at the hands of Sigtrig the Danish earl of Northumberland, and determined to slay

him, but was prevented by the earl's sudden and prema-
ture death.[1]

In every country the system of repudiation has gradually worn itself out, and generally in the same manner.
In Judæa, Rome, Arabia, India, China, and among the
Anglo-Saxons, the power of repudiation was at first unlimited, and could be exercised *in private*. The first restriction placed upon it in all these countries was the
requisition that the husband should divorce the wife publicly (if she wished it), *and for a given cause*. At first,
in all these countries, the most *trivial* cause sufficed. By
the Hindoo law, extravagance, attempting to procure
abortion, spoiling a husband's goods, or eating before he
had eaten, were sufficient excuses. The Chinese law
admitted seven grounds of repudiation, of which *talkative-
ness* was one!

When Rome was at the zenith of her glory, illustrious
Romans put away their wives and offered to the law the
grave reasons—of sterility, walking out with the head
uncovered, or going to a theatre without permission, talk-
ing to women of inferior rank, ill-temper, or a dislike of a
mother-in-law! The Jews put away their wives at pleasure, privately and causelessly, until Moses compelled
them to give a writing of divorcement; and even in our
Saviour's time, it was a matter of dispute between the
schools of Hillch and Shammai, whether a man might
put away his wife for any cause he chose, such as cooking
his dinner badly, or being less beautiful than her neighbours;—or whether the cause must be one thoroughly disgraceful to a wife, as public indecency, or some graver
offence. The historian Josephus, when he put away his
wife, who had borne him four children, assigned as a legal
ground that her manners were not pleasing. On this

---

[1] Layamon's *Brut*, vol. i, p. 104; *Annals of Ulster*, p. 67; Bede's
Geoffrey of Monmouth, l. ii, c. 4, 5, *Eccles. Hist.*, l. iii, c. 7; *Anglo-Sax.*
6; Flor. of Worcester, A.D. 926; *Chron.*, A.D. 645.

subject the Jews interrogated our Saviour, and were surprised when He denounced the barbarous marriage-laws of
their forefathers, and forbad them to put away their
wives save for the cause of adultery.[1]

The comparative gravity of the causes which satisfy
barbarous judicatures as legitimate excuses for repudiation
are tests of civilisation. In the seventh century, the
Anglo-Saxon husband had lost the right of putting away
his wife *without* cause assigned ; and though the reasons
he was accustomed to give were utterly insufficient, they
were not so frivolous as those permitted on the continent,
where Philip the first, having fallen in love with the wife
of the earl of Anjou, put away his queen, and assigned as
cause that she was "growing fat." The reasons which
were at one time considered sufficient in England probably were that the wife was either barren, deformed,
fetid, silly, passionate, luxurious, rude, an habitual
drunkard, a glutton, a gad-about, quarrelsome, or abusive.
Towards the end of the seventh century, it was declared
that no one of these was sufficient.[2]

The female sex were indebted to the clergy for the
limitations gradually imposed on the husband's power of
repudiation, but their assistance was at first of a timid
and limited character. The bishops taught "that if a
man repudiated his wife, he was not to marry another in
her lifetime, *if he wished to be a very good Christian.*"[3]
This sounds rather more like an admonition than a legislative enactment. They, however, declared that a man
ought not to put away his wife *without her consent* and
marry another ; and though they did not *then* punish
even by censure a man who did so, yet they excommunicated the second wife.

[1] Michaelis, *Laws of Moses*, vol. iii,
art. 120.

[2] See arch. Theod. *Canons*, A.D.
673, a. 10 ; and Bede's *Eccles. Hist.*,
l. iv, c. 5.

[3] *Capit., Karol. et Ludovici*, Lib.
6, c. 87. *Law of North. Priests*,
Thorpe, ii, 301.

It is to be feared that the exertions of the clergy in restricting the license of repudiation were limited by an over-anxious regard for the interests of the church. When either a husband or wife desired to repudiate his or her partner, and to bestow himself or herself and riches on a monastery, the church made no objection. In the eighth century, Sebbi, king of the East Saxons, desired to put away his wife and retire to a monastery, taking with him immense estates. The queen's consent was however necessary, and this she refused to give—a refusal which the clergy considered unreasonable and improper. Etheldrythe, a daughter of Anna, the famous king of East Anglia, was also encouraged by the clergy to deal very lightly by her marriage vows. This young lady had the misfortune to be very weak and very rich. She was consequently sought for as a wife, by princes who cared nothing for her person, and as a nun, by churchmen who cared as little for her soul. She endeavoured to please all parties. She took a vow of virginity with a permission to marry, and married with permission to observe her vow. Her first husband, Tondebert, earl of the Girvii, who probably obtained possession of her land, did not trouble himself about her or her personal property ; and on his death, she retired to Ely. She subsequently married Egfrid, a son of the king of Northumbria, a boy of about thirteen, whose friends desired her estates. He also for some time willingly respected her vow, but afterwards attempted to compel her to do her duty as a wife. She refused compliance with his wishes, and having succeeded in escaping from his kingdom, again took up her residence in a monastery. There, in defiance of her marriage vow, she emulated the strictest chastity of the cloister in the bonds of marriage. The clergy applauded her conduct, and no doubt obtained possession of her estates. The

F

king took a second wife ; and all parties appear to have
been satisfied with what was, in truth, a very discreditable transaction.[1]

The right of repudiation for a sufficient cause was not
confined to the male sex, but was exercised by women
whenever they were sufficiently powerful to do so effectually. The princess Gunhilda, daughter of king Cnut,
was famous as a lady of exquisite beauty, for whom all
lovers sighed, but whom none could win. Her brother
at length gave her in marriage to Henry emperor of
the Germans. The memory of the splendour of her nuptial pageant, the magnificence of the presents she received and of the nobles who waited upon her, lived for
centuries in popular song. For some time her married
life was happy, but, at last, her husband accused her of
infidelity. She demanded to be tried by wager of battle ;
and this, which was strictly her right, was immediately
conceded to her. She then chose as her champion a
dwarf named Mimicon, who had been in her brother's
service and was the keeper of her starling. The king
selected as his antagonist a giant of the name of Ro-
dingar. On the day of battle the dwarf succeeded in
ham-stringing his adversary, and ultimately proved victorious. The queen, therefore, was lawfully acquitted.
She immediately dissolved her marriage on the ground of
her husband's false accusation, and " taking the veil of
a nun, became a spouse of Christ, and grew old in the
service of God."[2]

At the time when the practice of repudiation was
wearing out, separations by mutual consent, which probably entitled the parties to marry again, were permitted.[3]

[1] *Histor. Eliensis*, lib. i. c. 8 and
9 ; Bede's *Eccles. Hist.*, l. iv, c. 3, s.
19 ; *Anglo-Sax. Chron.*, A.D. 679 ;
Matt. Westm., A.D. 679.

[2] Will. Malmes., l. ii, c. 12, s. 188 ;
Chronicon Joh. Bromton.
[3] *Concil. Hertford.*, c. 10 ; Spelman's *Concil.*, l. 573 ; Theod., *Pœnit.*,

Divorces were also granted for adultery, and for what
was termed by the clergy, spiritual adultery, viz., infidelity, idolatry, heresy, and schism.   To these causes it
is probable that the Anglo-Saxons, in imitation of the
cognate nations of the continent, added certain atrocious
crimes ; and also insanity, leprosy, and one or two in-
curable diseases.   It was also permitted, in case of either
party remaining a slave, or a prisoner of war beyond a
certain time, that the other should marry again.[1]   In the
later periods of Anglo-Saxon history, the custom of repudiation appears to have altogether ceased, and divorces
could only be obtained through the tribunals of the
country.[2]

xix, 20, Thorpe, ii, p. 17 ; Ecgb.
Dial., s. 13, Thorpe, ii, 93 ; Ecgb.
Excerp., 120 and 121 ; Ecg. Confess.,
35 ; Ecgb. Pœnit., iv, c. 55 ; Bede's
Eccles. Hist., l. iv, c. 5.   As to the
right of parties thus separated to
marry again, the minds of the Anglo-
Saxons seem to have been in an un-
settled state.   Archbishop Ecgbert
gives the following ambiguous answer to an inquiry as to the right of
a man so situated to marry again.
" Audi—' Quod Deus conjunxit, homo
non separet,' et item, ' Qui potest
capere, capiat.'   Sæpe namque tem-
porum permutatione necessitas le-
gem frangit.   Quid enim fecit David,
quando esuriit ? et tamen sine peccato est.   Ergo in ambiguis non est
ferenda sententia.   Sed concilia ne-
cesse est periclitari pro salute alio-
rum, hac conditione interposita, ut
ei qui se continentiæ devovit nullo
modo concedatur secundas inire nup-
tias."

[1] Epist. Papæ Johan. VII ad
Ethelredum Arch. Cant., Wilkins Concilia, vol. i, p. 195.

[2] It is true that we have one instance as late as A.D. 1051, in which
a king, and that a saintly one (Edward the Confessor), put away his
wife, but he at the same time de-
throned her, and confiscated all her

property, whether in land, gold, or
silver, and treated her as a criminal
and an outlaw.   This was done rather
in exercise of his power as a sovereign to punish a traitor, than of his
right, as a husband, to dismiss a
wife.   And it must be remembered
that the more powerful monarchs
took upon themselves to regulate
their matrimonial proceedings according to their own sovereign will, without any great regard to the laws of
church or state.   The accounts of the
repudiation of Eadgyth by Edward
the Confessor are very contradictory,
both as to its cause and manner.
The queen was attached to the Saxon
party of her brother Harold, and the
king's minister to that of the Normans.   At the instance of the latter,
the queen, after Harold's unsuccessful rebellion, was removed from
court, and publicly repudiated by
the king.   According to the Saxon
Chronicle, A.D. 1051, Flo. Wigorn.,
A.D. 1051, and William of Malmesbury, lib. ii, 13, she was deprived of
all her lands and treasures, was sent,
attended by one female servant, to
the abbey of Wherwell, and there
committed to the custody of the
abbess, who was a sister of the king.
According to a contemporary biographer of Edward (cited by Dr. Lin-

SECTION VIII.—MATRIMONIAL RIGHTS.

It has been already stated that, on an Anglo-Saxon marriage, the bride's relations gave security to answer for the defaults of her married life, and that the fines for offences committed against her were payable to them, and not to her husband. This may be accounted for by the fact that the wife did not become a part of her husband's family; but on his death, the mund, or authority over her, and the duty of protecting her, reverted to her own family. It may also be partly accounted for by the fact that *at first* the husband and wife had no joint property. The wife's separate property consisted of the father-fee and her morning-gift. Her interest in her husband's property after his death was very slight. If she survived him, *and had children*, she was entitled to half his property ; but *if she had no children*, she received nothing ; and the half which she received in the event of her having children was rather a provision for them than for her.[1]

As society improved, the interests of widows began to be duly protected, and at the time of Cnut their pecuniary rights were as carefully provided for by marriage settlements as they are at the present time. In a settlement made on the marriage of Wulfric and the sister of archbishop Wulfstan, the husband gave his wife all his land at Ealretun and Rebbedford for her life, and covenanted to procure her from a monastery a lease for three lives of the land at Cnihte-wic. He also gave her all his land at Eamilfin-tun absolutely, to give away in her lifetime or to dispose of by will, and he promised to give her thirty

gard from Stowe) she was conducted to Wherwell with royal pomp, and assured that her confinement was only adopted as a temporary measure of precaution.

[1] *Ll. Edmundi*, l. 3, 4, Thorpe, i, 255 ; *Ll. Henrici Primi*, lxx, 22, Thorpe, i, 574.

slaves and thirty horses. The settlement was witnessed by several archbishops and bishops, and was executed in duplicate. No family-solicitor of the present day could have wished for anything more formal.[1]

About this time (the era of Cnut), an Anglo-Saxon widow acquired a right, whether she had children *or not*, not only to her settled property, but to one-third of whatever had been acquired by herself and husband *jointly* during marriage, "except his clothes and his bed."[2]

It has been already stated that she forfeited everything if she married again within the year.[3]

About this time, also, the sex acquired a right which they probably did not despise, viz., to have, instead of the very scanty clothing of early times, a liberal wardrobe and a well-filled jewel-box. A lady of this era has left us a catalogue of her wardrobe, and we find that it contained mantles, gowns, and tunics of different colours; numerous cuffs and ribands; a golden fly beautifully adorned with gems, a golden vermiculated necklace, golden-headed beads, and a neck-cross. Another lady possessed necklaces and bracelets, wore rings with gems on her fingers, and indulged in the use of rouge or stibium.[4]

Among the Danes and Northmen a woman had a right to the custody of her husband's keys, and, if he refused to give them up to her, there was a specified form of action by which she could compel him to do so.[5] Cnut the Great extended this privilege to England, and under his reign married women acquired a right to have a storeroom, a chest, and a cupboard of their own, to keep them under lock and key, and to deny their husbands access to

[1] Hickes's *Diss. Epist.*, 76; Wanley's *Catalogue*, p. 302.

[2] *Ll. Ethelberti*, s. 81, Thorpe, i, 25; *Ll. Henrici Primi*, s. xx, Thorpe, i, 574; *Ll. Ripuar.*, tit. 37.

[3] *Ll. Cnuti Sec.* c. 74, Thorpe, i,

417; compare *Ll. Henrici Primi*, xi, s. 13.

[4] Turner's *Anglo-Saxon Hist.*, b. vii, c. 5.

[5] Steirnhook, *De Jure Suevorum*, p. 167.

them. This right, simple as it seems, suggests an explanation of the most important alterations in the relative positions of husband and wife that ever took place. In the
earliest times, if the husband stole, *both he and his wife*
were liable to be sold into slavery. Alfred the Great
relieved the wife from this penalty if she could *prove*
that she had not tasted of the thing stolen and knew not
of the theft. But, setting aside the impossibility of proving
a negative, the importance which the Anglo-Saxons attached to circumstantial evidence rendered this exemp-
tion nugatory ; for, where a man was *found in possession*
of stolen goods, he was not permitted to deny that he
stole them, and if they were found in the house of a
married couple *both* were deemed in possession of them,
both were considered guilty, and *both* were sold as slaves.

As in this age, marauding expeditions were the ordinary occupation of a gentleman, a wife would naturally
be anxious to get rid of any little articles which she
knew her lord had not obtained rightfully and for
which she anticipated a powerful claimant. There was
here a potent cause for domestic discord, which shews
clearly the incompatibility of the Saxon and Danish laws
as to matrimonial rights and responsibilities. When Cnut
therefore undertook to amalgamate the two codes, he
provided that unless stolen goods were found in one of
the wife's three lock-ups, she was not to be held liable for
the theft ; but if they were, she was to be sold into slavery
as formerly. He also aided the husband by enacting that
no wife should thenceforth forbid her husband to put
what he would in his own cottage.[1] This law, which,
without a knowledge of its origin, would seem very unac-
countable, must have contributed greatly to domestic

---

[1] *Ll. Inæ,* c. 7, Thorpe, i, 107 ; compare *Ll. Cnuti,* sec. 77, Thorpe,
Ll. Alfredi, l. ii, Thorpe, i, 47 ; and i, 419.

peace. In the tenth and eleventh centuries, the social position of women had every way improved. In the earliest ages, queens and princesses waited at table on their husbands. In the Brut, as well as in Beowulf, the queen is represented as serving the company; and we find the daughter of Hengist acting as cupbearer to king Vortigern. In the tenth century, instead of waiting at table, they sat at it, with their husbands and male friends—a privilege hardly ever accorded to the sex in a barbarous country. In a drawing in an Anglo-Saxon manuscript, representing a dinner party, the men and women are depicted as seated alternately, first a gentleman and then a lady, much in our present fashion. It was at a dinner party that Dunstan received from the queen-mother the offer of his bishopric.

Wives had also obtained the privilege of being present at the witena-gemot and at the county meetings; and they were permitted to sue and be sued in their own names in courts of justice;—a privilege they do not possess at the present day, except under peculiar circumstances in the city of London.

There is a curious story which enables us to fix the exact period when the great improvement in the social rank of women took place. Prior to the ninth and tenth centuries, the wives of the Anglo-Saxon kings had never taken the title of queen or been crowned. They enjoyed merely the title of the "king's wife" or the "king's lady." In A.D. 856, Ethelwulf, then a widower and in his dotage, made a pilgrimage to Rome, and on his return through France in July of that year he espoused Judith, the daughter of Charles le Chauve, a child of about twelve, and in the following October they were married by Hincmar, archbishop of Rheims. On this occasion, *a crown was placed upon her head*, and she was proclaimed "*queen*," which to the king and his nation had up to that time "*been an unknown custom.*" The social position of the Anglo-Saxon women had, however, so much advanced, that the West Saxons, who had before refused to tolerate a crowned wife, permitted Judith to wear her crown and to sit by the king's side on state occasions without a murmur.[1]

Thus we have seen that in the ninth and tenth centuries women ceased to be bartered away by their fathers, and acquired the right to dispose of themselves in marriage ; they ceased to be liable to repudiation at the will of their husbands ; acquired separate property, handsome wardrobes, and distinct keys ; ceased to be liable to be punished for their husbands' crimes ; and queens acquired their right to be so called, and to be solemnly and publicly crowned. These were very important facts in the history of the social position of the sex, and mark a great advance in civilisation.

For this amelioration in their condition, women were to a great extent indebted to the pains which the clergy took with their education, and to the intellectual accomplishments which they acquired, at a time when the male sex could study little but war.

It was, according to Asser, Osburga, the mother of Alfred the Great, who first awakened the literary tastes of her accomplished son ; and Ethelfleda, Alfred's eldest

---

[1] Ædewulf, rex occidentalium Anglorum, Roma rediens Judith filiam Karoli regis mense Julio desponsatam Kal. Octobribus in Vermeriæ palatio in matrimonium accipit, et eam, Jugmaro Durocortori Remorum episcopo benedicente, imposito capiti ejus diademate reginæ nomine insignit, quod sibi suæque genti eatenus fuerat insuetum. Patratoque regiis apparatibus utrimque atque numeribus matrimonio, cum ea Britanniam regni sui ditionem navigio repetit. Bouquet, *Recueil des Historiens des Gaules*, vol. i, p. 72. It has been alleged that Judith's receiving from Ethelwulf the title of queen, was one of the reasons why her son and certain bishops refused to surrender to him the authority they had usurped in his absence. But on the marriage of his daughter to Burhred, king of Mercia, she also obtained the title of queen. St. John's *Four Conquests of England*, vol. i, p. 240.

daughter, inherited her father's intellect and accomplishments, as well as his patriotic spirit and martial ardour. It was to his mother Ethelfrida, that Athelstan was indebted for an education which developed his natural energy and ability, and rendered him the first king of *all England*. The queen of Edward the Confessor was remarkable for her accomplishments ; and we are indebted to Ingulphus (or the borrower of his name) for an account of his juvenile acquaintance with this lady. It concludes with a " touch of nature," which shows that the way to a schoolboy's heart was the same then as now. " I have often seen her," he says, " while yet a boy, when my father was at the king's palace, and as I came from school, when I have met her, she would examine me in my learning, and from grammar she would proceed to logic (which she also understood), concluding with me in the most subtle argument, and then causing one of her maids to present *me with three or four pieces of money, I was dismissed, being sent to the larder, where I always obtained refreshments*."

Female accomplishments, however, did not preserve the sex from what we should now consider scandalous treatment. Our forefathers systematically beat their wives with great severity. During the whole of the Anglo-Saxon era and long afterwards, it was not only the right, but the duty of every husband to bestow " on his wife and his apprentices moderate castigation." There is no direct evidence to show what amount of chastisement was then considered *moderate*. The old Welsh law declares " that three blows with a broomstick on any part of the person except the head" is a proper allowance ; and a continental law of about the same date tells us that if the husband does not beat his wife with anything heavier than a stick or a birch broom, " he does not thereby disturb the peace of the menage," or in other words, break his matrimonial promise " to treat her well." One Welsh law limits the dimensions of the stick to the length of the husband's arm and the thickness of his middle finger.[1]

The high education bestowed on women during the last era of Anglo-Saxon civilisation, and the independent position they attained, tended to place them on an equality with the male sex ; and, combined with the chastity and sobriety which generally distinguished them, offered a sound foundation for the chivalrous respect and devotion of after times. It is difficult, however, to admit that this feeling was of Teutonic origin, or that it ever existed during the Anglo-Saxon era. At its conclusion, it was not exhibited even by the lover towards the object of his affection, as is sufficiently evident in the elaborate account which we possess of the courtship of William the Conqueror. On his return to Falaise after one of his many successful campaigns, William was publicly entreated by his subjects to marry, and to provide against the terrible contingency of a disputed succession. He was urged to unite himself to some powerful prince who might aid him in his innumerable wars. William pretended to hesitate and to take time to consider, though he had in his own mind determined to marry Matilda, daughter of Baldwin, earl of Flanders. He knew that his proposals would be distasteful both to her and to her father, but this did not deter him from formally demanding her hand. His offer was respectfully declined, though the true ground of its ill success was probably not stated. The lady was enamoured of the Saxon earl Brihtric, ambassador of king Edward at her father's court. To him she had made repeated offers of marriage, which were as repeatedly refused. William, who would not brook defeat

[1] See on this subject the *Ancient Laws and Institutes of Wales ;* Mi-   chelet, *Origines du Droit français,* tom. i, p. 49.

either in war or love, went immediately and secretly to
Bruges, where Matilda lived, and waited at the church
door till she came out. He then seized her, " shook
her not very tenderly," knocked her down with his fist,
kicked her over and over in the mud, and belaboured
her most furiously, " overwhelming her with blows."
Having concluded these delicate attentions, he mounted
his horse and rode away, without bestowing on her a
single word. Matilda was picked up by her attendants, carried home, and put to bed. Whether she was
fascinated with the duke's mode of wooing, or feared a
second offer of a similar character, does not appear ; but
while still confined to her bed through the maltreatment
she had received from her lover, she declared to her
father, " that sick in health, and dolorous of body from
the blows she had received, she had firmly decided to
marry no man but the duke William." On this intima-
tion of his daughter's feelings, the earl of Flanders with-
drew his opposition to the match. Matilda was married
to the Conqueror at the château d'Eu ; and, if we may
rely on Madame Guizot, " held him most dear to the very
day of her death." Her marriage afforded her, at least,
one source of gratification. On the conquest of England,
William offered to endow her with the lands of any Saxon
noble she chose to select ; and she immediately demanded
and received the estates of her once loved earl Brihtric.
She also obtained possession of his person and threw him
into prison, where he died mysteriously.

There is a rumour as to the close of Matilda's career,
which throws a shade over Madame Guizot's brilliant view
of her married happiness. It is said that when she grew
old, the king became attached to the daughter of a priest,
and that the queen, indignant at the amour, caused her to
be hamstrung and banished. When this came to the

king's knowledge, he indulged in one of those furious
bursts of passion which were habitual with him, and seizing Matilda, beat her to death with the headgear of his
horse. When his fury cooled, he attempted to atone for
his offence, by giving her a magnificent funeral and building a cathedral over her tomb. It is consolatory to know
that this account of her death is of very dubious authenticity; but for the purpose of appreciating the manners of the age, it is almost immaterial whether the tale
be really true, or merely so consistent with probability as
to have been readily believed at the time of its supposed
occurrence.[1]

With this story of the wedded life of the Norman William and of Matilda the descendant of the Saxon king
Alfred the Great, we conclude our review of the married
state of Anglo-Saxon women. Can we, even after our
cursory consideration of the subject, incline still to the
popularly received opinion, that "the Anglo-Saxon woman
was uniformly treated with chivalrous devotion and reverential love," or that there was no improvement in
domestic life between the time of Hengist and Horsa
and that of the Norman conquest?

[1] Continuation of Wace's *Roman de Brut,* in the *Chroniques Anglo-Normandes,* t. i, p. 73; *Domesday Book,* i, 101; Dugdale's *Monasticon,* i, 154; William of Malmes., lib. iii, s. 273; Bouquet's *Recueil des Histor.,* tom. xi, p. 188; *Essais Historiques,* par l'Abbé de la Rue, tom. iii, p. 437; *Guillaume le Conquérant,* par Mde. Guizot.

CHAPTER II.

THE CHILD.

SECTION I.—INFANTICIDE.

FROM the consideration of the relative position of husband and wife, we pass naturally to that of parent and child.

The Anglo-Saxons deemed it highly important that a child should be born on a lucky day, on which the whole tenor of his life was supposed to depend ; for, in their opinion, each day had its peculiar influence upon the destiny of the newly-born. Thus, the first day of the moon was preferred to all others for the arrival of the little stranger,—for they said, " a child born on that day is sure to live and prosper." The second day was not so fortunate as the first ; as the child born on that day " would grow fast, but not live long." If he were born on the fourth day of the moon, he was destined to be a great politician ; if on the tenth, a great traveller ; and if on the twenty-first, a bold marauder. But of all the days of the week on which to be born, Sunday was by far the most lucky, and if it fell on a new moon, the child's prosperity was destined to be unbounded.[1] Friday was an unlucky birthday, not only because it was the day of the

[1] Wright's *Biographia Anglo-Sax.*, vol. i, p. 101.

crucifixion of our Lord and Saviour, but because, according to Anglo-Saxon calculations, Adam ate the forbidden fruit on a Friday, and was also expelled from Paradise, and died and descended into hell, on that day.[1]

In these superstitions our forefathers firmly believed, and our fair ancestors had recourse to magic and potions, in order that their children might first see the light at a happy hour.[2]

No sooner was a child born than a question was debated concerning him which presents a lamentable proof of the misery and barbarity of the times. Should he be permitted to live, or should he be put to death? In the early Saxon period, the Anglo-Saxons did not consider infanticide a crime; on the contrary, under certain circumstances, they regarded it as a virtue.[3] They deemed it an act of parental tenderness to put a child to death who was born to a life of evident misery. "A child cries," they said, "when he comes into the world, for he anticipates its wretchedness. It is well for him that he should die."[4]

Among a nation living in a bitter and inhospitable climate, amidst forests and marshes, without pasturage or agriculture, dependent for existence on the uncertain produce of the chase, famine was of constant occurrence. It

[1] Solomon and Saturn, p. 183; Adrian and Rithæus, p. 199. Kemble's *Anglo-Sax. Dialogues.*

[2] Similar delusions exist even now among our peasantry. The following lines are said to be commonly sung both in the North and the South at the present day:—

"Monday's bairn is fair of face,
Tuesday's bairn is fu' of grace,
Wednesday's bairn's the child of woe,
Thursday's bairn has far to go;
Friday's bairn is loving and giving;
Saturday's bairn works hard for his living;

But the bairn that is born on the Sabbath day
Is lucky, and bonny, and wise, and gay."
—*Notes and Queries*, 1st Ser., vol. iv, p. 38.

[3] Tacitus says of the ancient Germans, "Numerum liberorum finiri aut quenquam ex agnatis necare flagitium habetur." *Germ.*, c. xix. Yet it was the universal custom of the continental nations to expose children, as indeed it was of all nations liable to famine.

[4] Michelet, *Origines du Droit français*, l. 1, c. 1.

was better, in their opinion, that a child should die as
soon as he was born, than that he should linger a few
days and then perish of starvation. It was the pressure
of necessity, not the want of maternal love, that drove the
Anglo-Saxon mother to a crime so abhorrent, even to the
worst of female hearts, as the murder of her child. When,
however, the Anglo-Saxon exchanged piracy and hunting
for pastoral and agricultural pursuits, famine became less
frequent ; and with a diminution of temptation, came a
diminution of crime.

No national custom ever dies a sudden death ; and infanticide passed into a practice so nearly akin to it, that
in modern times they would be considered one and the
same. It became common, instead of putting children to
death, to expose them in the woods or fields' to take the
chance of being devoured by wild beasts, or of being
found and reared by some benevolent person.[1] This custom, though a slight improvement on its predecessor, was
still too barbarous to last long without modification ; and
it soon became usual to exercise a little discretion in the
matter. It was considered idle to attempt to rear a sick
or weak child, for he would probably die of hardships
before he came to man's estate ; and it was worse than
useless to rear a timid one, who could only be a "*nithing*"
and a disgrace to a nation of brave men.

An infant was, therefore, subjected to some trial of his
temper, not unlike those by which the modern dealers in
fighting dogs test the breed of their puppies. He was
placed on a slanting roof, or on the bough of a tree, or in
some other dangerous place : if he laughed and crowed,
he was taken down and reared ; but if he was frightened
and cried, he was thrust out to perish.[2] This test was

---

[1] Grimm's *Deutsche Rechtsalter-
thümer*, p. 425.

[2] Howell's *General History*, par. i,
c. xx, p. 335. *Oxford Essays*, 1858,

deemed satisfactory by our ancestors; but as the child was too young to be conscious of danger, its value may be fairly doubted.

In the tenth century, when the custom of exposing infants was on the wane, it was usual to leave with the child some sign by which he might be recognised, probably with a view to the future exercise of the right which the law gave the father of redeeming him from a foster-parent.[1]

On one occasion, when Alfred the Great was hunting in a wood, he heard the cry of an infant in a tree, and ordered his huntsman to examine the place. The latter ascended the branches, and found at the top, in an eagle's nest, a beautiful child dressed in purple, and with golden bracelets, such as were worn only by nobles, on his arms. The king caused him to be brought down and baptized. From the situation in which he was found, he gave him the name of Nestigan. Alfred educated and provided for him, and one of his descendants figures in history as the mistress of king Edgar.[2]

In Greece, in Rome, and among the continental Saxons, while the child's fate was under debate he was laid upon the floor. If the deliberation ended in his favour, his father raised him in both hands and held him towards heaven, and after this ceremony he could not legally be abandoned.[3]

Any other recognition of the right of the child to live would have been equally valid. The one most insisted

---

p. 211 ; Michelet, *Origines du Droit français*, i, 7 ; Blackman's *Manners and Customs of the Icelanders*, p. 320.

[1] The incident of children exposed in this manner, with objects intended to lead to their future recognition, is frequently repeated in the medieval romances, or, as they are popularly called, romances of chivalry, of a later period.

[2] In the margin of a copy of Will. Malm., lib. ii, s. 156, this story is told, not of king Alfred, but of king Edgar. Hist. Soc. Edit., p. 251.

[3] Lucretius, *De Natura Rerum*, lib. 5. Michelet, *Origines du Droit français*, l. i, c. 1.

on, probably because the most common, was that of feeding it; for if the father fed it, he must have intended to rear it. We have an account of a parent who had determined on the death of his infant child, and to effect his purpose attempted to drown it in a water-butt. The babe clutched the edges of the tub with its fingers, and struggled for life. A woman, who was a spectator, touched with pity, snatched it up and ran away with it. She then gave it a little honey, and, on its being recaptured by its inhuman parent, pointed to the honey on its lips and defied him to kill it. The father was obliged to admit the evidence of its right to existence, and the child's life was saved.[1]

A custom so barbarous as the exposure of infants must soon have perished of its own inherent wickedness; but religion, superstition, law, and political economy, combined their forces for its destruction.

The church condemned every woman who was guilty of this sin to fifteen years penance;[2] and an ancient superstition caused it to be believed that it was lucky to find and adopt an exposed infant. The popular feelings on this subject will be best illustrated by an anecdote.

Of all the unhappy mortals of olden times, none was so universally unfortunate as Elfin, the son of an eminent Welsh chieftain. His father, disgusted with his constant ill fortune, banished him from home; but, to keep him from starving, bestowed on him a valuable fishery. No sooner had Elfin taken charge of it, than a property which had yielded a hundred pounds of silver annually, ceased to produce a single fish, and after a long and anxious trial he abandoned it in despair. As he wan-

---

[1] Grimm, *Deutsche Recht.*, p. 459.
[2] Theod. *Pœnit.*, xvii, 17, Thorpe, i, 10; Theod. *Pœnit.*, xviii, 8, xxi, 3, 5; Ecgb. *Confess.*, 30, 31; Ecgb. *Pœnit.*, ii, 2, iv, 21; *Modus Imp. Pœnit.*, 10.

G

dered away, he passed a weir, and on it saw what appeared
to be an otter. "Ah!" he cried, "it is you who have been
ruining my fishery. You must die." On approaching the
supposed otter, it proved to be a bundle of linen, which,
when opened, disclosed a lovely baby. "Tal-iésin! Tal-
iésin!" (what bright brows) exclaimed the weir-keeper;
"Taliesin shall be his name," said Elfin, "and I will adopt
him." He immediately wrapt the baby carefully in his
cloak, and, mounting on horse, carried it tenderly. In a
few moments, to his extreme astonishment, the child
began to sing, and prophesied that by his adoption a long
career of ill-fortune would be converted into one of brilliant success. The young foster-parent believed the wonderful infant, who in after life made good his promise,
and earned both for himself and patron wealth and honour.
"He sang miraculously," says the fable, "from the cradle to
the grave;" but, in truth, he sang with unrivalled eloquence and genius, and dying, left behind him a reputation, which, after the lapse of a thousand years, made
hearts throb and eyes brighten at the sound of the name
of "Taliesin, the bard."[1]

The kings did all in their power to encourage the
adoption of infants. King Ina fixed the amount to be
paid to every one who fostered a foundling;[2] and as, at
this period of history, the children most commonly abandoned were either illegitimate or orphans, he wisely
extended his liberality to every widow who, having exposed her infant, might be willing to take it back and
rear it.

The amount to be allowed for the support of a child
was regulated by the rank of the parent. For fostering
a ceorl's (or freeman's) child, the allowance was to be six

---

[1] Les Bardes Bretons par le Vi-   [2] Ll. Inæ, 26, Thorpe, i, 119; Ox-
comte de la Villemarqué, tom, i, p. 40.   ford Essays (1858), p. 213.

shillings in money, with a cow in summer and an ox in winter. For the child of a proprietor of ten hides of land, the provision was very ample ; and its details are curiously suggestive of the ordinary dietary of our fore-fathers. He was to be allowed annually, ten pots of honey, three hundred loaves, twelve ambers of Welsh ale, thirty of clear ale, two full-yeared oxen and ten wethers, ten geese, twenty hens, ten cheeses, an amber of butter, five salmon, twenty pounds of fodder, and one hundred eels.[1] This allowance was not for the nutrition of the child, but was the price which the foster-parent was entitled to demand for taking charge of it.[2]

On payment of this amount, the natural father had a right to redeem his son ; but if he failed to do so, the foster-parent acquired all his rights, and might (subject to the general laws affecting slavery) sell the child or let out his labour to reimburse himself.[3]

When the country became cultivated, a child's labour more than paid for his keep ; and every landed proprietor

---

[1] *Ll. Inæ*, 38 and 70, Thorpe, i, 127 and 147. An amber at the time of Edward I was four bushels. Ellis, *Domesday Book*, vol. i, p. 128.

[2] The custom of exposing infants was common among all the nations who overthrew the Roman Empire ; and in most of them the remedy adopted by the State was to encourage the fostering of children. Among the Wisigoths, if any one, *out of pity*, reared a child who had been *wilfully* exposed, and it was subsequently claimed by its parents, they were bound to find the fosterer a slave or pay the price of one. If the father either could not or would not do this, he himself was to become the foster-er's slave and the child was to go free. If any one received a child *from the parents* to foster, he was to be paid as many shillings per annum for his pains as the child was years old, until he arrived at ten years. After that time nothing was to be paid for him, as his services were considered a suf-ficient remuneration for his keep. *Ll. Wisigoth.*, lib. iv, tit. iv, s. 1, 2, 3. Fostri, altu alumnus; in den schwed. gesetzen ist foster ein im haus erzor-gener knecht, der milder behandelt wurde, als thræl und annödug. In the Swedish laws a *fostre* is a slave reared in the house, who was more gently treated than the *thræl* or an-nödug. Grimm's *Deutsche Rechtsalter-thum.*, p. 319. By the law of Rome, until the time of Trajan, a freeborn child exposed by its parents and brought up by a stranger became his slave. Plin., *Epist.* x, 7.

[3] This was forbidden by Diocletian, and afterwards by Justinian (*Cod. Justin.* iv, 43), but appears to have been practised long afterwards. Mil-man's *Latin Christianity*, vol. i, p. 371.

was willing to take charge of him. From this period infanticide became not only a crime but an extravagance.

A general willingness to foster children stimulated the habit, to which Anglo-Saxon mothers were already too much given, of abandoning the duties of maternity and putting children out to nurse. In his earliest communications to Gregory the Great, St. Augustine complained of their conduct in this respect; and the pontiff, in reply, denounced it in severe terms, imputing to Anglo-Saxon mothers sentiments common enough in Rome, but happily unknown in England.[1] The church endeavoured, by the infliction of penance, to suppress the practice altogether; but the kings contented themselves with correcting the abuses consequent upon it.

It is much to be feared that they who in Anglo-Saxon times received children to foster, not only often neglected their duty as guardians, but were sometimes guilty of the graver crime of homicide; and that their inhumanity was encouraged by the fact that, even when gross misconduct had taken place, it was very difficult of proof. When a young child died, or was injured, and the nurse was called to account, she could easily invent a series of accidents, the reality of which it might be impossible to ascertain. The favourite pleas of an Anglo-Saxon nurse were, that the child " had been overlaid when she was asleep," or that " she had hurt it when tipsy," or that " it had wandered too near the fire and been scalded." But for all these the law held her responsible, whether she were to blame or not.[2] This dealt with the question of negligence, but not with that of actual murder.[3] King Alfred endeavoured to remedy the

---

[1] Bede, *Histor. Eccl.*, l. ii, c. 27 ; Ranulph. de Diceto., Twysden's *Decem Script.*, p. 472.
[2] Theod. *Pœnit.*, xxxi, 36; Ecgbert,

Pœnit., Add. 4 ; *Mod. Imp. Pœnit.*, 41; Theod. *Capit.*, p. 76.
[3] When, on the death of Kenwulf, king of Mercia, his infant son,

greater evil. He enacted, that whenever a child put out to nurse died during nurture, the nurse should be presumed guilty of its death unless she could prove her innocence.[1]

Whether the efforts to remedy the evils incident on fostering were successful or not we have no means of judging; but the attempts of the clergy to put a stop to it *altogether* were certainly futile; it grew and flourished during the whole period of Anglo-Saxon history.

The reason of this is sufficiently evident. In the Danish-Saxon period, the incessant warfare, which rendered every man's house a place of danger, tended to the accumulation of young children in monasteries, whose sacred character protected them in civil broils, and whose military power defied all piratical excursions except those undertaken on a large scale. The schools established in these institutions were also a great attraction to parents. But during the more important wars between the Danes and Saxons, even monasteries were not safe abodes for children ; and at the time of Cnut it was customary to send them to the court of Normandy for education, or to place them in the house of some powerful earl that they might be trained in chivalry.

In Anglo-Saxon times, the nurse occupied a more important position than she does at the present day. She was regarded as a person of considerable consequence, and as an object of affectionate regard; and her rank and remuneration were proportionate to the esteem in which she was held.[2] When king Edgar came to the

Kenelm, succeeded to the throne, his elder sister, Quendreda, desired his destruction, that she and her husband might reign in his stead. At her suggestion, his fosterer, Ascebert, decoyed the boy into a wood on the borders of Shropshire, and there cut off his head and buried his body at a place still known as Saint Kenelm's Well. *Histor. Monast. August. Cantuar.*, p. 343; Roger de Wendover, A.D. 821 ; Camden's *Britan.*, p. 552.

[1] *Ll. Ælfredi*, c. 17, Thorpe, i, 73; *Ll. Henr.*, lxxxviii, 7, 8, Thorpe, i, 595.

[2] *Ll. Inæ*, c. 63, Thorpe, i, 145.

throne, he rewarded the wife of the earl who had reared him with liberal grants of land; and prince Athelstan, by his will, gave to Alfswythe his foster-mother, for her great deservingness, the lands of Wertune, which he bought of his father for two hundred and fifty man-cusses of gold by weight.[1] In the laws protecting the chastity of the royal family, the queens, the princesses, and the royal nurse were classed together; and any attempt upon the virtue of any one of these was declared high treason.[2]

Passing from the position and remuneration of a nurse to the duties which devolved upon her, we find her first charge was that of protecting the baby from fairies and evil spirits. There were probably many ways of performing this duty of which we know nothing; but, thanks to the disapprobation of the clergy, two very curious instances have come down to us. So soon as the child was born, it was the duty of the nurse to dig a long tunnel in the ground (in honour of our common mother the Earth, or Friga, the goddess of love and maternity), and through it to drag the child, carefully closing the aperture behind with thorns, so that evil spirits could not follow. At a later period, the Anglo-Saxon love of doing everything vicariously prevailed; and the nurse was at liberty to construct a somewhat larger tunnel, and to crawl through *in the name of the child*. In this case also the passage was to be closed promptly behind, that the evil spirits (who seem to have been as much afraid of pushing through brambles as if they had been made of substantial flesh) might not accompany her.

---

[1] *Histor. Rames.*, 3; Gale's *Script.*, 387, 405; Britton, c. 22.

[2] Sharon Turner's *Anglo-Saxon Hist.*, vol. iii, b. 7, c. 1. When a king's "companion" left the estate under his control, the only members of his numerous establishment whom he was allowed to take with him were his bailiff, his armourer, and his children's nurse.

When this ceremony was happily concluded, the infant was taken to a place where two or more roads met, and there placed upon the ground and dragged up and down, while prayers were said and incantations performed to propitiate the same goddess Eortha.[1] When all this was done, the child was considered to be under the protection of the goddess, and to be evil-spirit proof.[2]

SECTION II.—BAPTISM.

When the Anglo-Saxon people were converted to Christianity, and young children were baptised, it might have been anticipated that these superstitions would have been abandoned ; but in this, as in other things, there was a compromise between Christianity and paganism. Baptism was universally adopted, but it was regarded as a species of incantation, whereby a holy spirit was moved to protect a child from evil ones, and not as a sacrament whereby it was made a member of Christ and an inheritor of the kingdom of heaven.[3]

---

[1] Ecgb. *Pœnit.*, lib. iv, s. 20, Thorpe, ii, 211 ; King Edgar's *Canons*, c. 16, Thorpe, ii, 249 ; Grimm, *Deut. Mith.*, p. 676. It has been suggested that this was not a heathen but a Christian superstition. In the east the holiness of a second birth was supposed to be obtained by passing through the artificial body of a cow ; and it has been suggested that the practice mentioned in the text had some reference to the descent of a sinful man into the grave and a resurrection to righteousness. St John's *Four Conquests of England*, vol. i, p. 68.

[2] It is probable that this superstition was of Roman origin. Augustus Cæsar had caused lares or penates to be put up in every place where two or more roads met, and had appointed an order of priests, who were freed-men, constantly to conduct their worship. Hence the Romans had grown to attach a sanctity to places where roads intersected one another, and not improbably introduced the feeling into England. Evidence of the sanctity of the cross-roads under the Romans has, indeed, been found in our island. I may mention especially a Roman altar, dedicated to DEO TRIVII, discovered in the south-west of Herefordshire. See Wright's *Wanderings of an Antiquary*, p. 17. There is still among us a relic of the superstition as to the supposed sanctity of crossways, for persons who may not be buried in consecrated ground, are there interred (let us charitably hope) as the next most holy place.

[3] Soames, *Anglo-Saxon Church*, p. 114.

Archbishop Theodore and his friends, though they laboured to disabuse the public mind as to the magical character of baptism, insisted on its importance. They required all children to be baptised within thirty days after their birth,[1] a period which was subsequently reduced to ten.[2]

The ceremony of baptism was performed by immersion, unless circumstances rendered this mode of proceeding impossible. It differed in one respect from the form at present in use. Among us, the whole ceremony is performed by the priest; but among them, the priest placed the neophyte in the water, and the godparents removed him from it.[3]

Anglo-Saxon baptism created a much closer connection between the child and god parents than exists at the present time. The godson could not marry the godmother, nor could his godparents marry one another.[4] He was also entitled to compensation for injury done to his godfather or godmother as if it had been done to himself, although not to the same amount.[5]

The obligation of mutual affection created by this relationship was constantly used to give additional validity to treaties. When peace was concluded between Alfred the Great and Guthrun the Dane, the latter was baptised, and Alfred acted as his sponsor, whereby the spiritual

---

[1] *Ll. Inæ*, c. 2, Thorpe, i, 103.

[2] *Ll. North. Priests*, Thorpe, ii, 293. A kind of infant baptism was practised in the north long before the first dawn of Christianity had reached it. Snorri Sturleson, in his *Chronicle*, speaking of a Norwegian nobleman who lived in the reign of Harold Harfagra, relates that he poured water on the head of a new-born child, and called him Hakon, from the name of his father. Snor. Sturles., c. lxx. Mr. Soames states,

(*Anglo-Sax. Church*, p. 270,) that if the child was not baptised within the specified time, the parent was to forfeit all his goods; but it was not the *parent* but the *priest* who was to make "bot" with all his goods for negligence in this respect.

[3] Gregor. Turon., *Historia Franc.*, lib. x, c. 1.

[4] *Vide ante*, p. 33.

[5] *Ll. Inæ*, s. 76, Thorpe, i, 151; *Ll. Henr.*, l. xxix, 1, and l. xxx, 20, Thorpe, i, 584 and 586.

relation of father and son was created between them.[1] This neither of them could have disregarded by levying war on one another without disgrace.

It was the custom of godfathers to make very magnificent presents to their godchildren, and to provide for their maintenance and education ;[2] and the godchildren in return, if they were proud of their sponsors, took every opportunity of publishing the relationship.

SECTION III.—IMPOSITION OF NAMES.

Among the Anglo-Saxons, as among ourselves, children received their Christian names in baptism ; and in the selection of them, Anglo-Saxon parents displayed a discretion which contrasts very favourably with the practice of the present day. The names we give to children are, to the ears of all but scholars and antiquaries, utterly meaningless ; but among our forefathers every name had its signification. " In their names-giving," (says an old writer) "nobility, valour, truth, and charity, were remembered and recorded ;" and it was fondly hoped that a child would be stimulated to practise the qualities of which his name reminded him. Hence they loved such names as Ethelbert (the noble and bright) ; Edward (the happy protector) ; Ethelfretha (the noble and peaceful) ; Godwine (the friend of God), and many others. Among their favourite names were Edmund (the prosperous patron) ; Edwin (the happy friend) ; Herbert (the brightness of the army); and Ecgbert (the sword's brightness).

At the earlier period of their history, our forefathers were great admirers of the *wolf*. He was the bravest,

---

[1] Will. Malmes., l. ii, s. 121.

[2] Ellis, *Introduction to Domesday*, vol. i, p. 304. Illustrations might be given. There are charters signed by " Baldwin, *the king's godson*," and " William, *the godson*," with seals representing a king holding an infant over a font.

strongest, swiftest, and most *erratic* animal we then had
in England; qualities in which the Anglo-Saxon de-
lighted. To be "like a wolf" was then thought as honourable, as a century or two later it became terrible.
Children were therefore constantly christened after this
favourite animal; and we find many such names, as
Ulph, the wolf, Ethelwolf (the noble wolf); Berhtwolf,
(the bright wolf); Edwulf (the happy wolf); Ealdwulf
(the old wolf); Sigwulf (the wolf of victory); and Weal-
lendewulf (the wandering wolf).

Among the names given to little girls were some which
we still retain, as Edith (the happy gift); Adeleve, now
Adelaide (the noble wife); and Ellen (the excellent).
There were also many pretty ones which have gone out
of use, such as Wynfreda (the peace of joy); Dearwyne
(the darling joy); Dearsuythe (very dear); and Edfleda
(the stream of happiness); and many others, which would
form an agreeable contrast to our present meaningless
nomenclature. As the men venerated the wolf, and
named their children after him; so the women much
admired the elf or fairy, and assumed names of which
"elf" formed the first syllable. Among these, were
Elfgiva or Elfgifu (the fairy gift); Elfhilda (the warlike
fairy); and Elfthrytha (the threatening fairy).

The difference that existed between the three principal
eras of Anglo-Saxon history may be traced even in their
nomenclature. About the time of king Ecgbert, we find
a preference for names commencing with "Ethel," "the
hereditary noble." Thus we have Ethelwulf, Ethelbert,
Ethelbald, Ethelred, Ethelfleda, Ethelhelm, and very
many others. Originally these names could only be
properly borne by the younger sons of the hereditary
kings or earls: but during the Danish wars, when every
great man called himself an earl, every one considered he

had a right to christen his child "Ethel." With the time of Cnut came the prevalence of such names as Thurcytel, Oscytel, Tofig, Eric, Haldan, Harald, and Scurfa, all names of Scandinavian origin; and a few years later, even the names given to children in their baptism, betokened the impending end of the Saxon dynasty. Norman names were constantly used instead of Anglo-Saxon; and children were christened Tancred, Robert, Wilhelm, Hugo, Giso, and other such foreign appellatives.

The children did not take their father's name, nor had they any hereditary surnames. If there were two or three of the same Christian name at the same court, they were distinguished from one another by an additional name betokening some personal peculiarity. Thus we have Hewald the fair and Hewald the dark (who suffered martyrdom in an attempt to convert the old Saxons);[1] Ethelfleda the fair, Harold Harefoot, Edith Swan-neck, Wulfric the pale, Thurcyl Mare'shead, Edmund Iron-side, Godwin Town-dog. Sometimes their second names referred to their office, as Edric-Streona (treasurer); or Osgood Steallere (steward); sometimes to their parentage, as Sired Alfridson; and sometimes to their residences, as Godwin-at-Fecham, Eadric-at-Ho, Elfgar-at-Theapaham.

The Danes had the same mode of distinguishing men of the same Christian names as the Saxons. We read of Halfdan white-leg, and Ketil flat-nose, and we find "ugly," "squinteye," "long beard," "hag-nose," "hawk-nose," "spoon-nose," and "torch-eye," given to various persons as second names, for it may be observed that the great majority of these names are uncomplimentary.

Instead of surnames they had a system of nomenclature not unlike that practised in Wales. A northman

[1] Bede, *Eccles. Hist.*, l. v, c. 10.

whose name (to take one of their favorite names beginning with Thor) was Thorolf, and whose father was Thorstein, would be called Thorolf Thorstein*son* ; and if he
had a son Thorold he would be called Thorold Thorold-
son, each man taking as a sort of surname the christian
name of his father with the addition of *son*, but dropping
that of his grandfather.

All these were *additional* names *affixed* to those they
received in baptism ; but our ancestors were in the habit
of giving children pet names or nicknames, not in addition, but in substitution for those they received at the
font. Thus Ethelberga received the pet name of Tata
(the lively[1]), Ethelfleda that of Enede (the duck[2]), and
the abominable Eadwulf earned in his childhood the
name of " Yfilcild " or " bad-boy." It was in after life
that queen Emma received the name of the "gem of the
Normans,"[3] for which the Saxons substituted " Elfgifu "
(the gift of the fairies). We find another lady with the
substitutionary name of the Crow ; and the abbess
Hrodwaru, who (unless there were two of the same
name) was a married nun, had the uncomplimentary
name of Bugga, considered by Kemble to signify a well-
known noxious insect.[4] These nicknames they received
instead of their own, and they were so generally recognised
that with them they signed charters and other legal
documents.

SECTION IV.—EDUCATION.

At the present day the law of the land regards a youth
as an "infant" until he attains the age of twenty-one ;

---

[1] *Codex Diplomat. Ang.-Sax.*, nos.
732, 743, 747 ; the *Anglo-Saxon
Chron.*, an. 1010; Flor. Wigorn., an.
964.

[2] Bede, *Hist. Eccles.*, l. ii, c. 9.

[3] Flor. Wigorn., an. 964.

[4] *Codex Diplomat. Ang.-Sax.*, nos.
82, 210, and 124.

but our forefathers considered this early period of existence to terminate at "eight," at which age the infant became a " boy."

The infancy of children must, in all eras, be spent very much in the same manner ; and the account given of St. Cuthbert in his juvenile days, though illustrative of his own era, would do nearly as well for that of a high spirited child in any other. Bede says, " Even until the eighth year of his life, which is the first year of boyhood succeeding to infancy, he gave his mind to such plays and enjoyments alone as boys delight in. He took pleasure in mirth and clamour ; " (as most children do) " and as was natural at his age rejoiced to attach himself to the company of other boys, and to share in their sports ; and because he was agile by nature and of a quick mind, he often prevailed over them in their boyish contests ; and frequently when the rest were tired, he alone would hold out, and look triumphantly around to see if any remained to contend with him for victory. For in jumping, running, wrestling, or any other bodily exercise, he boasted that he could surpass all those who were of the same age, and even some that were older than himself. For when he was a child he knew as a child, but afterwards when he became a man he most abundantly laid aside all those childish things." In the early Saxon period boys were trained to running and jumping, and when their age permitted, fighting and hunting were added to these accomplishments.

From a very early period of our history the clergy interested themselves in the education of children ; and through their influence numerous schools were established in monasteries and elsewhere, in which the monks acted as teachers. Their extreme ignorance at certain periods, however, must have prevented their teaching anything but church music, or rather the chanting of psalms and a few prayers, which they repeated by rote without understanding them.

Under the auspices of archbishop Theodore an immense improvement in education took place. The schools were increased not only in size and numbers but in the rank of the pupils; and some of the more important seminaries were under the superintendence of scholars of the highest reputation.

Bishop Wilfred was one of those who devoted themselves to education. He had constantly under his care a large number of children, the sons of princes and nobles, who remained with him until they reached the age of fourteen, when he required them to decide whether they would become priests or soldiers, the only two occupations then open to gentlemen. If they selected the former, they were placed in monasteries to complete their education; and if the latter, he clothed them in arms, and presented them to the king. In their educational duties, the clergy received great assistance from their Irish brethren, many of whom were men of great learning and who came willingly to teach in English schools.

What the amount of knowledge disseminated by these schools was, may be a matter of some doubt, though we have ample accounts of the nature of the tuition. The instruction bestowed by archbishop Theodore is classed by Bede under three heads, poetry, astronomy, and arithmetic.[1] Other great schools, such as that at Malmesbury, were also established in the south, but the period of the southern scholarship which originated with Theodore was not of long duration, and a few years later the head-quarters of Anglo-Saxon learning had been removed to York, where, according to Alcuin, one of its

[1] Bede, *Hist. Eccles.*, l. iv, c. 2.

pupils, archbishop Aelbert taught grammar, rhetoric, juris-prudence, poetry, and, in addition, all the higher branches of learning.[1] We cannot, however, judge, from the few facts which have been handed down to us, what was the condition of the inferior schools, or what the bulk of the laity managed to learn.

Both the higher and the lower schools were abandoned under the terror and confusion of the Danish invasions, and when the illustrious Alfred ascended the throne his people seem to have sunk into general ignorance.

It is probable that the brothers of Alfred were as accomplished as most other children of the time, and their acquirements were limited to singing psalms and reciting popular poetry. They could neither read nor write. Alfred himself, through "the wicked negligence of his parents and nurses," had not been taught to read at twelve years of age.[2]

It is said, on the authority of the biography ascribed to Asser, that Alfred's mother Osburga (or his stepmother Judith) one day shewed him and his brothers a book of Saxon poetry, and offered to give it to the one who should first learn it. Stimulated by the proferred reward, or allured by the beauty of the illuminations, Alfred, though the youngest of the party, undertook the task. He carried the book to his master, who read it to him over and over again till he had learnt it by heart, when he joyously repeated it to the queen, and obtained the promised reward.[3] From this time, we are told, Alfred exhibited

[1] *Alcuin de Pontif. Eborac., Opera,* p. 728 ; Lorentz, *Life of Alcuin,* pp. 9-10.

[2] Asser *Vita Alfredi,* an. 884 ; Will. Malmes., l. ii, c. 4 ; Flor. Wigorn., A.D. 859 ; Simeon Dunelm., p. 676. Alfred was at least better off than the great monarch of the continent,

Charlemagne, who, notwithstanding all his efforts, never succeeded in learning to write well. Eginhardi *Vit. Carol. Mag.,* c. 25, Du Chesne, *Script. Rerum Franc.,* tom. ii, p. 187.

[3] Asser, *Vita Alfredi,* p. 474; Flor. Wigorn., i, 86; Sim. Dunelm. p. 676. Charlemagne acquired his literary

great zeal in learning, yet he could find no one competent
to teach him anything but what his biographer calls "the
daily course, that is, the celebration of the hours, and
afterwards certain psalms and several prayers." We
learn what this was from the following colloquy between a
teacher and pupil, in which the former asks, "What have
you done to day?" "We have done much," replies the
pupil; "this night when I heard the knell I arose from
my bed and went to church, and sang the nocturn with
the brethren, and then we sang the "*De omnibus
sanctis,*" and the "*Dægredlice lof-sanges,*" (the morning song of praise); after that the prime and seven
psalms with the litany and first mass, and then undern-
tide (or, tierce), and performed the mass for the day;
after that we sang the midday (sext), and then we ate
and drank, and slept; and then we arose and sang the
none, and now we are here before you to hear what you
have to say to us."[1]

It is not to be wondered at that such a mind as that
of Alfred should lament even at twelve years old that he
could find no one competent to teach him more than this.
As the nones commenced at two o'clock, and the service
must have occupied some time, it is clear that the children
could not have received any instruction before a late hour
of the day; and as at four o'clock they had to perform
vespers, very little time could have been given to study.

Alfred laboured diligently to re-establish the schools
which had been destroyed during the period of invasion
and war that had occupied the reigns of his predecessors
and the commencement of his own. He succeeded to a
very great extent, but to do so he had recourse to the

knowledge by the same process of
having books read to him. Inter
cœnandum aut aliquod acroama aut
lectorem audiebat. Eginhard, *Vita*
Caroli Magni, c. 4.

[1] See the curious tract, Alfric's
Colloquy, in Wright's *Volume of
Vocabularies,* p. 13.

doubtful expedient of bringing over to England large numbers of foreign children, whose parents were more accustomed to educational restrictions than his own war-like subjects, and whom he used as a species of decoy ducks. After his death the country was again destined to be the victim of fire and sword, and the institutions which he had taken so much pains to restore may almost be said to have perished with him.

Education, however, was still afforded to a limited number of children in the monastic establishments, and the attempt of the predecessors of Dunstan to enforce the rules of St. Benedict were highly advantageous to it. Under these, every monk was compelled to learn some trade, and many of them applied themselves so energetically, that they became the ablest artists, writers, architects, goldsmiths, blacksmiths, sculptors, and agriculturists in the kingdom. The laws of king Edgar made the education of children in monasteries conditional on their being taught some one of these useful occupations, and it is certain, from the perfection to which many mechanical arts were carried during this century, that the monks energetically discharged their duties in this respect. It is difficult to overrate the national advantage which was derived from every child being brought up to some pursuit by which he could add to his own and the national wealth, instead of being trained to the unproductive occupations of hunting, fighting, and singing psalms.

The Anglo-Saxons had but one mode of tuition, and that was the simplest in the world. They told a child to learn, and if he did not, they beat him. A stiff rod and a strong arm was all that a teacher needed. Alcuin, speaking generally, says, " It is the scourge that teaches children the ornaments of wisdom :" and referring particularly to his own case, he thanks the brethren of York

H

minster, that by "the discipline of paternal castigation, they had brought him to the perfect age of manhood." The learned monk must have much admired severity; for he had had ample opportunity of appreciating the scholastic system in use in his time. When he was too young to undergo the merciless floggings then in vogue, he was habitually subjected to the punishment reserved for tender youth. This consisted in cutting or pricking the soles of the child's feet with an instrument somewhat resembling a cobbler's knife, called an *acra*, an operation which was deemed more stimulating and less dangerous for very young children than beating with sticks.[1]

Flogging was not then looked upon solely as a mode of punishment, but also as a system of tuition. In the dialogue between a master and pupil, already quoted, the pupil applies to the master to teach him colloquial Latin: whereupon the master inquires how he would like to be taught—"would you like *to be taught by scourging?*" To this pleasant proposal the pupil is made to reply as no schoolboy ever did; that he would prefer "to be swinged for the sake of lore, rather than not learn." In the same dialogue, the master asks, "how are you awakened in the morning?" The pupil replies: "sometimes by the church bell, sometimes smartly by the master's rod." "Have you been flogged to-day?" he asks. "No, because I have acted warily." And how about your companions?" (the answer to this question is the only natural one in the whole conversation:) "Why do you ask ME? *I do not dare to tell tales out of school. Every one knows whether he has been swinged or not.*"[2]

---

[1] Du Cange, voce *Acra*; " Non istum verberibus, quia rudis adhuc est, acris...pedum tantum, in quibus duritia inest, calli tonsione cultelli castigemus." See also *Monast. Anglic.*, iii, 17.

[2] *Colloq. Arch. Alfr.* (Wright), p. 15. Young ladies were as liberally flogged as boys. When the uncle of Heloise entrusted her to Abelard for education, he expressly authorised him to inflict on her personal casti-

Personal chastisement was often administered in haste and passion. King Ethelred, when a child, offended his mother, who, having no whip at hand, beat him so severely with candles that he could never afterwards bear the sight of them, nor would he permit a candle to be lighted in his presence to the day of his death.

Scholastic punishment, however, could only be inflicted in the church in which the school was held. Once out of school, the boy was safe from castigation. An ingenious youth of the name of Aldene endeavoured to turn this regulation to account. He had good reasons for expecting severe chastisement at the next assembly of his school in the church of Norham ; and as he did not relish the prospect, he stole the church key, locked up the church, and, ascending a height which overlooked a deep place in the Tweed, threw the key into it. When the school should have reassembled, the church could not be opened, the boys were dismissed, and Aldene, for a time, escaped his flogging. But the church was, unluckily for him, dedicated to saint Cuthbert, who appeared to the rector in a vision ; and after reproaching him for the closing of his church, commanded him to go to Pedwell, a fishing station on the river, early in the morning, and purchase the first cast of fish brought on shore. He did so, and thereby obtained possession of a large salmon, in the throat of which he discovered the church key. The parishioners rejoiced at its miraculous recovery ; the key was blessed, kissed, and worshipped, and was for many years an object of veneration. Aldene's wickedness was discovered, and in all probability severely punished.[1]

The Anglo-Saxons believed not only that flogging stimulated industry, but that it had a specific action on the

gation, though she was then twenty-two years of age.

[1] Regin. Dunelm., *Libellus*, c. lxxxiii.

memory, such as particular drugs are known to have on certain organs of the human frame. If it were wished to impress any fact on a child's memory, it was told to him, and he was then well beaten, that on any occasion on which he was beaten afterwards, it might by the association of ideas recur to his mind.[1]

One lesson which it was particularly wished to impress on the memory, was the story of the massacre of the Innocents by king Herod. To effect this, every child was reminded of it at dawn on Childer-mass day, and at the same time was severely beaten, "that he might recollect and somewhat appreciate," says an old writer, "the hatred, persecution, cross, exile, and want, that was felt at the time of the birth of Christ."[2]

It was also customary, when it was wished to retain legal testimony of any ceremony, to have it witnessed by children, who then and there were flogged with unusual severity; which it was supposed would give additional weight to any evidence of the proceedings they might afterwards furnish.

The excess to which the system was carried is, however, best shown by the ordinary phrase used by Anglo-Saxon writers to express "my schoolboy days." They always said "when I was under the rod," calling the period after its most striking incident.

[1] To this notion we are indebted for the modern custom of "beating bounds," though the children, being now active instead of passive, enjoy this proceeding more than in olden times.

[2] Hospinian *de Orig. Fest. Christ.*, f. 160. Gregory, in his treatise on the "boy bishop," observes, "that it hath been a custom, and yet is elsewhere, to whip up the children upon Innocents' day morning, that the memory of Herod's murder of the innocents might stick the closer, and in a moderate proportion to act over the cruelty again in kind." Brande's *Pop. Antiq.*, vol. i, p. 536. This practice was called "giving the Innocents," and degenerated into a customary right for the young man who first saw a young woman on Saint Innocents' Day, to inflict on her personal chastisement of a not very decent character. It ultimately led to so much disorder as to call for legislative interference both in France and in England. King Henry VIII's Proclamation, July 22, 1540. See the *Contes de la Reine de Navarre*, Nouvelle 45.

But, even among schoolboys, extreme severity could not always be tolerated ; and it sometimes proved dangerous to those masters who were most detested for it. John Scotus Erigena, who was as notorious for his overbearing and violent temper, as he was famous for his wit and learning, superintended a school at Malmesbury, where, according to an old story, he treated his scholars with such extreme cruelty, that they mutinied, attacked him in the school, and wounded him so severely with their writing-styles, that he died a few days afterwards.[1]

The first person who doubted the efficacy of constant and promiscuous severity was the famous Turketel, abbot of Croyland. He took so great an interest in the education of all the children intrusted to his care, that he visited each of them once a day, and superintended their studies. On these occasions he rewarded those boys who distinguished themselves above the rest with figs, raisins, nuts, and almonds, or more frequently with apples, pears, and little presents, in order that, not so much with harsh words and blows, as by frequent encouragement and rewards, he might induce them to show due diligence in the prosecution of their studies.[2]

Reading and writing were not generally considered in the · Anglo-Saxon schools as the primary object of education, or as the necessary instruments of acquiring knowledge. This may have arisen from the extreme scarcity of books, and the impossibility of supplying them to pupils, a misfortune which must have greatly increased the difficulties of tuition. The teachers were compelled to adopt the sys-

[1] Will. Malmes., l. ii, c. 4 ; Rog. de Hoveden, A.D. 884; *Vita Aldhelm.*, *Anglia Sacra*, ii, 26 ; Sim. Dunelm. Twysden, *X Scrip.*, 149; Rog. Wendover, A.D. 884. Dr. Lingard contends that the John who was killed by his pupils at Malmesbury was not John Scotus Erigena, but John, abbot of Ethingley; upon which point Mr. Soames differs from him. Lingard, *Anglo-Saxon Church*, vol. ii, p. 247; Soames, *Anglo-Saxon Church*, p. 159.

[2] *Hist. Abb. Croyland*, A.D. 974.

tem of verbal instruction and of constant catechising,
usually practised in the middle ages. It was on this
plan that the few who were competent taught colloquial
Latin, church history, and arithmetic, which, with psalm
singing and a smattering of theology, was all that could
be learnt from any but the most eminent. They possessed a few elementary treatises on Latin grammar,
which were read aloud, over and over again, by the
master to the pupils until the latter got them by heart.
But a more favourite mode of teaching Latin was on a sort
of Hamiltonian system. The teacher would seem to have
copied out from a book placed in the middle of the room
certain Latin phrases on a scroll, and these he read
aloud to the assembled class, pointing out as he did so
each word and translating it. To assist him in his labours,
dialogues or catechisms on common topics were composed
in the Latin language, many of them having an inter-
linear translation or gloss, intended for the use of the
master.

The favorite mode of teaching arithmetic was by
problems not unlike those that are to be found in the old
treatise of Bonnycastle. The object in adopting this
mode of tuition was to assist the memory, which must
have been severely strained by the quantity to be remembered, and by the inability of the pupils to refresh their
memories by reference to books. The following specimens of arithmetical problems are taken from a manuscript of a date not later than the tenth or eleventh
century, and generally ascribed to a much earlier period.
The first is as follows. "The swallow once invited the
snail to dinner; he lived just one league from the spot,
and the snail travelled at the rate of one inch a day : how
long would he be before he dined?" Another is : "An
old man met a boy. 'Good day, my son,' said he; 'may

you live as long as you have lived, and as much more, and thrice as much as all this, and if God give you one year in addition to the others, you will be just a century old.' What was the child's age ?"[1]

The foregoing are very simple, and not above the capacity of a smart schoolboy. The next, which is probably of a later date, might tax the ingenuity of many who look down with contempt on the learning of our barbarous forefathers. " A man had three daughters of different ages, to whom he delivered certain apples to sell ; and he gave to the eldest daughter fifty apples, and to the second thirty apples, and to the third ten apples, and all these three sold a like number for a penny, and brought home the same amount of money : how many did each of them sell for a penny ?"[2]

The object of Anglo-Saxon education was rather to render the pupil acute and ingenious, than to crowd the memory with facts. With a view of sharpening youth (*ad acuendos juvenes*), they had dialogues of a disputatious character, in which master and pupil attempt to puzzle one another.

The following questions, and the answers expected to them, have been selected from an immense number as specimens of the Anglo-Saxon system of catechising.

Tell me how old was Adam when he was created ?—I tell thee, he was thirty years old.

Tell me how long was Adam in paradise ?—I tell thee, thirteen years ; and on the fourteenth he tasted the forbidden fig-tree's fruit, and that was on a Friday ; and through that he was in hell 5228 years.

[1] The following is current in various forms at the present day, but is hardly an arithmetical problem. "Three men and their wives came together at the side of a river, where they found but one boat, which was capable of carrying only two persons at a time ; each man was jealous of the other. How must they contrive to cross so that no man was left alone with his companion's wife ?" Wright's *Biogr. Liter.*, vol. i, p. 75.

[2] *Reliquiæ Antiquæ*, vol. ii, p. 75.

Tell me what man died and never was born, and afterwards was buried in his mother's womb ?—I tell thee, that was Adam the first man ; for the earth was his mother, and in the earth was he buried again.

What is a ship ?—A wandering house, a hostel wherever you will, a traveller that leaves no footsteps, a neighbour of the sand.[1]

What are fingers ?—The plectra of strings.

What is grass ?—The garment of the earth.

What are herbs ?—The friends of physicians and the praise of cooks.

What makes bitterness sweet ?—Hunger.

What is faith ?—The certainty of the unknown wonderful.

What is wonderful? I lately saw a live man standing and a dead man walking, who were never born.—A reflection in the water.

A stranger spoke to me, who had neither tongue nor voice, he never was in the past and never will be in the future.—It was a dream.

I saw the dead beget the living and the living consume the dead.—The friction of boughs begets fire, and fire consumes them.[2]

In addition to these *acute* dialogues, they used to stimulate the ingenuity of their pupils with literary puzzles. One of these is not unlike a game played by young children at the present day. They took a line of writing, and cut it up into separate syllables, and then disarranged the syllables and gave them to the child to put in order. The following absurd line puzzled not only those for whom it was intended but many generations of mature scholars, " Al pi pen ca bas tot habet ni nas quot habet gras," in which form it is (to borrow a phrase from Lord Mac-

---

[1] Kemble's *Anglo-Sax. Dialogues,*   [2] These questions are given in Salomon and Saturn, p. 183, *et seq.;*   Alcuini *Opera,* tom. ii. p. 354.

aulay) "not nonsense but gibberish." When the syllables are reduced to order it runs " Albas pica pennas tot habet quot habet nigras." (The magpie has as many white feathers as it has black ones).[1]

Of monastic education it may probably be said truly that the most valuable instruction given was colloquial Latin, which enabled the pupils to converse with the learned of other nations, and to make themselves understood when they went on foreign pilgrimages.

It must, however, be remarked that there seems to have been a popular prejudice against the extensive use of Latin, which had been first introduced by the foreign ecclesiastics ; and this prejudice was rather increased by the measures adopted by king Alfred. Finding that, through the decline of scholarship, few people could then understand the Latin writers, he sought to supply the want by furnishing translations in Anglo-Saxon. From this time the Anglo-Saxon language appears to have been more carefully cultivated than before.

At the time of Alfred the custom had commenced of placing children in the houses of kings or very powerful nobles, with a view to their education and subsequent advancement in life. The court of his grandson Athelstan was a famous educational establishment. In it three kings were trained, Haco, the son of Harold fair-hair, king of Norway ; Alan, king of Bretagne ; and Louis d'Outre-Mer, king of France. But after the time of Emma, the Gem of the Normans, a French education became fashionable, and it was customary to send the sons of Anglo-Saxon nobles to the court of Normandy to be educated, though the instruction they there received was not of a very intellectual character.

In the Norman castles children were taught to ride,

---

[1] Kemble's *Anglo-Saxon Dialogue*, p. 27; Harlcian MS. 3362, fo. 3.

hunt, and fight, as well as the duty of some one domestic servant, such as grooming horses, carving, or serving the cup at table. To these were often added the art of playing on the harp and singing to it.

The following lines from the romance of Horn Child state accurately enough the sort of teaching common in these great houses. The king of Westnesse is supposed to have adopted the " child," and to be giving directions for his education.

"The king came into the hall
  among his knights all.
  Forth he called Athelbrùs,
  his steward, and to him thus,
'Steward, take thou here
  my foundling for to teach
  of thy mystery,
  of wood and of river,
  and to tug o' the harp

with his nails sharp;
and teach him all that thou listest
that thou ever knowest;
before me to carve,
and my cup to serve ;
and devise for his fellows
with us other service.
Horn child, thou understand,
teach him of harp and of song.' "

SECTION V.—THE PARENT'S AUTHORITY.

There are few things in the history of society more interesting to the curious student of archaic law than the rules which in primitive times regulated the relative position of parent and child. In every country, however barbarous or enlightened, the parent possesses authority over the child ; and the child has in return a right to maintenance and protection at the hands of his father. But the authority of the father and the rights of the child vary in different countries, and in the same country at different times.

The authority of the parent varies both in *duration* and in *extent*. In early Rome, England, and Judæa, the father had the power of life and death over the child. In Rome, at the time of the emperors, this power had dwindled down to the right of bringing him before the tribunals *when* his conduct required it. Its duration varies as widely as its extent. It may continue during the whole of the joint lives of father and child, or it may terminate at any period of the child's life between ten and twenty-five. The *rights* of the son vary from a right to be maintained during childhood, *provided* he behave well, to an absolute obligation on the father to maintain him in idleness all his life, to be responsible for every crime of which he may be guilty, and to leave him the whole of his property at his death. It is in the patriarchal state of society that the power of the father over the child and the rights of children against the father are the most extensive. As a nation passes from the patriarchal state into the tribal, both power and rights are diminished; and they are still further decreased when the tribal state of society gives place to the national.

In endeavouring to trace the history of the paternal power (the *patria potestas* of the Romans) among the Anglo-Saxons, we will consider, first, the age at which it ceased; and, secondly, its extent and gradual diminution.

Among the Danes and Anglo-Saxons, in the early Saxon era, the power of the parent lasted during his life, but its duration gradually decreased, and it did so according to the general laws of social history.[1] Where these laws are not affected by abnormal causes, the period at which a child is considered of age is determined by the simple rule of *cessat ratio, cessat lex*. The object of parental authority is that the parent may be able to do for the child whatever is necessary to be done on his behalf, and which from his tender age he is unable to do for himself.

---

[1] *Oxford Essays*, 1858, p. 212. In Rome and Judæa, as in India and in China, there was a period when the father had a lifelong power over the child, and in all these nations, at a later era, we find social conditions closely resembling, (so far as the history of parental authority is concerned) the various phases of Anglo-Saxon history.

He must maintain and protect him, and discharge the requisitions of the society to which he belongs. Whenever the child is capable of doing for himself all that the state requires of him, or even the things which it deems most important, he is naturally of age.

The period of manhood will, therefore, vary in every country according to the duties which the state demands of its citizens. The feudalists considered the son of a *knight* of age as soon as "he could bear arms," and the son of a *burgher* when "he could count money and measure broadcloth ;[1] because these were the respective duties to which the state called them, and the ends for which they were politically intended.[2] The warlike Danes accounted a boy of age when he could do (what they considered) a man's work, and this was proved by his capacity to brandish his father's sword or bend his bow. The ancient Germans recognised the same principle. They, too, were a nation of warriors ; and at the earliest period of which we know anything of their history, fought with very light darts. A child of twelve years old could hurl them, and therefore at twelve years old he was declared of age. But the weapons with which they fought against the steel-clad warriors of Rome became rapidly heavier, and as a child of twelve could not use them, the age of manhood was changed to fifteen.[3] When

---

[1] Glanville, lib. vii, c. 9 ; Bracton, 86 b.

[2] King Theodoric the Goth, when called by a nation of warriors to determine the period at which a child came of age, replied, "Valour fixes the age of manhood. He who is able to pierce the foe, is bound to combat every vice."

[3] Montesquieu observes that Childebert II was fifteen years old when Gontram, his uncle, declared him to be of full age. "I have put," he said, "this javelin into your hands, to inform you that I now resign the kingdom into your care ;" and then turning to the assembly he said, "You see that Childebert is a man ; obey him." *Esprit des Lois*, l. xviii. So soon as Charlemagne was crowned emperor by Leo III, he caused the oath of allegiance to be taken by all his subjects who were twelve years of age. Kemble's *Ang. Sax.*, ii, 347. This was consistent with the Salic law, by which twelve is the age of majority. *Lex Salica*, tit. xxvi, art. 9.

heavier armour was introduced, it was further extended to twenty-one years.[1]

An Anglo-Saxon child became entitled to the possession of his property at ten years of age, but he could not deal with it until he was fifteen, and this was the age at which the Anglo-Saxons, at least at the later period of their history, were declared to have attained their majority.[2]

Among the early Germans, the "coming of age" was marked by a public ceremony, in which the young man was presented with a shield and a javelin; "the *toga virilis* of a warlike nation, and the signs and implements of manhood. From that moment the youth ranks as a citizen; while until then he is considered as part of (his father's) household, he is now a member of the commonwealth."[3]

SECTION VI.—LIABILITIES OF INFANTS.

As an Anglo-Saxon child was not at first recognised by law as a member of the community, he did not possess any of the rights of a freeman, and was not responsible, either to the state or to the church, for any offence he might commit. However natural and innocuous this rule may have been at first, when the ne-

---

[1] Gregor. Turon., l. vii, c. 33.

[2] Robins *on Gavelkind*, 185; Blackstone's *Comm.*, vol. ii, c. 0, p. 84. The law of gafolkind is a very curious instance of a local custom of an obscure tribe, opposed to the law of a great and civilized nation, remaining valid for one thousand years after the tribe had ceased to exist; and it is also an instance of the length of time that an obsolete law which provokes no great public scandal may remain unrepealed in England. For this law (although it extended over all England) we are said to have been indebted to the Jutes,

who settled mainly in Kent; and in Kent, where the Jutish custom of gafolkind exists, the rule still continues to be observed that an heir comes of age at fifteen.

[3] Tacitus, *De Mor. German.*, c. xiii. Audoin, king of the Lombards, was required by his followers, after a victory in which his young son had greatly distinguished himself, to treat him as of age, although he was not so in years; but Audoin refused to do so, until his son had been publicly armed in a solemn assembly. Warnefrid, *De Gestis Longobard.*, l. 23.

cessities of society were developed, its inconvenience was severely felt. The clergy were the first to attempt its alteration, by declaring (about the end of the eighth century) that a child of ten years old was morally responsible for his actions, and that if at that age he struck another so as to draw blood, he was to do penance. They also admitted him as a witness in the ecclesiastical courts.

The church was, in this matter, many centuries in advance of the state; possibly because the church deals with the conscience of the *individual*, while the state looked only to the *family* (or hundred) to which an offender belonged. The state did not punish boys for crime until the time of Athelstan, when the patriarchal system being entirely broken up, fathers refused to be any longer responsible for their children's thefts. Upon this, the city of London (in which the Danish element predominated) determined on severe legislation against juvenile offenders, and passed a law, whereby every person over the age of *twelve* who stole over the value of twelve pence should be put to death. This ordinance was disallowed by king Athelstan, who decreed that no person under the age of fifteen should be hung for theft.[1] So matters remained till the Saxon-Norman period, when the citizens of London renewed their hostility to juvenile offenders, and obtained an order that all children over twelve who stole above the value of eightpence should incur the penalty of death. There was an exception in these laws in favour of deaf and dumb children, who were declared never to come of age, but always to be under the authority of their parents, who were to be responsible for their actions; which tends to support the opinion

---

[1] *Ll. Athelst.*, l. i, v. 2, xiii, 3, *Sec.*, c. xxi, Thorpe, i, 389; *Ll. Henr.*, Thorpe, i, 229 and 241; *Ll. Cnuti*, lix, 20, Thorpe, i, 558.

that the power of the father was based on and limited by the necessities of the child.

From the consideration of the duration of the paternal power and responsibility, we pass on to its extent. Among patriarchal nations the father has the power of life and death over his children ; he can expose them in infancy, kill them when he pleases, sell them into slavery, force a wife on his son, sell his daughter to a husband, divorce his children of either sex, or transfer them to another family by adoption. No child can possess property in his father's lifetime, for whatever he earns belongs to his father or family. These were the laws of Judæa and of early Rome ;[1] but if they were ever those of the Anglo-Saxons (as is very probable), it must have been before the time of Hengist and Horsa, and consequently at an era of which nothing is known.

We have already seen that the Anglo-Saxon father had the right of exposing the child, but there is no evidence that he had, like the Roman and the Jew, the power of putting him to death after he had once undertaken to rear him. He had, however, *at first*, the power of selling him *whenever he pleased,* but this power was soon restricted. The first restriction upon the sale of children has ever been the same in all countries, namely, a prohibition to the father to sell the child, *except* under the pressure of extreme want. In a case of supreme necessity, says an old Frisian law, " when the child is naked as a worm, and without a roof ; when the black fog and the cold winter reach her ; then may the mother sell her child."

Nor can there be any doubt that in times of distress this right was commonly exercised. At the conclu-

---

[1] *Cod.* Justin., lib. viii, tit. 47, De patria potest., *Cod.* Theod., lib. iii, tit. 3 ; *Edict.* Theod. regis Goth., 794. The reader may also consult *Salomon and Saturn,* in Kemble's *Dial.,* p. 135.

sion of the fifth century, according to an old legend, the
father of saint Patrick being in great penury, availed
himself of it, and sold him and his two sisters to a Scot,
by whom the future archbishop was employed as a swine-
herd.[1]

As this power was too often exercised at the expense
of lawful offspring, it was still more likely to have been
so in the case of illegitimate children. There is a story
of a husband who after a long absence returned home,
and found his wife with a young son that could not
possibly be his. In answer to his inquiries she explained
that walking out one day in the extreme cold of the
north, a flake of snow had fallen on her bosom, from
which she became *enceinte*. Her husband appeared satisfied with the explanation, and shortly afterwards took
the boy with him to Italy, where he sold him as a slave.
On his return he accounted for his loss to his wife by
telling her that the child, like his father the snow, had
melted away in the sun, and that *that* which had been
born of the cold of the north had died of the heat of the
south.[2]

One of the first restrictions on the sale of children
related to the *age* at which they might be sold. Archbishop Theodore permitted a father, if pressed *by great
necessity*, to sell a son who was under the age of seven,
and to sell a daughter in marriage until she was fourteen,
but after these ages the children were not to be sold at
all.[3] At this period public opinion against selling children
probably became more powerful, for archbishop Ecgbert
(whose writings are almost copies from those of Theodore,
though seventy or eighty years later in date) repeats the
permission of the latter for the sale of children under a

[1] Roger de Hoveden, A.D. 491.
[2] Kemble's *Saxons in England*,
vol. i, p. 198.
[3] Theodori *Poenit.*, xix, 28, Thorpe,
ii, 19 ; and Ecgb. *Conf.*, Thorpe, ii,
153.

certain age, but adds that whoever avails himself of it should be excommunicated.[1]

The right of a father to sell his child into slavery involved a right of disposing of him in any other way he might think fit. Among these one of the most usual was that of placing a boy in a monastery, or a girl in a convent, to remain for life. When king Oswy was waging an almost hopeless war with Penda, king of the Mercians, he made a solemn vow that if he should be victorious in his next battle, he would dedicate his daughter Elfleda, then about a year old, to perpetual virginity; and with her he would give twelve farms on which to build a monastery. The king was successful, and strictly performed his vow.[2]

Although the clergy were, from the beginning to the end of Anglo-Saxon history, the steady opponents both of slavery and of the excesses of parental power, the fact that with every young person of rank placed in a monastery they received handsome endowments, rendered them tolerant of this practice of condemning children to servitude and of this gross abuse of a father's authority.[3] In the age of archbishop Theodore, a girl placed in a convent against her wish when under age was not allowed to leave on attaining years of discretion ; though for this no better reason was given than that Hannah offered Samuel to God when a child, and that he continued in the ministry of the temple during the rest of his life. But the rules of the Anglo-Saxon church in this respect appear to have varied at different times. The Catholic church, according to Dr. Lingard, did not, prior to the sixth century, hold the child bound by the determination of the parent ; but from that time to the pontificate of Celestin III (A.D.

---

[1] Ecgb. *Conf.*, xxvii, Thorpe, *Ancient Laws*, ii, 153; Ecgbert, *Pœnit.*, Thorpe, ii, 213.

[2] Bede, *Hist. Eccles.*, l. iii, c. 24 ;

Alcuin *de Pont. Ebor.*, v. iii ; *Histor. Rames.*, pp. 495, 497, 499.

[3] Ecgb. *Excerpt.*, c. 93, 94, & 95 ; *Domesday Book*, t. i, fo. 68, 596, 573.

1191), the contrary doctrine prevailed, and a child placed
in a monastery or convent by its parents or guardian
never attained a right to judge for itself.

It was natural that an affectionate parent of any intelligence should be slow to condemn a favourite child to a
life that might prove most distasteful to her ; and it was
equally probable that the clergy would endeavour to
obtain as noviciates the heiresses of wide domains and
noble fortunes. Between natural affection and the covetous zeal of the clergy, many a weak and superstitious
mind must have hesitated long; and numerous must have
been the devices which, in an age so fond of divination,
would have been employed to direct the wavering judgment. A curious instance of this occurred in the case of
Eadburga, the granddaughter of Alfred the Great. It was
the wish of her father, king Edmund, when she was very
young, to devote her to the cloister ; but a sense of the
cruelty of condemning to perpetual imprisonment an
infant who was too young to judge for herself, caused
him to pause. After some hesitation, he based his decision upon the following experiment. Eadburga, who was
but three years old, was conducted into a room, in one
corner of which a collection of juvenile trinkets had been
previously placed, and in another, a chalice with a book
of the gospels. It so chanced that the child ran to the
latter ; whereupon her father, who conceived that he had
thus received an answer from heaven, caught her in
his arms, exclaiming, "Thou shalt receive the object of
thy choice ; nor will thy parents regret, if they are thy
inferiors in virtue." She was, therefore, placed in a convent in Winchester, where she rendered herself eminent
for her piety and humility.[1]

In a country where the patriarchal system exists, a

[1] Will. Malmes., l. ii, c. 13.

person who is injured does not look for redress to the individual who has wronged him, but to the family to which the wrongdoer belongs. The family constitute a moral, political, and pecuniary partnership; and all transactions, even of wrong doing, are supposed to be carried on on behalf of the firm. One of the consequences of this is, that the son is responsible for his father's crimes, and also for his debts. This was the case in Rome and Judæa. Our Saviour alludes to this custom in the parable of the unmerciful servant, whose lord commanded him to be sold *with his wife and children.*[1]

During the whole of the earlier periods of Anglo-Saxon history, the child was liable to be sold into slavery for the payment of penalties incurred by his father; but in the beginning of the tenth century, no child *under* ten could be punished for his father's crimes, and no child *over* ten *unless* he were a party to them.[2] With the birth of the feudal system, this terrible liability rapidly disappeared. King Cnut (A.D. 1020) indignantly complained that it was anciently the custom that the child which lay in the cradle, though he had never tasted meat, should be sold into slavery for his father's crimes, *being held by the covetous to be equally guilty as if he had discretion.*"[3]

This enactment appears to mark an era in social history; for it shows that a child could no longer be lawfully punished because he was a member of an offending family, but that he was to be responsible for his own faults, and his own faults only.[4] The relief, however, which these

---

[1] St. Matthew, c. xviii.
[2] *Ll. Inæ*, c. 7, Thorpe, i, 107.
[3] *Ll. Cnuti Sec.*, s. 77, Thorpe, i, 421.
[4] It is to be feared that this law was disregarded on occasions of extreme necessity. Bishop Lupus says, " E terra venales missi sunt in longe in exilium, deditique in ditionem alie-

nam, et infantes e cunabilis minimo furti pretio plerumque per hanc gentem, ac sævissime contra leges, sunt mancipati." Langebec, *Script. Rerum Danic.*, ii, 468. A similar change occurred in the history of Jewish law. *Epist. Galatians*, c. iv, v. 1 & 2.

laws afforded was not complete ; because a man, guilty of crime, was liable to be outlawed, and as the child followed the condition of the father, he also became an outlaw. This grievance was *partially* remedied by Edward the Confessor, who relieved children born *before* a father was condemned from the consequences of his outlawry, and limited the penalty to such children as were born afterwards.

To the last period of Anglo-Saxon history, however, the child occupied the legal status of his father at the time of his birth ; and the son of a felon was born to his position of degradation. Nor in his father's household did he ever rise above the condition of a servant, but was always compelled to perform menial and other domestic duties ; a position in which he bore à curious resemblance to the Jewish child in the time of saint Paul.

It is curious that the paternal power among the Anglo-Saxons never extended, as among the Romans and other patriarchal nations, so far as to give the father a right to the earnings of the child ; nor did it ever enable him to compel a son to put away his wife.

At the time when the son was liable for the crimes of the father, the father was also liable for those of the son. If the son stole, his father or family must make good the damage done, though they could relieve themselves from this liability by delivering him up to the offended party. At a later date, they obtained the same immunity on payment of his " were," or legal value.

We have, in the preceding pages, endeavoured to trace the relative position of father and child from the beginning to the end of Anglo-Saxon history ; and it is clear that it was marked by considerable progress in domestic civilisation. At first, the child could be exposed as soon as born ; when reared, he could be sold into slavery ; he was liable to be punished for his father's crimes, and to be sold in payment of his debts. At the time of the Norman conquest all these barbarous liabilities had ceased ; and although the child was still regarded as occupying a position of extreme subjection or dependence, he had ceased to be a chattel or a slave.

CHAPTER III.

THE SLAVE.

THE Anglo-Saxon population may be considered under the two heads of those who were freemen and those who were not. The former consisted of the owners of land, or of those who had some other recognised source of independence ; and the latter, of those who were "in the hand" of another. Among these were included all men and children ; for a woman could never be altogether free, inasmuch as while single she was under the protection of her father, and when married under that of her husband.

The words "freeman" and "slave," as understood at the present day, are hardly applicable to the state of society under the Anglo-Saxons ; for a large proportion of freemen were in a position in which they would not now be considered altogether free ; and the majority of the slaves lived in a state of comparative independence.

The Anglo-Saxons divided the origin or causes of slavery into two classes—slavery by birth, and slavery by mishap ; although the former of these terms is not quite accurate.[1]

[1] *Ll. Henr.*, l. lxxvi, s. 3.

According both to Anglo-Saxon custom and to the law of the church, a man was a slave by birth whose father and mother were slaves at the time of his *conception*, not, as is usually stated, at the time of his *birth*. If a woman became a slave while in a state of pregnancy, the child was born free ; and if, on the other hand, a female slave was manumitted after she became pregnant, her child was born a slave.[1]

Our national customs and the law of Rome differed as to those of whose parents one was free and the other a slave. According to Anglo-Saxon law, the son of a freeman, by a slave mother, born in wedlock, was free ; while the son of a slave by a freewoman was deemed a slave. The child followed the condition of its father. The law of Rome and of the church was exactly the reverse. According to *that* the child followed the condition of the mother.[2]

The most common origin of slavery "by mishap" was war, which was once carried on with a ferocity happily unknown in modern hostilities. At first, every man in the defeated army was put to death ;[3] but a custom so horrible as this could not survive the dawn of civilization. The victors, at a very early period, generally abstained from indiscriminate slaughter, and systematically spared the lives of a constantly increasing proportion of prisoners, whom they reserved as slaves. It is not, however, to be

[1] Theodore, *Pœnit.*, xvi, 33; Ecgb. *Confess.*, c. 25 ; Bracton, lib. iv, c. 6, s. 4 ; Fleta, lib. i, c. 4.

[2] The Anglo-Saxons held, "Semper a patre non a matre generationis ordo texitur." Thorpe, i, 582. The Roman law was the reverse ; "partus sequitur ventrem." Fortescue *De Laudibus Legum Angliæ,* c. 42. Whether the illegitimate son of a female slave by a free father became a slave is, perhaps, doubtful. Hallam is of opinion that the child was free (*Middle Ages,* vol. i, c. 2, p. 2), and so is Thorpe (*Ancient Laws and Inst.*, v. i, p. 627) ; Kemble is of a contrary opinion (*The Saxons in England*, vol. i, b. i, c. 8.) It is exceedingly difficult to reconcile the various conflicting authorities on which they rely, particularly those of Bracton and Fleta.

[3] Tacitus, *Annales*, lib. i, c. 61, lib. xiii, c. 57 ; Fleta, lib. i, c. 3, s. 3 ; Grimm, *Deutsche Rechtsalter.*, p. 320.

supposed that wholesale massacres did not occasionally occur at every period of Anglo-Saxon history.

The first advance from the extreme of ferocious barbarity to which we have just alluded took place as early as the era of Hengist and Horsa,[1] but it was a long time before it made any important or well-established progress. From the earliest period at which any mercy was shewn to the conquered, it would seem to have been exhibited on a recognised system. The first persons whose lives were habitually spared were the camp-followers; and, as these were already slaves, they suffered nothing by capture but a transfer of their services from one master to another. It was afterwards usual to spare the ordinary soldiers; but all nobles and warriors of distinction were put to death.

There were probably two reasons for this. First, it was always in the power of the chieftains to stir up rebellions against the conquerors, and it was therefore expedient to be rid of them; and secondly, it was not usual between nobles either to offer or to accept the boon of life. To survive defeat and bonds would have disgraced not only the conquered noble, but all his kin; and he preferred death, even at his own hands, to so terrible a degradation.

The disregard of life displayed by both conquerors and conquered was opposed to the doctrines of Christianity; and the clergy consequently exerted all their influence, both to induce the victors to spare the lives of their prisoners, and to persuade the conquered nobles to accept the boon of life, even at the price of bonds and slavery.

[1] Bede, speaking of the conquest of the inhabitants of this island by the Saxons, tells us that "Some of the miserable remainder being taken in the mountains were butchered in heaps. Others, spent with hunger, came forth and submitted themselves to the enemy for food, being destined to undergo perpetual servitude, even if they were not killed on the spot." Bede's *Eccles. Hist.*, l. i, c. 16.

Their success in preventing the massacre of prisoners would have been greater, had it not been for the universal custom of hereditary vengeance, which required every man to slay the members of every family one of whom had killed any of his relations.

An instance of this occurred at the battle of the Trent, fought (A.D. 679) between king Egfrid and Ethelred, king of the Mercians. On this occasion a youth of good family, named Inna, was severely wounded and left on the field as dead. The following night he recovered sufficient strength to bind up his own wounds, and endeavoured to escape; but without success, for he was captured and delivered to an earl in the army of king Ethelred. With a view of saving his life, Inna denied that he was a soldier or a gentleman, representing himself as a poor married peasant who came to bring provisions to the army. On this statement his life was spared, and he was condemned to slavery. His manners and conversation, however, raised a suspicion against him; and on a promise of protection from the earl he was induced to confess the truth. Upon this the earl observed, "I knew by your answers you were no peasant. You deserve to die, BECAUSE *all my brethren and relations were killed in that fight*, but I will not kill you, as I will not break my word." He, therefore, took him to London and sold him to a Frisian trader; but the Frisian made a bad bargain, for, however securely he bound his prisoner, at a certain hour of the day his bonds fell off. His captors imputed this to his having about him some spell or charm, an accusation he denied. It was ultimately discovered that he had a brother named Tunna, an abbot, who, believing Inna to have been killed, regularly at Nones offered up prayers for his soul, and that it was always at this hour that his bonds were miraculously loosened. The historian

believed this tale to be true, and assures us that it ought
not to be passed over in silence, " for the narration of it
will conduce to the salvation of the souls of many."[1]

The inhabitants of a conquered province, who had taken
no personal part in the war, were also at the mercy of the
conquerors, and were dealt with very differently at different
times.   When the Norwegian Godred conquered the Isle of
Man, he gave his army the option of dividing the land and
the inhabitants among them, or of plundering the island
and returning home.   The majority of his soldiers preferred the plunder, with which they departed; but Godred
remained, made himself sole proprietor of the island, and
reduced the inhabitants to slavery.[2] This was an extreme
case, but the next is nearly as bad.   When the Mercians
conquered Northumbria, they reduced the whole of the
inhabitants into what they termed " hewers of wood and
drawers of water," and compelled them " to spend their
lives in ploughing and harrowing " for the benefit of the
conquerors.[3]   But when, in the time of king Alfred, the
Saxons overcame the Danes, the conquered suffered
scarcely any inconvenience, being permitted to retain
not only their possessions, but also their laws and customs.   This leniency may possibly have arisen from an
improvement in morals, or from the political wisdom of
the great king ; but far more probably from the still
formidable power of the conquered.

Among other sources of slavery were crime, debt,
gambling, superior legal power, voluntary surrender, and
illegal violence ; all of which were at one time carried
out to an extraordinary extent, and were, in fact, subjected to small limitation, but, in course of time, all
these various means of reducing people to slavery became

[1] Bede's *Eccles. Hist.*, l. iv, c. xxii.   [3] *Anglo-Saxon Chron.*, A.D. 876 ;
[2] *Chron. Manniæ*, MS. Cotton,   Flor. Wigorn., A.D. 876 ; Bede, *Eccl.*
Jul. A vii, fol. 32.   *Hist.*, lib. i, c. xv.

less fruitful. If a freeman were convicted of a crime, such as theft, and could not pay the penalty imposed on his offence, he became the " wite-theow," or convict-slave, of the offended party. The clergy availed themselves of this law to exercise a most cruel amount of tyranny and extortion. They declared witchcraft, incontinence, and other immoralities, to be offences *against the church*, for which the offender was liable to make them compensation or become their slave ; and they also claimed to try him before their own tribunals. This led to gross abuses. It frequently happened that a man, on the accusation of a bishop or abbot, was tried before his accuser, found guilty by him, and condemned to forfeit his estates to his judge, or to become a slave.

Toward the end of the ninth century, Denewulf, bishop of Winchester, granted the lands of Alresford to a kinsman of his own. After a certain time he found it convenient to resume not only the lands, but to claim his kinsman's savings. He caused him to be accused of fornication, tried him before his own tribunal, personally found him guilty, and then took possession of all his worldly wealth. In this plunder, if we may believe the canons of Winchester, a worldly-minded monarch unjustly desired a share, an encroachment on clerical rights which the indignant canons vigorously resisted. The matter was ultimately brought before the witena-gemot, who compelled the bishop to allow the king one hundred and twenty mancusses in gold out of the profits of the transaction. Neither of the parties to this robbery (nor, it must be confessed, the witena-gemot), appears to have bestowed a thought on the plundered sinner, who in his reduced position had no resource but slavery.[1]

On a similar principle to that by which a criminal who

---

[1] *Codex Diplom. Anglo-Sax.*, nos. 601 and 1296; Thorpe, ii, 9, note 4.

could not pay a fine became a slave, an insolvent debtor was handed over to his creditor to satisfy in person what he could not pay in purse, and a rich man increased his power without diminishing his wealth, by accepting the servitude of his debtors in discharge of their debts.[1] He was not, however, *compelled* to do so. If it were not convenient to him to invest the amount of his debt in his debtor's person, any one who chose to come forward and pay the debt had a right to stand in the creditor's place and take the debtor as his slave. Under this system a rich man could rapidly acquire serfs, and extravagant men were as speedily reduced to slavery.

Another source of servitude was found in the law which required every freeman beneath the rank of a thane to be either the recognized follower of some lord, or the member of a family or "frith-borg," who would be responsible for him. This naturally tended to serfdom, for no one would accept the permanent fellowship of a criminal or pauper who was constantly involving him in pecuniary penalties.

To the numerous unhappy beings who became slaves through insolvency and crime, we must add those who suffered the same lot through the national passion for gambling. The ancient German would play for everything he had in the world, and having lost all he could legitimately lose, would gamble for his wife and children. When these were gone, he would stake himself on the hazard of the die, and, if once more unlucky, would cheerfully surrender himself to the servitude he so justly merited.

To the various sources of slavery already mentioned must be added the excess of parental power, which enabled the parent to sell his children; and a severe

[1] Marculfi *Formulæ*, ii, 28; Thorpe, ii, 153 ; Du Cange *v.* Heribannum.

marriage-law, whereby a freewoman who married a slave became a slave also.[1]

But a still more melancholy source of servitude than any of these (for in all of them the sufferer was not altogether blameless), was the extreme poverty and distress which in a half-tilled country constantly arose from a failure of the crops, or from their destruction by the cruelties of incessant war. In such times, starving freemen flocked in multitudes to the monasteries, and resigned themselves to voluntary slavery, " that they might live and not die."[2] The monks fed all comers ; but they complained with unnecessary irritation that these unfortunates were apt, when the time of misery had passed away, to abandon their lords and return home, ungrateful for the protection they had received, and forgetful of their servile duties.

In addition to war and famine, the oppression of powerful earls and abbots often induced freemen to surrender their liberty into the hands of some superior who was capable of affording them protection. Painful as are all these sources of slavery, the saddest of all was illegal violence. The strong and rich habitually committed forays or razzias on their unoffending neighbours, and seized and sold them as slaves in defiance of the law both of church and state. In the seventh century, bishop Aidan, whose sanctity procured him profuse gifts from kings and earls, expended nearly all his wealth in ransoming those who had been unjustly sold into slavery.

---

[1] *Ll. Ripuar.*, lxxx, 18 ; *Ll. Sal.*, xiv, 7 and 11 ; *Ll. Burgund.*, c. xxxv, s. 3; Saxo Gram., lib. 5. This was certainly the law of the continental nations, but whether it was ever that of England may be doubted. It is stated by Bartholomæus (*De proprietatibus Rerum, c. Ancilla*) that a freeman who married a slave became a slave also, but he does not give his authorities for this statement.

[2] Gregor. Turon., vii, 45 ; *Ll. Frisionum*, tit. ii, s. 1 ; *Ll. Henrici*, c. 76 ; *Ll. Wisigoth*, lib. v. tit. 4, s. 10 ; *Ll. Longobard.*, lib. iii, c. 15 ; Kemble, *Cod. Diplomat.*, no. 925.

It has been already remarked that the condition of the conquered people who took no part in a war varied from one of slavery into one but little more severe than political subjection. The position of slaves and serfs was nearly as diversified. In the earliest period, the master had the power of life and death over the slave, and with it all the inferior rights which flow from it. In the exercise of this terrible power, both the early continental Germans and their Anglo-Saxon descendants abstained from acts of deliberate cruelty. It was not usual with the Germans to punish their slaves with whips or chains, or to oppress them with uncertain exactions. No law, however, protected their lives; and though they were never put to death deliberately, they were often slain in fits of passion.[1] The earliest laws of the Anglo-Saxons were in accordance with Germanic customs. They *permitted* the master to put his slave to death when, where, and how he pleased; and the first modification of this barbarous right, which emanated from the clergy, was so slight, that it could have had but little influence on national manners.

Archbishop Theodore declared that if a lady, *inflamed by rage*, beat her female slave to such a degree that she died within three days, the offender, " if she *intended* to beat her *to death*, was to fast seven years; but if she beat her to death without intending it, she was to fast three years."[2] The canons of king Edgar, published nearly three hundred years later, decreed the same penance whether the slave died within the three days or not.[3] It is to be feared that Anglo-Saxon matrons were very cruel mistresses. There are numerous instances of female slaves

---

[1] Tacitus, *Germ.*, xxv.

[2] Theod. *Pœnit.*, xxi, s. 12 and 13; Ecgb. *Pœnit.*, lib. ii, s. 4; *Ll. Henrici*, c. lxxv, 4; Thorpe, i,

579.

[3] *Ll. Alfredi*, 17, Thorpe, i, 49; *Modus Imponendi Pœnit.*, 12, Thorpe, ii, 269.

flying to the sanctuary of a cathedral to save their lives. A female servant of Theothic (the bellmaker) of Winchester was for *a very slight offence* placed by her mistress in fetters, chained by the feet and hands all night. Next morning she was taken out, and frightfully beaten, and again placed in bonds ; but the ensuing night she contrived to escape, and took sanctuary at the tomb of St. Swithin. Two or three other female slaves took refuge at the same tomb about the same time from the fury of their mistresses.[1]

The male sex, when guilty of cruelly maltreating slaves, were dealt with even more lightly than women. They were required to fast two years only ; and this fast was, of course, redeemable in the usual manner. For the barbarous crime of knocking out the eye or the tooth of a slave, the church *advised* the master to give him his freedom ; but it does not appear that he was compelled to make this reparation.[2]

This limited protection from the *blind fury* of his master was the first and only personal privilege a slave attained during the earliest period of the history of France, England, Rome, and Judæa. It was undoubtedly better than nothing ; but it was a very trivial limitation on the master's power of life and death, and the terrible catalogue of minor rights which flowed from it. By far the most important of these was that of selling the slave whenever he thought fit. The greater right was seldom abused, but the minor one was a constant source of domestic misery.

The history of the slave trade in England is one of the most discreditable features in the Anglo-Saxon annals. At how early a period it commenced, no man knows. When

---

[1] Wright's *History of Domestic Manners*, p. 56.

[2] These laws were evidently adopted from that of Moses, which punished the master of a foreign slave who struck him so violently that he died under his hand, and prohibited the striking out of the eye or tooth of slaves of Hebrew origin.

Britain was under the Romans, one of her main exports was British slaves; and after the Roman occupation ceased, there were few greater temptations to invasion either to Scot, Pict, Saxon, or Dane, than the desire to possess English slaves, whose personal beauty and reputation always commanded a high price in the continental markets.

There are few more remarkable instances of the truth of the saying, that " out of the greatest evils it often pleases God to bring the greatest blessings," than the fact, that to the slave-trade this country indirectly owes its conversion to the faith of Christ. Well known as the following story is, its importance will be an excuse for its repetition.

Towards the end of the sixth century certain foreign merchants arrived in Rome and publicly exhibited their wares. Among other goods were some young slaves, whose delicate complexions, beautiful features, and fine hair, attracted so much admiration, that even St. Gregory was tempted to visit them. When he saw them he inquired from what country they came, and was told from Britain, the inhabitants of which, he was assured, generally possessed the same attractive qualities. He next inquired whether they were Christians, and was answered in the negative. He sighed deeply, and said, " Alas! how sad it is, that the prince of darkness should have possession of men so fair, and that with so much grace of form the grace of the Holy Spirit should be wanting to them." He then asked what people they were called, and was told " Angles." " Right," he said, " they are angels in face, and should be co-heirs with the angels in heaven. What," he continued, " is the name of their province?" He was informed, that the people were called Deiri. " Truly they are *De Ira*," said the future pope, "for they are withdrawn from wrath, and are called to the mercy of Christ. What is the name of their king?" he asked, and was told " Ella." " Hallelujah!" he said ; "the praise of God must be sung in those parts." Nor did he content himself with this series of what might without irreverence be termed bad puns, but immediately applied to the pope for leave to undertake a mission to this country. He was not, however, destined to come himself, but he afterwards sent St. Augustine, whose labours, under God's providence, ultimately· led to the conversion of the Saxons to the Christian faith.

The Christian clergy no sooner obtained power in England, than they exerted it to the utmost, to put an end to the foreign slave trade, and in this endeavour they were aided by many of the most powerful of our kings. Ina, Alfred the Great, Cnut, and William the Conqueror, all legislated, *almost in the same words*, against selling slaves "out of the country, especially into heathendom." It is, however, to be feared, that their legislation had but little practical effect.[1]

During the period immediately prior to the conquest, the rich and powerful amassed large fortunes by committing razzias on their neighbours, seizing their persons, and selling them and their children to slave-dealers. These dealers bought them to sell to continental breeders of slaves, and they gave a higher price for female slaves than for male, and for females who had a prospect of becoming mothers than for any others. This led to the most infamous cruelty. "There was one custom," says William of Malmesbury, "repugnant to nature, which they adopted ; namely, to sell their female slaves, when pregnant by them, either to prostitution, or to public

[1] *Ll. Inæ*, ii, Thorpe, i, p. 111 ; i and iii, c. 15, Thorpe, vol. i, pp. *Ll. Ethelredi*, v, c. 2 ; vi, c. 9 ; viii, 305, 317, 338, 379, 483, 493. *Can.* c. 5 ; *Cnut. Sec.*, s. 3 ; *Will. I*, c. 4, *Sanctorum*, Wilkins, *Concil.*, i, iii.

K

slavery."[1]   Even ladies stooped to the acquisition of
money, by encouraging the violation and sale of their
own sex ; among these was a sister of Cnut, who accumulated considerable wealth by exporting female slaves
from England to Denmark.[2]

Above all others who distinguished themselves by this
horrible traffic were the merchants of Bristol.   "The
people of this town," we are told, "had a most odious
and inveterate custom, which they derived from their
ancestors, of buying men and women in all parts of England, and exporting them to Ireland for the sake of gain.
The young women they commonly got with child, and
carried them to market in their pregnancy that they might
bring a better price.   You might have seen with sorrow
long ranks of young persons of both sexes and of the
greatest beauty tied with ropes and daily exposed for sale."
Wulfstan, bishop of Worcester, at the time of the conquest, horrified at such practices, repeatedly visited Bristol, remaining two months at a time, and preached every
Sunday against this sin, until at last (we are told) he
induced the traders to abandon it, and to set an example
to the rest of England.[3]

As the life and liberty of the slave were in the power
of his master, it followed that his minor rights were also
vested in him.   If a freeman were slain, the penalty for
killing him was payable to his kindred ; but the compensation for the murder of a slave was paid to his master.
To the slave, too, was denied the right of purging himself
by oath of denial when accused of crime ; he was compelled to go to the ordeal, and if it proved unfriendly, he
must pay with his hide.   Sometimes his master chose to
buy him off, in which case he of course escaped ; but if

---

[1] Will. Malmes., lib. ii, c. 13.   [3] See the Life of Wulfstan in the
[2] Will. Malmes., lib. iii, c. 1.   Anglia Sacra, ii, 258.

not, the slave had no option, but "to go to the neck-catch," or "redeem his hide for himself."[1]

He could from a very early date do this by payment of a fixed sum, which was considered the value of his skin ; and in later times, the phrase, "pay with his hide," more commonly meant the sum of money payable to escape the infliction of chastisement than the punishment itself.

The chastity of the female slave was protected from violence, but the penalty inflicted was payable to her master and not to herself. If the offence were committed by a slave who could not redeem his hide, he was punished by mutilation.[2]

The great bulk of the servile population were *adscripti glebæ*, attached to the soil which they cultivated ; and when the land was sold or bequeathed, they or their services went with it. At the latest period of Anglo-Saxon

---

[1] *Ll. Wihtræd.*, s. 10, Thorpe, v. i, p. 39. It may be doubtful whether paying with the hide and going to the neck-catch were quite synonymous terms ; if they were not, the distinction probably was as follows : A slave condemned to pay with his hide was handed over to the offended party to be beaten to any extent his opponent chose. Usually the culprit was stripped naked, save a cloth round his loins ; his hands were tied behind him, and an iron ring was then placed round one ancle, and through this ring (and between it and his ancle) a strong stake or staple was driven into the ground, so that the sufferer was held fast to the spot by the ring and stake, with the facility of walking with one foot round the peg that held the other. When so fastened, the operator and a friend flogged him round and round with boughs or sticks until pity or fatigue induced them to leave off. Going to the "heals-fang," or neck-catch, was a slight variation from this, but was equally disagreeable. In this case a tree or post, about the height of a man, was placed in the ground, and a split placed at the top sufficiently wide to admit the culprit's neck. Into this slit his head or neck was forced, face downwards, and was retained in its place by the spring or closing of the split. To make this doubly sure, a transverse piece of wood was fitted into the back of his neck, the ends of which were secured to the opposite sides of the split of the neck-catch, so that his head was held tight in a triangular fastening. His clothes do not seem to have been taken off, but his hands were tied behind him, and he was flogged with a sort of cat-with-three-tails, composed of a handle about eighteen inches long, with three thongs of the same length, at the end of each of which was a hard knot about the size of a large marble. At the conclusion of the ceremony he was sometimes branded with a red-hot iron.

[2] *Ll. Alfredi*, Thorpe, i, p. 79.

K 2

history, they could not *legally* leave their land, though it sometimes happened when they had incurred penalties for which their lords might have been rendered responsible, that the latter permitted them to run away. In some cases they could be transferred from one estate to another, whether with or without their consent does not appear ; but, considering the disregard of law then general, their consent would hardly have been asked by any one who was powerful enough to effect his object without it.

A slave was not permitted to give evidence in a court of justice against a freeman ; nor could he marry without the consent of his master. With the approbation of the latter, slaves might intermarry, but if one of them afterwards became free the marriage was voidable, and the freedman or freedwoman might marry again.[1] If a man's wife or a woman's husband was reduced to slavery, the marriage was thereby dissolved, and the free party might marry another ; but the freeman who married a slave could not dismiss her and marry again *without her consent.*

The degrees of servitude and the gradual amelioration of the condition of slaves appear to have depended on their occupation and the employment for which they were required.

The Romans, who inhabited magnificent palaces and lived in the most extravagant luxury, employed slaves to perform every menial or domestic task, and were astonished to find that the continental Saxons entrusted the services of the home to their wives and children. They found the slaves employed in no domestic offices, but occupied exclusively in the cultivation of the land, or in keeping sheep, or in hunting or fishing for the benefit of their masters. None of them resided with their owners,

---

[1] Such second marriage was sinful in the opinion of the clergy, but its validity was not disputed even by them.

but each had his separate habitation, and his agricultural or pastoral duties.[1] When, however, the Saxons migrated to England, they had made some slight advance in civilisation, and a limited number of household servants had become useful.

The most severe form of servitude, however, fell to the share of the domestic slaves. They were constantly under the eye and the hand of the master; their work was never done, and every fit of passion might be vented upon them before his anger had time to cool. The prædial slaves, on the contrary, were employed at a distance. It was difficult to look after them, and there was no way of enforcing regular and systematic toil. Under these circumstances, it was advantageous to all parties that their labour should be fixed. They were consequently condemned to task work, to perform a stated amount of labour, or provide a fixed quantity of corn, honey, pigs, or eels. To this was often added the obligation of doing a certain number of days' harrowing, ploughing, and carting for the lord, and sometimes of finding him in firewood, and in horses and carts on particular occasions. The duties most commonly imposed on prædial slaves seem to have been ploughing, herding hogs, hedging and ditching, fishing, hawking, watching and warding, and going on messages.[2]

A slave who was in this position soon ceased to be altogether a slave, and became a tenant, paying rent in kind, and performing certain servile offices, in return for the use of the land which he was allowed to occupy.

It has been already stated that the laws afforded the slave a certain amount of protection from the sudden fury of his master, and intended to protect the chastity of the

---

[1] Tacitus, *Germ.*, c. 25. [2] *Rectitudines Sing. Person.*, Thorpe, i, 432.

female slave. In addition to this, the law at a later period provided for their competent subsistence. As the domestic slave resided with his master, and dined at the common table, he did not require any special provision ; but the prædial slave had to be supplied at his own habitation. The law decreed him a liberal allowance, requiring the master to furnish him with seven hundred and thirty small loaves each year, besides morning and noon meals.[1] At the time of the Norman conquest, the allowance to a female slave was seven pounds of corn, a sheep or threepence at winter, a tester of beans at Easter, and a goat in summer.[2]

The recognition of the Lord's day was one of the earliest sources of limitation on slavery. On that day a master could not compel the slave to work, under the penalty, at first, of forfeiting him to the king or reeve ; and, afterwards, of giving him his freedom. His master was also exhorted to leave him free from work twelve days at Christmas, and on the day on which Christ overcame the devil ; on St. George's day, and seven days before and seven days after Easter ; one day at St. Peter's, and one day at St. Paul's tide ; one whole week at harvest before St. Mary's festival, one day at the commencement of All Saints, and the Wednesday in the four Ember weeks. On these days he might work for himself and retain what he earned (that is, if his master would obey the church), but on the Sunday he was not to work under the penalty of the neck-catch.[3]

The savings of the prædial slave from his food and his earnings on feast-days formed his earliest property. This he at first held entirely at the will of his master, who took it away from him whenever he thought fit. The

---

[1] *Sal. and Sat.*, p. 192.
[2] Ellis, *Domesday Book*, vol. ii, p. 504.
[3] *Homily of St. Gregory*, App., p. 39 ; *Ll. Alfredi*, Thorpe, vol. i, p. 93.

early Anglo-Saxon bishops repeatedly exhorted their flocks not to exercise this right, but to leave the slaves' earnings untouched.[1] It is probable that their exhortations had considerable influence, for at the later periods of Anglo-Saxon history we find the slave in possession of property with which he sometimes " redeemed his hide" or " bought off the neck-catch ;" and in rare cases he wás permitted to purchase his freedom. His possession of property was, however, to some extent, permissive only, for on his death it reverted to his lord, and did not descend to his children. On the whole there can be little doubt that the condition of the serf was one far removed from slavery, and that it was not one of very great hardship, or unsuited to the state of society in which it existed. In corroboration of this opinion it may be remarked, that at no period of Anglo-Saxon history do we read of a rebellion of slaves or even of servile discontent.

From the earliest period the Christian clergy used their influence, not only to diminish the severity of slavery, but to limit its extent. They constantly freed the slaves who came into their possession, and they exhorted the laity to follow their example.[2] They were eminently

---

[1] Theod. *Pœnit.*, xix, 30 ; Ecgb. *Pœnit.*, Add., 35.

[2] Mr. Hallam seems to doubt the sincerity of the clergy in this respect (*Middle Ages*, v. i, c. 2, part 2) ; but I cannot help thinking without sufficient cause. The following letter from archbishop Brihtwald, A.D. 710, is too much to his credit to be omitted. " To his most reverend and venerable fellow-bishop Forthere, Brihtwald, the servant of the servants of God, sends greeting in the Lord. Since my request which I made in your presence to the venerable abbot Beorwald, to allow a captive girl to be ransomed, who is represented as having relations here, has turned out unavailing, contrary to my expectation, and they are again importunate in their entreaties, I have thought it most expedient to send this letter to you, by the girl's brother named Eppa, in which I beg you by any means to prevail yourself on the aforesaid abbot to accept three hundred scudi for the said girl from the hand of the bearer, and to deliver her to him to be brought hither, so that she may be able to pass the remainder of her life with her relations, not in the bitterness of slavery, but in the enjoyment of liberty. Your kindness in carrying out this matter will be rewarded by God as well as repaid by my own thanks. Our brother Beorwald too, I imagine, will lose nothing

successful with men who were on the point of death; for though the Anglo-Saxon, when in good health, was very reluctant to manumit a slave, he was willing to practise the posthumous charity of freeing him by his will.[1]

The clergy protested against slavery, not only by precept, but by example. In the seventh century, the famous bishop Wilfrid received from king Ethelwald a grant of Selsey (or Seacalf Island) with eighty-seven families; he found among them two hundred and fifty men and women who were slaves. All of these he immediately, by baptism, rescued from servitude to the devil, and by giving them bodily liberty also released them from the yoke of human slavery.[2]

That the motives of the clergy in emancipating slaves were, as a rule, pure and disinterested, ought to be presumed, though in some cases the proceeding appears to have been regarded by their fellow-clergymen with extreme suspicion. When the slave of a bishopric or abbey *paid* for his freedom, the price belonged to the bishop or abbot for the time being, though the loss of the slave's services was that of the diocese or abbey; and when the slave was emancipated by will for the good of the bishop's soul, or from any other motive, the loss still fell on the corporate body. It was, therefore, decreed about the middle of the eighth century that no bishop or abbot should free the slaves of his diocese, for " it was impious he should damage the church."[3] Nevertheless

---

of his just claim upon her by this transaction. I beg you, as I ought previously to have done, to remember me as often as you think of yourself in your frequent prayers. May our Lord Jesus Christ preserve your reverence in safety and add to your days." Hook's *Lives of Archbis. Canter.*, vol. i, p. 187.

[1] *Codex Diplom. Anglo-Sax.*, Nos. 314, 716, 721, 788, 931, 1342.

[2] Bede, *Histor. Eccl.*, l. 4, c. 13. Mr. Kemble states that this land was granted to Wilfrid by Caedwaelha (who conquered Ethelwalch), but this is not in accordance with the authority he quotes. Kemble's *Saxons in England*, vol. i, p. 211.

[3] It was forbidden by St. Isidore and by several councils of Toledo,

the Anglican church permitted every bishop or abbot to free all those who had become slaves *during his incumbency,* and if he did not do so in his life-time, they might be freed on his death. And when a bishop did not manumit his slaves by will, his death still served the cause of freedom, for every prelate or abbot who attended his funeral was required to free three slaves and to give three shillings to each of them for the good of the deceased prelate's soul, and in honour of his memory.[1]

The kings were equally desirous with the bishops to promote the manumission of serfs, but for a very different reason. A freeman was bound to carry arms and to combat the invaders of his country, but a slave was not permitted to do so and was useless for the purpose of national defence.

Many nations in times of great danger have freed and armed their slaves. The slaves who fought on the Athenian side at Arginusæ were manumitted and enrolled among the Platæans; and the Longobards on a similar occasion freed and enrolled their serfs.[2] Alfred the Great in his wars with the Danes adopted a similar policy, and, whenever he could, induced his nobles to free and arm the servile population.

The privileges claimed by the burghers of important towns was also another source of freedom. They insisted that no man who had lived among them as a citizen for a year and a day should be questioned as to his citizenship; and that if a slave had resided among them for that period he should be assumed to be a freeman.[3]

It has already been mentioned that at a *late* period of

---

particularly that held A.D. 633. See 67th and 70th Canon of that Council. *Concil.,* tom. x, p. 635-6.
  [1] *Council of Cealchythe, Can.* 10.

[2] Kemble's *Saxons in England,* b. i, c. viii.
  [3] *Ll. Wil. Conq.,* iii, c. 16; Ellis, *Domesday Book,* vol. ii, p. 65.

Anglo-Saxon history slaves were occasionally allowed to purchase their freedom. About the time of Edward the Confessor this privilege was so generally conceded that it became almost a right. It was, however, viewed more unfavourably by the Normans than by the Saxons; probably because the former held less liberal views as to the right of the slave to the enjoyment of his savings.[1]

The manumission of a slave, like every other act of importance among the Anglo-Saxons, was required to be performed with the greatest publicity. It is probable that there were two forms of manumission, one ecclesiastic, the other civil. The slaves of the church were solemnly freed at the altar, but by what ceremony is not known. At the latest period of Anglo-Saxon history, the lord who freed his slave produced him at a full meeting of the county, delivered him to the sheriff by the right hand, and then proclaimed him free from all yoke of servitude; he then showed him roads and doors, delivered to him the arms of a freeman, namely the lance and sword, and permitted him to depart whithersoever he would. The slave then presented his lord with thirty pence as " the price of his skin," and was thenceforth no longer liable " to pay with his hide," or " go to the neck-catch." It is probable that at this time the iron collar worn by the slave was filed off, and a cap of liberty given him that he might cover his head and conceal the ignominious shaving of his hair which marked his servile position.[2]

Manumission did not bestow on the slave all the benefits of freedom, unless with it he obtained a certain quantity of land or the rank of thane. He was compelled

---

[1] *Ll. Henr.* I, i., s. 78. Non potest aliquis in villenagio positus libertatem suam propriis denariis quærere, quia omnia catalla cujuslibet nativi intelliguntur esse in potestate domini sui. Glanvil., l. v, c. 5; see also Littleton, l. ii, c. 2.

[2] *Ll. Willelmi Conq.* iii, s. 15, Thorpe, i, p. 493; *Ll. Henrici I,* lxxviii, s. 1 & 3, Thorpe, i, p. 583; *Ll. Rotharis Longob. Regis,* cap. 225; *Hist. Ram.* 29.

to choose a lord under whose protection he must live, or
to join some guild or frith-borg who would be responsible
for his offences.   He was not permitted to give evidence
in a court of justice in favour of the lord who freed him,
or vote at a county meeting.[1]   At the earlier period the
compensation payable for killing a freed-man belonged
to his lord, but at a later period, when his position had
improved, it was paid to his relations.[2]

The relative proportions of freemen and slaves differed
very much, not only at different periods of history, but in
different parts of England.   At first, about one-third of
the population are supposed to have been serfs or servile
tenants.   As the nation advanced in civilisation the
proportionate number of slaves diminished.   The Domesday book gives only 26,500 slaves to 184,000 villeins
and bondsmen.   It also mentions 26,000 tenants and
soc-men, half of whom were free, and half of whom were
tributaries or demi-freemen.

The proportionate number of slaves and freemen varied
very much in different countries. In Yorkshire, Lincolnshire,
Huntingdonshire, and Rutland, there is not a single slave
registered in Domesday, and in Nottinghamshire the
slaves are in the proportion of one to two hundred and
fifteen freemen.   In Kent and the South-Saxon counties,
one-tenth of the registered population was servile, and
this proportion gradually increased as the borders of
Wales were approached.   In Cornwall and Devon, one-
fifth of the population were slaves, and in Gloucestershire, on the Welsh border, about one-third.   It may be
remarked that in this district, civil war, the great source
of slavery, had been incessantly waged between the
British and Saxon populations for many centuries.

We have observed that the condition of slavery rapidly

---

[1] Glanville, lib. i, c. 5.   [2] *Ll. Wihtred.*, s. 8, Thorpe, i, 38.

changed into one of servile tenure, and that the slaves gradually became tributaries doing suit and service. Hence
probably it was that, in the counties in which the slaves
were fewest, the serfs and villeins were most numerous.

The gradual amelioration of servile institutions was
marked, first, by the protection of the slave's life, and
then of his limbs; afterwards by a provision for his maintenance, and by limitations on his liability to be sold. It
was also marked, first by his *permissive* acquisition of property, and then by the increasing security of its tenure.
At the same periods of history, the extent of slavery was
limited by the diminution of the slave trade, the manumission of slaves from motives of conscience, or of military or economic expediency, and lastly, by the growing
right of the slave to purchase his own freedom. Every-
one of these steps forward is deserving of attention when
considering the history of civilisation.

CHAPTER IV.

THE FREEMAN.

THE non-servile portion of Anglo-Saxon Society is generally divided into two classes, the noble and ignoble, the
earl and the churl.

The privileges which distinguished the freeman from
the freedman or serf are said to have been the following.[1]
He had the right to carry on private war, or wage the
deadly fætha on his own account. If he owned land, he
might be a protector or lord ; and if he did not, he could
choose his own lord and change him at pleasure. He
could be a member of a guild or corporation, and could
use and occupy the public lands. He might take his part
in legislative or judicial assemblies, and was entitled, not
only to attend, but to assist, in the administration of public
worship. He had a right to go always armed, and, as
an outward sign of his rank, he had the exclusive privilege of wearing long hair.

All these rights were personal; but he could only exercise such of them as were of a political character in the
district in which he owned land. It would, however, be
a very great mistake to believe (as some have done) that

---

[1] These privileges are enumerated
in Kemble's *Saxons in England*, vol.
i, c. 5 ; and Turner's *Anglo-Sax.
Hist.*, b. vii, c. 9.

these privileges were the same from the end of the fifth
to the middle of the eleventh century. They varied as
much as it was possible ; and as their history serves to
illustrate the social progress of our Anglo-Saxon forefathers, it is proposed to trace their development one by
one.

<h2 style="text-align:center">SECTION I.—PRIVATE WAR.</h2>

One of the most important rights of an Anglo-Saxon
freeman was that of waging private war, or, in other
words, of personally revenging all injuries offered to himself or his relations. This right was at first absolute ;
but it was gradually limited by a series of social conveniences and legislative restrictions, until at the time of
the Norman conquest it had altogether disappeared.

In patriarchal states it is the duty of every freeman to
avenge the injuries of his family on that of the offender,
and he who neglects any opportunity of so doing, is
regarded as faithless to his kin, and treated as an out-
cast. The early English inherited this feeling from every
one of their various sources of descent.

The Germans regarded it as a sacred duty to adopt
both the enmities and friendships of their fathers,[1] and
the Frisians (who migrated hither in large numbers) dis-
inherited a man who refused to avenge a family insult.
The Danes were the most revengeful of all ; and at a
time when the Anglo-Saxons were easily satisfied by
pecuniary compensations, would rather suffer death than
forego vengeance. Numerous instances of this feeling
are to be found in the Danish sagas.[2]   When Grettir, a

---

[1] Tacitus, *De Mor. Germ.*, c. 18.
[2] I use the word " Danish " for
northern, and " Danes " for northmen, in obedience to established custom, without pressing any opinion
as to its accuracy.

famous Scandinavian outlaw, was slain, his brother Illugi preferred death at the hands of his murderers to foreswearing the revenge which he was bound to take. And the venerable and gentle Njal, when his sons had been killed, refused to leave the house which his enemies had set on fire, and quietly retired to bed with his wife and little grandson, that he might be there burnt to death, because he was too old to revenge his sons, and too proud to endure the shame that would have befallen him had they perished unavenged.[1]

The obligation of hereditary vengeance (or of prosecuting the deadly fætha, as it is more properly termed,) is the most striking of all the social peculiarities of patriarchal states. In all of them the system was at first the same. Vengeance was not desired on the offender personally, but on the family to which he belonged, or on the great chief who governed and represented it.[2] The result of this was that every family or tribe was liable to punishment and warfare at the hand of every other for an offence given by some member of their body to one of another tribe. It is obvious that this must have produced endless strife and bloodshed, and that no social system could be developed unless its evils were controlled. To effect this in a manner which should not afford immunity to offenders, when there was no executive power, was one of the most difficult tasks of early legislators. The expedient to which they most generally had recourse was to limit the right of vengeance to the nearest relation of the murdered man, who was called the avenger of

[1] Dr. Dasent's *Burnt Njal.*, vol. ii, p. 178.

[2] Sale's *Koran*, Prelim. Diss., sec. i, Malcolm's *Hist. of Persia*, vol. ii, p. 461. Niebuhr, *L'Arabie*, p. 28. A curious instance both of the punishment of a tribe for the fault of a few members, and the obstinacy with which they usually refused to surrender a delinquent, is to be found in the history of the men of Gibeah, and the almost total destruction of the Benjamites by the other tribes of Israel.—*Judges*, c. 20.

blood, and to prohibit the rest of the family from prosecuting the feud.   This was the course pursued by Moses in
Judæa, and by Mahomet in Arabia, and with some modification by the Britons, the Scandinavians, the Franks, and
the continental Saxons, all of whom limited the right of
vengeance to the persons to whom the family estate descended, or to a small number of the nearest relations.
It is curious that this restriction was never introduced
among the Anglo-Saxons.   On the contrary, the number
of persons entitled to avenge offences was, as time went
on, rather increased than diminished ; and in the time of
Athelstan, the lord and fellow guildsmen, and even spiritual relations, had obtained the same rights in this respect
as were originally conceded to kinsmen only.

A far more important restriction on the system of vengeance is the limitation of the number of persons *on*
whom it is to be taken.   At first it might be inflicted on
every member of the offender's family ; but at the beginning of the tenth century the kin of a criminal were
relieved from liability, *provided* they delivered him up to
justice ; and at the end of the same century, *provided*
they were innocent of his transgressions.[1]

These Saxon relaxations of extreme severity were unacceptable to the Anglo-Danes, who in the middle of the
eleventh century insisted on the punishment of criminals,
" *or* their nearest of kin, head for head."[2]   Slight as
this relaxation was, a slave never obtained the benefit
of it.   If he committed an offence and could not buy
himself off, vengeance was to be taken on him, *and*,
on the continent, on *seven*, and in England, on *six* of his
nearest relations.[3]   As an evidence of the spirit of par-

---

[1] *Ll. Sax.*, tit. ii, s. 5 ; *Ll. Wallicæ*,   Thorpe, i, 596.
lib. iii, c. 1; *Asega-Buch*, vi, s. 9; *Ll.*   [2] *Ll. Ethel.*, ii, 3, Thorpe, i,
Edmundi, s. i, Thorpe i, 249 ; *Ll.*   286.
Henrici Primi, lxxxviii, s. 12, in   [3] *Ll. Saxonum*, tit. ii, 55.

tisanship which marked the age it may be added, that it
is expressly stated in all the Anglo-Saxon laws on this
subject, that if the kin of a thief "stood up for him"
(which they usually did), they should not be freed from
their ancient liability on his account.[1]

The responsibility of every individual for the offences
of his family must have been intolerable to a man who
was encumbered with a number of ill-conducted relatives; and the law, in pity of his sufferings, afforded
him a means of escape. He was permitted to call a
public meeting, at which he denounced their offences,
took a bough in his hands, and, holding it over his head,
broke it in pieces and, scattering them to the winds,
typically banished his family. From that time forth he
was, both as to liability and inheritance, a stranger to
them. His family had a corresponding right; and could
in a similar manner banish him. If they did so, he was
bound to find a lord, a burgh, or a guild, to become
security for him; and if he could not do this, he became
" *a friendless man.*"

The value which the Anglo-Saxons attached to friendship may be inferred from their ordinary phraseology.
A friendless man was synonymous with " a stranger," or
" an outlaw," and an outlaw was said to wear a " wolf's
head." Every man who met him had a right to kill
him; and, in the Danish districts, whoever omitted to do
so, when he met him with equal weapons, became himself
an outlaw, and might be killed by the first person who
chose to do justice. He was hunted from village to
village as people would hunt a wolf, and knocked on the
head without mercy. His children, if he were a man,
were called " wolf's droppings," and if the mother were
the outlaw " cave-begottens," and were slaughtered as

1 *Ll. Edwardi*, s. 9, Thorpe, i, 165 ; *Ll. Athelst.*, s. 8, Thorpe i, 205.

wild beasts' cubs wherever found.   In short, he became a
sort of vermin, whom everybody was bound to destroy.

Limitations on the taking of vengeance were also introduced as to *the places* in which it might be taken.
The offender was safe in a church, or at a public meeting,
and when going to or coming from either, provided he
kept the direct road.[1]   Nor was he to be slain in the presence of the king or of an archbishop.   Among the Danes,
it was not allowable to enter on a man's land with a view
of punishing him.   If he remained upon it, or within a
bowshot of its boundaries, he was safe; if he went further,
he might be lawfully slain.   There is a tale of a man of
the name of Örn, who was outlawed and was to be put
to death, but he kept so strictly upon his own land that
no one could touch him.   At last the avengers of blood,
who were disgraced by his impunity, had recourse to
stratagem.   They drove a herd of wild cattle to his
pasture and lay in ambush at the point where they knew
they would be driven off ; in his eagerness to expel them
Örn overstepped his limits, and the avengers slew him, as
they thought, lawfully.   But his brother procured a bow-
man of incredible strength, who contrived to shoot an
arrow from the boundary of his farm beyond the spot on
which he · was killed.   This proved him to have been
slain in sanctuary, and the avengers of blood became
liable to punishment as murderers.[2]

Alfred the Great made some curious arrangements of
a similar character.   He forbade the avenger of blood to
break into the offender's house until he had besieged him
seven days ; and if his strength did not suffice for the

---

[1] *Ll. Fris. Add. Sapien.*, c. i.
[2] Dasent's *Burnt Njal*, vol. i, p.
74.   It may be remarked that the
law of Moses was very similar to
that of the Scandinavians. If a murderer could be induced to come one
thousand ells from the walls of a
Levitical city, he might be lawfully
slain, but he was safe within that
limit.

siege, the ealdorman was bound to assist in maintaining it. If at the end of that time the besieged surrendered his weapons, he went unscathed for thirty days, during which time his friends might make peace for him. If, however, he did *not* surrender himself or his weapons within the week, his house might be broken into and he might be slain.[1]

There were also limitations as to the persons *for* whom vengeance might be taken. A murderer, an outlaw, a thief, and a runaway convict-slave, were considered " friendless men," and might not be avenged.

The modes of limiting the system of personal vengeance which have been mentioned are mere palliations. They admit the propriety or even necessity of it, and merely check its excesses, or remove its most offensive results. It was expedient to do more than this, and to find some substitute which, while it punished crime, satisfied the offended party and prevented feuds. Nothing could be so effectual for this purpose as a system of pecuniary compensation payable by the criminal to his prosecutor ; and consequently a series of regulations based upon this idea were adopted in nearly every country passing from the patriarchal into the tribal state.

The Anglo-Saxons were far less revengeful than the Orientals, and even less so than the Danes. The Mosaic law does not even *permit* forgiveness. " An eye for an eye, and a tooth for a tooth." " He who sheddeth man's blood, by man shall his blood be shed." " Ye shall take no expiation for the blood of a murderer ; he shall surely be put to death." " The avenger of blood shall slay him wherever he meets him,"—were the stern laws of the Jews. The law of the Arabs was the same. Till the time of Mahomet, it was criminal to forgive ; and

[1] *Ll. Alfredi*, Thorpe, i, p. 91.

the most the prophet attempted was to *permit* of pardon. But the ancient Germans were " not implacable in their resentments. Injuries were adjusted by a settled mode of compensation. Atonement was made for homicide by a certain number of cattle, and by that satisfaction the whole family was appeased."[1] The customs of the Anglo-Saxons were based on those of the Germans. With a view of giving full effect to the system of expiatory compensations, they valued every man's life at a fixed amount, called his wehrgeld or were. This was the sum to be paid for killing him, and was the amount at which he might redeem his own life when forfeited.[2] It varied according to his rank or wealth. Thirty thousand thrymsas were payable for a king, and fifteen thousand for a prince of the blood or an archbishop, while seventy sufficed for a landless freeman, and fifty or sixty for a slave.[3] When the system was first introduced, the murderer had nothing to do but to pay the " were," and with that his liability ceased. But at a later period he had in addition to pay a fine to the king for a breach of the peace ; and shortly afterwards, a fee to the bishop for wounding the conscience of the church ; and at a still later period, a neck-catch fee to the nearest male relation, who, had he been handed over for execution, would have had the pleasure of putting him to death ; and also, in certain cases, manbote to the dead man's lord.[4]

In the payment of compensations for murder one difficulty occurred. It often happened that when the

---

[1] Tacitus, *Germania*.

[2] *Glossary to Anc. Laws and Inst.* v. *Were.* There has been some difference of opinion as to the derivation of the words wehrgeld and were. By some they are derived from " wehre," courage or worth, and signify a man's value ; and by others they are derived from wehr, defence (from which we have the words beware and warrant), and signify the money which protects or guarantees a man's life. Guizot *De l'Etat social et politique de la France*, p. 168. Thorpe, vol. i, 123 and 189.

[3] *Ll. Ethel.*, vi, 28, 42 ; *Ll. Edward. Conf.*, 6.

[4] *Ll. Inœ*, 70-76 ; *Ll. Cnuti E.* 2.

offender attempted to leave his sanctuary for the purpose of paying it, his enemies, who lay in ambush for him, fell upon and killed him. To remedy this it was decreed that he should be at liberty to give security for payment to some friend of the dead man's kin ;[1] and that when this was done, he was to be permitted to attend the public meeting, and there to produce a fixed number of sureties for payment by instalments. The first of these was paid at the open grave, and the remainer at appointed periods. He also gave security for the payment of all other fines and fees due from him.[2]

The system of pecuniary compensation *for murder* was found to work so well, that it was soon extended to all provocations. All grave offences and many trivial ones, all mutilations, wounds, rapes, arsons, thefts, trespasses, and even insults, were valued, so that the punishment of them might be redeemed by payment of a fixed sum proportionate to the rank or wealth of the offended party. Mutilations or wounds, being the most ordinary offences, were most carefully appraised. The price was generally regulated by their severity and importance, with, however, one exception ; personal injuries which did not produce disfiguration were slightly punished, compared with those that did. A bruise above or below the mantle was double the price of one which it concealed, and a wound in the head, which the hair could be made to cover, was half the price of an exposed one ; a front tooth was worth six shillings, an eye tooth four shillings ; while the first double tooth was valued at three shillings only, and the grinders, the knocking out of which involved no disfigurement, were put down at one shilling a-piece. But if the assault was on a large scale,

---

[1] *Ll. Edmundi*, c. 7, Thorpe, i, 251.
[2] *Ll. Edw. & Guthrun*, s. 12, Thorpe, i, 175 ; *Ll. Gulielmi Conq.*, s. 7, Thorpe, i, 471 ; and see Palsgrave's *Ang.-Sax. Commonwealth*, ii, p. 113.

the price of teeth was reduced, and the whole jaw might
be knocked out for eighteen shillings.

Fingers were valued almost as elaborately as teeth.
The first finger, which was necessary for the use of the
bow, and the ring finger, which was used for ornament,
were worth fifteen shillings and seventeen shillings respec-
tively, while the other fingers were valued at much less.
A hand maimed externally was to be paid for with twenty
shillings, but if internally, with ten shillings ; and every
injury below the hair, the sleeve, or the knee, was to be
paid for doubly.

A broken shoulder-blade, which the clothes covered,
was valued at twenty shillings, and a great toe, the loss
of which was generally visible (as few but great men
wore shoes), was charged at the same price. A tongue,
an eye, and a foot, were alike valued at sixty-six shillings
and sixpence, and a nose at sixty shillings, while an arm
or a leg was valued at eighty shillings. For breaking a
man's arm fifteen shillings were to be paid ; and for cutting off his ear, twenty-five shillings, unless he had previously lost its fellow, in which case thirty shillings were
payable. Thigh wounds were the cheapest, namely a
shilling a stab ; while wounds in the nostril varied from
three times to six times this price. There was hardly
any possible *personal* injury the price of which was not
carefully regulated, but the above instances will give a
sufficient notion of the general valuation of wounds and
blows.[1]

All other grave offences were carefully estimated. For
the violation of a king's free female servant, fifty shil-

---

[1] I omit the authorities for the
statements in the text as to the
amounts to be paid for particular injuries. They will be found scattered
through the first volume of Thorpe's
Ancient Laws and Institutes. If
we bear in mind that at the time
these penalties were fixed a cow
was valued at a shilling and a sheep
at the same price, it is difficult to
conceive how these enormous penalties could ever have been paid.

lings were exacted : for that of a long-haired maiden, sixty shillings, unless she had previously suffered a similar misfortune, and then it was reduced to thirty shillings. Proportionate compensation was fixed for offences against women of every station, freewomen, superior and inferior slaves, according to their own rank or that of their connections. The penalties for offences against the sex were increased by Alfred the Great, and still further augmented by Cnut. Housebreakings, thefts, assaults, and insults, were specially valued ; and most of the favourite practical Anglo-Saxon jokes were prohibited and punished.

The compositions payable for homicide and other offences are generally spoken of as the price or value of a man, of his wife, child, leg, arm, foot, tooth, etc. ; and so, perhaps, they ultimately became ; but originally they were framed on an estimate of the power of the offended party to take revenge, and the probability of his so doing.

No part of the composition for murder was, for many centuries, payable to the *female* relatives of the slain, " because from the weakness of their sex they could not carry on the feud ;" although, at a *late* period, the widow obtained the miserable pittance of ten shillings. Nor was it necessary to pay anything to the relatives of a murdered slave, provided the offender was prepared to run the risk of their being able to revenge themselves.[1]

The payment of these compensations was at first optional on the criminal and his family. They could pay them if they pleased ; and if not, they might bear the feud.[2] When first introduced, they were regarded by the

---

[1] *Ll Longobard.*, l. i. tit. 9, s. 18 ; *Ll. Inæ*, c. 74 ; Spelman's *Glossary*, *voce Faida; The Anc. Laws and Inst. of Wales*, p. 233.

[2] Charlemagne put an end to this throughout his dominions, and compelled all parties both to pay and accept them ; but it may be doubted

nobles as undignified arrangements, to which humble men submitted because they were too weak to take or defy vengeance, but which men of rank despised. The first instance in which royal personages were induced to adopt them was in the seventh century, when archbishop Theodore with great difficulty prevailed on king Egfrid to receive, and Ethelred king of the Mercians to pay, compensation money for the homicide of Elfwin, king Egfrid's brother.[1]

Although the nobles considered it beneath their dignity to pay or receive compositions on their own account, they were anxious that their retainers should do so. They did not approve of their spilling in feuds among themselves the blood which they were bound to shed in their masters' quarrels. They, therefore, endeavoured to enforce the system of compositions.

The first step towards compelling their acceptance was taken in the seventh century, when Ina, king of the West Saxons, imposed a penalty of thirty shillings on any one who took revenge prior to demanding compensation.[2] In the ninth century, the penalty was increased to five pounds ; and, at a later date, the demand of compensation was required to be publicly made *three times* in the presence of good witnesses.[3]

But though it became compulsory to *accept* the composition, it was never an absolute legal necessity to *pay* it. A man had his choice either to make amends, or to bear the feud ; whence, says Edward the Confessor, the English have the proverb, " Buy the spear from your side, or bear it."[4] This option nominally existed to the

whether this was ever effectually done in England.

[1] Bede's *Eccles. Hist.* l. iv, c. 21.
[2] *Ll. Inœ*, s. 9, Thorpe, i, 109.
[3] *Ll. Alfredi*, s. 42, Thorpe, i, 91 ; *Ll. Ethelr.*, iv, 4, Thorpe, i, 301 ; *Ll.*

Henrici Primi, lxxxii, c. i, Thorpe, i, 589.
[4] *Ll. Edwardi Conf.*, xii, Thorpe, i, 447. The law of the Roman Decemvirs was the same:—" Si membrum rupit, *ni cum eo pacit*, talio esto." As

last; but practically it became necessary to pay; first, from the force of custom; and, secondly, from the growth of the executive and judicial power. It was to the interest of the relatives of the offender that he should pay, as they were thereby relieved from liability; and it was also to the interest of governors, as whoever paid a composition, paid at the same time a fine to the king, and generally a fee to the bishop, and a fight-fine to some other dignitary. If a man could not pay, his pursuer had a right to the assistance of the earl or king in obtaining possession of his person; and when he obtained it, he might put him to death or retain him as a slave.

In the Saxon-Danish era, the hundred in which a criminal lived was bound either to make good his offences or to deliver him up. It is probable that when both parties belonged to the same district, this duty was fairly performed; but when the murdered man was a detested Dane, or a still more hateful Norman, nobody ever chose to know how he came by his death. To protect his Danish subjects, Cnut declared the hundred responsible for every man who was found dead on public land, unless he was proved to be an Englishman; and, at a later period, William the Conqueror enacted similar laws in regard to his French subjects.[1] Nothing can be stronger evidence than this of the bitter enmity which the South Saxons bore to both Danes and Normans.

The burghs, which claimed a right to protect all their members, were very slow to make compensation to any but their fellow-townsmen; and were still more reluctant to deliver up the guilty. They usually preferred "to bear

---

was also the law of the Frisians. *Ll. Fris.*, l. 2, c. 5.

[1] *Ll. Edw. Conf.*, s. 15, Thorpe, vol. i, p. 448; and compare with these authorities, Bracton, lib. iii, *De Co-*rona, s. 15; *Dialogus de Scaccario*, lib. i, c. 10. The presentment of Englisherie, whereby the hundred escaped this penalty, was not abolished till 14 Edward III, stat. i, c. 4.

the feud," and set not only common people, but even earls and kings, at defiance. This often led to their severe punishment. When the monks of Thetford murdered their abbot, king Edred, instead of attempting to punish the offenders, whom he probably knew that he could not capture, slaughtered the townsmen ; and when two of Harthacnut's body-guard were murdered at Worcester, the king, without any previous demand of compensation, ravaged the county for four days, and on the fifth he burned the city. On the same principle Edward the Confessor ordered the destruction of Dover, because the followers of his brother-in-law Eustace, count of Boulogne, had been there killed.[1] In none of these cases did the towns offer to surrender their offending townsmen.

The various restrictions imposed on the carrying on of the *fætha*, and particularly the system of pecuniary compensation, rapidly undermined the custom of personal vengeance ; and the public administration of justice by the Conqueror and his ministers, by rendering it unnecessary, gave it its death-blow.

There is scarcely any general custom that was not at some period beneficial, and, however ruinous it may afterwards become, there are sure to be opponents to its abolition. Whatever mischief the deadly fætha did, it had the good effect, according to a contemporary bishop, of stimulating family affection, and knitting more closely the bonds of friendship. While it lasted, father and son, brother and brother, and loving friends, did not hesitate to lay down their lives one for the other ; and when the custom became obsolete, these once affectionate beings cared no more for one another than for strangers. No man or custom, however infamous, dies unlamented. When Nero

---

[1] Florenc. Wigorn., A.D., 1041 ; Sax. Chron., A.D. 1048. The reluctance to surrender offending friends to justice was universal ; nobody did so save under terror of superior power.

perished, a hand unseen strewed flowers upon his tomb ; and when the most barbarous of English customs passed away, there were good and wise old men who mourned its death.[1]

SECTION II.—THE LORD AND HIS MAN.

It has been often said, that one of the distinguishing rights of the Anglo-Saxon freeman was that of choosing his own lôrd and of changing him at pleasure.[2] But this statement, if it is to be deemed correct, must be limited to a very short period of history.

In patriarchal times, it was customary for the family of a great chief to admit into its circle a large number of " children by adoption," who had the right of leaving whenever they chose, and were liable to expulsion. While the patriarchal system lasted, the family was responsible for all its members and protected them from injury ; but when this state of society passed away, the government required that every man should offer tangible security for keeping the peace and making atonement for offences. This security was called " frith-borg"; and there were several modes in which it might be given. The most simple was the ownership of ample landed estate, available for the payment of compensations and fines. But if a man did not possess land, there were three other ways by which the same object might be attained. He might become the " man" of some powerful lord, whose estates were sufficient security, not only for himself, but for all his establishment ;[3] or he might become a burgher of some corporate town ; or, if he preferred it, a member of a guild or club of approved responsibility.

[1] *Epist. Lupi*, printed in Hickes's *Thesaurus*.

[2] Hallam's *Middle Ages*, vol. i, c. 2, p. 1 ; Kemble's *Saxons in Eng-* land, v. i, c. 5.

[3] This process was called by lawyers " commendatio," and the man was " commendatus."

It is clear that, though the two last alternatives might have been available to townsmen, the peasant was practically confined to the first. It is, therefore, not at all to be wondered at that, from the time of saint Augustine downwards, the number of poor independent freemen in the agricultural districts gradually diminished, until, at the close of the Anglo-Saxon era, nearly every man and woman were either " protectors" or " protected."

As a protected position was *originally sought* by a poor freeman, and was not, as *afterwards, forced on him*, it was natural he should be allowed to select his lord ; and there can be no doubt that *at first* he had a legal right so to do. But after a short time it was found that it was more profitable to lords to protect " men," than for men to procure lords ; and all sorts of temptations were held out, and excuses made, to induce a poor man to choose as his lord the landed proprietor near whose estate he dwelt.

At the earliest period of Anglo-Saxon history a *freedman* became the "man" of the master who had emancipated him, and had no right of choosing another lord, a disability which, in the opinion of the age, derogated from perfect freedom. Many powerful men, therefore, when they freed their slaves, expressly gave them this right. But even in these cases the poor man was constantly robbed of his privilege on the pretence that there were debts due, or fees payable, to the lord's heir or ministers. To such an extent was this carried, that, in the tenth century, the freed-man had practically lost one of the most important rights that the laws professed to secure to him. Alfred the Great was probably well aware of this fact ; for by his will, in which he enfranchised all his dependents, and gave them express liberty to select their future lord, he says, " I, in the name of

the living God, bid that no man hinder them, either by
demands of fee or any other thing, from choosing as
lord whomsoever they will."[1]

Notwithstanding, however, the efforts of Alfred, the
poor freeman's right was soon completely lost.   In
Domesday Book the privilege of leaving his land and
changing his lord is spoken of as one of the distinguishing marks of the gesithcundman, or demi-noble ;[2] and in
Saloman and Saturn we read, "Lo! a wealthy noble
may easily choose for himself, according to his mind, a
mild lord, a prince of noble birth, but *a poor man cannot do so.*"[3]

If the humble freeman's right to choose his own lord
was soon lost, it is obvious that his power of changing
him at pleasure would perish still more rapidly.   As
early as the seventh century, he was forbidden to leave
his lord without the sanction of the alderman of the shire,
under a penalty of sixty shillings, an amount which was
doubled in the reign of king Alfred.[4]   The new lord who
illegally accepted him was also liable to a fine.   These
laws remained in force until after the Norman conquest.[5]

In addition to this *civil* system of "commendation"
(or becoming a lord's man), there was a *military* one, by
which, in the earliest time, a man attached himself to a
leader for a campaign or a war only; and afterwards
generally, as a military follower.[6]   These men had at first
a right to come and go at pleasure, and they retained it
longer than the poor civilian.   But even with them, when
warfare became more systematic and lasted longer, they
were allowed to change their chief but once a year, and

---

[1] *Codex Diplom., Anglo-Sax.*, vol. ii, No. 314.

[2] Palsgrave's *Anglo-Saxon Commonwealth*, vol. i, p. 15.

[3] *Saloman and Saturn*, part ii, p. 169.

[4] *Ll. Inœ*, c. 39, Thorpe's *Ancient Laws*, i, 127; *Ll. Alfr.*, c. 37, Thorpe, i, 87.

[5] *Ll. Henrici*, lxi, 1 and 17, Thorpe, i, 560.

[6] Tacitus, *German.*, c. 14.

this they were obliged to do on New Year's Day, by
public notice to their lord, in presence of two of their
fellow soldiers specially selected as witnesses.[1]

It is probable that at first the duty of the man to his
lord was purely military. He was bound to fight for
him in all his battles, and to follow him in war ; but
from an early period, in addition to this, he made him
presents at Christmas and Easter, which were soon commuted into pecuniary payments or fixed agricultural services. These obligations constantly increased. Every
few years brought some new addition to the lord's demands, until the follower became subject to all the exactions of the feudal system and was little better than a serf.[2]

The duty of the lord to his man was to protect his
person and property from illegal violence, and from all
who sought with the strong hand to make him responsible
for offences.[3] If the lord were powerful, this did not, *at
first*, involve him in much responsibility. If the complainant was weak, he adopted the simple and economical
course of kicking him out of his house ; and if he was
strong, he could either surrender his man (with which his
liability ceased), or, if it was worth while to retain him,
he could assist him in paying his compensation money.
But unless this was paid in full, the master was *legally*
bound to surrender him to his antagonist.[4]

[1] *Cnuti Magni Leges Castrenses,*
Langabek, iii, 149 and 161.

[2] The celebrated jurist, Ranfre-
dus, who lived in the time of Frederic II, says of these protected or
commended men : — " Commendati
dicuntur, qui veniunt sub alienis
partibus, et habitare volunt in civi-
tate tua, elegit patrocinium tuum,
et dicit, Domine, volo esse tuus
commendatus ut habeamus tuam
defensionem annis singulis, et ser-
viam in Pasha vel in Natali duas
gallinas vel libram piperis vel aliquid

aliud. De istis multos invenies apud
Neapolim in villis eorum et Bono-
niæ. Isti de jure nihil aliud debent
conferre ; sed Neapolitani ab illis
multa exigunt et fere omnia quæ
exigunt domini a vassallis." This
would have been as true in Anglo-
Saxon and feudal times of England
as of Naples.

[3] Ellis's introduction to *Domesday
Book*, vol. i, p. 178 ; Preface to
Brady's *Hist.*, p. 56.

[4] *Ll. Ethelb.*, l. i, Thorpe, i, 281 ;
Ll. Cnuti, Thorpe, i, 397.

When the country had made some progress in political organisation, the position of the lord was incidentally modified. A man who became liable to make compensation for a crime, became also liable on conviction to pay a fine to the king ; and at a later date also to make compensation to the clergy for the pain his wickedness had caused them.

It has been already stated that a lord could relieve himself from his liability for damage done by his man by surrendering his person ; but, though this satisfied the accuser, it did not discharge the fine due to the king on every conviction. It was, therefore, necessary, to find some mode of evading this payment. As the fine was payable on conviction *only*, if there was no trial there could be no fine ; and thence it happened, that no sooner was the man of any powerful lord accused of an offence, than he disappeared, either from prudential motives of his own, or from the economical ones of his master. By this the king was deprived of his fines, and the clergy were cheated of their fees. For this grievance, therefore, they lost no time in finding a remedy. They declared that when a man disappeared after accusation, and before trial, the lord should pay the king's fine in the same manner as if he had been found guilty, unless he could clear himself of all knowledge of his escape. As a slight counterpoise to this infliction, it was decreed, that if any one laid a formal accusation against a man before he had demanded compensation from *his master*, he should pay the king's fine in the lord's stead.[1]

At the earliest period of Anglo-Saxon history, a protected-man might live on his own land, but during the Saxon-Danish era nearly all freeholders had been com-

[1] *Ll. Cnuti*, 28 and 31, Thorpe's *Will.*, I, 52 ; *Ll. Henr.*, xli, 6, and *Ancient Laws*, i, 393 and 398 ; *Ll.* xv, 4.

pelled to surrender their estates to the crown, church, or great earls, and receive them back again as tenants. At the later periods, therefore, every man resided on his lord's land, and a system of "commendation," which had had its origin in the necessity of protection and legal responsibility, passed into one founded on the position of landlord and tenant, and the conveniences of a military system. This led to many changes in the relative position of lord and man ; but they belong rather to Norman than to Saxon history.

SECTION III.—GUILDS.

It has been already stated that one of the modes in which a poor freeman might give public security for his good behaviour, was by becoming a member of a guild of recognized responsibility.

These guilds, when first formed, held forth no promise of the important part they were destined to play in the jurisprudential history of the country. They were merely associations formed for the purpose of social intercourse, supported by voluntary contributions. The subscriptions to them were paid in beer or mead, honey or malt ; and the fines for offending against their rules were paid in the same coin. The regulations of one of these drinking clubs are given in a subsequent chapter ; and they shew with how much foresight our ancestors provided for the gratification of their love of conviviality.

The first addition which the clubs recognised to the duty of drinking was that of singing ; and there are extant rules of early clubs formed for the combined purpose of tippling and music. As neither the conviviality nor the style of singing tended to practical morality, the clergy, on the conversion of the guildsmen to christianity, endeavoured to substitute psalms and spiritual hymns for the warlike and bacchanalian songs previously in vogue. They also recommended the members, either in person or by deputy, to sing a quintain of psalms, or a certain number of masses, on saints' days and festivals.[1] As the Anglo-Saxon, provided he might drink deep enough, was not choice as to his toasts, and if permitted to sing loud enough and long enough had no insuperable objection to any tune or topic, the clergy were more successful in this than in some other of their moral innovations.

But little by little the offices of the guilds were extended, and they were so in the same manner as those of modern clubs. They undertook to enforce for one another those rights which the law neglected. Modern clubs have adjudicated on affairs of honour, personal discourtesies, or scandal among their members, simply because these were grievances for which the law did not provide; and the ancient guilds in the same spirit extended their objects and duties with a view of supplying the shortcomings of the law.

Our forefathers had the same passion for splendid funerals, which, to the disgrace of modern civilisation, still exists ; and for this feeling the law did not provide. One of the first occupations which the guilds added to that of conviviality, was the superintendence of the burial of members. They bound themselves to recover the body of every fellow guildsman who died far a field, to form a procession for bringing it home, and to wake and bury it with musical honours. The assistance of the clergy was necessary on these occasions, and consequently the payment of soul shot and a certain sum for

---

[1] Sancti Anselmi, lib. ii, epist. 7 ; *tiq. Dan.* c. 8; *Chron. Monast. de Bello,* Du Cange, *v. Gilda;* Bartholin., *An-* p. 21 ; Dugdale's *Warwick,* p. 123.

masses were among the earliest recognised charges on
the corporate funds.

The guilds also, at a very early period, undertook a duty
which drew on them the displeasure of the kings and
earls.   When no mercantile man could either read or
write, and all contracts were necessarily verbal, it was of
primary importance to obtain witnesses to all transactions between townsmen.   With this view, buying and
selling occasionally took place publicly at the club-meet-
ings.   All the guild were present as witnesses, and much
chaffering and bargaining doubtless went on ; but when
the parties were agreed, liquor was called for, and the
seller and buyer drank a " leth-kop " or " bargain-cup "
together.   When this was done, the bargain was concluded, but prior to this either party might abandon it.
The buyer and seller then treated the company.[1]

At a very early period the earls and reeves claimed a
right to be the attesting witnesses of all important transactions, *and to be paid* for their trouble.   The proceedings of the guildmen deprived them of these emoluments.
Hence arose, both in England and on the continent,
a series of laws which at first appear unintelligible ;
whereby guilds are required to be held publicly in towns,
and all purchases to be transacted before the port-reeve,
or some other officer, so that the fees payable on purchases might be secured.

This, like most other matters in those days, ended in a
compromise.   The burghers retained the right of buying
and selling, *inter se*, at their guild-meetings ; but the
officer of the king or earl was invited to be present.   He
of course received his share of the liquor, and as he was

---

[1] Si quis aliquid emit et dat mer-
cipotum, nec emptor nec venditor
possunt revocare. Grupen, *Antiq.*
Hanover., p. 234 ; Thorpe, i, 422,
note ; *Ll. Henrici Primi*, lxxxi,
Thorpe, i, 588, and note.

a person of dignity, probably a great deal more than his share. The reeves, however, never thought that they received as much as they ought, and constantly demanded more and more. This claim was also compromised, and they received in lieu of liquor a fee called " drink-lean " on every transaction, and this was declared by repeated laws to be a fixed and invariable amount.[1] On the continent, but not in England, this drink-lean ultimately became one of the seignorial rights of the feudal lords.

At the period of which we are about to speak, the guilds had become a species of religious and convivial association, at which business was occasionally transacted, but they had no political, and but little social importance;[2] yet they were in possession of characteristics that cannot fail to command attention. They were voluntary combinations of Anglo-Saxon freemen, and the only ones that then existed ; they were in strict subjection to the law of the land, and yet in accordance with the spirit of a lawless age; they had an executive organization when no other executive existed, and a system of local self-government which has survived to the present day. They possessed the germ of great things. Bestow on such a body political power, or compel them to usurp it, and the result is clear. The importance of the political position they ultimately attained is so great, and the history of it is involved in so much obscurity, that the reader will possibly pardon a slight digression in an attempt to trace it.

In the development of the political institutions of barbarous nations, the judicial power exists before the legislative, and both prior to the executive. There are judgments before there are laws, and there are both judgments

[1] *Ll. Cnuti Secul.*, c. 82, Thorpe, i, 423 ; *Laws of Northumb. Priests*, Thorpe, ii, 303 ; Du Cange *v. Mercipotus.*
[2] *Ll. Henrici*, lxxxi, s. 1. This law suggests the original character of guilds. It begins : " In omni potatione, dacioni, vel empcioni, vel gilde." Thorpe, i, 588. Carew's *Cornwall*, p. 68.

and laws before there are ministers for carrying them into execution. Long after every man ceases to be a judge in his own cause, or the legislator of his family, he continues to be his own policeman and sheriff's officer. The kings, the chiefs, or the public assembly, provide a tribunal, but they create no machinery for bringing offenders before it or executing its sentences.

In Rome, in India, and among the Scandinavian and Teutonic nations, it was, at one time, the duty of an injured individual to seize the offender and drag him into court. This was also his duty in England, though he had the additional privilege of distraining his goods, if he could, and detaining them till he appeared. It was on this principle of throwing all executive duties on the complainant, that after sentence was pronounced, the judge did not inflict any punishment, but handed the criminal over to the prosecutor, that he might (in the words of Charlemagne,) " do with him whatever he liked best." And if the offender was condemned to any specific punishment, as death, mutilation, or flogging, it was not a public officer, but his antagonist, who executed the sentence ; and if condemned to slavery, he became the slave of the prosecutor, not of the state.

As with the judicial, so it was also with the legislative power. The kings or parliaments laid down the most general laws, and left the great towns and other bodies to enact bye-laws, to explain and apply them. At first they provided no machinery for giving effect to their legislation ; and when they did, it was of a very crude and almost useless character. There were, for instance, endless laws against theft, but no means of arresting the thief, save what a man might find in his own right hand, and the aid of his friends.

It was in this phase of civilisation that the guilds

gradually undertook executive, if not legislative, functions; and endeavoured to provide for the short-comings of the government. Their first steps were very humble. To the occupations of drinking, singing, and burying, they added the task of recovering all property stolen from any member of their body. This they effected by main force, and in large bodies ; and not content with recovering their own property, they slew the thief and confiscated his goods. Charlemagne, who had advanced notions of the duties of a governor, put a summary stop to these proceedings ; but in England the guilds, by a well judged arrangement, retained their self-appointed jurisdiction. By giving half the thief's goods to his widow they pacified his family ; and by dividing the other half between the crown and themselves they secured an immunity for their illegal proceedings, and paid themselves for their trouble.[1]

In the ninth century their jurisdiction was still further extended. Ecgbert and Alfred the Great had divided England into tythings and hundreds, and had imposed important duties on them. They were rendered responsible for the crimes committed by every one of their members unless they delivered him up to justice ; they were required to track the spoor of stolen cattle until they shewed where they left their district ; they became liable for all, or a certain proportion of, fines, fees, and penalties, incurred by any of their members ; and they had the privilege of prosecuting the deadly fætha, and of exercising executive power if they could.

When this state of affairs first arose, the new territorial divisions accepted the burdens imposed on them ; but they were unable to discharge their duties, because they

[1] *Capit. Carol. Magni*, tit. ii, c. 14 ; *Ll. Longobard.*, i, tit. 17, l. 7. By these laws the purposes of guilds were limited to eating and drinking, and assisting one another in case of fire, shipwreck, or other misfortunes.

had no mechanism for the purpose. The guildsmen, therefore, being the only organised body, constituted themselves into a sort of committee of the hundred, and in that character undertook its functions and liabilities. Yet they were not, as has sometimes been supposed, one and the same body; because the hundred was always a compulsory association and the engine of the state, while the guild was always a voluntary one and the executive of the people.

Guilds ultimately became almost innumerable, and were formed wherever it was necessary to provide bye-laws for the management of any particular class of persons, or mechanism to carry general laws into effect. There were guilds of clergy, of thanes, of military men, of merchants and other bodies, all formed for the purpose of making regulations in matters of detail for the guidance of their members, yet all formed with a superstitious recollection of their origin. All of them provided for conviviality.[1] One of the first rules laid down by the merchants of London was that they should all meet once a month to brew a certain number of tuns of ale; and the clerical and military guilds were not one whit less thoughtful of joviality than the citizens. They nearly all of them provided for psalm or glee-singing,[2] for the burial of their members, and for the performance of masses. They recovered the goods of members, defended their legal rights, and prosecuted their feuds. They generally engaged to subscribe a charitable fund for the relief of the poor, and to assist one another in distress,

---

[1] The Normans probably considered conviviality one of the main objects of some English guilds. A law of Henry I (lxxxi, s. 2), latinises "guildsmen" by "combibentes;" and Walter Mapes gives "bibatoria" for "guild-halls." Quales Anglici in singulis singulas habebant diocesibus *bibatorias*, *guild-hus* anglice dictas. (*De Nugis Curialium.*)

[2] I have not in these pages used the word "glee" in its modern technical sense; but in its ancient one, of a merry song of any sort.

particularly on occasions of house-burnings, sickness, or death.

But by far the most important duty they undertook was that of mutual suretyship. They bound themselves, and the law compelled them, to produce an accused member before the tribunals, and in default to make good his offences. This obligation was at first unlimited; but after a certain period, if they could clear themselves of all knowledge, both of the offender's crime and his flight, their liability was reduced. At this time, if the member had kin who would pay for him, the guild escaped altogether; and if he had no relations, they were compelled to pay only a certain portion of his penalties; but if they could not clear themselves of all complicity, both in his crime and flight, they had to pay in full.

In return for their liabilities, the guilds acquired a right to compensation from every one who killed or injured a member. If a reeve or earl neglected to do a guildsman justice, they not only compelled him to do it, but claimed from him a fixed fine, which, if he would not pay, they took by force.

So universal and so powerful did these guilds at last become, that no man was too eminent to be a member of them. Cnut the Great was a member of a military guild, and having on one occasion slain one of the brethren in a fit of passion, he submitted himself to the judgment of its court, and paid the nine-fold compensation inflicted upon him.[1] It is probable that this proceeding was not so completely a matter of condescension as it has been generally represented. One of his successors acted differently, and suffered for it. He had killed a member of a guild at Hætheby, in Sleswig, and, afterwards pressed by the necessity of travel, determined to stop and rest in the town.

[1] *Hist. Leg. Castren., Reg. Cnuti Magni*, c. iv, app.; Langebek, v. iii, p. 146.

His courtiers and knights attempted to dissuade him, assuring him that the guildsmen practised the Hez-lagh most strictly. The king replied that the guildsmen were nothing but a parcel of trumpery tanners and cobblers, and that nobody need be afraid of them. He persisted in his purpose, but had no sooner entered the town, than the tocsin was sounded, the guildmen assembled, seized the king, slew all who attempted to defend him, and then put him to death.[1]

The guilds usually consisted of full members, ordinary members, and youths or apprentices, paying subscriptions and possessing rights and positions of dignity according to their membership. At their meetings stringent regulations were made for the preservation of order. Full members were allowed to introduce a fixed number of guests, and if they exceeded their number were fined. Fines were also imposed on those who took a higher seat than belonged to them, or who " misgreeted in anger " any member.

A very large proportion of the guilds appear to have been broken up about the time of the Norman conquest. The clergy had obtained a complete ecclesiastical organisation, and did not need them. The military had also been formed into regular armies, under barons who exercised jurisdiction over their retainers, and who were intolerant of voluntary associations that were a check on their authority. In the country the guilds had never been so popular as in the towns, and in the depressed condition of the serfs under the Norman régime they hardly could have existed. They continued to flourish in the great towns, but their objects and constitution were most materially altered ; and though they never neglected the duties of conviviality, they became most

---

[1] Bartholinus, *Antiq. Dan.*, c. vii, p. 131.

powerful combinations for the protection, regulation, and development of particular trades.[1]

Another right which is said to have belonged exclusively to the Anglo-Saxon freeman was that of making use of the public forests and commons, which slaves and foreigners were not permitted to do.

If this right ever existed, it must have been very limited in character. There were not among the Anglo-Saxons at the earlier period of their history any lands which belonged to the state ; for a *state*, in the modern sense of the word, did not exist. There was, from the earliest times, round every patriarchal estate, a broad belt (or *mark*) of forest land, on which every member of the sept had a right of cutting firewood, feeding hogs, and fishing for eels—the three great wants of the age : but a member of another tribe was not permitted to trespass on the mark. At first the supply of this land was so greatly in excess of the demand for it, that when any of the family thought fit to clear a portion and treat it as his own, there was no motive for dissatisfaction. Any one who envied him the possession of his encroachment could go and do likewise.

But as population increased, the value of commons and folkland increased with it, and its occupation was in consequence more carefully regulated by law. It is probable that, at the time of St. Augustine, any member of a tribe

[1] Compare, on this important subject, the *Judicia Civit. Lundoniæ*, c. vi, ii, s. 6, Thorpe, vol. i, p. 237 ; *Ll. Edw. Conf.*, xx, Thorpe, i, 450; Kemble's *Saxons in England*, vol. i, p. 238, *et seq.*, and 511; Turner's *Anglo-Saxon Hist.*, vol. iii, p. 98 ; Hicks' *Dissert. Epist.*, pp. 21, 22 ; Palgrave's *Anglo-Saxon Commonwealth*, vol. i, p. 197 ; Lappenberg's *Anglo-Saxon Kings*, vol. ii, p. 92; Soames's *Anglo-Saxon Church*, p. 269.

was allowed to take possession of it ; but he did so subject to the rights of his companions as to sporting and
pasturage, and subject also to a liability of being ejected
if the land were required for general purposes. The tribe
had also a right of disposing of the folk-land and bestowing it on those who rendered them any distinguished
service, or of using it to buy off the northern invaders.[1]

It is probable that, at the latest period of Anglo-Saxon
history, the kings considered that they had a right to
dispose of the folk-land as they pleased ; but at an
earlier period they always obtained the consent of the
tribe or district to which it belonged. And even when
it had been granted away, *as folk-land*, it remained subject to certain rights of hunting and pasture reserved to
the crown, though not to those of the land-owners of the
district.[2] After the Norman conquest, the lords of manors
claimed to be the owners of all common-land not vested
in the crown, and they compelled all freemen to pay for
escartes or encroachments on the waste. The rights of
common subsequently acquired were not based on the
ancient rights of allodial proprietors, but on the tacit
consent of lords to encroachments on manorial rights.

SECTION V.—POLITICAL RIGHTS.

The right of taking a part in the legislative proceedings of his country was also the privilege of the Anglo-
Saxon freeman. The consideration of this topic, as far as
it is purely political, is beyond the scope of these pages.

---

[1] Beówulf, l. 5977 ; Bede's *Epist.
ad Ecgb. Archiep.*, s. ii ; *Opera Min.*,
ii, 216.
[2] *Codex Diplomat. Anglo-Saxon.*,
Nos. 86, 119, 276, 288. When folk-

land was converted into boc-land, it
was generally freed from these liabilities ; or, at least, they were limited,
(Kemble's *Saxons in England*, b. i,
c. 11.)

It is elaborately treated in many works devoted to constitutional history, and in none more ably than in sir Francis Palgrave's *Anglo-Saxon Commonwealth.*

Neither will we discuss here the freeman's right of being his own priest, or of taking an administrative part in the celebration of public worship : it is a question altogether theological. It is, however, obvious, that on the conversion of the nation to Christianity, the clergy would gradually have excluded the laity from the ministration of holy ordinances.

The Anglo-Saxon freeman also claimed the right of going constantly armed. The Romans, who never wore their swords but in time of war or when travelling, were much struck with the fact that the Germans never transacted any business, public or private, unless they were completely armed. They were probably not sufficiently acquainted with them to know that they carried arms, not with a view to constant appeals to force, but that by wearing them they might be recognised as freemen.[1] An unarmed man was presumed to be a serf, and therefore to disarm a freeman was one of the grossest insults that could be offered him.[2] Neither a boy nor a slave could wear arms ; but when a boy came of age, or a slave was emancipated, he was publicly presented with a sword and lance, which he afterwards always carried with him. The clergy also, in direct violation of ecclesiastical law, went constantly armed, and sometimes refused to lay aside their weapons even when ministering at the altar. This was a subject of reprehension from their ecclesiastical superiors.[3]

The extreme scandal that arose from fighting during

[1] Tacitus, *De Mor. Germ.,* c. 13. Thorpe, i, p. 600.
[2] *Id. Cnuti Sec.,* c. 61, Thorpe, i, [3] *Northumb. Priests' Laws,* s. 37, p. 409 ; *Ll. Henri. Primi,* xc, s. 9, Thorpe, ii, 297.

divine service, induced the superior clergy to insist that
not only the inferior clergy, but also the laity, should
attend church unarmed. The weapons were to be deposited in the porch prior to entering, and to be resumed
on leaving. Hence it is that the church-porch it still in
many places called the weapon-house.[1]

There were but few incentives to fighting in church,
but the temptation to fight at the public judicial assemblies, in which all causes were heard and decided by the
voice of the majority, was very great. These meetings
were often the scenes of the most violent disputes. The
plaintiffs and defendants came to them attended by large
bodies of armed friends, who not only canvassed for the
votes by which causes were decided, but endeavoured by
force to prevent their antagonists from voting. These
meetings were in consequence constantly broken up by
violence, and many lives were lost, not only in the frays
that took place at the time, but in the deadly fætha that
arose from them. For this reason the freemen were required to deposit their arms with an appointed officer
prior to entering the assembly, and received them back
on departing. Hence it was that the assemblies and the
districts to which they belonged were called "weapon-
takes," a name they have retained to the present day.[2]

The Anglo-Saxon was forbidden to carry arms when
doing penance ; and an unsuccessful attempt was made
to induce him to lay them aside when he went to a
drinking-match. With these exceptions, the right of
every freeman to carry arms remained unrestricted from
the time of St. Augustine to that of William the Conqueror.[3]

[1] Mallet's *North. Antiq.* p. 278.
[2] Dr. Dasent's *Burnt Njal*, pref. ;
Mallet's *North. Antiq.*, p. 295.
[3] Theod. *Pœnit.*, c. iii, s. 2, Thorpe,
ii, 5. *Ll. Hloth. et Ead.*, s. 13 and 14,
Thorpe, i, 33.

SECTION VI.—THE HAIR SYMBOLICAL OF FREEDOM.

It would, at first glance, appear absurd to include among the most important rights of an Anglo-Saxon freeman the privilege of dressing his hair in a particular manner; but it is easy to shew how it might be of immense importance in an age of barbarism.

When reading and writing are unknown, everything must be expressed by symbols; and those symbols are naturally selected which are most easily noticed and generally understood. It was for this reason that the Anglo-Saxons chose certain modes of wearing the hair, as the outward signs of particular stations in society, and as the expression of a right to important privileges. Long and flowing hair was, *at first*, evidence that the wearer was a noble, and *always*, that he possessed, unforfeited and unimpeached, all the rights of an Anglo-Saxon freeman. It conferred dignity on the wearer; and the highest and most illustrious were proud of it. It was the distinction in which the Merovingian kings of France most gloried; and Harold Fair-hair and Cnut the Great considered that the length and beauty of their hair added to their lawful claims to popular admiration.[1] A fashion which had so much to recommend it, was certain to be carried to excess; and Anglo-Saxon dandies in the tenth and eleventh centuries indulged in a length and profusion of locks which gave them an effeminate appearance, and provoked the censures of the church. It is from these censures that we learn the extravagant lengths to which the fashion was carried. The Council of London (A.D. 1102) required all long-haired men to be cropped, " so that at

[1] Turner's *Anglo-Saxon Hist.*, vol. iii, p. 43 ; *Anglia Sacra*, t. i, p. 254.

least a part of their ears might be visible and their eyes uncovered."[1] If any one entered a church who had disobeyed this injunction, the service was at once stopped, and not resumed until he left. As, however, this led to constant interruptions, archbishop Anselm ordered the services to be continued, and the hirsute intruder to be publicly warned, that if he worshipped God unshorn, he worshipped against God's will and to the damnation of his soul.[2]

When so much importance was attached to the wearing of long hair, it was natural that beards and moustachios should also be highly estimated. In the earliest period, they were worn of an immense size,[3] and were particularly esteemed by such of the population as were of British descent. The want of them was considered by the laity as a mark of weakness and vulgarity, and by the clergy as evidence of effeminacy and dissolute life. The Anglo-Saxon priesthood at first persisted in wearing them in defiance of canonical prohibition, and boldly insisted that men without such adjuncts could not enter the kingdom of heaven.[4] Dunstan, however, compelled the clergy to obey the law of the church, and to shave themselves in an orthodox manner.[5]

The Normans did not wear beards or moustachios, and on the adoption of Norman manners in England under Edward the Confessor, these became less fashionable among the aristocracy; but the general public were never brought to tolerate their absence. The spies whom Harold

---

[1] *Concil. Londoniense* (A.D. 1102), c. xxiv; *Concilium Turonense*, (A.D. 1083) in the *Concilia Gallica*, t. ii, p. 658.

[2] Epistle of archbishop Anselm to William the archdeacon, Wilkins's *Concilia*, vol. i, p. 238.

[3] William of Malmesbury speaks of them as "pilis incessanter fructi-cantibus," lib. iii.

[4] Alcuin (*De Officio Divino*) says, "Molles sunt qui vel barbas non habent sive alterius fornicationem sustinent." Theod., *Pænit.*, xxviii, 3; Ecgbert, *Pænit.*, iv, 68.

[5] *Canons under King Edgar*, c. 47, Thorpe, ii, 255; *North. Priests' Laws*, 34, 40.

sent into the Norman camp prior to the battle of Hastings, reported that the army must be composed of priests and women, for there was not a beard or moustache to be seen; but Harold knew the Normans too well to be deceived by such a report.[1]

As the various modes of dealing with the hair had all a mystic signification, it is, perhaps, pardonable to follow the topic at greater length than it may at first appear to deserve. There was hardly any important era in an Anglo-Saxon's life which was not marked by some fixed change of fashion.

A child's hair was never cut or dressed until he came of age, except as an insult or practical joke. His coming of age was marked by a ceremonious shortening and dressing of his hair by his father, or, if his father was dead, or thought fit to entrust the operation to other hands, it was done by some one who was willing to adopt him and become his nominal father.[2] Sometimes the operation was performed on young princes by archbishops, or even by the pope himself, whereby the operator became the spiritual father of the youth, and was supposed to be bound to him by parental ties nearly equal to those of a real father. And as public dressing and arranging of the hair was part of the established form of parental recognition and adoption, so the cutting it off in public was the formal rite by which a parent disowned a son, whom he immediately afterwards beat and turned out of his house. His cropped hair was public notice to all comers of his disgrace; and this was the more likely to attract general attention, as the status of slaves and

---

[1] Will. Malmesb., lib. iii. The Gauls considered the Roman army a collection of serfs and social scum, because they wore their hair short. Apol. Sidon., *Epist.* iii; Bosquet, i, p. 790.

[2] Juvenalis *Sat.*, iii, 186; Suetonius, *Vita Calig.*, c. x, *Vita Neronis*, c. xii; Paul. Diacon. *De gestis Longobard.*, lib. vi, c. 53; Gregor. Turon., lib. vi, c. 24.

criminals was rendered palpable to the vulgar by a similar process.[1]

No slave was allowed to wear long hair. He was compelled to keep it always close-cropped; partly because long hair was the recognised mark of a freeman, and partly because it was impertinent in him to remain covered with hair in the presence of his superiors. When he was manumitted he received a cap of liberty, that he might conceal the insignia of his previous servile position until nature provided him with external evidence of freedom.

If it were necessary to the dignity of a long-haired Saxon that slaves should be kept close-cropped, it was still more necessary that criminals should be shaved. Every convict who could not buy himself off, and whose friends disowned him, was compelled to suffer "in his hide and his hair." In pursuance of this sentence, his hair was originally pulled out by the roots, or carefully shaved off; but, when our forefathers became imbued with Roman fashions, a small ridge was left at the top of the head. The clergy caused this to be extended into transverse ridges so cut as to present the form of a cross. The Normans (on certain occasions), not content with the mockery of cutting a criminal's hair in this absurd manner, dipped his head in warm pitch and powdered it with feathers. These proceedings were no laughing matter when every "manifest thief" might be lawfully slain by the first person who met him.

If the right of wearing long hair was important to men, it was doubly so to women; for with them it was not only a mark of rank, but of chastity. Every young freewoman while unmarried was said "to be in her hair,"

---

[1] See Du Cange, v. *Decalvatio*; and compare Constant. Afric., l. ii, *Pan-* *tech.*, c. 16; Ordericus Vitalis, lib. viii.

which she wore long and loose; and, when she married, she was required to dress it in a different manner. If she misconducted herself, it was cut off altogether.[1]

At the earliest period of Anglo-Saxon history after the introduction of Christianity, when a maiden married or entered a convent, and became thereby the servant of God or man, her hair was cropped like a slave's, as evidence that she had accepted a position of servitude ; and at a later period it was shortened and bound up to shew that, though not exactly a slave, she did not possess the freedom of an unmarried woman. It has already been stated that when wives obtained a superior social position to single girls, they regarded this mode of wearing the hair, which was originally a mark of servitude, as a crown of honour.

From the earliest period to the latest, a portion of the public punishment of an unfaithful wife was to deprive her entirely of her hair. This penalty was always accompanied by the most severe personal chastisement.

It is curious to observe how much of the development of Anglo-Saxon character is to be traced in the apparently trivial matter of male and female hairdressing.[2]

[1] Spelman's *Gloss.* v. *Capillati ; Gloss. Ancient Laws and Inst. v. Homola.* Baronii *Annales Ecclesias.,* t. xii, p. 71.

[2] With reference to guilds, which form one of the topics of this chapter, it may be stated, that the origin of *mercantile* guilds *in towns* has been ascribed to the *collegia* and municipal institutions of the Romans. It may, however, be observed, that the main object of the formation of the Roman *collegia* was the holding of property as a corporation, which was not the object of Anglo-Saxon guilds ; and that the names of the office-bearers of the guilds were of Anglo-Saxon, not Latin derivation. The question, however, is an obscure one, on account of the want of evidence.

CHAPTER V.

THE NOBLE.

It is the duty of the jurist, rather than that of the student of domestic life, to trace the rise, progress, and decay of the Anglo-Saxon aristocracy; yet their history had so important a bearing on the home, that it cannot be passed over in silence.

The Anglo-Saxon nobles were, according to distinguished authorities, divided into two classes, who have been designated "nobles by birth" and "nobles by service." The former existed from the very earliest period; flourished in patriarchal times; decayed in an era of transition; and perished when families and tribes became a nation. The latter were the offspring of an age of incessant warfare, in which military exigencies increased the power of the crown and gave rank and wealth to successful soldiers.

The mode in which a patriarchal aristocracy arose among the Anglo-Saxons is very easily explained.

When in Germany or Scandinavia an increasing population found the means of subsistence insufficient, either the whole nation marched in search of a more extensive and fertile territory; or, with a view to diminish their numbers, a few large families emigrated.[1]

---

[1] Machiavelli, *Istorie Fiorentine,* lib. viii, p. 418; Geoffrey of Monmouth, lib. i, c. 1; Saxo Gram., *Histor. Dan.,* lib. vi, c. 9.

Sometimes these emigrants were volunteers, sometimes they were selected by lot, and sometimes the junior members of the family were compelled to emigrate. If they chose to depart by sea, the head of any family, who was sufficiently wealthy, purchased and provisioned a ship, of which he became both captain and owner, and thereby a viking. In. this he embarked not only his children, nephews, and grandchildren, but such freemen as, being too poor to purchase a ship, were willing to become his retainers for the sake of a passage and subsistence.

Occasionally the viking sailed alone, but more commonly in company with two or more other vessels, commanded by chiefs descended from the same ancestor.

At the earliest period of their colonization of this country, the Saxon immigrants settled down peaceably, without disturbing others or being themselves disturbed. Their mode of proceeding was usually this. They sailed up some river and landed, and then pushed through the forests (which at that time covered nearly all the country but the marsh lands) until they found a spot suited for agricultural or pastoral purposes. Here they took possession of a certain portion of land, which they cleared, and thereby made their own, and with it they obtained a right to use a broad belt or boundary of forest land for the purposes of fuel and hunting. If the party thus settling was commanded by more than one patriarch, the cleared land was divided by lot among the heads of houses, and became their allotted or "allodial" land. It did not, however, belong to the chief absolutely, because all the grown-up members of the family were interested in it as partners-by-affinity ; but its exclusive control and management, and the apportionment of its produce, belonged to him. The guests, retainers, and servants who accompanied the expedition had no interest in it.

N 2

This estate was called the "ethel," or hereditary land of the family ; and all who were entitled to share in it were deemed "hereditary landowners." These constituted the earliest Anglo-Saxon aristocracy. Their personal dignity arose from their descent from a founder of a family, and their rights as nobles from the ownership of allodial land.

When through increasing numbers the family estate became insufficient for the support of all, the younger members abandoned it, and taking with them such retainers as they could induce to accompany them, founded fresh settlements elsewhere. By so doing the emigrant did not lose his personal rank as an "ethel," though he forfeited all interests in the family estates, and all his *political* rights as a noble in the district in which they lay.

The right of emigration was not confined to the young nobles. Every retainer of the family could, *at first*, leave when he pleased ; and if he could obtain land, either by occupation or violence, he became a landowning-freeman or churl. He could then claim many of the privileges of a noble ; but unless he were descended from a recognised founder of a family, no amount of wealth, *at first*, entitled him to noble rank.

In the transition period, when the patriarchal aristocracy was breaking up, this rule was slightly relaxed. A churl who purchased an earl's estate ranked as a plebeian ; his son who succeeded to it was regarded as noble-worth, though not as a noble ; but the grandson, if he continued owner of the estate, was recognised as a full noble or ethel.

The nobles had no hereditary title, but like the Cornelii or Fabii of the Romans, bore the general appellation of the race to which they belonged. Their Christian names sometimes suggested their rank by being compound-names of which "Ethel" formed the first half—as in Ethel-ward, Ethel-wulf, Ethel-bert, Ethel-red, Ethel-fleda, Ethel-burga, and many others.[1]

The head of the family was called the earl or ealderman (the elder), and he had *originally* supreme power over his household, being at once king, judge, general, and priest. All these powers, however, rapidly vanished as the patriarchal system broke up ; and even his title of earl lost its original signification, and was conceded to all his relations, however young, who chose to usurp it. He was also, as the chief proprietor of the family estate, designated as lord (hlaford), or breadowner, and the wife who superintended his household, lady (hlafdig), or bread-divider.

The privileges of the ancient ethels were very few. The most important was the right to insist that the kings should be elected from their class ; and the next in value was that of being present at and taking precedence in the witenagemot. In the Danish era, this involved the privilege of preparing the business of these meetings, and taking the initiative at them.

A far earlier privilege, and one that in the most barbarous times was valued above all others, was that of being killed when taken prisoner, without being bound

---

[1] The name of an Anglo-Saxon family was formed by the addition of "ing" to that of its founder. Thus the posterity of the Scylde, of whom Beowulf was one, were called Scyldingas ; the descendants of Uffa were known as Uffingas, and the noblest family of the Mercians were distinguished as Iclingas. The estate or residence of which we have spoken as "belonging to the family," was commonly called their "ham" or home, and its name was formed by the addition of this syllable to the family patronymic. Thus, the family of Beorm, known as Beormingas, possessed themselves of land in Mercia to which they gave the name of Beorminga-ham, now corrupted into Birmingham ; and the Buckingas to a territory called after them, Buckinga-ham, and now Buckingham. Many other places in England retain the names given them by Anglo-Saxon families ; as Badlingham, Warningham, Harringham, Walsingham, Brantingham, etc. Kemble's *Saxons in England*, vol. i, b. 1.

like a slave, or their long hair soiled by the touch of ignoble hands. To die in battle was at one time an Anglo-Saxon noble's proudest aspiration; while to be bound as a prisoner involved dishonour and loss of caste, not only to him but to all his family. At the battle of Cambrai, between Clovis and *his relative*, Ragnacharius, the latter was taken prisoner and chained. The conqueror reproached him with having accepted his life. " You have brought disgrace," he said, " by suffering bonds not only on yourself, *but on our whole race.* It were far better you had died." And then lifting his double-edged axe into the air, he gave effect to his admonition by striking off his head. He then turned to Richarius, his brother, who had been also taken prisoner, and said, " If you had aided your brother as a brave man ought, he would never have brought the disgrace of bonds *upon all our house;* " and thereon he slew him also.[1] In return for the privileges which the earls enjoyed, certain responsibilities and duties were imposed upon them. In addition to their liability for all offences committed by their family, they were expected to keep peace, and to attend to the interests of the crown and the general welfare of the people. It was also their duty to collect and command the military forces of the district on occasions of foreign invasion or civil war.

Thus far we have considered the duties, powers, and privileges of the hereditary ethel, when his star was in the ascendant; it now remains to examine briefly the circumstances under which his rank and influence waned and disappeared.

His power arose mainly from his ownership and control of the family estate, on which all the family were dependent for bread. The first symptom of the breaking up of the patriarchal system in all countries is the introduction

---

[1] Gregor. Turonensis, *Hist. Franc.*, lib. ii, c. 42.

or permission of *private* property, belonging not to the family as "partners by affinity," but to individuals. Its origin has been everywhere the same. Whatever a man by any special interest added to the family estate, he was allowed, at first, a special interest in; and, at a later period, was permitted to regard it as his own. Thus, among the Romans and the Jews, the earliest private property was the booty a man took in war; and among the Hindoos, whatever a member added to the common stock by some art unknown to his brethren, was regarded as his private property. Among the Anglo-Saxons, at a very early period, whatever a younger member of a family personally acquired by war or industry became his own; and though a family estate could not be alienated, land thus acquired, provided the owner had no children, might be sold or devised.

When population began to increase, and families to break up, these acquired lands became infinitely more extensive and valuable than the ancestral estate. There is an instance of this in the case of the Buckingas, whose original family estate did not probably exceed a few acres, but who rapidly extended their possessions over the county which still bears their name.

The number and value of these new estates rendered the younger members of a tribe independent of their chief, and put an end to his authority as lord or bread-owner. His right to command the family militia still remained; but as he had no means of compelling the attendance of his followers or enforcing obedience to his orders, his military authority was a mere delusion. When the Danish wars rendered it necessary to organise thoroughly the military resources of the nation, our greatest kings, such as Ecgbert and Alfred, laboured to substitute a territorial division and a local militia for unorganised tribal guerillas, and to give them educated and experienced officers in lieu of the patriarchal chieftains.

This brings us to the period when the hereditary ethel ceased to exist; and in which the "thane," or "noble by office," took his place. It is impossible to fix the exact date at which the king's military attendants rose from the position of servants to that of nobles, because this rise was very gradual; but their greatest advance was made during the earlier period of the wars between the Saxons and the Danes. There are ample materials for tracing the social history of "the nobility by office," from its servile beginning in German forests, to its royal rank and splendour at the time of Harold.

It was the proudest distinction of a Teutonic chief to be surrounded by a band of young companions whom he had attracted to his home by his reputation for hospitality, valour, and open-handedness. They came to him as reverential pupils and retainers, who hoped through him to learn the art of war, and to attain the fame that hallowed all the companions of a hero and a conqueror. They bound themselves to him as friends, pupils, and servants, anxious to participate in his triumphs and ready to share all his dangers.[1] In return for their services, the chief lent them arms and horses, which, on their treason or death, reverted to him. He also provided them with clothes, and generously divided among them whatever he gained in battle.[2]

In times of peace, which were rare (for the normal state of society was one of war), these youths, unless some daring adventure tempted them away, remained at the side of their chosen leader. They resided with him,

---

[1] Beowulf, l. 5763; Annal. Lauris., A.D. 796; Pertz, Mon. Germ., i, 182.
[2] Eginhard, Pertz, Monum. Ger-

man., i, 183; Saxo Gramm., Hist. Dan., lib. i, c. 1, and lib. xvi; Valerius Max., lib. iv, s. 8.

and at his expense; and they assisted his wife and children in the performance of those domestic duties which were their daily task.

It is natural that in so doing each should take to himself some special department, as is the custom of servants at the present day. One of them filled the important post of a "mara-schal" (horse-servant) or marshall, and superintended the purchase and training of the chieftain's stud. Another became his "stallere," or stall-man, and looked after the stables. A third took charge of the lord's bedroom, and was called by the learned *cubicularius*, or chamberlain, and by the ignorant, a "bower-thane." The chieftain had also his hrægh-thane, or clothes-servant; a dish-thane, who waited at table; a carver, cup-bearer, and many others. Among these officers there were two who subsequently rose to great importance— his hord-ere (hoarder), or money-box keeper; and a constant attendant, whose office marks the barbarity of the times, his private executioner, or headsman.

Menial as were the tasks which the chief's "companions" performed, they received, in return, attentions nearly as humble. It was the duty of the queen and princesses personally to make and mend their clothes. When Siegfried went on his fatal matrimonial expedition into Burgundy, the royal Síglint personally clothed him and his companions;[1] and when king Frotho was a widower, his thanes were in so ragged a condition that they mutinied, and coming to him in a body insisted on his immediately marrying again, as while he was without a queen they had no one to make them new clothes, or even to sew up the rents in their old ones.[2]

The title first borne by a "companion" was that of "ge-sith" (or sizar), which in the Danish era was changed

---

[1] Nibelunge Nôt, 66, p. 10, Lachman. [2] Saxo Gramm., *Hist. Dan.*, p. 68.

for that of thegen, or thane. This name signified a *voluntary* servant, and was given to the "companions" to distinguish them from the "theows," the involuntary servants or slaves. The extreme humility of their primary position is proved by the fact that their wehrgeld (or life-value) was the same as that of a poor landless freeman ; and that even in the tenth century, when they had much risen in dignity, unless they owned land, it was only one tenth that of an earl.

It must not, however, be for a moment forgotten, that whatever were the rank and offices of the thanes in time of peace, their *duties* were mainly military. They sought the chief solely that they might be trained in the art of war, and they were retained almost exclusively with a view to military services. To monarchs perpetually engaged in war, who had generally to rely for troops on raw levies of ploughmen and shepherds, these trained soldiers were of the greatest utility, and their value was greatly enhanced by their enthusiastic devotion to their chief, and by their incorruptible fidelity.

The story of Lilla, the thane of Eadwine (king of Northumbria), who interposed his body between the assassin's dagger and his royal master, is well known, and is merely one of many similar anecdotes. About the end of the eighth century, Cyneheard, a prince of Wessex, having some pretensions to the crown, collected his thanes and attacked king Cynewulf, who was visiting at the house of his mistress at Merton, and there slew him. He offered to a few of the king's thanes, who were in attendance upon him, land and wealth if they would retire, but they indignantly refused to survive their lord, and perished in a desperate effort to avenge his murder. On the following morning, an overwhelming force of the late king's friends arrived. They offered to the prince's thanes the same terms that he had proposed to the king's, but they, in their turn, refused the bribe, preferring to die with their prince to incurring the dishonour of abandoning him.[1]

When England was incessantly harassed by Danish invasion, the kings spared no efforts to increase the number of these military retainers, and to improve their position. King Alfred, in addition to all customary provision, distributed among them one third of that portion of his revenue which he devoted to secular purposes. When Ecgbert and his successors divided the country into military districts, they naturally placed in command over them officers on whose personal fidelity and military knowledge they could implicitly rely. The troops furnished by a single "tything" or "hundred" might be prudently left to the control of an officer of their own selection; but the combined forces of a district required to be placed under one who was competent to the management of large bodies of troops; and the trained and veteran soldiers of the king being alone equal to the task, at once obtained all the most important commands.

In the time of Ecgbert there was no general army. There was nothing but a local militia which very reluctantly left their own neighbourhood. This was an additional source of power to the thanes, as it caused them to reside for a very considerable part of the year in the military district which they commanded. Here, from representing the crown in a military point of view, they soon grew to represent it in political and civil affairs; and in addition to commanding the king's troops, they collected his revenue and administered justice in his name.

[1] Ethelward, *Chron.*, A.D. 755; Roger of Wendover, A.D. 785; Matthew of Westminster, A.D. 786; Florence of Worcester, A.D. 784; *An-glo-Saxon Chron.*, A.D. 755; Henry of Huntingdon, A.D. 784; and William of Malmesb., *De Gestis Rey.*, i, s. 42.

All their offices they most grossly abused to their personal profit. They jobbed every military appointment within their gift, they administered justice only on payment or compulsion, they levied taxes and fines according to no law but that of their own will ; they kept the estates which they confiscated to the crown as their own property ; and they accounted for as much of the royal revenues as suited their convenience. Having by these and similar means obtained the position, wealth, and power of the ancient earls, they usurped their title ; while these last, whose dignity was still recognised, but whose means were terribly curtailed, educated their children in the king's household that they might become thanes. Thus it came to pass that the titles of earl and thane gradually became synonymous ; or rather that the earl retained his title and became a thane, while the thane continued to perform his duties and called himself an earl.

As the thane lived for a considerable portion of the year in his own district, and yet did not surrender the domestic office which he held in the king's household, he was of course compelled, when absent, to execute its functions by deputy; but this did not provoke criticism; as there was nothing an Anglo-Saxon did—whether it were fasting or feasting, praying or swearing, being tried or being punished—which he might not do vicariously.

The officers in the king's household rose in dignity as well as in wealth. In the ninth century, the royal butler presided at the witenagemot ; and his daughter married her sovereign and became the mother of Alfred the Great.[1] The stallere or groom took the title of " comes stabuli," which was retranslated constable. He carried the king's flag after him in war, whence he acquired the position of " standard-bearer of England," the highest office in the

---

[1] *Chronic. Mailros.*, Gale, vol. i, p. 142.

country. It was at the marriage of a daughter of his stallere (Tovi the proud) that Harthacnut drank himself to death. The offices of bower-thane and hordere (chamberlain and treasurer) had been combined at a very early period, probably because the treasure chest was kept in the king's bedroom; and the duty of the office was extended from merely keeping the key of the king's money-box to regulating the management and disposal of its contents. The hordere had, at the latest period, more controul over, and interest in, the royal treasures than the king himself. On one occasion, when Edward the Confessor was ill in bed, Hugoline, his chamberlain, came into the room, and having put something into the hoard, retired, leaving it unlocked. The king noticed the fact, and so did a scullion boy who was in attendance, and who, believing the king to be asleep, immediately opened the chest, filled his bosom with gold, and quietly carried it off. Having deposited his plunder in safety, he again ventured into the chamber and repeated his experiment with the same success. Not knowing when he had enough, the young rogue visited the room a third time, and was about to add to his ill-gotten gains, when the king, alarmed, not for the safety of the money, but for that of the thief, exclaimed, " Have a care, boy, have a care, and be off with the sum you have : if Hugoline returns and catches you, he will not leave you a penny." Even the executioner in the Saxo-Danish era became a great noble. At the court of Cnut, the office was filled by no less a person than Eric, king of Norway; and on one occasion at least he exercised his duties personally and in the king's presence. The marshal, the wardrobe-thane, the seal-bearer or chancellor, all rose rapidly in power and dignity; and the same may be affirmed of all the royal household thanes or servants, the royal harper alone ex-

cepted.   At an early period he obtained the right to rank
as a royal thane, but, from some unknown cause, he does
not seem to have shared the good fortune of his comrades.

There was, however, one qualification, without which
no earl or thane could exercise the political functions of
a noble.   He must be a landowner ; for though noble
descent had come to be of small account, and successful
soldiers had acquired all civil authority, yet the fundamental political notion of the Anglo-Saxon, that all political rights arose from the ownership of land, was never
abandoned.

An earl who sold all his land retained his nominal
rank, but forfeited all his privileges, and was bound to
become the " man" of a lord in the same manner as the
humblest freeman ; and a thane, even if also an ethel,
unless he owned forty hides of land, could not vote in
the assembly of nobles.   We have in the history of Ely
an account of a young noble of the name of Godmund, who was enamoured of the daughter of "a most
powerful earl."   The lover wooed and won his mistress,
the parties were espoused, and the wedding-day was
fixed; but on the eve of the day the lady discovered
that her intended, not owning forty hides of land, could
not vote in the assembly of nobles.   She immediately
declined to fulfil her engagement.   The young man, overwhelmed with shame and despair, repaired for advice and
assistance to his brother Elfric, abbot of Ely.   The abbot
fraudulently executed to him a conveyance of more than
the required quantity of land, being a portion of an
estate belonging to the monastery.   Armed with this precious deed, Godmund returned to his lady love, and was
happily married.   Unfortunately for his liberal brother
the abbot, the monks were not long in discovering the
fraud and calling him to account.

The rise of the royal thanes to power introduced a new element into Anglo-Saxon society, and one that had very considerable influence upon it. They no sooner obtained establishments of their own, than they proceeded to form their households on the model of the king's. They in their turn had *their* thanes, whom they called treasurers and chamberlains, stewards and marshals, who filled in the houses of the thanes the offices which they held in that of the king. There were queen's thanes, archbishop's thanes, earl's thanes, and many others; and all these gradually asserted their right to be considered nobles. This was not acceptable either to their superiors or inferiors, but as there was some foundation for their claim, they received the title of minor thanes, and were looked on as a sort of half-spurred noble. There were also *minimi thaini*, or very small thanes, who seem to have been game-keepers, a body of men who were of more importance in Saxon-Norman times than at present.

The period at which earls and thanes became one is easily ascertained. A patriarchal earl was an earl by divine right. God made him an earl, and no man ever pretended to unmake or remove him; but a thane was appointed by the king or witenagemot, and whoever appointed him had a right to cashier him. We do not hear of any attempts to do this until the time of Alfred the Great, who threatened to discharge all who did not improve their minds, and did remove at least one of them. Edgar also exercised the right of dismissal, as did all the more powerful of his successors.

The social change from the patriarchal earl to the official thane was a very great one. The earl was the head of a large family by all of whom he was loved and venerated, and all of whom he fed and protected. He was to them what Abraham, Isaac, and Jacob were to the households they ruled. The thane was a very different person, and bore more resemblance to a Turkish pasha of fifty years ago than to an hereditary noble. He was often of low birth, bred in the prince's household, and raised to power from motives of fear, hatred, or caprice. The thanes, like the pashas, often exhibited great talent, and a high sense of military honour; but like them they practised every possible system of extortion on the miserable beings who came under their jurisdiction. If they obtained wealth without power they were constantly "squeezed" by their king; and if they grew too powerful, they became insubordinate and set the crown at defiance. The earls ruled by the influence of the domestic affections, and their followers were controlled by a sense of duty based upon them; the morality of the thanes was founded on an intense feeling of the obligation of personal fidelity. To them we are indebted for our noble hatred of treason, and for that elevated self-respect and sense of honour which are the most common, and, perhaps with many, the most powerful, of moral principles.

The political consequences of the change are foreign to our purpose. But it may be briefly observed that it is the natural result of long-continued civil war to concentrate military power in the hands of a few individuals; and that at the time of the Confessor, three earls, Godwin of Sussex, Leofric of Mercia, and Siward of Northumbria, wielded almost all the civil and military power of the kingdom, and reduced the king to a cypher. The fatal results of this, and of the jealousies between them, are familiar to all. Harold, earl of Sussex, was left to combat single-handed the Norwegians in the north and the Normans in the south, and his rivals repented of their ill-will or inertness too late to save themselves and their country from total subjugation and unparalleled misery.

CHAPTER VI.

___

THE PRIEST.

___

DURING the Anglo-Saxon period, the word " clergy " had
a far more extensive meaning than it has now. It included not only all who are now considered clergymen,
but a vast number of persons corresponding to the parish-
clerks, chorister-boys, beadles, bell-ringers, and pew-
openers, of the present day. According to ecclesiastical
law, the clergy then consisted of seven orders of persons,
with distinct rank and offices. There were door-keepers
or ostiaries, readers, exorcists, acolyths, sub-deacons,
deacons, and priests.[1]

The ostiary was the door-keeper of the church,
whose duty it was to ring the church-bells, to open the
door to all who were believers, and to refuse admittance
to all who were not. The duty of the lector was to
read the small portion of the service which was not sung
or read by the deacon. The exorcist, as his name
denotes, was required to exorcise evil spirits, adjuring
them in the name of the Almighty to depart from those
they troubled. The acolyth held the candle at divine
service, at the reading of the gospel, and at the consecra-

___

[1] Ælfric's *Canons*, 10-17; Ælfric's   *Concil. Trident.*, sess. xxii, c. 11; Bel-
Pœnit., 34 ; Ecgbert. *Excerpt.*, 160 ;   larmin., *de Clericis*, lib. i, c. 11.

tion of the Eucharistic bread. He was said to hold it
not for the purpose of driving away obscure darkness,
but to typify "the light of Christ, who is our light."
The duty of the sub-deacon was merely to carry back-
wards and forwards the sacred vessels, and to wait upon
the deacon. The deacon attended on the mass-priest,
placed the oblations on the altar, read the gospels at
divine service, baptized children, and houseled or absolved
the people. A priest who had no deacon to wait on him,
was said "to have the name, but not the attendance, of a
priest." The duty of the presbyter or mass-priest was
to consecrate the housel or sacramental bread, to preach
to and teach the people, and to be an example to all
Christians by the purity of his life. The priests and
bishops were of the same *order*, but different in point of
dignity. It was the bishop's duty to ordain priests and
" bishop children," to consecrate churches, and " to guard
God's rights."[1]

The clergy were divided into two bodies; namely,
ecclesiastics, consisting of priests and deacons, who were
under episcopal rule; and the "headless" or "vulgar
clergy," who had no chief or rule of life. The latter
body were of course composed of the first five of the
orders just enumerated.

The *ecclesiastics* were sub-divided into "regular" and
"secular" clergy. The regular clergy consisted of those
monks or religious men, who, having taken upon them
the vow of some order, performed the offices of the
priesthood in their respective monasteries. The secular
clergy were those who were not of any religious order,
and on whom the care of parishes generally devolved.
The canons of such cathedrals as were not of monastic

[1] Ælfric, *Epist. ad Wulfsin*, Thorpe, 379; Lingard's *Anglo-Saxon Church*, ii, 349; *Epist. ad Wolstan*, Thorpe, ii, ii, 17.

foundations were called secular canons, and the incessant disputes between them and the monastic clergy had a considerable influence over the Anglo-Saxon home. The most important difference in their notions of domestic life arose from the fact that the parochial clergy were generally married men, while the monks were bound by vows of celibacy. The former taught their parishioners to be dutiful sons, affectionate fathers, and home-keeping husbands ; while the latter exhorted their disciples to observe vows of continence, to practise devotional exercises, and go on foreign pilgrimages.

The comparative *ecclesiastical* rank of the different orders of clergy may be ascertained by the pecuniary satisfaction to be paid to *the church* for killing them. For an ostiary, one pound was to be paid ; for a lector, two pounds; for an exorcist, three pounds; for an acolyth, four pounds ; for a sub-deacon, five pounds ; for a deacon, six pounds ; and for a priest, seven pounds.[1] For a bishop there was no fixed legal payment ; but the mulct, penance, and other punishment, were to be settled on each occasion by public consultation.[2]

In addition to their ecclesiastical position, archbishops and bishops enjoyed high temporal rank. They were summoned to all national councils, in which their superior abilities and education generally gave them a marked preponderance. The archbishop had the royal privilege of giving his word, where other men were required to make oath ; and of granting nine days' respite to all who

[1] Thorpe, *Anct. Laws and Inst.*, ii, 295 ; *Munimenta Gildhallæ London.*, ii, 629.

[2] The difference in their respective stations may also be inferred from the length of time they were required to do penance for certain offences, the punishment increasing in duration according to the rank of the offender. Where a *slave* was condemned to fast two years, a "canonicus" was to fast five years, a sub-deacon, six ; a deacon, seven; a priest, ten ; and a bishop, twelve years. *Theod. Pœnit.*, ii, Thorpe, ii, c. 3 ; *Canons under king Edgar*, 2, Thorpe, ii, p. 267.

were guilty of murder or manslaughter. He also had the royal right of coining money and of maintaining troops of his own.

The comparative *social* rank of the clergy and laity may be judged by the compensation to be paid, not to the *church*, but to their *kindred*, for killing them. The amount payable for an archbishop was half that of a king ; for a bishop, the same as an earl ; for a mass-priest, that of a thane or gentleman ; and for the vulgar clergy, the same as for common men.[1]

The occupations of a bishop in the Anglo-Saxon period far exceeded those of prelates of modern times. It was his custom to sit with the judge of the civil court as assessor in the administration of justice ; although his presence in this character, particularly when sentence of mutilation or death was passed, was clearly contrary to the canons of the Catholic church.[2] On these occasions, it was his special province to administer oaths and to provide against perjury ; and he was also to superintend the administration of the ordeal so as to prevent fraud. He was to offer his arbitration in all disputes, and promote peace. At a very early period, his labours in this respect were probably beneficial ; but at a later date, the claim of bishops to *arbitrate* in nearly all differences (aggravated by their misapplication of a technical rule of the Roman civil law, whereby there could be no appeal from the decision of arbitrators selected by the parties), became a source of tyranny and injustice. It was also the office of the bishops to protect the poor against the rich ; and the weak against the strong. In discharge of the first duty, they claimed the superintendence of all weights and measures ; and in that of the second, the right of de-

---

[1] Thorpe, i, 157. Wer-gilds.   Wendover, A.D. 1164; *Ll. Eadg. Sec.*,
[2] Spelman's *Concil.*, i, 295; Roger   ii, s. 5 ; *Ll. Cnuti Sec.*, ii, s. 18.

ciding all differences between the lord and his prædial slaves or servile tenants.

In the heyday of ecclesiastical supremacy, there was no limit to the rights or power of a bishop. In the words of the ecclesiastical institutes, "To the bishops belongs every direction both in divine and worldly things;" and in accordance with this doctrine, ecclesiastical laws and charges required kings and princes to yield them servile homage and implicit obedience.

There were among the Anglo-Saxon clergy men of transcendent merit, who commanded the veneration of the age in which they lived, and who are justly honoured by posterity. The zeal, piety, and learning of St. Augustine, Wilfrid, archbishops Theodore and Ecgbert, Benedict Biscop, Aldhelm, Alcuin, St. Boniface, the venerable Bede, St. Dunstan, Alfric, and St. Cuthbert, would have merited distinction at any time and in any country, and their general influence over the intellect and morals of the nation was a blessing for which we cannot be too thankful. To such men all homage is due. It were treason to Christianity and civilisation not to speak of their labours with the admiration they deserve ; but of the inferior or headless clergy, particularly at certain periods, it is impossible to speak in laudatory language; and even the character of the superior ecclesiastics varied greatly at different eras.

During the century which succeeded the advent of St. Augustine, little is alleged against the clergy but lust of power and wealth, and that, in the gratification of these passions, they were guilty of what would now be deemed harshness and injustice. But men must be judged by the morality of the age in which they live ; and cruelty and injustice were means to which, at that time, very few persons, whether clerical or lay, ever hesitated to have

recourse. The piety, self-denial, and zeal of the superior
clergy of the seventh century, are generally spoken of in
the highest terms ; but, in the eighth century, they began
to experience the effects of too great prosperity. The
assumption of political power and the acquisition of unnecessary wealth were ruinous to them. The former
alienated the free-spirited Anglo-Saxon laity, and the
latter drew into their body a large number of dissolute
and idle persons, who cared for nothing clerical but the
loaves and fishes. The enormous amount of treasure that
was accumulated in cathedrals and monasteries added
eventually to their misfortunes ; for the piratical northmen soon discovered that these sacred fanes were the
most profitable places to attack and plunder.

In the time of king Ecgbert and his sons, the Anglo-
Saxon church was reduced to the lowest ebb of virtue,
knowledge, power, and wealth. Its great and shining
lights were dead, and had not left to their successors the
illumination of their spirit ; their famous monasteries,
such as Lindisfarne, Peterborough, and Ely, had been
razed to the ground, and their gold, and silver, and jewels
carried off, even from the violated tombs of their saints
and martyrs : the books, which the early bishops had so
zealously collected, were burnt or lost, the more learned
and virtuous of the monks were slain or scattered, and
the revival of the Anglo-Saxon military spirit had recalled her princes and nobles from the cloister to the
battle-field. The severity of monasticism had disappeared, and those who had adopted the spare and simple
garments of St. Benedict were slaves or hirelings, who
wore them only as a cloak for idleness and license. As
to their learning, " so clean was it ruined," says king
Alfred, " that there were very few on this side the Humber who could understand their service in English, or

declare forth a letter out of Latin into English; and I think there were not many beyond Humber. So few such there were, that I cannot think of a single one to the south of the Thames when I began to reign."[1]

Their morals were on a par with their learning. Singing light songs, wandering about, fighting, and furious intoxication, appear to have filled up their ordinary round of life. Their excesses were such that, in the words of a distinguished writer, "had there not been some among them who resisted the general depravity, and distinguished themselves by lives strict in proportion to the profligacy of the rest, or had not the ignorance or barbarism of the times been so great that the most absurd superstitions found a ready reception, it would be difficult to conceive how a religion could continue to be held in estimation whose ministers surpassed other men, not in virtue, but in vice."[2]

Against this torrent of evil the wise and good king Alfred exerted all his influence. He invited distinguished clergymen from abroad, and appointed them to high office; he sought and raised to eminence the little he could find of native piety and learning; he founded monasteries and schools, and supplied them with books and teachers; and he spared neither wealth nor personal labour to raise the morals and the intellect of the clergy from the utter debasement in which he found them. To precept and persuasion, he added the potent teaching of example; studying, translating, publishing all that he could find to enlighten or elevate his people. His labours were crowned with temporary success; but the character of the Anglo-Saxon clergy was never effectively reformed until they suffered the iron discipline of archbishop Odo

---

[1] Preface to his Translation of the *Regula Pastoralis of Gregor. I.*

[2] The words quoted are those of Lorenz, *Life of Alcuin*, p. 15.

and the great St. Dunstan, who, whatever their vices may
have been, have certainly the merit of having raised their
order from well-deserved contempt to the position of
moral and intellectual superiority, which it has ever since
maintained.

In considering the influence of the clergy over the
domestic life of the Anglo-Saxons, we must examine it
apart from that of the divine ·religion which it was its
privilege to teach. What the effect of pure Christianity
would have been on such a moral and intellectual state
of mind as existed in England at the commencement of
the seventh century, is an inquiry far too solemn and
profound to be considered incidentally in pages devoted
to meaner topics ; but the influence of a particular body
of men, teaching unknown truths, introducing novel
customs, claiming absolute authority, and bringing to
bear on all they did the energy and power of unity and
discipline, cannot be altogether passed over in any dis-
quisition, however humble, on the history of social improvement.

Before we consider, as it will be necessary to do, certain *special* modes of ecclesiastical influence, two *general*
facts connected with it require to be noticed. The first
is the isolation of the clergy, and the second the language
of the church. The regular clergy were a body apart
from the people. They were, or ought to have been,
without wives and children—those sacred pledges which
bind men in affection to their kin. England was not
their nursing-mother ; their mother was the church. Their
affections and their passions were not devoted to the
welfare of their native land, but to that of an ambitious
corporate body whose head was a foreign bishop. Their
home and country was the church. This alone would
have sufficed to have separated them from the laity

in interests and affections ; but the constant superintendence of the Anglo-Saxon clergy by Italian and French
bishops increased their alienation.

The moral influence of the higher order of ecclesiastics
over the vulgar clergy and the laity was further diminished
by the fact, that the language of the church was Latin,
and that of the people Anglo-Saxon. The great Italian
missionaries were as a rule ignorant of the language of
the nation they came to convert.[1] A bishop, whose zeal
had brought him from Rome to England, abandoned his
mission in despair, and on his return assigned as one of
the causes of his want of success, that he spoke nothing
but Latin, of which the natives did not understand a
word. This difficulty, though undoubtedly great, was
not insuperable, as St. Augustine, whose mission was
eminently successful, taught through interpreters procured in Gaul, who possessed but an imperfect knowledge
of Anglo-Saxon.

The earliest bishops were nearly all strangers. A succession of Romans occupied the cathedral thrones of
Canterbury, Rochester, and London, and for a certain
time that of York also. East Anglia was under the superintendence of Felix, a Burgundian ; and Birinus, a
Frank, was the apostle of Wessex. All these spoke a
strange language, and though one or two of them attempted to acquire the Anglo-Saxon language, they were,
as a rule, ignorant of it.

---

[1] Alfric, *Pref. Genesis*, p. 1; Bedæ,
Epist. Albino, 55; Bede, *Ecc. Hist.*, l. i,
s. 23, and l. iii., c. 3 ; Lappenb., *Ang.-
Sax. Kings*, vol. i, p. 135 ; Lingard's
Ang.-Sax. Church, vol. i, p. 156. In
A.D. 664, Agilbert, bishop of Dorches-
ter, declined to address an assembly of
clergy because he could only do so
through an interpreter.—Dr. Hook's
Lives of Arch. Cant., vol. i, p. 132. The
early missionary bishops seem to have
thought it unnecessary, or at least
very disagreeable, to learn the language of the people to whom they
preached. Irenæus, bishop of Lyons,
in the second century, laments the
necessity of having to learn Celtic.
—Hallam's *Middle Ages*, vol. iii, c.
9, p. 1; Milman's *Latin Christianity*,
vol. i, p. 403.

This was felt by their converts as a grave misfortune, and some of the more powerful among them had recourse to violent remedies. Ægilberht, a Frank, who was ignorant of Anglo-Saxon and consequently taught in Latin, succeeded Birinus as bishop of Wessex. King Coinwalch, "disgusted by his foreign talk" (*pertæsus barbaræ loquelæ*), first divided his bishopric in halves, and then removed him from it altogether.[1]

But England was not long indebted to Rome or France for the whole of her episcopate. As early as the eighth century, a great proportion of the bishops were Anglo-Saxons, and of course spoke their native language.[2] They would have been more influential for good had they been always selected on purely religious grounds, rather than, as was too often the case, from political or pecuniary motives. Among them were many of royal, noble, and military rank, a few of whom were men of undoubted piety and learning, but the many were as ignorant of Latin as their predecessors had been of Anglo-Saxon, and did not understand the prayers they recited or the scriptures they read.[3]

Bede translated the Lord's Prayer and the Creed for their instruction, and other celebrated ecclesiastics provided them with the Psalms, the Gospels, and portions of the Old Testament in the vulgar tongue. But it was some centuries before all these were written, and there never was, as far as we know, a complete translation of the Bible into Anglo-Saxon during the Anglo-Saxon era.[4]

In addition to all influence which may be considered as general, there were several institutions or customs

[1] Bede's *Eccles. Hist.*, iii, 27; William of Malmesb., *De Gest. Pontif.*, l. ii.
[2] *Anglo-Saxon Chronicle*, A.D. 690. Before this, the bishops had been Romans; subsequently, they were English.

[3] Lupi *Epist. apud* Hickes; Du Chesne, *Hist. Franc. Script.*, ii, 749; *Concil. Rom.*, c. iv (A.D. 826); Labbæi *Concil. VIII*, 106.
[4] Lappenberg, *Anglo-Sax. Kings*, vol. i, p. 200.

established by them which deserve especial notice. Among these are the *partial observance of the Mosaic law, the study of Roman laws and literature, the system of penances and pilgrimages,* and, above all, *monastic institutions.*

As it is not proposed to discuss in these pages any subject that is purely theological, jurisprudential,- or literary, some of these important matters are merely enumerated.

It is very difficult to ascertain what the views of the Anglo-Saxon clergy were as to the extent of the obligation of the Mosaic law. It is possible that they appreciated the extreme difficulty of treating one portion of a law as obligatory, while another part of the same law is admitted not to be so. The division of the Mosaic law into moral, municipal, and ceremonial, as a test of the places and times in which it is obligatory, was either unknown to them, or imperfectly understood. They generally omitted the second commandment from the Decalogue, and they differed materially from the modern orthodox, as to the obligation of certain regulations not now considered binding upon Christians. They forbade the eating of unclean meats, as horseflesh, magpies, and even hares. They permitted the eating of hog's flesh, which the Jew abhorred, but forbade the drinking of liquor into which a little pig had fallen, until it had been sprinkled with holy water and fumigated with incense. They also prohibited the drinking of beer into which a mouse or weasel had fallen. They allowed the converts to eat fish, but not animals found dead. Honey was not to be used if the bees killed in it *remained a whole night.* Fowls and other animals suffocated in nets were not to be eaten, even although a hawk should have bitten them. Domestic poultry which had tasted human blood was not to be eaten until three months afterwards. A man who *knowingly* ate blood in his food was to fast seven days ; and any one who did so *ignorantly* was to fast three.[1] They imposed several restrictions on the female sex and on the intercourse between husband and wife, to the latter of which, however, there is no reason for believing that the laity paid any attention.

To trace the influence of the clergy upon Anglo-Saxon jurisprudence and literature would be to write their history. There is scarcely a person (with the exception of king Alfred,) who laboured successfully for their advancement, who was not either a clergyman or a monk. As the literary and jurisprudential history of the Anglo-Saxons is not within the scope of this work, we will pass on to the clerical institutions which bore more directly on the general character of the nation, namely monasticism, penance, and pilgrimages.

[1] *Pœnitent.* Theod., Thorpe, ii, 40-41 ; *Council of Cloveshoe, Can.* 40 ; Wilkins, *Concilia*, vol. i, p. 124 ; Ecgbert. *Pœnit.*, c. 38, Thorpe, ii, 215 ; Soames' *Anglo-Saxon Church*, p. 253.

CHAPTER VII.

THE MONK.

THE fundamental idea of monasticism is hostile to the "Home." It involved the abnegation of all family ties ; and had its origin in the moral error of denying the existence of all social duties, and in a sad perversion of some of the most important doctrines of the Christian religion.

In the century that immediately succeeded the crucifixion of our Saviour, when his disciples, like their Divine Master, were despised and rejected of men, none but those who were actuated by a firm conviction and earnest faith, became members of a body which was the object of public scorn and bitter persecution. But when the new faith began to triumph, many were added to its votaries whose motives were of a less noble character, and who, although they cared little for its principles, were not unwilling to share its prosperity. These neither practised the devotion nor suffered the self-denial required of them. Their sloth and their laxity were a scandal and a wound to the body they had joined. Hence it was that in the third and fourth centuries many members of the church were looked upon by their more zealous brethren as merely nominal or professing Christians, whose coldness provoked contempt and merited censure.

In the opinion of some, the church was divided into two distinct bodies, one of which they regarded as "vulgar," and the other as "ascetic" Christians; and for whom (as it was alleged) Christ had established different rules of sanctity.[1] The former were permitted to indulge in all the idleness and luxury of the decaying civilisation of Rome; while the latter carried self-denial into self-torture, and a disregard of this world into a neglect of every social duty.

A loose and imperfect practice of religion satisfied the conscience of the majority. The prince or magistrate, the soldier or merchant, sought to reconcile his religion with the exercise of his profession, the pursuit of his worldly interest, and the indulgence of his passions; but the ascetics, who obeyed, as they imagined, the clear precepts of the gospel, were inspired by the savage enthusiasm, which represents man as a hopeless criminal, and God as a merciless tyrant. They seriously renounced the business and the pleasures of the age, abjured the use of wine, of flesh, and of marriage; chastised the body, mortified their affections, and sought a life of misery here as the price of happiness hereafter. In the reign of Constantine they fled from a profane and degenerate world, established regular communities of the same sex, and of a similar disposition, and assumed the names of hermits, monks, and anchorets, expressive of their lonely retreat in a natural or artificial desert.[2]

At first the stern ascetic bent his lonely way to some miserable rock washed by the ocean, to some solitary cavern in the desert, or to a dreary islet in a pestilential marsh. Here he lived alone, spending his time in divine

---

[1] Winckelman, *Hist. de l'Art*, i, c. 2, 51.

[2] Gibbon's *Decline and Fall*, vol. vi, c. 37; Churton's *Early English Church*, p. 87; Maitland's *Dark Ages*, p. 159; Milman's *Latin Christianity* vol. i, p. 162; and Fosbroke's *Monasticism*.

contemplation, abstinence, and self-torture. In some cases he stood for weeks, months, or even years, in one unchangeable attitude ; and in others, denied himself the use of any food but a few vegetables, and water which he purposely defiled.

The reputation which these enthusiasts obtained for superior sanctity induced the vulgar to give them credit for supernatural wisdom ; and not only were they surrounded by a crowd of humble disciples, but even kings sought their counsel and direction in temporal as well as spiritual affairs. By this the pride of the hermits was flattered, but their solitude was destroyed, and their negation of the world belied.

Egypt, the fruitful parent of superstition, afforded the first examples of monastic life ; and offered a soil, both moral and physical, suited to the rapid development of the new institution. The sands of Lybia, the rocks of the Thebais, and the islands of the Nile, which nature had dedicated to solitude, were peopled with monks. A single district was occupied by five thousand anchorets, and still preserves the ruins of more than fifty monasteries. One small island was the habitation of one thousand four hundred monks, under the direction of Pachomius, who at solemn festivals had under his spiritual care no less than fifty thousands individuals. The ancient sarcasm against Egypt, provoked by the worship of beasts, birds, and insects, was varied ; and in lieu of saying, that it was easier to find on the banks of the Nile a God than a man, it was said, that their cities were less populous than their deserts.

From Egypt the monastic institution rapidly spread itself throughout Palestine, and from Palestine to Rome, and from Rome to Gaul, and either from Gaul, or directly from Rome, it found its way to England.

Prior to the time of St. Augustine monasteries had existed at Iona, one of the Hebrides, and at Bangor, in Flintshire ; but of these very little is known.

The South Saxons were indebted to St. Augustine for the establishment of monastic institutions. He was himself a monk, and no less than thirty of his small band were selected from the monasteries of St. Gregory. Soon after his arrival, he founded two monasteries in Canterbury, one within and the other without the walls ; and he subsequently established others at London and Rochester.

The northern part of England received monastic institutions from a different source. About forty-eight years after the arrival of St. Augustine, Aidan, and a band of Scottish monks from Iona, established a monastery at Lindisfarne, a small island on the coast of Northumberland, and in common with most heads of early monasteries assumed the rank and functions of a bishop.

The diversity in the origin of the northern and southern monasteries was the cause of numerous and fierce disputes. The Scottish monks persisted in teaching the doctrine and discipline of St. Columba ; and what was far more important to the laity, refused to submit to the authority of St. Augustine, or to the church of Rome. Hence arose endless discussions about trivial matters, of which the time of keeping Easter, and the form of clerical tonsure, were the most important.[1]

On the establishment of monasticism in England, there were few things to which the monks attached more importance than the sites of their monasteries ; and in their selection they displayed sound judgment and exquisite taste. Everywhere they paid homage to the charms of

[1] The form of the tonsure was so completely a badge of party, that when Wilfrid left the Celtic party for the Italian, the first thing he did was to submit his head to the scissors of a Roman barber. Eddius, quoted by Dr. Hook, *Lives of Archbishops of Canterb.*, vol. i, p. 15.

nature ; but in their passion for the beautiful they never forgot the useful, the duty of seclusion, or the necessity of self-preservation. They generally selected spots which were lovely and fertile, but never one which was not secluded and safe. An island on a rugged shore, like Lindisfarne, would, they vainly hoped, be protected by its insular position from the incursions of the moss-trooping Scot ; and by the dangers of the coast, from the visits of the piratical Dane. Ely and Peterborough were erected on islands in the middle of meres, which at that time were inland seas, and were, from their position, places of comparative security.

The site of a monastery was also so chosen that its neighbourhood might afford an ample supply of water for its inhabitants, broad meadows on which cattle might be pastured, and forests that provided firewood and materials for repairing the interior of the abbey and constructing its numerous outhouses.

Of the selection of one of these sites we have the following account : On the death of a nobleman attached to king Edgar's court, his brother, a wealthy earl who had led an irregular life, sought the spiritual advice of bishop Oswald. The bishop told him that nothing would be so grateful to God as the erection of a monastery, and urged him to select a suitable situation on his estates and to build one. The earl replied that he had some hereditary land surrounded with marshes and remote from human intercourse, near a forest full of noble trees, with open glades of turf and meadows of fine grass for pasture. The bishop went to view it, and finding that the waters made it an island, approved the spot, and on it a monastery was immediately erected. Abbo, a celebrated scholar from Fleury, was appointed to superintend it ;

P

and thus, on what was but a few months before a deso-
late waste, stood the celebrated abbey of Ramsey.[1]

At the earliest period of Anglo-Saxon history, the
churches and monasteries were buildings of the most
lowly character. Nothing could have been more humble
than the cell which St. Cuthbert built for himself at
Farne. The building was circular, about four or five
poles in diameter. The wall outside was about the
height of a man, but inside a greater depth was obtained
by excavating the rocky floor. The walls were constructed
of turf and rough stones, some of which were so large
that four men could not lift them ; but St. Cuthbert, it
is said, with the assistance of the angels, raised them up
and placed them on the wall. The roof of the house was
thatched with turf, and had a large hole in the middle,
which was at once chimney and window, for St. Cuthbert, when he looked out from his cell, desired to gaze on
heaven only. The interior was divided into two apartments, the one an oratory and the other a kitchen ; and,
for the accommodation of the brethren who came to visit
him, he constructed an out-house near the landing-
place.[2]

The earliest churches and monasteries were not much
more splendid than St. Cuthbert's cell : they were formed
of split wood and covered with reeds. The abbey of Lindisfarne and the first cathedral at York were thus built ;
and it is probable that the humbler churches and monasteries were constructed of wicker work wattled with clay.[3]
It would be difficult to trace step by step the improvement
in the construction of monasteries. The Italian priests
and the Anglo-Saxon pilgrims soon taught the natives to

---

[1] *Hist. Ram., Anglia Sacra*, p. 396;   and *Hist. Eccles.*, lib. iii, c. 25.
Chron. Monast. de Bello, p. 7.   [3] Giraldus Cambrensis, *Itin. Camb.*,
[2] Bede, *Vita Sancti Cuthberti*, c. 17,   p. 890.

erect churches and monasteries of stone, and to imitate the buildings which they had seen in France and Italy.[1]

Among the more striking improvements in ecclesiastical buildings were the substitution of leaden roofs for those made of reeds, and the occasional lining of the walls with lead. The construction of windows was also a great improvement, though they were at first merely square holes with transverse poles or beams covered with linen. The progress in ecclesiastical architecture was exceedingly rapid. The foreign bishops brought with them workmen from all parts, and marble columns and glass windows soon appeared, to the astonishment of the uncultivated Saxon. The monastery of Hexham, built by St. Wilfrid in the seventh century, was the wonder of the age.[2]

In the eighth century monasteries engrossed all the wealth of the country. Their interiors were specimens of such barbaric splendour that they excited the universal envy of the laity and fired the passions of the plundering Dane. On solemn festivals every vessel employed in the sacred ministry was of gold or silver; the altars sparkled with jewels and ornaments of precious metals, and the vestments of the priest and his assistants were gorgeous with embroidery; even the walls of the churches were adorned with beautiful paintings and the richest tapestries. In the church built by Bugga in Wessex, before the year 700, the principal altar was covered with curtains of cloth of gold; the cross was of gold, with silver ornaments and gems; the chalice and the patene were a cup of gold chased with precious stones, and a dish of silver of great magnitude. In the church of York

---

[1] The missionary Paulinus substituted a stone church for the wooden one originally erected by Edwin at York. Bede, *Eccles. Hist.*, lib. ii, c. 14.

[2] Eddius, *Vit. Wilf.*, c. 17 and 22; Bede, *Eccles. Hist.*, lib. iii, c. 25; Bedæ *Opera Minora*, p. 143, *Eccles. Hist.*, lib. v, c. 21.

stood two altars entirely covered with plates of gold and silver. One of them was also ornamented with a profusion of gems, and supported a lofty cross of equal value. Above them were suspended three rows of nine lamps in a pharus of the largest dimensions. Even the books employed in the offices of religion were decorated with similar magnificence. St. Wilfrid ordered the four gospels to be written with letters of gold on a purple ground, and presented them to the church of Ripon in a casket of gold, in which were enchased numerous precious stones.[1]

At first the monks were exclusively laymen, but at an early period St. Athanasius admitted some of them to holy orders, that the brethren might have among them ministers of religious worship ; while on the other hand numerous members of the clergy took monastic vows ; so that, a large proportion of monks having become clergymen, and a still larger number of the clergy having become monks, the word monastery appears after a certain period to have been applied indifferently to clerical and monastic establishments, and the clergy and the monks to have been generally confounded together.[2]

In the earliest monasteries the monks took no vows, and in all probability did not live according to any fixed rule ; but in those established by St. Augustine the rule of St. Gregory was obeyed. At a very early period, however, the rule of St. Benedict was introduced into England, and was universally adopted in the south ; and in the following description of the daily life of the monks it is assumed that these rules were duly observed.

At the earliest period, the monks, though bound by no

---

[1] This description of the interior of monasteries is copied almost verbatim from Dr. Lingard's *Anglo-Saxon Church*, vol. i, p. 265. See also the *Monasticon*, vol. i, pp. 40, 104, 165, 222; and, as to the extravagance with which books were bound, Maitland's *Dark Ages*, No. xiii.

[2] Soames' *Hist. of the Anglo-Saxon Church*, p. 131.

vows, were expected to practise those virtues which were afterwards more clearly defined and more strictly enforced. Before all things it was necessary that the monk should be obedient to his abbot, chaste in life, and careless of worldly wealth ; and, on the introduction of monastic vows, obedience, chastity, and voluntary poverty, were the three main duties imposed by the rules of every order.

The monk was required to be obedient to his abbot in everything ; not only in the greatest affairs of life, but in the smallest matter of daily conduct. This obedience was to be unhesitating and confiding, and to be yielded in a cheerful and devoted manner. If, however, the abbot's commands were clearly at variance with the will of God, the monk was at liberty to disobey, but it was at his own peril.

At first no vow of continence was required from either monk or nun. There were monks who were married men and nuns who were married women ; nor even after the introduction of vows of chastity was the marriage of a monk or nun absolutely void, though it rendered the offender liable to expulsion from the monastery.[1] The rule of St. Benedict, however, required perpetual continence from its disciples ; and the most stringent means were taken to secure obedience in this respect. Sobriety at meals, long and painful watchings, and constant prayers and exhortations, perpetually recalled to the minds of the monks that they had renounced the world and its concupiscence. They were commanded to sleep in the same room, in which a lamp was burning all night, so that the conduct of each individual might be open to the observation of all. The gates of the convent were

---

[1] August., *de Bono Viduit.*, c. v (*Op.* iv, p. 1408) ; Bingham's *Christian* SS. *Benedict.*, vol. vi, p. 375, f. 2) ; *Antiq.*, vol. ii, p. 322 ; Soames's *Anglo-Saxon Church*, p. 265. Concil. *Aurel.*, i, c. xxi (Labb., vol.

shut against the intrusion of strangers, and the monk whom business called abroad into the outer world was constantly attended there by two companions. They who strictly observed the duties of continence were considered the "immaculate spouses of the lamb," and were believed to have earned for themselves the high rewards described in the Apocalypse as belonging to those who " have not been defiled with women."

The practice of voluntary poverty was the third condition required in the monastic state. The early Christians had all things in common ; and the instances in apostolic times in which rich men sold all they had and gave it to the church are numerous and well known. Hardly any virtue was more peremptorily insisted upon by the founders of monasticism than that of voluntary poverty, yet there was scarcely any to which their disciples paid less attention.

Saint Columba, the father of the northern monks, taught them, that not only was to *have* more than mere necessaries a damnable sin, but that *even* to *wish* for it was equally wicked.[1] While St. Benedict asserted that they only were truly monks, who, like their fathers, lived by the labour of their hands.

· Whatever might have been the case abroad, we know of no period in which monastic establishments were conducted in England without a view to the acquisition of wealth. From the very beginning, the monks exerted themselves to obtain grants of land from the kings they converted, then to have those lands freed from all dues and taxes, and then to collect from all sides dependant labourers, servants, and slaves. To repentant sinners they held forth that there was no duty so pleasing to God as to bestow wealth upon the church, and to reduce their

---

[1] *St. Columb. Reg.*, c. 4.

families and children to poverty in adding to the superfluity of the monks. So successful were they in these
labours that at one time half the land in England, and
two thirds of the moveable property, are supposed to have
belonged to clerical and monastic bodies ; while the
retinues, establishments, and furniture of the bishops and
abbots surpassed in magnificence not only those of nobles
and princes but even those of kings.[1]

In defence of this apparent disregard of the obligation
of poverty, it was said that monastic poverty consisted
only in the abnegation of *private* property, and that however wealthy a monastery might be, yet as the wealth
was the property of the corporation and not of individuals, the monk was the penniless member of a wealthy
body.

According to the rule of Saint Benedict, at least as
observed on the continent, the monks should have had
all things in common, even to their wearing apparel.
The abbot was to find them all that was required, which,
in England, besides board and lodging, seems to have
consisted of clothes, a handkerchief, a knife, a needle, a
steel stylus and tablets to write on, a mat, a straw bed,
a piece of serge, a blanket, and a pillow. All these things
were the property of the monastery, and on the continent the monk who talked of *my* shoes, or *my* gown, was
severely punished. But in England this last rule was
not enforced ; a monk who could obtain a license from
his abbot was at liberty to enjoy not only his own private
clothes, but land, money, and whatever else he could
procure.[2]

In addition to the particular virtues of obedience,

[1] Alcuin, i, 291, *Epis.* ccxxv.
[2] In many grants of lands by monks
or their relations to the monasteries
which they joined, the income of the
land is reserved to the monk for his
life, sometimes generally, and sometimes for the express purpose of finding him in clothes and other articles.

poverty, and chastity, to which the monks bound themselves, there were numerous observances which the church demanded from them as a necessary part of the duties of monasticism. First and foremost among these was abstinence, or a careful avoidance of all superfluity in eating and drinking.

The dietary of the Anglo-Saxon monks ought to have been of the most spare character. Two meals a day—a dinner and a supper—was all that was allowed them ; and for these meals two dishes of pottage, one pound of bread, and a few apples or wild fruits were to suffice. To this the abbot had power to make additions in case of illness or hard labour. The meat of four-footed animals was forbidden to all but the sick. On the continent this rule was relaxed in favour of children, but it was not so in England. The general allowance for boys was considerably less than that for men, and everything approaching " overfill" or " overswill" was above all things to be avoided. Fish formed a considerable portion of their daily food. The rent payable for their farms was often reserved in eels ; and we find tenants paying as many as seventeen thousand, and, in one instance, twenty-three thousand eels annually. In some parts of the country these rents were reserved payable in herrings. The manor of Lewes paid thirty-eight thousand herrings annually to the monks of Winchester ; and fishing boats and tributary fishermen formed part of the establishments of the monasteries of Ely and Ramsey.[1] The monks were not content to be dependent on nature alone for their favourite food. They constructed large fish stews, or *vivaria*, in the neighbourhood of their monasteries, in which they bred enormous quantities of fish. A

---

[1] Ecgbert, *Excerpta*, Thorpe, ii ; Wright's *Biograph. Brit. Lit.*, vol. i, p. 441; Ellis's *Introduction to Dooms-day*, vol. i, p. 141.

single stew is spoken of as supplying twenty thousand eels annually.[1]

Among the mischiefs which are stated to have arisen from the entry of kings and nobles into monasteries, was the abolition or neglect of the rules for simplicity of diet. When king Ceolwulf (A. D. 704) retired to the monastery of Lindisfarne, he obtained a license for the monks to drink wine and ale, which, according to the rules of their founder, St. Aidan, they could not have done.[2]

The introduction of intoxicating liquors into monasteries was a great misfortune, and gave rise to grave disorders. The monks, like the mass of the Anglo-Saxons, did not know what moderation meant, and habitually drank to excess. The Council of Cloveshoe put a slight restriction on their license in this respect, by forbidding them to drink intoxicating liquors before the ninth hour of the day, to get drunk themselves, or to *force* others to do so. Dunstan temporarily succeeded in modifying their bad habits ; but under the Danish kings the monks were more crapulous than ever ; and though the Norman contempt for drunkenness must have tended to their reformation, yet the Anglo-Saxon monks never bore a satisfactory character in this respect.

[1] Ellis's *Domesday Book*, vol. i, p. 143, *et seq.* The monks did not carry the meagreness of their diet to an extent injurious to health, for many of them appear to have lived to an extreme old age. If we may believe the *Chronicle of Croyland* (which few people do), when Turketul, who is alleged to have been chancellor of England under king Edred, visited Croyland, he found among the brethren three monks, Turgar, Brune, and Aio, each one hundred and fifteen years of age, a fourth, named Snarling, aged one hundred and forty-two, and a fifth of the name of Claren-bald, who is stated to have died at the incredible age of one hundred and sixty-eight. *Hist. Croyland,* A.D. 946-975.

[2] The rule of St. Benedict was rather more liberal, and permitted each monk to drink a "hemina" of wine per diem, and increased the allowance of bread from twelve to eighteen ounces. As king Ceolwulf did nothing more at Lindisfarne than was done in nearly all the monasteries in England, his conduct does not appear to have merited the severe observations bestowed upon it. How much a "hemina" was is uncertain.

Saint Benedict established no particular rule as to the dress of the monks. He merely required that it should be similar to that of the labouring poor, and suited to the climate. In England a cowl and a tunic were considered sufficient, the cowl being thicker in winter and thinner in summer. In addition to this a scapular or upper garment was used, which was substituted for the cowl when the monks were engaged in hard work. In the eighth century the monks neglected their rules as to dress, adopted the costume of the laity, and indulged in numerous fopperies, which offended their ecclesiastical superiors.

Archbishop Cuthbert complains that they imitated secular men in the fashionable banding of their legs,[1] and in wearing cowls round their heads in the fashion of a layman's cloak ; and the Council of Cealchythe (A.D. 785) condemns their custom of "wearing costly garments dyed with Indian tinctures."[2] But there were many habits of this sort contrary to ecclesiastical law, which neither the monks nor the clergy could ever be induced to abandon. Among these were the customs of carrying arms and wearing long hair, as marks of ingenuous birth ; and of constantly wandering about, which was always a favourite amusement with every class of Anglo-Saxons. The nuns were as fond of travelling as the monks, and their indulgence of this propensity led to a great amount of scandal. In the seventh and eighth centuries the law forbad any man to afford wandering monks hospitality for more than one night, unless they carried a travelling license, and prohibited the nuns from taking up their lodgings at the houses of laymen.[3]

---

[1] "In vestitu crurum per fasciolas." Concil. Cloves., c. 28; Wilkins's Concil., vol. i, p. 98 ; Oculas in circumdatione capitis, Id.

[2] Concil. Cealch., c. iv; Wilkins's

Concil., vol. i, p. 46; Walter de Mapes, De Nugis Curialium, Distinct., i, c. 25.

[3] Ll. Withr. Eccl., s. 8 ; Concil. Cloves., c. 29.

The Anglo-Saxon love of singing was another weakness which tempted the monks to a disregard of the regulations of their order. Even the rigid Saint Dunstan was never so obedient to his own rules as to abstain from harping and singing the "most vain songs of the gentiles." As a passion for music cannot be pleasantly indulged in solitude, the monks were tempted to invite into their monasteries wandering minstrels, whose characters were not of the best, and to make parties to ale-shops, where they amused themselves with drinking, singing, and tumbling, in a manner rather inconsistent with the gravity of their profession.

But the church not only pointed out to the monks what they were *not* to do, but carefully taught what they *were* to do during nearly every hour of every day. Six hours were allotted to sleep. Soon after midnight they were to arise and chant the nocturnal service, and during the day they were seven times summoned to church to perform parts of their canonical duties ; seven hours were to be employed in manual labour ; two in study ; and the remainder was to be devoted to necessary nourishment. On the Sabbath (Saturday), the domestic economy of the monastery was to be attended to. Supplies for the kitchen and cellar were to be provided, and on that day the monks were required by Dunstan to grease their shoes and wash their clothes.

It has just been said that "seven hours were to be given to labour." As the monks had professedly abandoned all right to separate property, and the establishment at first pretended to reject the idea of collective wealth, the inhabitants had to support themselves by manual labour. Every monk had therefore an occupation. Sometimes he made wooden sandals, or twisted osiers into mats or baskets. Sometimes he was employed in agricultural labour, and the fields which his industry had won from the forest or morass were cultivated by his hands ; or, perhaps, the draining of the fens of Ely, or the marshes of Croyland, occupied his time. As knowledge progressed, superior duties fell to his share : he was the builder, the architect, or the sculptor of his convent ; and he laboured to bring to perfection any art that served to adorn or benefit it. No rank or eminence exempted a monk from these humble duties. Saint Dunstan was a celebrated blacksmith or worker in metals, and his pupil, Saint Ethelwold, followed the same occupation.

When the clergy and the monks became one body, the monks' labours were extended. They were employed in scholastic duties, and those who were sufficiently accomplished occupied their time in copying portions of the scriptures, decrees of councils, and lives of saints ; to which employment was added that of transcribing (and sometimes forging) charters and grants of land in favour of their monasteries.

No institution could have grown more rapidly or flourished with greater luxuriance than monasticism did for a time in Anglo-Saxon England. As monasteries were built, young and old, high and low, rich and poor, crowded into them ; and numerous and extensive as the foundations were, they were inadequate to receive the enormous numbers who clamoured for admission. In Northumbria alone, at the time of St. Wilfrid, the monks were numbered, not by tens or hundreds, but by thousands.

To the poor and oppressed people of Anglo-Saxon England the attractions offered by the monasteries must have appeared almost irresistible. The numerous estates granted by kings and nobles to ecclesiastics became in their hands far more valuable than they had been under lay-proprietors. In the first place, they were discharged from all

rates, taxes, tolls, fines, fees, and impositions, which, at
that time, exceeded anything of which we dream at the
present day. In some instances, indeed, the kings compelled them to contribute to the *trinoda necessitas* of the
realm, that is to say, to the keeping up of roads and bridges,
and defraying military expenses ; but this payment was
resisted by the clergy as a monstrous extortion, and as
certain to draw down eternal punishment on the king
who demanded it.

The freedom of their property from taxes was of less
direct than *indirect* importance. At a time when *most*
freemen were compelled to surrender their land and to
become tenants or feudatories, the church claimed that all
estates conveyed to them should be (as their own were)
free from taxation. They could, therefore, accept sur-
renders of lands and regrant them free from taxes at a
rent equivalent to what the taxes would have been, without detriment to the owner, who received the benefit of
their protection, and merely paid the church for rent what
he would otherwise have paid the king for taxes. Their
estates were also free from the plunder and destruction of
civil war. While the lands of every layman were laid
waste in the incessant turmoil of the age, the monastic
property was respected. The pagan Danes, and they
only, plundered the church.

Monasteries had also the right of affording sanctuary,
so that no criminal or debtor could be seized within their
jurisdiction, and the homicide flying from the deadly
feud was for a certain time protected from vengeance.
So numerous were the criminals who embraced the monastic profession to escape the punishment due to their
crimes, that the church at last forbad murderers to be
admitted to monastic vows, though they do not appear to
have interdicted other offenders.

The superior skill of the monks in all handicrafts tending to personal or domestic comfort was another attraction. Every one was compelled to follow some occupation, and their immense number, aided by the habitual subdivision of employments, enabled them to carry every art to a perfection elsewhere unknown. Many of the superior ecclesiastics had been educated at Rome or in France, and brought with them into England numerous articles of comfort and luxury previously unknown, but with which an experience of the then superior civilisation of the continent had rendered them familiar.

The inhabitants of monasteries also escaped one of the most intolerable grievances of the age, the obligation of appearing in arms whenever a superior went to war with his neighbour ; and were also exempted from the more legitimate obligation of resisting foreign invaders. We must, however, do them the justice to add that they seldom availed themselves of the latter privilege (save in the eighth century), and that there were as a rule no braver warriors than the monks and clergy.

The numerous privileges of the monastic orders induced men of every rank and character to adopt the cowl. In the era immediately preceding the reign of Ecgbert, the nation appears to have been carried away with a mania for monasticism. No less than ten kings and eleven queens abandoned their royal duties and retired to monasteries ; and nobles and freemen followed their example in very large numbers.[1]

The existing establishments were altogether insufficient to accommodate so vast a multitude ; and kings, princes, and earls vied with one another in founding new monasteries and endowing them in right regal and princely fashion.

[1] Bede, *Epis. Ecgbert. Arch.* with this Roger de Hoveden, A.D. 736 *Ebor.*, s. 10 and 11; and compare and 763.

The influx of the nobles into monasteries was as injurious to monasticism as to aristocracy. The monks corrupted the nobles, and the nobles the monks. The one lost the military habits necessary to protect their country from the piratical Danes ; while the others, forgetting their vows of sobriety, temperance, and chastity, emulated the luxurious vices of the nobles.

The chastisement this drew upon them from the Danish arms, the plunder and destruction of their sacred fanes, and the slaughter or dispersion of the monks, was possibly, after all, a social and political benefit. The clergy, who were steeped in ignorance and vice, re-acquired in the terrible school of adversity some of the energy, self-denial, and virtue which had once adorned their body ; and hundreds of nobles and freemen, who could no longer eat the bread of idleness, flocked to the standard of Alfred, and chased from their native homes the human wolves who devastated them.

By the time the arms and policy of that great king had partially restored peace to England, a great reaction in public opinion as to monastic institutions had taken place. They were as vehemently hated and despised at the end of the ninth century as they had been admired and loved a hundred years before. The mischiefs they had done had been appreciated ; but this was not all. They *had been* very rich and were now poor ; had been powerful protectors, and were now impotent ; had been luxurious and lax, and were becoming regular and strict.

During the Danish invasion the number of the monks of Croyland dwindled from a hundred to thirty ; and instead of increasing in number on the restoration of peace, they continued to decrease till, in the time of Edred, they consisted of an abbot and two monks only. Nor was it easier to people new monasteries than to procure

inmates for the old ones.   When Alfred the Great desired
to fill his new establishment at Ethelingey, he found that
the well-born of his subjects universally rejected a monastic life, and he was compelled to people it with boys
and slaves.   Even these did not present themselves in
sufficient numbers, and he at last sought occupants for
his new foundation in the ecclesiastical establishments of
Gaul.

But, from the time of Alfred, downwards, the monastic
bodies gradually increased in riches and dignity, and
with these their unpopularity vanished ; till at length, in
the time of Edgar, they had attained such wealth and
power as to endanger not only all political liberty, but
almost the rights of private property.

CHAPTER VIII.

THE NUN.

MONASTERIES at first were not inhabited exclusively by men. The majority of them were at their foundation double monasteries, in which both sexes lived in social intercourse. Such were Faremoutier, Chelles, and Andeli, in France (where a large number of Anglo-Saxon ladies were educated), and our own monasteries of Whitby, Barking, Coldingham, Ely, Wenlock, Winbourne, Beverley, and many others.[1] It does not appear that at first the monks and nuns were in any manner separated from one another ; but from an early period it was customary to appoint one portion of the building as the sleeping-place of the male, and another as that of the female inhabitants. After a short time, one side of the establishment was regarded as the residence of the men, and the other of the women ; but both monks and nuns roamed through the whole building at pleasure.

Towards the end of the seventh century women were forbidden to sleep on the male side of the monasteries, or men on that of the women ; and in the eighth century the erection of double monasteries was forbidden, though the prohibition appears to have been disregarded.[2]

[1] Lingard, *Anglo-Saxon Church,* vol. i, p. 214.

[2] Sixth General Council (the *Quintisext* in Trullo), can. 47; Beve-

Q

Long before this period the more earnest of the ladies who superintended Anglo-Saxon monasteries had placed restrictions on the visits of the male sex to the female side of the monastery. They did not, however, prohibit men of the dignity of Saint Cuthbert and the venerable Bede from the minute personal examination of every portion of their establishments.

There was, in the beginning of the eighth century, a double monastery at Winbourne, surrounded by lofty walls, of which one part was occupied by men and the other by women. No woman was permitted to enter the monastery of the men, nor was any man to come into the convent of the women, with the exception of the priests who came to celebrate mass. Even the abbess herself, if it were necessary that she should receive advice or give orders, spoke to men through a window ; and so desirous was she of preventing any intercourse between the sisters and persons of the other sex, that she refused admission not only to laymen and clergymen, but (which was not usual) even to the bishops themselves.[1]

There was another double monastery at Whitby, in which a sisterhood of nuns and confraternity of monks obeyed the famous Hilda, an East Anglian and Northumbrian princess. This lady was famous throughout the land for her piety, charity, and learning. The nuns under her care enjoyed the highest reputation for every Christian virtue, and no less than five of the monks of Whitby were raised to the episcopal dignity during the life of the foundress.

The principal obligations of the nuns were the same as those of the monks, viz., chastity, poverty, and obedience, and their religious exercises did not materially differ.

---

ridge, tom. i, p. 213 ; Gibbon's *De-cline and.Fall*, vi, 258.

[1] *Vit. S. Liobæ*, in Act. SS. Benedict., sæc. iii, p. 246.

They worked in the gardens and fields much in the same manner as the monks, but their indoor occupations were, of course, different. Both acquired a smattering of literature and a slight knowledge of music, and both employed themselves in tuition. The nuns wove, and made the clothes of their establishment in accordance with the rules of their order, and to these they added many garments they had no authority to wear. Among them were white and violet chemises, veils and tunics of delicate tissue, richly embroided with silver and gold, scarlet shoes, and many other articles of female finery. They also worked the splendid vestments of the mass-priests and bishops, and wove the tapestry that adorned the churches. Many of their performances were of great magnificence. On a groundwork of scarlet or purple they would represent flowers, foliage, fruit, buildings, beasts, and birds ; and they occasionally wrought the storied mantles worn by kings at their coronation, on which mythological and historical subjects were delineated. Their handiwork shews that they must have studied the art of design, and though they were occasionally assisted in their compositions by such gallant gentlemen as St. Dunstan, a considerable portion of the merit must have been their own.

The habits of some of the most celebrated nuns were far from cleanly. The abbess Edda declined to wear any linen between her person and her woollen garment, which she changed *annually*, or to wash oftener than three times a year. The nuns of Sempringham were allowed to wash their heads seven times a year, and *not more*, on which occasions they were to wipe their faces with a cloth. They were never permitted to wash their feet unless they had been working in the marsh, but a cloth was provided in the cloisters with which they might rub their feet and hands. The heads of the children under their care were not washed during Lent. St. Cuthbert, the sainted model of English monks, only washed his feet at Easter, and if his annual self-examination was unsatisfactory, he omitted the usual ablution. It would be easy to quote a multitude of instances illustrative of the dirty personal habits of the monks and nuns, but the subject is not inviting. It is sufficient to say that an absence of personal cleanliness was considered evidence of self-denial and sanctity.[1]

At the earliest period, the abbesses were selected on account of their piety ; but, when the convents grew rich, they were chosen from less worthy motives. A valuable abbey was considered an excellent endowment for a woman of rank, who had lived to a certain age unmarried, and for whom it was necessary to make provision. Even kings did not disdain the headship of a convent for their widowed sisters or unmarried daughters ; and towards the end of the eighth century, we find nearly all the principal convents under the superintendence of royal ladies.[2]

The appointment of these royal ladies to offices, to the

[1] *Monasticon Anglic.*, v. ii, p. 697. Du Cange v. *Capitalavium.* There was an exception in those cases in which from their habits they had become "scabie occupatæ," an event, which from its being expressly provided for, we may conclude to have been of common occurrence; they were then allowed to wash oftener. A monk who inhabited the Feroe Islands, speaking of the long light of their summer nights, says, " sed quicquid homo operari voluerit, vel pediculos de camisia abstrahere, tanquam in presentia solis potest." Dicuil, *De Mensura Orbis Terræ.*

[2] Bede, *Eccles. Hist.*, l. iii, c. 2, and l. iv, c. 23. Etheldrytha, daughter of Anna, king of the East Angles, was abbess of Ely, in which office she was succeeded by her sister Sexburh. Abbe, a sister of king Oswiu, was abbess of Coldingham in Berwickshire ; and Hilda (who has been already mentioned), a grandniece of king Eadwine, enjoyed a similar dignity at Hartlepool, in Durham, and subsequently at Whitby, in Yorkshire. In the latter she was succeeded by her niece, Elflæda, also a daughter of king Oswiu. Ethelburga, a daughter of a king of the East Angles, was abbess of Farmoutier-en-Brie ; as afterwards was Earcongota, a daughter of Earconberht, king of Kent. It would be very easy to multiply examples of abbesses of royal birth. Lappenberg, *Anglo-Saxon Kings*, vol. i, p. 195.

duties of which they were comparatively indifferent, was open to grave objection, but it was innocent when compared to the system of selection that afterwards prevailed. The headship of a convent or abbey was then considered a convenient situation for any female of high rank of whom it was expedient to be rid ; and persons were consequently selected for the office whose conduct demanded their exclusion from general society, and whose birth or rank forbad their suffering condign punishment.[1]

About the end of the eighth century, Charlemagne appointed an Anglo-Saxon ex-queen abbess of a monastery on the express ground of her exceeding wickedness. The lady who received and merited this infamous distinction was Eadburh, the widow of Beorthric, king of Kent, and daughter of Offa, king of Mercia. She was renowned throughout England for her beauty, talents, and ambition. Married at an early age to one who was her inferior in every respect but birth, she ruled her husband with an absolute and jealous authority. She carefully removed from his court all who thwarted her, either by bringing false accusations against them and procuring their execution, or by the more direct agency of poison. Among those who possessed influence with her husband was a young earl of the name of Worr. He was famed for personal beauty, valour, and wisdom ; and the affection the king entertained for him, aided by his general popularity, rendered his influence formidable to the queen's supremacy. On some occasion of public hospitality, she prepared for him a stoop of poisoned liquor, and courteously presented it to him. The king, who was present, claimed his right as head of the nobles to drink first, and having done so, passed the cup to the young earl, who emptied it. Both died in consequence,

---

[1] *Anglo-Saxon Chron.*, A.D. 919; *Anglia Sacra*, ii, 113.

leaving the guilty queen exposed to the indignation of the royal family, whose chief she had accidentally killed, and of the nation, whose favourite she had intentionally murdered. Unable to face the storm she had raised, Eadburh collected her treasures and fled to the court of Charlemagne, where she employed her beauty and her wealth to obtain a favourable reception. The emperor of the west had dreamt (as continental emperors have more than once dreamt in vain) of adding England to his already too extensive empire ; and with this view he had unsuccessfully negociated matrimonial alliances between his own children and those of king Offa. Either from motives of policy or ambition, or, perhaps, by a mere caprice, he received the beautiful widow very courteously. He suggested to her that she would probably find married life more agreeable than widowhood, and asked whether she would prefer as a husband himself or his son. Eadburh replied, with more frankness than discretion, that in the matter of husbands she preferred young men to old, and that she would take his son. Charlemagne, either piqued or pretending to be so, told her that had she chosen him he would have married her to his son, but as she preferred his son she should have neither. For some time he permitted her to remain unnoticed at his court, until, scandalized by her wicked life, he placed her at the head of an excellent monastery. In her new and responsible position, Eadburh conducted herself as badly as might have been expected, and, being detected in a discreditable amour with one of her countrymen of low birth, was expelled the convent. This unhappy queen then wandered from place to place, until at length she, who was the daughter of one great monarch and the wife of another, ended her days a common beggar in the streets of Pavia.[1]

[1] Roger de Hovenden, A.D. 749 ; William Malmesbes., l. ii, c. 2 ;

Great as was the difference in the character of the abbess Hilda, in the beginning of the seventh century, and that of queen Eadburh, at the conclusion of the eighth, it was not greater than the difference in the character of the nuns over whom they presided. The ladies, who at the first establishment of monastic institutions dedicated themselves to God, generally bore the highest reputation for chastity, self-denial, charity, and devotion ; while those who occupied the monasteries in the later half of the eighth century, led lives not only inconsistent with their vows, but with morality and decency.

The least fault laid to their charge was a neglect of the humble habit which they ought to have worn and the adoption of the dress of the irreligious. For this they are reproached with unnecessary severity. The venerable Bede complains that in his day they spent all their time in weaving fine garments, "either to adorn themselves like brides, or to gain the friendship of strange men." St. Aldhelm is more minute in his reproaches. He complains that they had adopted altogether a worldly dress, with the simple addition of a veil fastened with ribbons to the head, crossing over the chest and falling to the feet behind.[1]

In one convent the lady abbess appeared in a scarlet tunic with full skirts and wide sleeves and hood, over an undervest of fine linen of a violet colour, and with shoes of red leather. Her face was rouged, and her hair curled

---

Asser, *De Rebus Gestis Ælfredi*, p. 471; Matth. of Westminster, A.D. 802 ; Simeon of Durham, p. 673; *Chron. de Mailros.*, apud Gale, i, 140. Asser says, "A domino meo Ælfredo, Angul-Saxonum rege veridico, etiam sæpe mihi referente audivi, quod et ille etiam a veredicis multis referentibus, immo ex parte non modica illud factum commemorantibus, audierat." Lingard's *Anglo-Saxon Church*, vol. ii, c. 12.

[1] St. Aldhelm. de Laud. Virgin., 307, 364 ; Lullus, *Epist. inter Bonifacianas*, xiv, p. 63; Lingard's *Anglo-Saxon Church*, vol. i, p. 210 ; and Hook's *Archbis. Canter.*, vol. i, p. 33.

with irons over the forehead and temples ; ornaments of gold encircled her neck, heavy bracelets adorned her arms, and jewelled rings were upon her fingers. Her nails were worn long and cut to a sharp point to resemble the talons of a hawk.

In the latter part of the eighth century, Alcuin in vain exhorted the nuns to sacrifice the empty gratification of dress to a sense of duty, and to prefer the virtues of their profession to the display of hoods of silk, of bands round the waist, of rings on the fingers, and of fillets round the feet.

Even St. Dunstan never succeeded in curbing the female love of elegant costume. During the reign of king Edgar, Ethelwold, bishop of Winchester, saw at her father's court the abbess Edith, magnificently dressed, in utter disregard of her monastic vows. "Daughter," said the prelate, "the spouse whom you have chosen delights not in external pomp. It is the heart that he demands." "True, father," replied the abbess, "and my heart I have given to Him. While He possesses it, He will not be offended with external pomp."[1] The reply was not that of a worldly-minded woman, but of one who was famous for charity and piety during her life, and whom, after her death, the church enrolled in the catalogue of saints. It nevertheless shews, that the lady abbesses, as a body, were not willing to submit to ecclesiastical regulations as to their costume.

In the middle of the eighth century the character of the nun was at its lowest ebb. The love of dress, " with a view to attract strange men," which Bede prophesied

---

[1] Gotselin., *Vit. St. Eadgithæ*, apud *Vit. SS. Bened.*, sæc. v, p. 637, quoted in Lingard's *Anglo-Saxon Church*, vol. ii, p. 266. According to William of Malmesbury the lady's answer was, " I think that a mind may be as pure beneath these vestments as under your tattered furs." William of Malmesbury, *De Reg.*, lib. ii, s. 218, p. 371.

would be the ruin of the nuns, and the indecent conversation in which they indulged, bore the fruit that
might have been expected. The loss of all modesty was
followed by that of decency, and that of decency by sin
and open shame. During several centuries we find that
the royal mistresses were almost exclusively drawn from
the convent ; and that nearly all the monarchs reproached
by bishops or pontiffs with matrimonial infidelity selected
the partners of their guilt from the virgins consecrated to
God.[1] One sin led to another ; and incontinence was
too often followed by the graver crime of infanticide.[2]

Nunneries were almost abandoned about the middle of
the ninth century, and it was not till the later part of
the reign of Alfred that efforts were made for their re-
establishment. Alfred and his queen founded nunneries
at Shaftesbury and Winchester, and found it much easier
to people them with nuns than to procure monks for the
monasteries. Although from this period to the time of
Edgar convents gradually increased in number and
wealth, they can hardly be said to have flourished. Incessant civil warfare, and the repeated invasions of the Danes,
were drawbacks to their prosperity. During the reign of
Edgar, however, their number was greatly increased, their
discipline was partially restored by the energy of Dunstan, and wealth, power, and dignity, flowed in upon them.

In considering the influence of clerical and monastic
institutions on domestic life, it is fair to exclude the era

[1] Dr. Hook (*Lives of Archbishops
of Canter.*, i, 217) tells us that Ethelbald's harem was filled with nuns
whom he had seduced : and Boniface
says, " Quod hoc scelus ignominiæ
maxime cum sanctimonialibus et
sacratis Deo virginibus per monas-
teria commissum sit." Bonifacii
Opera, i, 132.

[2] Dum illæ meretrices, sive monas-
teriales, sive seculares, male conceptas
soboles in peccatis genuerint, eas
sæpe maxime ex parte occidunt, non
implentes Christi ecclesias filiis adop-
tivis, sed tumulos corporibus et in-
feros miseris animabus satiantes.
Bonifacii *Opera*, i, p. 133 and 137 ;
William of Malmesbury, b. i, c. 4 ;
Council of Aix-la-Chapelle, c. 14 ;
Wilkins, *Concilia*, i, 88.

of king Ecgbert, in which cathedrals and monasteries were filled with a body of men who were priests and monks in name only.

The influence which the clergy exercised in improving the relative position of husband and wife, in restraining the marriage of near relations, and in limiting the right of repudiation, has been already mentioned. To them children were almost exclusively indebted for all the education that could be obtained ; and their noble struggles against domestic slavery did much to alleviate the sufferings of the conquered and oppressed.

Liberal as was the hospitality of kings and nobles, that of the monks was even more so. Every traveller found at the monastery a hearty welcome, and every starving beggar obtained food and succour. All the literature and learning of the country was contained within these sacred walls, and every art and science, of which anything was known, was there, and there only, cultivated.

It was to the monks that our fathers were indebted, not only for all they knew of architecture and painting, but for many improvements in agriculture, draining, road-making, building, smiths' work, cabinet work, and other practical matters.

In the monasteries the science of medicine was carefully studied. For many centuries the physician was commonly a monk, and the monastery was not only the workhouse, but the hospital and dispensary of the district.

That the clergy and monks were ambitious and rapacious cannot be denied, and that they had recourse to iniquitous means for obtaining power and wealth is equally certain ; but these vices were rather the vices of an age than the peculiarities of an institution. That monasticism had any great influence in promoting the sobriety of the age may be fairly doubted. The laity

were as drunken as they could be, and the bulk of the
clergy were no less so. Its effect on female morality
was not more advantageous. A celibate clergy, careless
of continence, and the unnatural restrictions of conventual
life, had a mischievous influence on the character of
women; whilst the doctrine that there is something pious
in uncleanly personal habits and an untidy home could
not have tended to domestic comfort ; nor was the marvellous skill in needlework which was acquired by the
mass of English women through the teaching of the nuns,
a sufficient set-off to the absence of cleanliness which their
precepts and example inculcated.

CHAPTER IX.

THE PILGRIM.

THE habits of the Anglo-Saxons in the time of St. Augustine were so migratory, and their love of travel and adventure so strong, that a very small temptation was sufficient to induce them to undertake pilgrimages to foreign lands. The early converts had a natural desire to visit the places rendered sacred by the birth, miracles, and crucifixion of our Saviour ; and they were taught to look upon Rome, the burial-place of St. Peter and St. Paul, and the seat of Christ's successor and vice-regent upon earth, with almost equal reverence. The interest which the Anglo-Saxon converts, in common with all others, felt in gazing on the tombs of the apostles and martyrs, was enhanced by the belief that the souls of the dead hovered around their graves, and that when standing on the spot where the bodies of the saints were buried, they held communion with their spirits.

The first Anglo-Saxon pilgrim, of whom we have any record, who succeeded in reaching Jerusalem, was St. Willibald, of whose sufferings and adventures we have a most interesting account dictated by himself to a nun of Heidenheim, and admirably retold by Dr. Lingard in his *History of the Anglo-Saxon Church.*[1]

---

[1] Lingard's *Anglo.-Sax. Church*, vol. ii, p. 117, *et seq.*

The earliest pilgrimages appear to have been voluntary, and to have been undertaken either with a view to obtain pardon for sin, in discharge of a religious vow, or for the gratification of religious sentiment. Of the accounts left us, several present touching stories of simple piety.[1]

At an early period, however, many pilgrimages were compulsory, being ordained by the church as penances, or recommended by the state as a courteous form of banishment. These penal or penitential pilgrimages were introduced into England from Ireland about the beginning of the eighth century.[2] They were at first imposed as the penalty for striking a bishop or other dignified ecclesiastic, and might be redeemed by submission to the tonsure and taking monastic vows. They were then extended to the offence of having possession of goods stolen from the church, and as an optional substitution for the loss of a hand and indefinite imprisonment. These were, however, merely ecclesiastical regulations, and it may fairly be doubted whether in the eighth century the church had the power of giving practical effect to its sentences. It was not till the time of Dunstan that compulsory pilgrimages were decreed by the civil law. In his era, any one who killed an ecclesiastic or his own nearest kinsman, was compelled to perform a pilgrimage to Rome, and there place himself at the mercy of the pope, and suffer such sentence as his holiness might decree.[3]

There was one essential difference between the voluntary and penal pilgrimages; the former were made in comparative comfort, while the latter had always to be undergone in some painful manner. The penal pilgrim

---

[1] See the account of the pilgrimage of the aged Ceolfrith, abbot of Wearmouth. Bede, *Vita Sancti Ceolfrith Abbatis, Opera Minora*, p. 318-344.

[2] Ecgb. *Excerpt.*, c. lxii and lxxix; Ecgbert. *Pœnit.*, iv, 6, Thorpe, ii, 377; Theod. *Pœnit.*, iii, 6, xxi, 9.

[3] *Modus Impon. Pœnit.*, s. 27, Thorpe, ii, 273.

was forbidden to eat meat, to use hot water, or to cleanse his hair or nails. In addition to this, he sometimes had to make the journey naked and in chains, or to receive stripes on his hand every day.[1] These last were usually commuted for the punishment of kneeling down at certain times, and dashing the palms of the hand against the ground. The pilgrims so punished were known by the name of "palmati."[2] If the penances were inflicted for the murder of a near relative, the sword with which the offence was committed was hammered out into a chain, which was twisted round the neck and limbs of the offender.[3] The effect of the hard iron, which rapidly became rusty, wore into the flesh, and produced ulceration, must have been terrible. Reginald of Durham gives a most horrible account of one of these pilgrims, who was miraculously released from his fetters at the tomb of St. Cuthbert.[4] King Ethelwulf, on his pilgrimage to Rome, obtained a decree from the pope that no Englishman was thenceforth to suffer this punishment out of his own country.[5]

The penal pilgrimage, like every penalty inflicted by the Anglo-Saxon church, might be bought off for money; and the rich and powerful could escape punishment at a cost proportionate to their means and the cupidity of their spiritual advisers.[6]

If pilgrimages owed their origin to religious feeling, this sentiment soon became alloyed with worldly considerations; and these increased so rapidly, that at last

---

[1] Charlemagne forbad these naked pilgrimages. Non sinantur vagari isti nudi cum ferro, qui dicuntur sedata penitentia ire vagantes. Du Cange, v. Peregrinati.

[2] Ecg. Pœnit., iv, c. 6, Thorpe, ii, p. 377; Theod. Pœnit., iii, 6, and xxi, 9; Theod. Capit., p. 311; Pœnit. Canons, c. 38; Du Cange, voce Pal-

mati.

[3] Acta Benedic. Sœc., iv, t. ii, p. 72; Lappenberg, Anglo-Saxon Kings, vol. ii, p. 26.

[4] Reginald. Dunelm., Libellus, etc., c. 94.

[5] Lappenberg's Anglo-Sax. Kings, vol, ii, c. 8.

[6] Nov. Gloss. Du Cang., v. Peregrini.

the religious element could hardly be said to preponderate. Many pilgrims left their native country from prudential motives. Persons who were pursued by the deadly vengeance of the relatives of those they had slain ; or who had levied unsuccessful war, open or covert, on the powers that were ; or had incurred debts they could not pay, found it expedient to adopt the garb of the pilgrim, and wander to Rome, Jerusalem, or Compostella. The commercial spirit, ever strong in the Anglo-Saxon character, turned many pilgrimages into journeys of mercantile speculation ; and the ambition and warlike habits of the more powerful barons often converted them into military or political forays.

It has been repeatedly stated in these pages that there was nothing that an Anglo-Saxon might not do vicariously. As he might perform any other penance by deputy, it was natural and consistent that he should make pilgrimages· in the same manner. The exercise of this privilege gave rise to a class of professional pilgrims, who earned their living by doing penitential pilgrimages for those who had been condemned to them. It is easy to guess how these substitutes performed their work. In addition to the pilgrimages the motives of which were either good or indifferent, there were, at the latest period, many that were undertaken solely with a view to extortion or debauchery. Whenever a bishop or an earl thought fit to announce that he was about to start on a pilgrimage, he claimed the right of raising by a tax on his tenants the probable expenses of his journey. In those times a man could not travel without a considerable retinue of servants, and he required numerous expensive gifts wherewith to purchase the goodwill of the kings or princes through whose territory he passed, so that the amount demanded of his tenants was generally very considerable. As every irresponsible privilege is sure to be abused, it became the custom of those lords who were in want of money to be suddenly conscience-stricken, to vow a pilgrimage to Rome or Jerusalem, and having levied upon their tenants the probable cost of their journey, to wander as far as London or Paris, and then discover some insurmountable obstacle to their going any farther. This abuse was carried to such an extent that the "levying of aids," with a view to pilgrimages, was forbidden.[1]

In the beginning of the eighth century the mania for pilgrimages to Rome was at its height. Kings abandoned their thrones, bishops their flocks, nobles their estates, and serfs fled from their duties, that they might behold the splendours of the Imperial City, and receive the benediction of St. Peter. Ceadwalla, king of the West Saxons, resigned his throne and departed for Rome, where he received baptism from the hands of the supreme pontiff, and "being still in his white garments fell sick and died."[2] His successor, Ina, also abandoned his kingdom, and undertook a pilgrimage to Rome, "where he grew old, clothed in a plebeian habit, among beggars." "The same thing" (the venerable Bede tells us) "was done about the same time through the zeal of many of the English nation, noble and ignoble, laity and clergy, men and women."[3]

The passion for pilgrimages diminished rapidly during the reign of Ecgbert and his sons. The ravages of the Danes, the destruction of religious seminaries, and the dispersion of the clergy, had cooled the religious zeal of the nation ; and the genius and perseverance of England's

---

[1] Gaufridi de Coldingham, *Hist. Dunelm.*, p. 723 ; *Concil. Cabilon.* (an. 813), c. 45.

[2] The baptismal white headdress, or chrysome, was removed on the eighth day after baptism. *Ang.-Sax. Chron.*, A.D. 688.

[3] Bede, *Hist. Eccles.*, lib. v, c. 7.

greatest monarch had enlisted all the energy and spirit of the country in its military defence.

From the reign of Ethelwolf to that of Cnut, we hear nothing of royal pilgrimages, and in the reign of king Alfred there was one year in which not a single pilgrim started for Rome, and the letters usually entrusted to them had to be sent by special messengers ; but when a period of comparative peace and prosperity returned, the passion for foreign pilgrimages revived also. It reached its height in Cnut's reign, who fostered it both by precept and example. From his time downwards we repeatedly hear of royal pilgrimages, but oftener as vowed than as performed.

To the last of these we are indebted for one of the most stately and famous monuments that adorn our metropolis. Edward the Confessor, wearied with the anxieties of his royal life, vowed a pilgrimage to Rome, of which his nobles and council prevented the performance. Unable to undertake the journey himself, he sent the bishops of Sherborne and Worcester in his stead, on whose intercession Leo IX released him from his vow, on condition of his erecting a minster in honour of St. Peter and St. Paul. In discharge of this obligation, he erected on the ruins of a church built by Sæberht, king of Essex, the splendid abbey of Westminster.[1]

Pilgrimages were not undertaken without great preparation. Previous to departing on his journey, the pilgrim made a formal confession of his sins, and received absolution ; though, if he were a grievous sinner, this was not granted him till his penance was partially performed and he had shown signs of repentance.

Pilgrims were everywhere known by their costume,

---

[1] *Saxon Chron.*, A.D. 1066. Flor. ap. Twysden, *Decem Scriptores*, p. Wigorn., A.D. 1065. Ailred. Rieval. 379, s. 9.

which was nearly the same in all countries. The two distinguishing articles were the *pera* or scrip, and the *bourdon* or staff.

The scrip was merely a pouch or wallet, in which were carried articles of absolute necessity, and it ought to have constituted the whole of the pilgrim's baggage. These scrips were originally of untanned leather, and of the coarsest and most humble construction; but those whom too much humility, even in garments, did not suit, indulged in scrips of gold.[1] They were attached to a scarf which passed over the shoulder, and were generally worn hanging down in front, though the Anglo-Saxon wore his at the side.[2]

In addition to the scrip, the pilgrim always carried what was called under the Normans a *bourdon* or staff. At first this was merely an alpen-stock, or plain staff, about six or seven feet long, with a nail at one end as an assistance in climbing, and a knob at the other, possibly for defensive purposes; and a little above the middle was a second knob, which afforded a convenient purchase to the hand in holding or flourishing the staff. After a certain period, the bourdon appears to have been made of two pieces of wood joined together and fastened near the middle by a thick band or ring; and one of these pieces was occasionally hollowed out at the end so as to serve the purpose of a pipe for pitching the key-note when the pilgrims sang psalms.

This simple instrument was destined to gradual improvement and to an honoured life. After a short time

---

[1] Du Cange, v. *Scarcella*.

[2] These scarves were worn by crusading pilgrims and knights *over the breastplate*, whence they became a part of the regular costume of an officer of rank, and were the origin of the military scarves worn at the present day. The French are said to have worn white scarves; the Spaniards to have preferred them red; the Bavarians and Catalans black; and the inhabitants of the Rhine countries, the Danes and the English, blue. Grose's *Military Antiq.*, vol. i, p. 362.

it was used by the pilgrims to sustain the "drone base," or "bourdon," under the voice-part of their songs, the continuity of which renders the noise of bagpipes so detestable, but which the Anglo-Saxons then, as the Highlanders now, found peculiarly agreeable. As from their numbers the majority of Anglo-Saxon singers could do nothing but join in chorus, and as they naturally attached supreme importance to their own share in the performance, the name of bourdon was eventually bestowed on the chorus, which was then a constant iteration of a leading sentiment, and has descended to us slightly corrupted in the common phrase, "the burden of the song."[1] The "bourdon" was improved until it became a species of flute, known as "the pilgrim's staff," by which name it is mentioned as late as the reign of king Henry VIII.[2]

Some pilgrims, possibly more prudent than musical, applied the hollow of the staff to another purpose. They used it as a sort of porte-monnaie, in which they concealed their money. This practice is said to have originated with the pilgrims to Compostella, a notion which is borne out by the Solomon-like judgment delivered by Sancho Panza when he shrewdly administered judgment in his island of Barataria.

In addition to the articles already mentioned, the pilgrims wore, as a distinguishing garment, a long coarse robe of shaggy stuff, called "sclavina," from its being ordinarily worn by slaves. The female pilgrims wore a similar garment, called "scrobula," which reached to the

---

[1] Hawkins's *Hist. of Music*, vol. iii, p. 274; Burney's *Hist. of Music*, vol. ii, p. 326.

[2] A curious reason for the use of the pipe in pilgrimages is found in the state trials (Trial of William Thorpe), "I say to thee, that it is right well done that pilgremys have with them both syngers and also pypers, that whare one of them, that goeth bare-foote, striketh his too upon a stone and hurteth him sore and maketh hym to blede, it is well done that he or his fellowe begyn then a song, or else take out of his bosome a bagge-pype, for to drive away with such myrthe the hurt of his fellowe." Harleian MS., No. 1419, fol. 200.

ground. Neither sex wore linen, but substituted woollen garments for those usually made of that material, and both sexes went barefooted.[1]

The conduct of the pilgrims on their journey was not always such as to merit approbation, though some palliation may be found for it in the notions of religion which then existed. Prayer at the shrines of saints, psalm-singing, insulting Jews, and personal uncleanness, were esteemed religious practices : while gambling among the men, and licentiousness among the women, were often indulged in to while away the tedium of their journeys.[2]

In all the accounts which we have of pilgrimages, the earnest prayers and enthusiastic ejaculations which were uttered, the tears which were shed, and the kisses which were bestowed at the tombs of the various saints whose last resting-places were visited, form a considerable portion of the narrative. At Rome, Jerusalem, and Compostella, the pilgrims usually indulged in many days of pious ecstacy and exciting religious exercises.

They deemed it a duty to annoy and insult Jews wherever they met them. The Jews had insulted, persecuted, and slain our Saviour, and to revenge these crimes on the descendants of the offenders was incumbent on all who bore the cross.

Dirty personal habits were also considered highly meritorious. The pilgrims rarely washed; and the Anglo-Saxons, probably, less often than the rest, because they

---

[1] Theodori Archiep. *Pœniten.*, i. " In orientalibus vero, id est Germaniæ Saxoniæque partibus, ... si parricida extiterit, perigrationem suscipiens, nudipes laneisque indutus perambulat, pane et aqua atque holeribus contentus." See also Canons under Edgar, *De Modo Imponen. Pœnit.*, s. 10, Thorpe, ii, p. 281.

[2] During their journey they amused themselves by singing psalms and less grave songs. One song called " Ultreia" was so famous with them, that to sing " Ultreia, ultreia" was another phrase for going a pilgrimage. Unfortunately we know nothing of this song but its name. Du Cange, *v. Ultreia;* Duchesne, *v. Ultreia.*

hated cold baths, which were unsuited to their climate, and warm water was forbidden. Among the many acts of piety for which Godric of Finchale was famous, there was none on which he prided himself more highly than his disregard of cleanliness ; he boasted that he had abstained from all ablutions from the time he left England until he washed in the river Jordan.

As the Anglo-Saxon prided himself on the length and beauty of his hair, he considered it praiseworthy to leave it undressed and unattended to during the whole of his journey. He also abstained from cutting and cleaning his nails.[1]

Pilgrims were exempted from paying toll on any roads or rivers along which they passed, and had the right to have their baggage carried gratuitously in merchants' vessels.[2] They had also a claim to hospitality wherever they travelled, from all persons, willing or unwilling.[3] The monasteries always welcomed them, and gave them three days' bread and lodging and rest, without questioning them whence they came or whither they were going ; and in addition to the establishments at which they were casually relieved, there were numerous hospitals founded with a sole view to their assistance.[4] The earliest and most renowned of these hospitals was one founded at Rome, A.D. 727, by Ina, king of Wessex, whose abdication and journey to Rome have been already mentioned. It was for several centuries famous for its magnificence and misfortunes under the name of the " Schola Saxonum." It was burnt down and rebuilt an almost incredible number of times, and existed at a very recent period under the modernised title of " Hospitale di S[to] Spirito in Vico di Sassio."

---

[1] *Script. post Bedam*, 464, a.
[2] Baronii *Annal.*, an. 755, xlvi.
[3] *Capit. Caroli Mag.*, c. 27.
[4] The hospital of Ledbury in Herefordshire was so founded. Dugdale's *Monasticon*, vol. ii, p. 453.

The early pilgrimages were almost exclusively to Rome or Jerusalem ; the later were often to the shrine of St. James of Compostella or to that of some native saint. The Anglo-Saxon pilgrims to Jerusalem generally went by sea to Marseilles, and made their way thence to the holy city. Sometimes they went overland, but both ways were beset with dangers. The journey by sea was dangerous from its duration, the miserable character of the ships, their overcrowded state, and the comparative ignorance of navigation which then existed. A very large proportion of the pilgrims who travelled by sea perished by shipwreck or starvation. Those who journeyed by land encountered no less perils. The length of a pilgrimage from England to Jerusalem was estimated at three thousand miles, though, after the conversion of the Hungarians to Christianity in the tenth century, the length of the journey was shortened and the dangers diminished. The most perilous part of the journey to Rome was the passage of the Alps. Here nature and man combined to try the courage of the pilgrim, for, when he escaped the severity of the climate, he fell into the hands of men even more inexorable. The passes were infested by bands of brigands, in the pay of robber chieftains, who waylaid the travellers and deprived them of everything they possessed. It was in vain that captive bishops poured forth among the terrors of the Alps the eloquence that had charmed great cities, or that they preached the duties of hospitality, and expounded to ignorant heathen the solemn decrees of great Catholic councils for the protection and veneration of pilgrims. Their captors cared for none of these things, and when they permitted their venerable victims to escape with their lives, had nothing on their consciences but a vague suspicion that they had treated them with culpable indulgence. St. Elphege fell into the hands of these

wretches as he entered Italy, and was robbed of everything he had.[1] The bishops of York, Hereford, Wells,
and the earl of Northumberland, were hardly more fortunate, and were plundered in the same place on their
return home. Ealdred, bishop of Winchester, who was
not too well qualified for the duties he undertook, was,
through the influence of the Anglo-Saxon party, made
archbishop of York in the reign of Edward the Confessor.
He started for Rome, to obtain the pall from the supreme
pontiff, accompanied by earl Tostig, the brother of
Harold. On his arrival, the pope refused him the inves-
titure he sought, either in consequence of Norman influence, or of the charges of simony and ignorance brought
against him. Returning over the Alps, the bishop and
earl fell in with robbers, who stripped them of everything
but their clothes. This enraged the brother of the great
Saxon earl, who indignantly complained that, though the
pope exercised tyrannical authority over kings and princes
(provided they were suppliant), he had not real power
enough to keep in order the beggarly gangs of thieves who
infested his highways, and he added a vow that, until
matters were mended, not a farthing of Peter's pence should
find its way from England to Rome. So great was the
estimate of the earl's power, that to assuage his wrath and
deprecate his threats, the pope sent Ealdred the pall,
which he had only just refused him ; a proceeding which
cost much less than establishing an Italian police. On
the occasions just referred to, the travellers escaped with
their lives, but this was far from being the general rule.

The pilgrims endeavoured to diminish the dangers of
the journey by travelling in immense numbers ; but the
precautions that protected them from the sword increased
their liability to famine and pestilence. It was impossible

[1] Osbern, *Vit. S. Elphegi*, p. 129.

that every miserable village at which they stopped could afford accommodation for so numerous a body ; nor could they have been welcome even in the largest and wealthiest towns, as they objected to pay for either food or lodging, and claimed to be entertained " for charity and the love of God." This claim was the more unreasonable, as they sometimes carried with them considerable wealth. We have a very curious account of one of these gigantic pilgrimages.

In the reign of Edward the Confessor it was noised through Europe that an immense pilgrimage was to be undertaken to Jerusalem from the central cities of Germany. The rumour reached the court of William, duke of Normandy, and fired the imagination of Ingulphus, afterwards abbot of Croyland, who, as private secretary to the duke, held supreme rule there. Ingulphus, having collected a party of thirty knights and prelates, who recognized him as their leader, with their necessary attendants, travelled to Mentz, where they arrived in time to form part of the enormous band, or rather army, of pilgrims then starting for the Holy Land. On the feast of St. Martin, A.D. 1069, no fewer than seven thousand persons, under the guidance of the archbishop of Mentz and the bishops of Utrecht, Bamberg, and Ratisbon, started on their pilgrimage. There was not at first much evidence of humiliation, poverty, or penance, in their mode of travelling. The ecclesiastics journeyed in great state. At every place where they stopped, they wore their palls and splendid vestments, and ate and drank exclusively from gold and silver vessels. They travelled prosperously until they reached Constantinople, where they visited the church of St. Sophia, "and kissed its sanctuaries, infinite in number." From Constantinople they passed over into Asia Minor, and here their troubles began. The Arabs, attracted by a rumour of their immense riches, fell upon them on Good Friday, plundered them of a large portion of their wealth, and slew the greater number of them. The rest took refuge in a deserted castle, where they defended themselves for some time with stones and staves, and were ultimately rescued by a chieftain whom they bribed to escort them to Jerusalem. Here they were in as great danger as in the mountains, and after much peril and anxiety they purchased an escort to Joppa, where they fell in with a fleet of Genoese merchantmen, who landed them in Apulia. Thence they made their way to Rome, worshipped at the shrines of the apostles, and then departed homeward. In Italy, the pilgrims, who had suffered so much together, parted in great sorrow, and with a multitude of kisses, some for Germany and some for France. Of the seven thousand who had started on the journey, not two thousand returned home. Among the survivors was Ingulphus, who has left a narrative of his adventures, from which this account is taken. Towards the close of the Anglo-Saxon era, Jerusalem was as dangerous as the route thither, for the Saracens had overrun the Holy Land, and whenever they could they seized and sold the pilgrims as slaves.

The custom of making pilgrimages had a considerable influence on the domestic character of the Anglo-Saxons ; improving it in some respects, and in others doing it great damage. It brought to the Anglo-Saxon home a large amount of intellectual knowledge, and many comforts, but it tended to diminish those domestic virtues which are its greatest blessing.

The value of the knowledge for which we are indebted to the pilgrims can hardly be exaggerated. Many of their journeys, though nominally religious, were undertaken almost entirely with a view of procuring books for monasteries ; and the pilgrims returned laden, not only with theological works, but with the classic writings of Greece and Rome. To these they added scientific books on various subjects, and among others medical works, of which the Anglo-Saxons were much in need. They did not confine themselves to the importation of books ; they brought with them holy relics, gold and silver ornaments, and garments. To them we are indebted for the introduction of stained glass into England, the importation of foreign marbles and innumerable articles of every degree of value, from musical instruments and medical drugs down to such humble matters as lanterns and shoe-blacking. Against these advantages we have to set off several grave mischiefs. The military defence of the country was endangered by the absence of her bravest and most adventurous sons ; and the church suffered by the withdrawal of her most learned and zealous clergy. The country was also impoverished by the enormous sums taken abroad to purchase protection in the countries through which the pilgrims passed, and to make offerings at the shrines they visited. These payments diminished so much the amount offered to the churches in England, that the clergy soon began to preach the superiority of domestic over foreign pilgrimages.

The pilgrims filled one most important office ; they were at once the postmen and newspapers of the age. They carried not only all private letters, but the dispatches of sovereigns, and bore verbal messages for the far more numerous body of the public who were unable to read or write. They also collected historical, theological, and political information, and retailed it for the benefit of their friends at home. That they acquired

and brought home a great deal that was true, cannot
be doubted, but that they invented an incredible mass
of falsehoods is equally certain. It was through their
liberality of invention that the once honoured name of
"storyteller" acquired the unflattering signification it
now bears ; and there were eminent religious teachers
who considered that the inveterate habit of telling un-
truths which the pilgrims acquired more than counterbalanced any good they derived from their labours. "If
they went one month on pilgrimage," we are told, "they
spent the next six in jangling, half tale-telling, and half
lying." The influence of these journeys was disadvan-
tageous to the Anglo-Saxon home in two respects. It
encouraged in the men a love of wandering, and a taste
for undomesticated habits ; and it induced in the women
a disregard for that severe chastity which at one time
they so universally practised at home.

Pilgrimages, at a time when no conveniences for travelling existed, were peculiarly unsuited to women, and they
must have suffered great hardships on their journeys.
Carriages were not to be had, and they had to travel on
foot, with the aid of an occasional lift on the shoulders of
the men. There were no inns, unless a few miserable ale-
shops in villages, scattered far and wide, could be so called ;
and the pilgrims had to depend on the hospitality of the
monasteries which at long distances from one another
were to be found on the route ; so that they frequently
slept on the bare ground. There was no opportunity of
observing those decencies of life, which are necessary to
female modesty, and the loss of modesty and decency
resulted in vice and open shame.

The conduct of the Anglo-Saxon female pilgrims was
so bad, that it aroused the indignation of the bishops
through whose dioceses they passed, and so early as the

seventh century, St. Boniface, the apostle of the Germans, wrote to Cuthbert, archbishop of Canterbury, exhorting him to put an end to female pilgrimages altogether. He complains that there was not a single town in France, Gaul, or Lombardy, where there were not English female pilgrims earning the wages of prostitution.[1]

There can, however, be but little doubt that, on the balance, the influence of foreign pilgrimages was advantageous to the domestic life of the Saxon. The immense increase of knowledge, the expansion of ideas, the experience of improved architecture, furniture, food, clothes, and every convenience of civilised life, more than counterbalanced the moral disadvantages, which, after all, were mainly confined to those who actually went abroad.

[1] *Epist. S. Bonifacii;* Spelman, *Concil.* i, 241. Dr. Lingard and Dr. Hook think that St. Boniface exaggerated. The Anglo-Saxon female pilgrims were probably not worse than their neighbours. In other parts of the world, female pilgrim and courtesan are almost synonimous terms; and the roads to Haridwara and Mecca are as fatal to the reputation of oriental ladies at the present day, as the way to Rome proved to those of Europe from the seventh to the tenth century. St. John's *Four Conquests,* vol. i, p. 327.

CHAPTER X.

PENANCES.

AMONG the numerous institutions which the clergy established in England, few ought to have had more influence
on the manners and customs of the country than that of
" penance."

The offences which rendered the sinner liable to it
were so numerous, its forms so various, and its duration
so long, that there can have been few churchmen, however
excellent, who, if the law had taken its course, would not
have passed the greater part of their lives as public penitents.

Happily for the Anglo-Saxons, the ancient and elaborate
doctrine of the Roman church, as to penance and penitents, had been very much modified long before its introduction into this country. The stages of penance and the
orders of penitents which occupy so many folios of early
catholic doctrine, the several ranks of weepers, hearers,
substrators, and costanders, with their penalties and privileges, were never known here.[1] The system of penance

---

[1] According to the Greek church,
penitents consisted of προσκλαίοντες,
ἀκροώμενοι, ὑποπίπτοντες, and συνιστάμε-
νοι, called by the Latins, flentes,
audientes, substrati, et consistentes.
According to some, there was a fifth
and highest order, who were in a
state of μέστωσις, or " completion,"
and were awaiting an opportunity of
full reconciliation by communicating.

was quite extensive and elaborate enough without them; indeed, so extensive and elaborate as generally to defeat its own ends, and render obedience to its behests impossible.

The date of its first introduction into England is a little uncertain, but it obtained its full development under archbishop Theodore, in the seventh century. Every crime known to the law, and every sin recognised by moralists, and a great many actions which were neither one nor the other, rendered the offender liable to it.

The crimes which were visited with the greatest severity were the killing or injuring a bishop or priest, robbing the clergy, rape, murder, perjury, and theft. These were all undoubtedly grave crimes, and have always been properly punished by the civil law; but in addition to these recognised offences, the doctrine of penance dealt with a series of immoralities which the law disregarded, and to which the Anglo-Saxon church gave the harsh title of "capital sins." They were eight in number, namely, pride, vain-glory, envy, anger, despondency, avarice, greediness, and luxury.

The first two of these offences require no explanation; but under the third, envy, was included a sin which must, if our fathers resembled their children, have subjected many amiable persons to punishment. Not only was "detraction" punished by three days' fasting on bread and water, but "willingly listening to scandal" incurred the same penalty. Angry words, or even mental anger unexpressed, demanded penance; and he who felt illwill towards another, was required to make him satisfaction, with a merry face and joyful heart.

The fifth "capital sin" was despondency, or as it was called in old English "accidie." He who had been guilty of this offence was enjoined to keep constantly before his mind the joy of spiritual blessings and of eternal happiness ; and if he permitted his want of liveliness to damp the cheerfulness of another, he was to make him amends and fast a day on bread and water.[1] This fast was not a long one, but yet it was hardly calculated to promote hilarity. He who was guilty of avarice was not only to fast, but to give profusely to the poor ; and if he objected to this distasteful penance, he was to fast three years. Penal gluttony was of three kinds, eating too soon, eating too much, and eating too well ; and consisted in dining before the appointed hour, eating to satiety, or indulging in exquisite or too nourishing food. The man who was guilty of the third species was to live contentedly on the coarsest food and do penance three years.[2]

In all these cases the penances were for improvement in life and morals, but they were sometimes inflicted for acts that were perfectly innocent. If a man in giving evidence swore to the best of his belief, and his statement afterwards proved untrue, he was condemned to penance; and if a man in public battle or in self-defence killed another, he was to fast forty nights.

According to the Anglo-Saxon church, penance should, in all grave cases, have been preceded by sorrow for sin, and, also, by confession, either public or private.[3] When the offender had confessed, the bishop or priest pronounced his penance according to the rules laid down in Pœnitentials published by authority.[4] If the offences were slight

---

[1] Unlæde bith and ormód
Sethe á wile
Geómrian on gihtha ;
Se bith Gode fracothest.

Wild is he and mindless
who will for ever
mourn in spirit ;
most rebellious to God.
Salomon and Saturn, p. 160.

[2] Theodori *Pœnit.*, i to xiv.
[3] Ne ænig man ne mæg synna buton andetnesse wel gebetan. Æfter andetnesse man mæg and dædbote Godes mildheortnesse ræthe geearnian, gif he mid innewearde heorte

hrofige. And thæt behreowsige thæt he thurh deofles lare ær gefremede to unrihte. *Saxon Pœnit., MS. Laud.*, 482, fo. 5.
[4] The most important Anglo-Saxon Pœnitential that has come

he absolved the penitent on his promise of obedience and
amendment ; but if the sin were grave, he did not absolve
him till the penance was in part or altogether performed.
It seems, however, that the rank and wealth of the penitent had sometimes an influence on this point.

The most common penance was fasting on bread and
water a certain number of days, months, or years ; but, for
sins against the clergy, the criminal was generally condemned to enter a monastery, and for those calculated to
provoke revenge, he was sent on one or more pilgrimages.
The penitent was usually required to abstain from going
armed, wearing shoes, or using warm baths, from eating
flesh, using stimulants, and going to church ; he was to
visit holy places, publicly and constantly to confess his sins,
implore the intercession of all he met, and to kiss no one.

Penances were also invented as occasion required to
suit the case of particular individuals. When Robert the
Devil repented of his crimes, and desired to lead a new
life, the Norman clergy, from whom he sought absolution,
confessed their inability to fix a proper penance for so
great a sinner, and referred him to the pope. He went
accordingly to Rome, and the supreme pontiff personally
heard his confession, but found himself also unequal to
the task of naming his punishment. He, therefore, sent
him to a celebrated hermit of whom his holiness took
counsel in matters of great difficulty. The hermit was
no less puzzled, and before replying prayed for divine
direction. Early in the morning he fell asleep ; an angel
then appeared to him, saying to him in this wise, " Holy

down to us is that of St. Theodore,
archbishop of Canterbury (A.D. 688).
There is also one by Ecgbert, archbishop of York, who died A.D. 766;
but it seems little more than a copy
of that of St. Theodore. There is
another Pœnitential published in

Bede's works (*Opera*, viii, 968, ed.
1612), and ascribed to him, but its
authenticity is very questionable.
There was also the Pœnitentiale Ro-
manum. These three were in general
use. Milman's *Latin Christianity*,
b. iii, c. 5.

fader, here and take hede of the message that God commandeth the; yf that Robert will be shryven of his synnes, he must kepe and counterfete the wayes of a fole, and be as he was dombe; and he may etc no manner of mete, but that he can take it from the dogges; and in this wyse, without spekynye, and counterfetynge the fole, and no thynge etynge but what he can take from the dogges, must he be tyll tyme that it plese God to show him that his synne be forgyven."[1]

There were special penances for very grave offences, such as wearing iron chains round the body, lying naked at the feet of the person offended, going always with a rope round the neck, and abstaining from every species of cleanliness. As there was supposed to be something essentially pious in dirty personal habits, the penitent was required to go "with foul mouth, filthy hands, dirty neck, undressed hair and beard, unpared nails," and clothes as uncleanly as his person. There was one special penance which must have been more popular with the clergy than the laity,—it was that of selling all the sinner possessed, bestowing one-third on the clergy, giving one-third to the poor, and retaining the remaining third for the support of himself and family.[2]

The fasts imposed on rich penitents were so numerous and of such long durations, that there could have been but few men who ought not to have fasted a great many more years than they had any reasonable prospect of living. For this state of affairs there were two remedies; fasts might be bought off or redeemed, and they might be performed vicariously.

A wealthy sinner could redeem his penance by building a church and endowing it with lands, by the emancipa-

[1] Thoms' *Early English Prose Romances,* vol. i, p. 36.

[2] Bingham's *Christ. Antiq.,* vol. vi, p. 461; Thorpe, i, 281, ii, 7.

S

tion of slaves or other works of charity, or by the purchase of intercessory masses.[1] Penances might also be redeemed by pecuniary payments, and at the time of king Edgar the following tariff was established :

One day's fast=one silver penny, or two hundred and twenty psalms.

Twelve months' fast=thirty shillings, or to purchase the freedom of a slave of that value.

Seven years' fast=two hundred and fifty psalters of psalms in twelve months.

Twelve days' fast=one mass.

Twelve months' fast=thirty masses.[2]

At a later date, the price of penance was fixed by a special bargain between the priest and his penitent.

To wealthy offenders the system of vicarious fasting was by far the most convenient. "A powerful man," when under penance, was permitted to give a huge feast to as many persons as he could bring together, and to entertain them as long as he pleased, on condition that, either before or afterwards, they assisted him in performing his fast. The directions given in king Edgar's canons are these : A powerful man is to take to him twelve men, and let them fast three days on bread, green herbs, and water ; in addition to these, he is to get, *in whatever manner he may*, seven times one hundred and twenty men, who shall also fast for him three days ; "then," says the canon, "there will be as many fasts as there are days in seven years." Having performed this mockery of a penance, "the powerful man is *to try earnestly to shed tears* and bewail his sins;" and this conclusion of his penance was, perhaps, the most difficult part of it.[3]

---

[1] *Saxon Pœnit.*, MS. *Laud.*, 482, fol. 40 b ; *Canons under king Edgar*, s. 14, Thorpe, ii, 283.

[2] *Canons under king Edgar*, ss. 18 and 19, Thorpe, ii, 286.

[3] Petri Damiani *Epist.*, lib. i, ep. 12, and lib. v, ep. 10; *Chron. Monast. Abingdon.*, ii, 63; Thorpe, ii, 287.

The mischiefs of vicarious penance were such as might have been anticipated. The whole object of penance was lost sight of; and in lieu of its being regarded as a remedy for sin, wherein confession sucketh out the poison from the wound and penance *heals* it, it was looked upon as a compensation or equivalent for sin. A notion was adopted by the laity, not only that a man was at liberty to sin, provided he was prepared to take the consequences and do penance afterwards; but also that a man, who, conscious of his frailty, had laid in a large stock of vicarious penance in anticipation of future necessity, had a right " to work it out," or spend it in sins.

Towards the end of the eighth century, a certain worldly rich man brought this question to an issue by peremptorily demanding immediate and gratuitous absolution for some sin he had committed. He alleged that if he lived three hundred years, and sinned as hard as he could, he had already earned a right to absolution by the enormous amount of vicarious fasts, psalms-singing, and alms-giving, for which he had paid, to say nothing of what he might have done himself. This demand provoked the just indignation of the Council of Cloveshoe, and the practice of purchasing a stock of vicarious penance and expending it in sin, was most properly and severely condemned.[1]

A penitent was under several grave religious disabilities. He could not claim any office of the church necessary to the enjoyment of his temporal rights; for instance, if a king, he could not be crowned; if a subject, he could not be married by any ecclesiastical ceremony.[2] On the continent it was made an excuse for dethroning kings actually crowned, as was the case of Wamba, in

---

[1] Spelman's *Concil.*, i, 247; *Concil. Cloves.*, c. 27, 28; Wilkins' *Concil.*, i, 98.
[2] *Concil. Arelat.*, c. xxxi; Labbe,

Concil. iv, 1013; Ambrose *de Pœnit.*, lib. ii, c. x; Hieron. *in Joel.*, c. ii (Venet. 1768, vol. vi, p. 193.)

Spain, and Louis le Debonaire, in France; but in England this was never attempted. Dunstan, indeed, forbad king Edgar when under penance to wear his crown, but this in no way affected his royal rights or power.

The system of penance was an enormous addition to the power of the clergy, which was already too great. It enabled them to interfere in politics, between husband and wife, and between master and servant; to exercise an irresponsible tyranny in the imposition of punishment, and to sell a discharge from it at any price and in any manner most convenient to themselves, subject to nothing but rules of their own making, of the construction and application of which they were the sole judges.

CHAPTER XI.

SUPERSTITIONS.

SECTION I.—PRIMITIVE CREED.

SUPERSTITION is one of those vague words to which a great variety of meanings has been attached. In the following pages it is used in the limited sense of an erroneous belief in supernatural beings or causes. Having its origin in an instinctive desire to trace the causes of events, and in the finite character of human knowledge, it is as universal as human nature ; and modified by the various circumstancas that influence society, it is to be found more or less intensely developed in all times and places.

As a rule, the more ignorant and timid a nation is, and the more it is under the influence of grand and terrible phenomena—such as storms, volcanoes, earthquakes, and pestilence,—the more superstitious the people are. To this species of superstition a change of creed brings no relief. The disease yields only to a general advance in knowledge. As civilisation increases, and the true sources of natural phenomena become known, an erroneous faith in supernatural causes gradually disappears ; the superstitions of medicine and jurisprudence slowly vanish, and those alone remain which cannot be conclusively resolved by human reason.

As the knowledge of physical science possessed by the Anglo-Saxons was of the most limited character, superstition, as might be expected, trespassed on the domains of metaphysics, astronomy, meteorology, medicine, jurisprudence, agriculture, and even of domestic economy and maternal duty.

If a maiden knew too little of the human heart to retain the affections of her lover, she tried the efficacy of love-potions. If a wife was, from physical defects, incapable of becoming a mother, she had recourse to philtres, as disgusting in their composition as they were barren of result. Eclipses and comets were deemed the work of monsters or hostile gods, who required to be propitiated by sacrifices or alarmed by clamour. The physician who could not cure the simplest diseases, sought a remedy in incantations or in the relics of saints ; and the judge, whose want of judicial acumen prevented him from deciding as to the guilt of a criminal, had recourse to the trial by ordeal, or, in the Norman era, to the equally absurd test of judicial combat.

Though superstition is truly said to be the child of curiosity, ignorance, and fear, yet there is another feeling not less universal, without which it would never have assumed any of its most usual forms. There is planted in the breast of man a belief in the existence of some supreme and almighty Power, the creator of the universe, and the ruler of human events ; and almost as universal is the desire to know His will, and to obey His commandments. As this first great cause is of all causes the most unfathomable, the most sublime, and the most awful, it is natural that minds at once inquiring, ignorant, and timid, should be filled with a thousand fantastic delusions as to the nature and attributes of God. Thence it arises that, though among nations equally ignorant the substance of superstition will be ever the same, yet its form and colour will vary according to their idea of the deity and of his relations to man.

There were three great eras in the history of Anglo-Saxon superstition. The first was the time of paganism ; the second, that when the chiefs were converted to a species of Christianity, and the people were said to be so ; and the third, when Christianity, sadly corrupted, was the established religion of the country.

Prior to their conversion, our forefathers worshipped the sun, moon, earth, or stars, and regarded with pious veneration all material objects from which they derived unexpected blessings. They adored the fountains that supplied them with refreshment, the trees that afforded them food and shelter, and the rare plants whose medicinal qualities they had learnt to value. These were gods to them, long before they became acquainted with the mythical deities of Scandinavia and Germany.

When the Saxons settled in England, they, of course, brought with them their mythology and pseudo-gods. The most important of these were Thor, the northern Jupiter ; Woden, the god of war ; and Friga, the goddess of love and reproduction. They also worshipped the goddess Rheda, or the spring, and Eostre (the east or brightness), in whose honour the paschal week is still called Easter. Among the evil deities whose wrath was deprecated, were Zernbock or death ; Loke or Lucifer ; Occhus Bocchus, symbolised by the common type of evil, a goat, and preserved to us in the traditions of the nursery under the name of "old bogie ;" and Occhus Nech, the water-fiend, familiar to us under his modern title of "old Nick." There was also Mara, a demon who tortured men with pain and evil visions in the night, and who is too well known by her modernised name of the "night-mare."

The occupations of these fiends were of a very coarse character. They did not consist in leading man into sin by exciting his passions or deluding his intellect, but in inflicting on him temporal loss and physical pain. "Sometimes," says an old poem, "they seize and drown the sailor ; sometimes they enter the body of a snake, sharp and piercing ; they sting the neat going about the fields ; they destroy the cattle. Sometimes in the water they pull down the horse and hew him with horns, until his heart's blood in a foaming bath of flood falls to the earth. Sometimes they fetter the hands of the doomed one. They make them heavy when forced in war against a hostile troop to preserve his life—they write upon his weapons fatal magic marks."[1]

In addition to the evil deities of the first rank, the Anglo-Saxons believed in evil spirits of a humbler class. Among these were the water-nixies—the daughters of Nech—who play so important a part in German fairy-tales. These beautiful water-spirits tempted the young hunter or fisher by their tender blandishments to seek their embraces in the waves, and then drowned him in the paternal flood, or vanished and left him to perish. Of a similar character were their brothers the Nicors, who charmed the maidens that strayed along the banks of the rivers, and then seized and drowned them. Of a more amiable disposition was the Danish Stromkarl, who from the jewelled bed of his river watched with delight the children gambolling in the adjoining meadows, and singing sweetly to them in the evening, detached from his hoary hair the sweet blossoms of the water lily, which he wafted over the surface to their hands.[2]

---

[1] *Salomon and Saturn*, Kemble's *Anglo-Saxon Dialogues*, p. 144.

[2] Kemble's *Saxons in England*, b. 1, c. 12.

All these gods and spirits were feared and worshipped, and to all of them were sacrifices offered and prayers addressed ; and though the belief in their powers was modified by the partial conversion of the Anglo-Saxons to Christianity, yet it was never altogether abandoned.

SECTION II.—CONVERSION.

In common conversation, the Anglo-Saxon nation is said to have been converted to Christianity by St. Augustine and his immediate successors ; but this phrase conveys an erroneous impression, as to the extent as well as to the nature of the change which took place in the creed of the people in the seventh century.

The persons to whom the gospel was preached were generally the king and queen, and sometimes the leading earls or eoldermen. These were persuaded and baptized, and the people, who carelessly followed the example of their chiefs, were reckoned as converts.

Among those who adopted the new faith, there were many, particularly of the female sex, who were earnest and sincere. Some of them abandoned thrones, wealth, and luxury, to practise in the convent the austerities of monasticism, while others wandered barefooted in pilgrimage to the tombs of the apostles ; but a large proportion of the chiefs were not blessed either with an extensive knowledge of Christian doctrine, or with an earnest or permanent faith. In many cases, when they found the laws of Christianity opposed to their interests or a restraint upon their passions, they re-adopted their heathen deities, and indulged in the customs of their fathers. This was the course pursued by Ethelbald, when he determined to marry his father's widow, and by many others.

The converts were also baptized without sufficient discrimination. A pirate, when captured, was permitted to save his life by submitting to the ordinance; and was afterwards expected in plundering excursions to spare ecclesiastical property. One of these marauders, to whom baptism was proposed, and who was expected to object to it as a harsh condition, replied, " He had no objection; he had been baptized nineteen times before, and he supposed the twentieth would not hurt him." This man was probably a bad specimen of a convert, but it is to be feared that there were many not much better.

The belief of a large proportion of the early Anglo-Saxon Christians in the fundamental truths of Christianity was very limited. They did not, in fact, become Christians, but they superadded a species of Christianity to their original heathendom. They received the sacrament of baptism and attended Christian worship; and at the same time they formed congregations, even in the immediate precincts of the temple, to worship the sun and moon, and to perform sacrifices to devils. In some cases, the very same church was used for the worship of the true God and for idolatrous services.[1]

---

[1] Bede's *Eccles. Hist.*, l. ii, c. 15. King Ercombert, nearly a century after the conversion of his family to Christianity, was the first person who thought it necessary to level the temples of the heathen gods and to destroy the idols they contained. Will. Malmesb., l. i, c. 1. In considering these matters, it must be recollected that St. Augustine did not endeavour to force his converts to abandon at once all their pagan beliefs and practices, but was content that they should gradually adopt in their stead Christian doctrines and customs. In the answer of pope Gregory the Great to St. Augustine's application for specific directions in certain matters, and particularly in reference to the carelessness of the Anglo-Saxons as to consanguinity in marriage, the pope forbids his dealing severely; adding, " For at this time the holy church chastises some things through zeal, and tolerates some things through meekness, and connives at some things through discretion, that so she may often by forbearance and connivance suppress the evil she disapproves." Their system was by no means inconsistent with the doctrine of the popes, under whose judicious management the festival of Pan Lupercus was merged in that of the purification, the temple of the Roman gods became a church of the blessed Virgin, and the statues of its ancient occupants, respectable representatives of the twelve apostles. *Sal. and Sat.*, i, p. 7.

SECTION III.—MIXED SUPERSTITIONS AND OBSERVANCES.

The Anglo-Saxons during every period of their history firmly believed in supernatural appearances. Every man, either sleeping or waking, had seen a spectre, although it was esteemed a great misfortune ; and scin-craft, or the art of raising spirits, was severely punished.[2] They had a great horror of dreams, to which they attached an extravagant importance. They looked upon the phantoms seen in them, not as delusions, but as existing beings sent to torment them by the goddess Mara, whom they believed to have been induced to persecute them by spells and incantations. As an antidote against them they used magical herbs, of which the mugwort (*artemisia*) was the most esteemed; and, if it is a powerful aid to digestion, it may have been of value, for the most potent spells for provoking the visits of " Mara of the night," were the heavy suppers of half cooked pork in which the Anglo-Saxons habitually indulged.

They were also firm believers in ghosts, but they did not imagine, as some of their descendants have done, that the disembodied spirits of the dead wandered about the earth to warn or terrify their former friends or foes. They fancied that the departed spirit, or the devil in his stead, entered into the corpse of the dead man, and that, rising from the violated grave, the ghost—half fiend, half flesh—walked the earth at dead of night, till the rising dawn drove him to his place of sepulture.

Alfred the Great, not long before he died, founded a monastery, in which he wished to be buried, near the cathedral of Winchester. At the time of his death, the

<hr />

[1] Will. Malmesb., l. ii, c. 4, Mr. Hardy's note, edit. Histor. Soc.

monastery was unfinished, and the king was temporarily
interred in the cathedral. With this arrangement the
deceased monarch (as the monks alleged) was dissatisfied,
and, as evidence of his displeasure, his departed spirit
nightly re-animated the royal corpse, and roamed the
precincts of the cathedral. To pacify his father's ghost
(and the monks), king Edward finished the new minster,
and removed thither the king's remains.

To these miraculous reanimations witches and wizards
were peculiarly liable. A most amusing account of a
battle for the body of a penitent witch, between the monks
and exorcists of Beverley on the one hand, and Satan and
his imps on the other, which lasted three days and three
nights, may be found in William of Malmesbury. The
enemy of mankind came off victorious, and having placed
the screaming dead body on a black horse, saddled with
sharp iron hooks, he bore it away no man knew whither.[1]

The sole remedy for this improper interference with
the dead by the prince of darkness, was to dig up the
body and burn it ; for the fiends broke open church doors,
bars, vaults, and stone coffins, and carried off thence the
dead bodies of the wicked, whom they immediately tortured. Nothing but the cremation of the body was
deemed a certain safeguard from violence. This notion
was probably East-Anglian, as the Danes not only condemned all witches and wizards to death, but caused
their bodies to be burnt, that their ghosts might not re-
visit the glimpses of the moon.[2]

The bishops did their best to suppress this superstition.
In the reign of William the Conqueror, a man died in
Buckinghamshire, leaving a widow and some relations,
and was duly buried in consecrated ground. On the
night subsequent to his burial, his re-animated corpse en-

---

[1] Will. Malmesb., l. ii, c. 13.   [2] Mallett's *Northern Antiquities*, p. 299.

tered his wife's bedroom, and not only frightened her, but nearly crushed her beneath its weight. This conduct the ill-regulated ghost repeated on subsequent nights, until the widow procured nocturnal companions. He then haunted several houses in the neighbourhood, always departing at cock-crow, unseen of many, but visible to some. As no sufficient remedy could be found, the vicinage applied, through the archdeacon, to the bishop for leave to dig up the body and burn it. The bishop disapproved of the proposal; but he granted a full episcopal pardon to the departed sinner, which was placed on the breast of the corpse. So efficacious was this, that the ghost never afterwards entered the widow's bedroom or troubled any one.[1]

SECTION IV.—MAGIC AND WITCHCRAFT.

A belief in the existence of supernatural beings, inferior to and independent of the true God, leads to an attempt to obtain the benefit of their agency and power, and is the natural origin of magic and witchcraft.

The most ancient mode of incantation consisted in the simple process of chanting or singing imprecatory verses, and must have been very harmless. The systems which succeeded this must have been very numerous; some were protective, and some aggressive; some amatory, some judicial, and a large proportion medical. A few of them were precatory, and were used to propitiate the pseudo-gods. Of these last, the following custom, which is denounced by archbishop Theodore, is among the most curious.

On the kalends of January the people held meetings for the purpose of merriment, and on these occasions the

[1] Will. of Newb., *De Rebus Anglicis*, lib. v, c. 22.

young men disguised themselves as calves or stags, by
putting on the skins and heads of these animals, and in
this state they practised magical ceremonies to propitiate
"the earth," or goddess of fertility, and to procure an
ample harvest.[1]

The Anglo-Saxons endeavoured to obtain supernatural
protection from elves and demons by the use of amulets
composed of "runes," or certain signs engraved on their
arms, or on pieces of wood or other materials. There were
pious impostors whose sole business it was to design and
compose them according to the special purpose for which
they were required. There were runic amulets to procure
victory, to preserve from poison, to relieve women in
labour, to cure bodily diseases, to dispel evil thoughts
from the mind, to dissipate melancholy, and to soften the
severity of a cruel mistress. The same signs were always
used, but their combinations were varied. For some purposes they were written from right to left; for others
from top to bottom; or in the form of a serpent, or contrary to the course of the sun, etc. After the conversion
of the nation to Christianity, the clergy sanctioned the
use of these charms, but they substituted texts for runes,
and the science of composing Christian amulets was as
carefully studied as the heathen art had previously flou-

---

[1] Theod. *Pœnitent.*, xxvii, s. 19,
Thorpe, ii, 34. It has been supposed
that this practice had its origin in
the Roman "Compitalia," said to
have been founded by Tarquinius
Priscus in honour of the Lares com-
pitales, and celebrated on the kalends
of January; and that it was, in its
turn, the origin of the feastings, etc.,
still observed on Plough Monday, and
of the Catholic ceremony of the feast
of fools. The Council of Auxerre
had decreed (A.D. 378), "Non licet
kalendas Januarii vetula aut cervolo
facere." Labb., *Concil.*, v, 917. Isidore, about the end of the sixth century says, "Tunc enim miseri homi-
nes, et, quod pejus est, etiam fideles,
sumentes species monstruosas, in
ferarum habitu transformantur, alii
fœmineo gestu demutati virilem vul-
tum effœminant." (*De Eccles. Offic.*,
lib. ii, c. 40, *Bib. Patr.*, x, 200.) A
similar passage occurs in Alcuin, *De
Divino Officino*, *Bib. Patr.*, x, 200.
See Maitland's *Dark Ages*, No. ix, p.
151 *et seq.*, where a capitular of Atto,
bishop of Vercelli, and a correspond-
ence between St. Boniface and pope
Zachary as to the superstitious observance of the kalends, are referred
to. See also Du Cange, v. *Kalendæ*.

rished. These amulets were commonly made of ribbon, in which a text of scripture or some religious sentence was sewed, or worn round the neck, or bound round some part of the person, and were believed to be antidotes against disease.[1] Of the superstitious practices adopted for the gratification of revenge, the earliest and most famous was called " stacung " (sticking), and as originally practised it was by no means an ineffective style of incantation. It consisted in sticking spikes or thorns into the detested person, with the expression of a wish that the wounded part might mortify or wither away. As the Anglo-Saxons were very reckless in the infliction of wounds, and as the spikes were inserted vigorously in the most tender parts of the person, the incantation was commonly successful, and the victim perished, in *their opinion* of the curse, but more probably of the wounds.[2] In the tenth century a widow and her son practised this species of magic with iron pins on one Elsie, who naturally or supernaturally died from the experiment. The widow, who had an ample estate, was tried for the offence, found guilty, and drowned at London Bridge ; the son escaped, but was outlawed, and their lands were forfeited to the king.[3] This mode of incantation, however, was not always safe for the parties who practised it ; for the person to be bewitched often laid violent hands on the necromancer, and revenged by anticipation his intended death. Its form was, therefore, modified and improved, and with due regard to the favourite Anglo-Saxon principle of acting and suffering vicariously. In the improved process an image of the person to be injured was manufactured of wax or indurated clay, and then either needles were driven into it, or it was placed before a fire and melted,

---

[1] Bedæ *Vita S. Cuthberti*, c. ix.

[2] Ecgbert, *Pœnit.*, lib. iv, s. 17 ; *Modus Imp. Pœnit.*, s. 38.

[3] *Codex Diplom. Anglo-Sax.*, vol. iii, p. 125, where the king's charter giving away the lands is set out.

or slowly mutilated and chopped to pieces, with impreca-
tions or incantations, and the accursed person was expected
to perish or melt away in the same manner as his image.[1]

Though incantations were generally used for evil purposes, they were sometimes employed from more amiable
motives. A married woman who desired to retain her
husband's affections, or a girl who wished to ensure the
admiration of her lover, had recourse to philtres or love-
potions.

King Alfred, in one of his translations of the metres of
Boetius, says,

> " A maiden with secret arts
> A friendly witch will seek,
> If she cannot
> In public grow up
> So that men will woo her with bracelets."

The philtres used on these occasions were often of a
very dangerous description ; and we constantly read
of the beloved object dying from the effect of them.[2]

[1] John of Salisbury, *De Nugis Cu-*
rial., lib. i, c. 12. This custom continued in use in England to a comparatively modern time. In the
reign of Henry VI, a necromancer
and witch were charged with having,
at the request of the duchess of Gloucester, " devised an image of wax representing the king, which little by
little consumed, intending thereby
to waste and destroy the king's person." In 1589 a Mrs. Dyer was charged
with practising a similar conjuration
against queen Elizabeth, whereby her
majesty suffered excessive anguish by
pains of her teeth ; and king James,
in his *Dæmonology* (book ii, c. 5),
says that " the devil teacheth how to
make pictures of wax or clay that,
by roasting thereof, the persons that
they bear the name of may be con-
tinually melted or dried away by
continual sickness."

[2] There is an account of a woman
who, having married a widower, was
desirous of weaning his affections
from his child by his first wife. She
sought a witch " who knew how to
change men's minds by arts and en-
chantments," and having bestowed
on her the customary promises and
rewards, she inquired how her husband's affections might be changed.
The wise woman prepared a love-
philtre, to be mixed with the husband's meat and drink. " His mind
in consequence became affected ; all
his love for his child was transferred
to his wife, so that not only did he
cease to notice it, but repulsed its
caresses." The wife was not satisfied
with her success, and ultimately murdered the child, and being miraculously convicted of the offence
through the agency of the abbot of
Ramsey, her husband was compelled,
as a penance, to make over a valuable estate to that abbey. *Historia
Ramesiensis*, c. 84. *Pœnit. MS.*, Bibl.
Publ. Camb., Ii, 1, 33, p. 396.

Married women, when they expected to become mothers, especially if they were of high rank, frequently consulted witches and wizards to ascertain whether their child would be male or female. There is a curious instance of this in Layamon's *Brut*.[1]

The Anglo-Saxons had great faith in lucky and unlucky days, and there was hardly any action for which some particular day was not deemed favourable. The first day of the moon, especially if it fell on a Sunday, was the most fortunate for nearly every purpose. Our forefathers also believed in omens and auguries, and in dreams, which they pretended to interpret.[2] They practised a humble species of astrology by the study of the position of the sun, moon, and stars, and pretended to foretell future events by the flight of birds; but their favourite mode of divination was by casting lots. They cut the branch of a tree into slips, and having marked them, scattered them on a white cloth; then, if the inquiry were a public one, the high priest, or, if a private one, the father of the family, having prayed to the gods, thrice raised each piece and interpreted them when raised, according to the marks found upon them.[3] At a later period, the pieces of wood were put into a box and drawn out at hazard. After the conversion of the Anglo-Saxons to Christianity, the Roman mode of practising this divination was introduced. Certain names or events were written on small pieces of wood, and were placed in an urn partially filled with water, and so small at the top that only one piece of wood could come to the surface at a

---

[1] Layamon's *Brut*, vol. i, p. 12.

[2] If a man dreamed that he had a burning candle in his hand, it was a sign of good; if that an eagle flew over his head, it was a sign of some dignity awaiting him, and the higher the eagle flew the greater the honour. The rolling of thunder at particular times had also its significance; if it happened in the evening, some great man was born, and other events were foreshadowed according to its time and place.

[3] Tacitus, *De Mor. Germ.*, c. 10.

T

time. The urn was then shaken, and the piece of wood that first came to hand was deemed to express the response of the gods.

The Roman clergy also introduced the famous mode of divination called "*Sortes Sanctorum.*" It consisted in opening the Psalms or Evangelists, hap-hazard, and accepting the first passage that the eye fell upon, as a divine response to some previous question. This system of augury was commonly made use of at the consecration of bishops; but in this respect, as in others already specified, the practices of the clergy were at variance with the laws of the church, which, from the fourth to the fourteenth century, thundered in vain against this folly.[1]

At the earliest period of their history, the Anglo-Saxons knew very little of medicine or surgery, and, therefore, trusted to charms and incantations to remedy the more important injuries and diseases ; and even in those cases in which some slight medical skill was evinced, supernatural remedies were used to give it greater efficacy.

They knew the medicinal properties of the mugwort and the savin, betony, and garden cress ; but to render them efficacious the two first had to be culled at particular times ; the betony to be gathered in August without the use of iron ; and the garden cress must have been " such as grew of itself and man sowed not."[2] After their conversion to Christianity, they continued the use of mugwort as a charm against devil-sickness and to keep off evil spirits, but it was gathered with a Pater noster and Credo in lieu of an ancient incantation.[3] Other herbs were also used as charms ; and medicines on certain occasions were drunk out of the church bell.

[1] Theod. *Capit. et Fragm.*, Thorpe, ii, 84 and 85 ; Gregor. Turon., *Hist. Franc.*, lib. iv, c. xvi; *Concil. Agath.*, c. xliii, Labb., iv, 1390 ; *Concil. Venetic.*, c. xvi, Labb., iv, 1509; *Concil. Aurel.*, l. cxxx, Labb., iv, 1409.

[2] Wright's *Biographia Ang.-Sax.*, vol. i, p. 101.

[3] Ecgb. *Pœnit.*, lib. ii, s. 23; *Pœnit., MS.*, *Bib. Pub. Camb.*, Ii. 1, 33, f. 4.

The following prescription shews in how curious a manner the monks, who were the chief physicians of the age, mingled medicine and superstition. "Take thrift-grass, betony, penny-grass, carrue, fane, fennell, christmas-wort, and borage, and make them into a potion with clear ale, sing seven masses over the plants daily, add holy water, and drop the draught into every drink that he shall drink afterwards, and sing the Psalm *Beati im-maculati*, and *Exsurgat*, and *Salvum me fac Deus*, and then let him drink the draught out of the church bell, and, after he has drunk it, let the mass-priest sing over him "*Domini sancti pater omnipotens.*"[1]

The Anglo-Saxons do not appear to have known much more of surgery than of physic, though it is curious that they knew how to prevent disfigurement from small-pox. The pustules were each pricked with a thorn and then smeared with thick wine, or honey and butter, which is said to have proved generally efficacious. Bleeding was a favourite remedy with them in many disorders, but was in general so clumsily performed as to be more dangerous than the disease. Its efficiency was supposed to depend on the day of the month on which it was performed. On certain days it was altogether useless, and on others was only efficacious if performed at particular hours. The operation was prohibited "when the light of the moon and the tide of the ocean were increasing." John of Beverley severely reproved the abbess Hereberga for allowing her daughter to be bled at this season, and was with great difficulty induced to pray over and miracu-lously heal her.[2]

All the remedies we have spoken of are to a certain extent medicinal, and might have been beneficial, though

---

[1] Wright's *Biographia Anglo-Sax.*, vol. i, p. 104.   [2] Bede, *Eccles. Hist.*, lib. v, c. iii.

they were applied in accordance with superstitious notions; but there were many which were merely superstitious, and could not under any circumstances have been of use to any one.

The most ancient of these is a remedy for fevers in children, which consisted in exposing the child on the roof of the house, or placing it in the oven, with certain mysterious and magical ceremonies, the details of which are not known.[1] Another instance may be found in the treatment, not of human beings, but of cattle. Hanging up the bones of dead animals with certain incantations was supposed to be a remedy against pestilence among sheep and oxen.

The treatment of diseases of which nothing was understood, such as epilepsy, or insanity, was wholly superstitious. They were supposed to arise from the influence of demons, and were dealt with accordingly. The Anglo-Saxons had a notion common to many nations, that evil spirits could not be conjured out of one man unless they were conjured into another, or into something else. The disease was, therefore, commonly charmed into a stick, and the stick thrown across a highway, that it might be effectually separated from the sufferer. It was supposed that the disease, or evil spirit, would enter into the first person who picked it up.[2] When the Christian clergy became influential, they took upon themselves the exclusive duty of curing insanity and epilepsy; and as they knew no more than the laity of the proper medical treat-

---

[1] Theod. *Pænit.*, xxvii, s. 14; Ecgb. *Confess.*, s. 33, Thorpe, ii ; *Pænit.*, *MS. Bibl. Publ. Camb.*, Ii. 2, 33, f. 394.

[2] Wright's *Biographia Angl.-Sax.*, vol. i, p. 103. It is curious how general this superstition is. Among the peasantry on the borders of Wales it is, or was not long ago, common to charm away warts by pricking them with a thorn, and then throwing the thorn across a highway. It is believed that the warts will pass to the first person who picks up the thorn. Children are forbidden to touch pieces of paper and other things which they find lying in the road, for fear that they should thereby catch some disease.

ment of these complaints, they were compelled to have recourse to superstitious ceremonies. There was in the church a distinct order of clergy called exorcists, whose duty it was day by day to lay hands on the insane with a view to the expulsion of the devils by whom they were supposed to be possessed ;[1] and there were numerous forms of prayer, or incantations, which were supposed to be of great power.[2]

The use of the relics of saints was recommended by the clergy as a cure for nearly every disease. A hair of a saint's beard dipped in holy water and taken inwardly was recommended as a powerful remedy for fever ; and blindness was said to have been repeatedly cured by rubbing the eyes with relics. A broken arm was mended by the application of the wood of a cross erected by St. Oswald ; and a girl was cured of a palsy by being rubbed with the dust of the spot on which he was slain. An abbess was healed of a disease which baffled all physicians by wearing the girdle of St. Cuthbert ; and innumerable cures were effected by holy water into which chips of an oak blessed by St. Oswald, or pieces of bishop Earconwald's horse litter, had been dipped. The miraculous cures said to have been performed by saints and bishops are so numerous that the accounts of them probably occupy

---

[1] See *ante*, chap. vi.

[2] " + In nomine Patris quesivi te.
+ In nomine Filii inveni te.
+ In nomine Spiritus Sancti delebo te.

+ Circumcingat te Pater + circumcingat te Filius + circumcingat te Spiritus Sanctus. + Destruat te Pater + destruat te Filius + destruat te Spiritus Sanctus. + Crux Christi te + Vultus Domini Nostri. + Super aspidem et basiliscum ambulabis, et conculcabis leonem et draconem. Adjuro te malum ex quocunque genere et per Patrem + et per Filium + et per Spiritum Sanctum et per sanctam MARIAM genetricem ejusdem Dei et Domini nostri Jhesu Christi et per c.xl.iiii.m. innocentes et per vii. dormientes Maximianum, Malchum, Martinianum, Constantinum, Dionysium, Johannem, Serapionem, et per omnes sanctos Dei, ne percutias vel affligas carnem istam. Parce famulo Dei, et Pater noster, et Quicunque vult, et evangelium. In principio—Maria Magd.—recumbentibus. Si quis diligit me—cum venerit." *Notes and Queries*, 2nd Series, vol. viii, p. 245.

more than one half of the writings of Bede and many other of the early chroniclers.

SECTION V.—ORDEALS.

Potent as was the influence of superstition on the practice of medicine, during these early ages of imperfect mental culture, it was equally powerful in that of jurisprudence.

When the Anglo-Saxons were unable to decide as to the guilt of an accused person, they had recourse to what they called the "*judicium Dei*," or trial by ordeal. To obtain the benefit of this mode of procedure, it was necessary that the accuser should swear that he believed the accused to be guilty, and that this oath should be supported by that of a certain number of friends, who swore to their belief in his statement, or to his general truthfulness.[1] In certain cases the accused was allowed to rebut the charge by a counter-oath asserting his innocence, supported by that of a certain number of "compurgators" or friends, who swore that they believed his oath to be " clean and upright." The decision was sometimes given in favour of him who produced most compurgators, or rather most oath-value ; for the value of a man's oath depended on his rank, that of a bishop, an earl, a mass-priest or a thane being worth a great number of the oaths of humbler men. If the matter could not be thus concluded, the defendant had to undergo some one of the trials by ordeal. Of these there were four kinds.

The first was called trial by the " cor-snæd " or corsned. The corsned was a small cake of consecrated barley-bread,

---

[1] A man might, however, be accused merely "per famam patriæ," or on general rumour, and compelled to clear himself by the ordeal. Glan-ville, lib. xiv, c. 1 ; *Grand Cust.*, cc. 4 and 68 ; Fleta, lib. i, c. 21 ; *Ll. Henr.*, i, c. 43 ; *Mirror*, c. 2, s. 22.

which the accused, after swearing to his innocence, was required to swallow. If, when he took it into his hands, he trembled and turned pale, and, when he attempted to swallow it, his jaws became fixed or his throat contracted, and he was unable to do so, he was pronounced guilty; but if he could eat it comfortably he was acquitted. This was the easiest form of ordeal, and was the one by which the clergy were usually tried. It seems very improbable that any man of strong nerves could ever be found guilty by it, though the instance of earl Godwin is sometimes quoted in favour of its efficiency. The earl was accused by the Norman friends of Edward the Confessor of having been a party to his brother's (prince Alfred's) murder, and *is said* to have claimed to be tried by the corsned. He swore, as it is alleged, to his innocence, and attempted to swallow the consecrated bread, but was choked in the act, and died on the spot. The story is not entitled to much credit, being probably one of the innumerable falsehoods invented by the Normans to damage the reputation of the great earl.

Another form of trial by ordeal was by cold water. When this was adopted, the accused was stripped, and his hands tied cross-wise to his feet; he was then sprinkled with holy water, and permitted to kiss the cross. A rope was then tied round him, with a knot two and a half ells from his body, and he was thrown into a pond. If he sank low enough to draw the knot under the surface he was declared innocent; if he floated, he was declared guilty. The result of this experiment must have depended very much on the vehemence with which the accused was thrown into the water, and the manner in which the ropes were held.[1]

---

[1] This form of ordeal was practised by the vulgar in one class of cases long after it ceased to be legal. Suspected witches were tried by self-ap-

There was also the ordeal by hot water. A cauldron of water with a fire under it was placed in a remote part of a church, and at a certain depth of water (fixed according to the gravity of the offence) was a stone or piece of iron. No one entered the church after the carrying in of the fire but the priest and the accused, and, when everything was ready, two friends on each side entered the church to see if the water boiled. If they were satisfied of this, they were joined by a fixed number of others, and these stood along the church on opposite sides. The priest then sprinkled them with holy water, and gave them the gospels and the cross to kiss. After this no one was to speak, but to pray to God to reveal the truth. The priest then sang the litany, and at the conclusion of the ceremony, at a signal from the priest, the accused plunged his arm into the hot water and drew out the stone. His arm was immediately bound up in a clean cloth and sealed with the seal of the church; and if, on being untied three days afterwards, the wound was clean, he was pronounced innocent; if foul, he was declared guilty.

The ordeal of hot iron was another mode of trial, and in this the same rules were observed as to the attendance of the priest and friends as in the trial by hot water. Near the fire a space was measured off equal to nine times the length of the prisoner's foot. This might possibly make a length of seven or eight feet, and this distance was subdivided by lines into three equal portions, by the first of which, where the prisoner stood, was a small heap of stones or stand of some description. So soon

pointed judges by the water ordeal, and were sometimes drowned in the course of the experiment. King James I regarded the test as sound. After enlarging on the monstrous impiety of witches, he tells us that, as they had by sin shaken off or refused to be immersed in the water of baptism, water miraculously refused to allow them to be immersed in it, and when thrown into a pond, they floated on the top instead of sinking. Brande's *Popular Antiquities*, vol. iii, p. 1 *et seq.*

as the mass was begun, a bar of iron, the weight of which depended on the crime charged, was laid in the coals, and at the last collect it was taken off and put on the stand. The accused, at a signal given by the priest, took it up and carried it the nine feet in three steps, and then let it go. His hand was then bound up in the same manner as in the hot water ordeal, and the state of the wound at the end of the three days determined the guilt or innocence of the accused.[1]

These ordeals were entirely under the control of the priesthood, and they could have had no difficulty in managing them in any way they pleased.[2] The abbey of Glastonbury is said to have been so superior in sanctity to all others, that but one man of the multitudes who were there tried by ordeal was ever found guilty. Whether this arose *solely* from the sanctity of the place is a point on which modern sceptics may differ in opinion from the good old monk who tells the story.

The opinion existed then, which is still generally held, that these trials were fraudulently conducted. When William Rufus caused forty Englishmen of good quality and fortune to be tried by the ordeal of hot iron, they all escaped unhurt, and were of course acquitted. Upon this the king declared that he would try them again by his own court, and would not abide by this pretended judgment of God, which was favourable or unfavourable at any man's

---

[1] The iron ordeal or iron proof for accused females, consisted in walking over nine redhot ploughshares. *Ll. Angl.*, tit. xiv ; *Annal. Winton.* ap. Du Cange, voce *Vomere ;* Cf. Theodor. Monach., *Hist. Reg. Narv.*, c. xxxiv, ap. Langebek, t. 5, p. 340 ; *Capit. ad Leg. Salic.*, c. ix; *Capit.*, l. iv, App. ii, c. 3; *Ll. Longobard.*, l. i, c. 10, s. 3 ; *Ll. Hen.*, i, c. 89. The service used at the ordeal is given at length in Spelman's *Glossary*, voce *Ordalium*, and at the end of

the appendix to Brown's *Fasciculus.*

[2] *Northumbrian Priests' Laws*, s. 39. In the opinion of nearly every historian, the clergy managed the ordeals according to their pleasure, and without any regard to justice ; but Dr. Lingard states that this imputation is unjust, and is supported by no contemporaneous authority : he argues that no systematic fraud could have remained undetected for six centuries.

pleasure. Henry II was so firmly convinced that these trials were unfairly managed, that he condemned any man acquitted by the ordeal to undergo half the punishment he would have undergone had he been found guilty; thus, in a case in which, had he been found guilty by the ordeal, he would have lost his hand *and* been banished, he was, when acquitted, to be banished only.[1]

At the *earliest* period of Anglo-Saxon history the accused had his choice between the various modes of ordeal; but early in the tenth century incendiaries and morth-slayers[2] were deprived of this privilege, and were compelled to submit to whichever form of ordeal the accuser selected.[3]

As the ordeal by hot iron was thought more honourable than that by boiling water, king Edward directed a man accused for the first time to be tried by fire, but one who had previously been convicted of theft, by water. And at the time when this mode of trial was rapidly wearing out, the ordeal by fire was expressly reserved for gentlemen, and that by water for churls.

Even in the trial by ordeal the Anglo-Saxon was permitted to discharge his duty vicariously and might undergo the ceremony by deputy instead of in person. When Remigius, bishop of Lincoln, was accused of treason against William the Conqueror, his servant went through the trial by ordeal successfully, and thereby cleared his master from the charge, and restored him to the king's favour.[4]

The Normans did not approve of ordeals. They knew no "judicium Dei" but the trial by battle, and they spared

---

[1] Lyttleton's *Hist. of King Henry II*, vol. iv, p. 279; Reeve's *History of the English Law*, vol. i, c. 4.

[2] "Morth" was an *attempt* at *secret* homicide, and answers to the *meurtre de guet à pens* of the French law. It has no equivalent in English.

[3] *Ll. Athelstan.*, iv, s. 6, Thorpe, i, 225; *Ll. Ethel.*, iii, 6, Thorpe, i, 297 and 313.

[4] Spelman's *Glossary*, voce *Ordalium*.

no pains to substitute it for the more ancient ceremony of the Anglo-Saxons. In a few cases they permitted the ordeal to such Englishmen as, when challenged to the trial by battle by a Norman, were unable to fight, to old men, maimed men, and women ; but, as a rule, if the accused party was unable or unwilling to do battle, he was compelled to find a deputy.

The trial by ordeal was also opposed by the popes and the higher Norman clergy. When the Council of Mentz attempted to introduce the trial by hot ploughshares in the case of suspected servants, pope Stephen the fifth immediately wrote to the bishop in condemnation of it ; and pope Alexander the second absolutely forbad it by a decree which is still extant. These prohibitions, however, had only a moral and no legal effect in England.

The trial by ordeal was never formally abolished by the legislature, but, being unsuited to the advancing spirit of the age, gradually fell into desuetude. It lingered among English customs during the eleventh and twelfth centuries, and probably ceased in the reign of king John, or in the beginning of that of Henry the third.[1] It owed its introduction into England to the grafting of Christian rites on heathen superstition ; it was at first acceptable to the laity on account of its utility in deciding disputes that must otherwise have been settled by violence, and it was afterwards valued by the clergy on account of the power and profit it brought them. It fell into disrepute partly through the distaste of the warlike Normans to any in-

[1] I think that it may be fairly considered to have ceased in the reign of Henry III. There is no evidence that it was ever used after the directions given by him to his justices in eyre to discontinue it. It is true that this order was not a legislative act, but it was quite within the administrative power of the crown as then understood. The fact that in a few charters of later years a grant of " thol, theam, *ordel*, etc.," occurs, is of no great weight, as lawyers were then, as now, in the habit of inserting a drag-net of general words at the end of particular descriptions, without much reflection on their utility.

strument of decision but their swords, and partly through the powerful opposition of the popes, but mainly because an increased knowledge of jurisprudence had familiarised the nation with more sensible and trustworthy modes of ascertaining the truth.

CHAPTER XII.

VICES AND VIRTUES.

DIFFERENT races of men, and different nations, are usually found to possess particular vices and virtues to a greater degree than others, which thus not only become characteristic peculiarities, but have a marked influence on their national character and manners, and require, therefore, to be duly considered in treating of their social history. Among such peculiarities of our Anglo-Saxon forefathers we may point out especially the qualities of honesty, temperance, hospitality, valour, cruelty, and chastity.

SECTION I.—HONESTY.

It is not probable that any nation in the state of civilisation in which the Danes and Saxons were at the earliest period of their history, should have any great regard for the rights of property. They were professedly pirates and brigands, who lived by taking possession of the lands and goods of others ; and they naturally recognised no rights but such as were derived from physical force. " That he shall take who has the power, and he shall keep who can," expressed their code.

Their system of migration was entirely founded on this idea. When a family sailed for a foreign land, they carried with them a consecrated pillar of wood, a door post of their old house, or some memory of home. On approaching land they threw it into the sea, and wherever it was cast ashore they disembarked, and challenged the proprietor of the land to fight them for it. When the owner was of kindred origin, the challenge was accepted as good temperedly as it was offered. The combat took place, the victor became the owner of the land, and the vanquished, however disappointed, had the satisfaction of knowing, that as he would have done unto others so it had been done unto him.[1]

This view of the rights of family to territory naturally extended itself to those of individuals ; and bred a floating notion that there was no great moral objection to take from another anything he was unable to defend. Let the cause have been what it may, it is certain that at the earliest period of their history the Danes and Saxons were arrant thieves, and that from first to last they were what in modern times we should consider cheats and swindlers. The infinite number of the laws against robbery, and their constantly increasing minuteness and severity, are conclusive evidence on this point.

The scientific view, which the Anglo-Saxons took of robbery by violence, is a curious illustration of the state of society. They divided thefts into three classes, corresponding very nearly to our ideas of robbery, brigandage, and razzias. The first was an offence committed by not more than seven men in a body, and was theft pure and simple ; the second was robbery by a "hloth," or gang, consisting of more than seven and not more than thirty-five ; while a band who plundered in greater numbers

[1] Dr. Dasent's *Burnt Njal;* Mallet's *Northern Antiquities*, p. 286.

constituted an "here," or little army, who were levying war on their own account.[1]

The punishment for these offences was very different, for it increased according to their dignity, or rather according to the extent in which they disturbed the public peace. Thieves were more mildly dealt with than brigands, and brigands than free-booters.

King Edgar was a terrible enemy to these moss-trooping gentry. His laws against them were ferociously cruel, and were enforced with an energy and determination of which the country had previously known nothing,[2] That they were beneficial cannot be doubted; and the story of his having caused golden bracelets to be hung up in highways, where none dared to touch them, is probably a fable which expresses in a poetic form a substantial success.

The species of property which thieves most coveted was (with the exception of jewelry and coins) cattle and slaves; and this shows that cattle-dealing and slave-dealing were among the most profitable of Anglo-Saxon occupations. Stud-mares and bee-hives (if we may trust to an inference drawn from the frequency of legislative interference) possessed great attractions for dishonest people; perhaps because the former were valuable and easily carried off, and the latter were incapable of identification. If, however, we add together all the laws against theft, other than those against cattle-stealing, we shall find that they do not amount in number to one-fourth of those enacted against this more common offence.[3]

[1] *Ll. Inæ*, 13, 14, 15, Thorpe, i, 111. A similar distinction existed on the continent, though there forty-two and not thirty-six constituted an army. *Ll. Bavar.*, tit. iii, cap. 7; Wachter's *Gloss.*, v. *Reile;* Thorpe's *Gloss.*, v. *Haraidum.*

[2] Edgar's laws against thieves were horribly severe. Their eyes were put out, nostrils slit, ears torn off, hands and feet cut off, and finally, after the scalp had been torn away, their bodies were exposed to birds and beasts of prey. *Vita S. Swithini*, *Acta Sanctorum* (Jul. 2). *Decem Scriptores*, vol. i, col. 87, 1.

[3] *Ll. Hloth. and Ead.*, c. 5 and 7, Thorpe, ii, p. 31; *Ll. With.*, c. 26; *Ll. Athelstan.*, i, iii, 6; *Ll. Alfredi*, c. 16.

Although the amount of house-breaking and cattle-lifting which takes place in a barbarous country is, to a certain extent, evidence of the *quantity* of national morality, it is no evidence of its *quality*. To estimate the honesty of a people, it is not only necessary to know to what extent they endeavoured to observe the duties it imposed, but also what they considered those duties to be.

Throughout the tenth and eleventh centuries (particularly during the reign of Edgar) the kings and bishops laboured to compel the people to be just and honest; but many of even their notions as to honesty and justice were exceedingly obscure. One of their leading ideas would seem to have been that men should act openly and above board, and that privacy or secrecy was *primâ facie* evidence of fraud. They declared that all purchases should be made in public before the reeves or other responsible authority; and that every man who brought cattle into a town must publicly declare, of his own accord, where, when, and from whom, he bought them.[1] A traveller who trespassed on another's land *privately* might be killed as a *thief*, though if he blew a horn he was merely a trespasser.[2] A man who cut down another's timber in any noiseless manner was punished as a robber; but if it were cut down with an axe, he was merely responsible for the damage.[3] "For," says the law, "an axe is an informer not a thief, and so is a horn." However illegal the mode of acquiring property may have been, publicity seems to have been regarded as a palliation of the offence, if not as a species of justification.[4]

---

[1] It is probable that this was done as much, or more, with a view to obtain fees, as from a love of honesty and justice.

[2] *Ll. With.*, 28 ; *Ll. Inæ*, 20, 21.

[3] *Ll. Athel.*, i, 3; *Edward and Guth.*, s. 3; Thorpe, i, 167 ; *Ll. Ethlredi*, ix, 27, Thorpe, i, 347; *Cnuti Ll. Ecclesias.*, s. 5, Thorpe, i, 363, ii, 465.

[4] The Danes extended this curious notion even to the gravest crimes. If a man-slayer concealed the body, he was guilty of murder, but if he openly confessed his crime, he escaped with the penalties of man-slaughter. *Ll. With.*, 28, *Ll. Inæ*, 20, 21, Thorpe, i, 117; Mallet's *North. Antiq.*, p. 362.

While, however, clandestine theft was severely punished, every species of cheating was considered allowable. The enormous mass of pseudo-charters granting lands to bishops and abbots, which are even now extant, are evidence of the extent to which forgery was practised by the clergy. It is *possible* that they considered it innocent when employed in so righteous a cause as enriching the church.

Numerous instances of most disreputable acuteness are mentioned in these pages, all of which have been handed down to us by the friends of the offender in honour of his memory. Nothing is, however, more conclusive of the moral ignorance of the age than the violence and open corruption practised in the administration of justice. Disputes were decided either by collective tribunals (such as county meetings), or by individual judges. In the former, armed violence prevailed, and in the latter, bribery. At the " things," or judicial meetings, the litigants attended armed with as many friends as they could muster. Judgment was given by the votes of the majority, and neither party hesitated to expel an antagonist's voter by force of arms. Individual judges, if not influenced to the same extent by regard for kith and kin, were most corrupt and greedy. The earls and bishops who discharged judicial functions were habitually parties to thefts committed by their dependents, and *for a consideration* protected them from punishment;[1] while thanes and sheriffs accepted money and grants of land as an introduction to their good graces. The judges, as well as the sheriffs, publicly accepted bribes from disputants and criminals;[2] and all

---

[1] St. Wilfrid by his will left one-fourth of his goods to the abbots of Ripon and Hexham, that they might therewith purchase the protection of kings and princes in their law-suits, and Ingulphus records the grant of land to a sheriff that he might favour and protect their abbey. Eddius, *Vita Wilfr.*, c. 4; *Chron. Croyland*, A.D. 1013; *Concil. Cealchythe*, c. 13 ; *Ll. Æthelredi Eccles.*, c. 8 ; Hook's *Arch. Canter.*, vol. i, p. 475.

[2] Alcuini *Opera (Epist.,* 110), p. 161, *Epist.,* 102, p. 152 ; *Ll. Bcior.,* tit. 2, c. 17; *Ll. Ripuar.,* tit. 88 ; *Adden. Lud. Pii,* 3, tit. 57, 64.

efforts to obtain the restoration of property, or the redress of grievances, were idle against those who had, and knew how to use, an ample purse.

Alfred the Great laboured diligently and honestly to check this abuse, as did his son Edward ; but their successors endeavoured to restrain it in a manner open to suspicion of insincerity. Athelstan required all thanes and reeves who accepted bribes to pay him a fine, and "to bear the disgrace ;" but he did not remove them from their office.[1] Cnut pushed the matter a little further. He fixed an amount (a hundred and twenty shillings) with which judges who accepted bribes should compound with him, *and* he deprived them of their offices ; but he expressly provided that they might repurchase them of him if they could and would.[2] These laws seem more likely to cause a division of plunder between the king and the judge, than to put a stop to bribery.

Corruption was not confined to the royal judges. The bishops loved money as dearly as the laity, and obtained it as dishonestly. In one of his royal progresses, Cnut was accompanied by a bishop of the name of Etheric. When they arrived at the royal burgh of Massington, where they intended to pass the night, it was found inadequate for their accommodation, and many of the suite, among whom was the bishop, availed themselves of the hospitality of a Dane, who was lord of the manor of Athelton. The host provided them with every luxury of the table, on which they feasted from midday till evening. The tables were then removed, and eating gave place to drinking. The bishop complimented the Dane on his estate, the loveliness of its situation, its numerous streams, its jocund meadows, the luxuriance of its pas-

---

[1] *Athelst.*, iv, 1, Thorpe i, 223. [2] *Cnuti Ll. Secul.*, 15, Thorpe, i, 385.

tures, and its wealth in every blessing of rural life. At the same time he commanded the butler to ply the Dane with liquor, and to pass the stoop to him out of his turn. The host, having been made very jovial, boasted of the value of his estate, told the number of its flocks and herds, detailed its rental, and stated the services paid by his dependants. The bishop very carelessly observed that he should like to buy just such a manor. At this the drunken Dane began to scoff—the penniless churchman buy his estate, and at that distance from his bishopric, too—well, he might have it cheap, for anything he cared —say, forty marks of gold, but the money must be paid before cockcrow ! Upon this the bishop, ably turning jest into earnest, closed with the offer, and called his followers and the Dane's wife to witness the bargain. At first the bishop seems to have thought with the Dane that it was utterly impossible to get the money in time ; but in the course of the night he succeeded in borrowing it. When the morning came he tendered it to his host, and claimed a conveyance of the estate. The Dane, having slept off the effect of his inebriety, " wickedly " refused to complete his bargain, whereon the bishop cited him before the king's judges. *On these he bestowed ten marks in gold*, and they awarded the purchase-money to the Dane, and the land to the bishop. The decree of the judges having specified the *land* only, the malevolent seller spitefully stripped the manor of all its serfs and cattle, leaving to the bishop nothing but the ground and bare walls. These he afterwards presented to the monks of Ramsey, who, in admiration of his subtlety, one after another, kissed his feet and bathed his knees with tears.[1] When the great teachers of morality had no clearer notion of honesty than this bishop displayed, it is not probable

[1] *Hist. Rames.*, Gale's *Scriptores*, iii, 441.

that their disciples possessed any very lucid ideas of its obligations.

The legitimate restraint on the dishonesty of the earls and bishops was the crown—the fountain of justice ; but some of the kings, not content with merely fining offending judges, so as indirectly to procure part of their plunder, condescended directly to accept bribes ; and with sorrow it must be added that the queens took their part in these iniquities.

A charter of Edward the Confessor in favour of the abbey of Ramsey boldly admits that the king had been bribed by the abbot to make the grant it contains. Nor was this the only occasion when that monarch listened to the eloquence of the abbot's gold. Towards the end of his reign, an English nobleman named Ailwin-the-black, of high rank and great possessions, lay upon his death-bed. Alfwin, abbot of Ramsey, visited him in his dying moments to administer the last consolations of religion, and availed himself of the opportunity to obtain from him a grant in favour of his abbey, of his four estates at Clapham, Kembeston, Kerdington, and Cravingfield. Upon Ailwin's death, the abbot proceeded to take possession of the estates, but the validity of his grant was " wickedly resisted " by Alfric, the dead man's next of kin. The dispute ought to have been decided by the county-meeting, but having regard to the high rank of the claimant, and the influence of the nobles in these assemblies, the abbot concluded that it was dangerous to leave the matter in their hands. He therefore applied to the king, and pointed out the justice of his claim and the wickedness of any opposition to it. To his arguments he added, " from the resources of a well-stored purse, twenty golden marks, with which he bought the king's favour ;" and to make assurance doubly sure, he also " presented queen

Editha with five marks of gold, that she might impress his suit upon the royal ear." On the "familiar solicitation of the queen," the king yielded. Ailwin was induced by his representations to refer his suit to his arbitration, and had no sooner done so, than Edward informed him of his intention to decide against him, and to award the lands to the abbey. The monks have recorded this tale to shew their title to the land, and the shrewdness of their excellent abbot.[1]

If the kings and bishops thus judged unjustly, what could be expected from the petty reeves who *administered justice* (?) to the humbler classes ? It is clear that nothing like honesty in its administration could have existed ; but whether the dishonesty arose from a wicked determination to do what was known to be wrong, or from an ignorance of what honesty dictates, is a point on which there may be a difference of opinion.

SECTION II.—TEMPERANCE.

A marshy land and a cold damp climate seem to provoke men to intemperate habits ; and drunkenness, which is comparatively unknown in southern Europe, has ever been the favourite vice of the chilly north.

The Germans in their primæval forests indulged in this habit to an extent that astonished the soldiers of imperial Rome ; and Tacitus, who desired to hold up their barbaric virtues as a model to his luxurious countrymen, thus describes and extenuates their practices. "To devote day and night to deep drinking," he says, "they deem a disgrace to no man. Disputes, as will be the case with people in liquor, frequently arise, and are seldom limited to abusive language. The quarrel generally ends in blood-

---

[1] *Histor. Rames.*, cc. 113 and 114, Gale's *Scriptor.*, vol. iii.

shed.   Important subjects, such as the reconciliation of
foes, family-alliances, the election of chiefs, and even
peace and war, are generally canvassed at their carousals.
The moment of conviviality, when the mind opens itself
in frank simplicity, or grows warm with brave and noble
thoughts, is, in their opinion, the true season for business.
Strangers to art and ignorant of subtlety, they speak
their sentiments without disguise.   The pleasures of the
table expand the heart, and call forth every secret.   On
the following day the subject of debate is again considered, and thus two different periods have distinct uses.
They debate when warm, and when cool decide."[1]

This habit of constant intoxication, which Tacitus so
skilfully palliates, they brought with them to England,
where it was destined to flourish during the whole period
of their history.   "Excessive drinking," says Malmesbury,
speaking of the Saxons, "was one of the common vices of
all ranks of people, in which they spent whole days and
nights without interruption."

The Danes were (if possible) still more desperate
drunkards.   In their own country they had carried this
habit to so great an excess, that even their religious ceremonies were systematically concluded with drunken
orgies.   When their sacrifices were ended, they filled and
emptied a stoop in honour of Odin, the god of victory
and war; others to Njord, and to Frege, the goddess of love
and fertility ; and to Bragi, the god of eloquence ; and
then continued to drink in honour of their gods till they
could drink no longer.[2]

On their conversion to Christianity, the clergy attempted
to put an end to this system of pious intoxication, but
finding it impossible to do so, they determined to give it
a Christian sentiment.   The converts were permitted to

---

[1] Tacitus, *De Mor. Germ.*, c. 22.   [2] Mallett's *Northern Antiquities*, c. 10.

drink at the conclusion of religious services, as they had been accustomed to do, but were required in their toast-drinking to substitute for the names of their false deities those of the true God and his saints.

Their drinking-meetings were conducted with great ceremony. The guests being seated in rows opposite to one another, a slave filled a beaker for each guest, and, when every man was served, they all rose together, sang a verse in honour of St. Stephen, St. Eric, or their patron saint, and then emptied their beakers. The cans being refilled, they commenced drinking minnæ, or memory cups, in reverence and honour of the dead. A verse was sung in worship of our Lord and Saviour, and the memory-cup reverentially emptied in His honour. Then followed a verse in praise of the Holy Virgin, and a beaker was emptied to her memory. When these toasts were disposed of, they drank brag-botes, or hero-cups, in honour of departed warriors, prefacing each with a verse or song in praise of his deeds. In the intervals between the toasts, it was customary for some one of the guests to rise, and after a speech in praise of himself, to make a vow to perform some act of desperate valour. The vows they made when drunk, we are quaintly told, they often repented when sober. No "shirking" was allowed in drinking. Every man was compelled to empty his cup, and a man who spilt more of his liquor than he could cover with his foot, was fined an "ora."[1]

Anglo-Saxon notions of hospitality were inimical to sobriety. It was the duty of the host to offer liquor to every guest, and if possible to induce him to drink to intoxication. The kings and nobles on their journeys stopped to drink at every man's house, and indulged until they were incapable of taking care of themselves. This

---

[1] Bartholinus, *Antiq. Danic.*, lib. i, c. 8.

is proved by the laws, which impose a double penalty on
any one who injures them on these occasions, and by the
number of royal assassinations which took place when
monarchs stopped to drink.[1]

In a country where deadly feuds were numerous, where
life was held very cheap, and drunkenness was universal,
it was natural that the period of a man's intoxication
should be one of danger ; and there were national peculiarities which rendered it doubly dangerous among the
Anglo-Saxons. To drink from the large stoops or cans
then in use, it was necessary to lift them with both hands,
and in this posture a man offered to his foe an excellent
opportunity of stabbing him, which was too often made
use of. There are many instances of this, of which none
is more generally known than that of the murder of
Edward the Martyr by the orders of his step-mother.

As a protection against this custom, a system of
" pledging " was introduced, relics of which remain in
our familiar customs to the present day. A man, when
about to drink, asked his neighbour to be his " pledge,"
or guardian. If he consented to do so, he rose, drew his
sword, and guarded the drinking man,[1] who afterwards,
in his turn, "pledged," or guarded his companion while
he drank.

The convivial meetings of the Anglo-Saxons were of
the most riotous description, and constantly ended in
quarrelling and bloodshed. To this their passion for practical joking largely contributed.

Among the most common jokes were throwing a rat or
weasel into the stoop of liquor as it was passed round to
the company, or taking it up and pouring the contents on
the head of one of the guests, or dashing them in his
face. If the last specimen of fun was attempted, it was

[1] Pontopidon, *Gesta et vestigia Danorum*, ii, 209; *Ll. Ethelb.*, c. 3, Thorpe, i, 5.

creditable to the joker to hit the sufferer in the eyes, as that hurt and annoyed him much more than a general ducking would have done.[1] These jokes led to so much fighting, that they were all at last forbidden by severe enactments.[2]

It was not till towards the end of the seventh or at the beginning of the eighth century that efforts were made to check universal intoxication, and the honour of the initiative belongs to Theodore, archbishop of Canterbury, and Egbert, archbishop of York. Their exertions, which sprung purely from religious motives, were aided by the kings, not with a moral view of diminishing intemperance, but from a political desire to prevent riots and bloodshed.[3]

The habits of the laity were at that time sadly intemperate, and those of the clergy were not less so. The edicts of the archbishops tell the tale of clerical intemperance more effectively than any description of it could do, and are not open to any suspicion of exaggeration or ill-will. When they determined to check it, they most properly commenced with the bishops. A bishop who was drunk to vomiting while administering the holy sacrament, was condemned to fast ninety days ; and one who was so intoxicated, as, pending the rite, to drop the sacred elements into the fire or into a river, was required to chant a hundred psalms as penance. All bishops who were " constantly and deliberately " drunk, were degraded from their office.[4] The laity were more mildly dealt with. If a man compelled another to become intoxicated *out of hospitality,* he was to do penance for twenty days ; if

---

[1] *Ll. Hloth. et Eadric,* c. 12. If any man with a cup and beer cast it on another under the eyes, let the bot be six angels. If he hold it and pour the beer on him, three angels. *Hemstra Boten, ap. v. Schwartzen-*burg, i, 107.

[2] Thorpe, i, 33, note.

[3] *Hloth. et Eadric,* 12 and 13.

[4] *Ecgb. Arch. Ebor. Pœnit.,* iv, 33, 45, 46, 47, 48 ; *Concil. Clovesh.,* xxi.

from *malice*, the same penance was enjoined as for man-slaughter. One exception from the rules of temperance was permitted, which is both curious and suggestive. "If any one," says archbishop Theodore, "in joy and glory of our Saviour's natal day, or of Easter, or in honour of any saint, become drunk to vomiting, and in so doing has taken no more than he was ordered by his *elders*, it matters nothing. If a bishop commanded him to be drunk, it is innocent, unless indeed the bishop was in the same state himself."[1] In legislating upon drunkenness, it was necessary to mark the exact state of inebriety which was to constitute a legal offence. The archbishop, there-fore, declares that a man is to be considered drunk " when his mind is quite changed, his tongue stutters, his eyes are disturbed, he has vertigo in the head, with disten-tion of stomach, followed by pain."[2] The mild edicts of Theodore were ineffectual in checking clerical intoxica-tion. Archbishop Egbert repeated and amplified them; and at a later date, Boniface, the venerable Bede, and the Council of Cloveshoe, complained bitterly of the habitual drunkenness of the clergy.[3]

During the era of misery which was occupied by foreign invasion and civil war, nothing could be done for the improvement of morals; but in the middle of the tenth century, king Edgar, or St. Dunstan in his name, endea-voured to restrain the general custom of excessive drink-ing. He prohibited the clergy from frequenting ale-shops, and imposed heavy penalties on every act of clerical in-toxication. For the benefit of the laity he is said to have introduced a very curious custom. Among men who loved liquor dearly, and who were constantly strug-gling to make one another tipsy, it was necessary that

---

[1] S. Theodor. *Pænit.*, xxvi, De ebrietate et vomitu, s. 9.
[2] Idem, s. 14.

[3] Wilkins, *Concilia*, i, 93; Bede, *Epist. Episc. Ecgb.*, s. 4.

every man should drink his own share of the liquor and no more. Where each man had his own glass this was easily managed, particularly when, as among the Anglo-Saxons, it was pointed or circular at the bottom, and would not stand on the table. Every one drank glass for glass, and on each occasion it was emptied. To prove that there were no heel-taps, it was then turned over, and the last drop poured on the drinker's thumb, or, as it was termed, he made " a pearl on his nail."[1] But where one common can was passed round, it was not easy to compel each man to drink exactly his own share ; and, with a view to effect this, either king Edgar or St. Dunstan introduced the custom of " drinking to pegs."

Pegs or pins were placed in the tankards at equal distances from one another, so that each space contained the same quantity of liquor, and every man was required at each draught to drink from one peg to another, no more and no less. If any man drank beyond his " peg," he might be desired to drink to the next ; so that an inexperienced toper, who could not measure his draughts, might be compelled, if the company wished it, to empty the tankard. It may be doubted whether this ingenious device contributed to sobriety, as the Council of London (A.D. 1102), at the instance of archbishop Anselm, forbad the clergy " to go to tippling bouts, or to drink to pegs."[2]

After the death of king Edgar the influence of the Danes on English social habits constantly increased. In war and in peace, in public and in private, the passion for three or four days of continuous intoxication

[1] Ray's *Proverbial Sayings*, p. 69

[2] William of Malmesbury, lib. ii, c. 8; *Act. Pontif. Cant.*, Twysden, p. 1647 ; Grose's *Classical Dict. of the Vulgar Tongue* (voce pinna); Cowell's *Law Dictionary;* Spelman's *Glossary*, " *Ad pinnas bibere.*" Wilkins, *Con-*

cil., 1. 383. Many of these tankards still exist. Some of them were made of oak and others of silver, and all of them held about two quarts. They had on the inside a row of seven or eight pins, one above another, from top to bottom, the space between the pins holding about half a pint.

prevailed, and was equally fatal to them in each position. Many years before this time, Alfred the Great, disguised as a gleeman, had entered their camp during one of their feasts, examined their position, and, returning to his own soldiers, had fallen upon and slaughtered them. In victory they suffered from this vice almost as severely as in defeat. In one of their latest and most powerful expeditions, they had succeeded in plundering an immense tract of country, and in particular had carried off the gold and silver plate, ornaments, and other treasures, from the wealthy abbey of Peterborough. In their way home they placed all their plunder in a church, where they held a feast to celebrate their success, and while intoxicated burned down the church and destroyed their gains.[1]

On no occasion did they indulge in greater profusion than at their wedding feasts, which usually lasted three or four days. At the wedding of Alfred the Great, festivities were so much prolonged, and carried on to so great an excess, that the king, who was, probably, the most temperate man present, was attacked by an illness from the effects of which he never recovered. King Alfred, however, was less unfortunate than one of his successors.

At a feast given by Osgod Clapha, at his "ham," or house, in Lambeth (since called Clapha-ham, or Clapham), on the marriage of his daughter Gytha to Tovi the proud, king Harthacnut drank to intoxication. Towards the conclusion of the feast he rose to propose a health, staggered, and fell back upon the ground. He was removed speechless to an adjoining room, and died a few days afterwards.[2]

The last of these wedding feasts mentioned in the *Anglo-Saxon Chronicle* ended almost as unhappily. William the Conqueror gave the heiress of William Fitz-

---

[1] *Anglo-Saxon Chron.*, anno 1070.   Flor. Wigor., anno 1042, 8th June ;
[2] *Anglo-Saxon Chron.*, anno 1042 ;   Will. Malm., lib. ii, c. 12.

Osborne in marriage to earl Ralph, and created him earl
of Norfolk and Suffolk. The earl took his bride to Norwich, the very centre of Anglo-Danish power and customs, and there held the wedding feast; but, says the
chronicle,

> "There was that bride-ale
> That was many man's bale."

In their cups the feasters grew too valiant, and determined
to throw off their allegiance to king William, who was
then in Normandy. The rebellion then plotted was
sufficiently formidable to compel the king's return to
England; he suppressed it with vigour, and having
obtained possession of the majority of the revellers, he put
out the eyes of some and punished others ignominiously.[1]

The Normans, who were a polished and temperate people, looked on these rough drinking-bouts with disgust;
but the extreme severity with which they put them down
may have arisen from the fact that they were commonly
held as a cloak for seditious assemblies called together to
plot rebellions. The banquets of the Normans were remarkable for splendour, the number and rarity of their
dishes, and their skill in cookery; but their feasting was
conducted with moderation, and no excess in drinking
was usually allowed. Under their influence intemperance
for a time decreased in England, but after a few reigns
the Saxons seem rather to have corrupted their Norman
conquerors than to have benefited by their example.

Intemperance would seem to have accompanied the
Anglo-Saxons from their native Germany; to have been
nourished by a damp climate and marshy soil; to have
been temporarily checked by the power of such of the
higher clergy as were of Italian or French origin; to
have been carried to its greatest excesses through the

---

[1] *Anglo-Saxon Chron.*, anno 1075; Will. Malm., s. iii, anno 1074.

practice and example of the Danes ; to have been again checked by the influence of the more civilised Norman ; and then, after a short time, to have burst out with undiminished virulence.

SECTION III.—HOSPITALITY.

Among the barbaric virtues of the ancient Germans, which attracted the admiration of civilized Rome, hospitality occupied an eminent place. Of Germany, Tacitus tells us that, "hospitality and convivial pleasures were nowhere so liberally enjoyed. To refuse admittance to a guest was deemed an outrage against humanity. The master of the house welcomed every stranger, and regaled him to the best of his ability. If his stock fell short, he became the visitor of his neighbour, and conducted his new acquaintance to a more plentiful table. Men did not wait to be invited, nor was it of any consequence, since a cordial reception was always certain."[1]

This virtue they brought with them to England, where it was strengthened and confirmed by the precepts of Christianity and the example of the clergy and the monks.[2]

The Anglo-Saxon monarchs were famous for their hospitality, particularly at festive seasons. At Christmas, Easter, and Whitsuntide, they kept open house for several days, entertaining all comers, high, low, rich, and poor, and the nobles imitated their example.[3]

The hospitality of the monks, if not equally profuse, was more systematic. The monasteries were open at all times and all seasons for the relief of travellers ; extra

[1] Tacitus, *De Mor. Germ.*, c. 21 ; Spelman's *Concilia*, tom. i, 276, 601.
[2] *Anglia Sacra*, tom. ii, p. 199 ; Theod. *Pœnit.*, xxv, 4 ; *Eccles. Inst.*, Thorpe, ii, 423.
[3] Leofa, who murdered king Edmund, though a robber and outlaw, appears to have entered the king's hall and seated himself at the royal table without any objection being made ; and Hereward the Saxon, when he went as a spy to the court of the king of Cornwall, joined the festive board almost unnoticed and unquestioned. Will. Malmesb., l. ii, c. 7; *De Gestis Hereward.*, c. 6.

buildings were provided for their reception, and officers appointed whose duty it was to see that they were liberally entertained, and that they conducted themselves discreetly.

There is, however, no practice, let its excellence be what it may, which is not liable to abuse. The acuteness of the Anglo-Saxons, and their custom of converting every voluntary gift or service (if often repeated) into a legal obligation, led to a gross abuse of the privileges of hospitality.

It was the custom of certain "powerful men" to receive under their roof, nominally as guests, but really as dependents, wandering criminals, who had been disowned by their own families, and could not obtain the necessary sureties for good conduct.[1] These men committed theft and other offences, and when their lords were required to make compensation, they disputed their responsibility on the ground that the offenders were *guests* and not *servants*. To remedy this it was at a very early period declared, that travellers who remained two nights in the same house were to be regarded as visitors, but, if they stopped three consecutive nights, they became members of the establishment, for whose misdoings the head of the house was answerable.[2] This law led to a customary limitation on the duration of friendly visits ; and, many centuries after its enactment, Edward the Confessor quoted as a favourite saying of the English, "two nights have a guest, three nights own him."[3]

But the custom of feigning a hyperliberal hospitality was not the most important abuse of the habits this virtue engendered. From a very early period the kings and

[1] See *ante*, p. 157-160.
[2] *Ll. Hloth et Ead.*, s. 15, Thorpe, i, 33; *Ll. Cnuti Sec.*, c. 28, Thorpe, i, 393.
[3] *Ll. Edwardi Confess.*, c. xxiii,

Thorpe, i, 452.
Verum dixit anus, quod piscis olet triduanus ;
Ejus de more simili fœtet hospes odore.
          Reliquiæ Antiquæ, i, 91.

nobles laboured to convert the free-will offerings of an
hospitable people into a legal obligation ; and these attempts, from their political and social importance, merit
more attention than they have generally received.

Of the non-political causes of war between the kings
and nobles, questions of hunting were the most important ;
but between the towns and the nobles the attempts to
enact compulsory entertainment was the grand *social*
cause of discord.   They were to a great extent the origin
of the continental wars of the eleventh and twelfth centuries, between the burghers and the nobles, and particularly of those between Frederic Barbarossa and the allied
towns of northern Italy.[1]   But there was one remarkable
difference between the continental and the Anglo-Saxon
history of this claim.   Abroad it was extended, enforced,
and ultimately recognised ; while in England it was resisted, gradually limited, and at last abandoned.[2]

Both in England and on the continent, the lives of the
most energetic monarchs, such as Charlemagne, Cnut, and
our own Edgar, were occupied with incessant journeys
through their wide dominions ; and wherever they went

---

[1] Sismondi, *Histoire des Repub-
liques Italiennes*, tom. i.

[2] *Capit. Pipini*, A.D. 793; *Baluz.
Capit.*, 535, h. i, ii; *Ll. Burgund.*, c.
xxviii, s. 1 to 6 ; *Capit. Car. Mag.*, i,
tit. 75 ; *Ll. Ripuar.*, tit. 65, s. 3 ;
Libertas Civitatum, c. 2; *De Libertate
Civ. London.*   The reason of the difference may be this.   On the continent, the right of entertainment probably arose from the Roman "jus
hospitalitatis" established by the
later emperors, whereby every one in
Germany and France was required to
entertain the soldier billeted upon
him, and to surrender to him the use
of, at first, one third, and afterwards of
one half of his house.   When the Lombards and Burgundians overran the
Roman territory and began to treat
it as their own, they found this system established, and adopted it.   A
barbarian soldier was quartered on
every Roman householder, who was
compelled not only to give up to him
half his house, but to make over to
him for his sustenance one third or
one half the produce of his farm so
long as his visit lasted.   Hence it was
that when the feudal system was developed, hospitality became an absolute seigniorial right, limited only by
the custom of particular places.   But
the Roman "jus hospitalitatis" was
established at so late a period, that
it could not have had much effect in
England; and the Romans left this
country without being conquered
and reduced to the tributary position
they occupied under the Burgundians and the Lombards.   There was
therefore in England no foundation
for a seigniorial right to unlimited
hospitality.

they claimed to live at free quarters, and to be lodged and fed at the expense of their subjects. This right was cheerfully conceded when the kings travelled on military or political affairs. But kings, of inferior power to those we have named, oftener travelled for amusement than business. They went on long hunting excursions, and compelled the residents of the neighbourhood to supply gratuitous board and lodging for themselves, their courtiers and huntsmen, and for their dogs and horses.[1] This infliction was, as against the owners of folc-land, strictly legal, and was willingly submitted to when the king was personally present; but it became intolerable when the king's foresters (having become a numerous body scattered over all England) insisted on the same rights of hospitality, when hunting for their own amusement, as they would have received had the king been present.[2] It was also aggravated by the custom of the earls and thanes claiming for themselves, on a minor scale, all the rights and privileges of royalty.

The monks, who were the wealthiest and the most hospitable of landed proprietors, were the greatest sufferers by these abuses, and as they were powerful and always energetic in self-defence, they vigorously resisted them. Their position, however, had its moral difficulties. While they wished to deny the existence of the right of enter-

[1] Du Cange, v. *Hospitalitas.*

[2] Speaking of folc-land, Allen says, " The possessors of folc-land were bound to assist in the reparation of royal vills and in other public works. They were liable to have travellers and others quartered on them for subsistence. They were required to give hospitality to kings and great men in their progresses through the country, to furnish them with carriages and relays of horses, and to extend the same assistance to their messengers, followers, and servants, and even to the persons who had charge of their hawks, horses, and hounds. (Allen's *Rise and Growth of the Royal Prerogative,* p. 144; and see Kemble's *Saxons in England,* vol. i, p. 294.) I doubt whether the Anglo-Saxons paid as much practical respect to nice distinctions in the nature of tenures as some imagine. There was a general inclination to treat rights as co-extensive with the power of enforcing them; and all were compelled to entertain the king who could not resist his demands.

X

tainment, as against the crown and the nobles, they desired to enforce it, in their own favour, against their
tenants. Many of their farms lay at a distance from
their monasteries, and they were not at all inclined to
abandon their right to entertainment when they went
on periodical tours of inspection ; though their tenants
had the same objection to entertain them as *they* had to
entertain the nobles.[1]

In the ninth and tenth centuries the obligation of hospitality had been so abused that it had become thoroughly
unpopular with all who were bound to discharge it ;
though it was fondly regarded, or, at the best, very reluctantly abandoned, by those who claimed the benefit
of it.[2] The more powerful monasteries obtained charters
or grants from the kings, either freeing their lands altogether from this liability, or expressly limiting its extent.[3]
As early as A.D. 821, the monastery of Abingdon obtained
a charter which released them from the obligation of entertaining either the king, his fæstingmen, huntsmen, fal-
coners, horses, or dogs.[4] And there are numerous charters
of nearly the same date of a similar character.[5]

Many of them, however, contain curious exceptions.
One, granted by a king of Mercia, continues the obliga-

---

[1] *Concil. Beccanceld.*, Wilkins' Con-
cil., i, 90 ; *Concil. Narbonense* (A.D.
1054), c. 16; *Histor. Monast. de Bello,*
p. 122.

[2] It was grossly abused in other
countries, and was consequently restricted. In Scotland, by *Statutis
Davidis Secun.*, c. 8 and 45. In
France, by Charles le Chauve, A.D.
872, *Capit. Caroli Calvi*, iii, tit. 4,
art. 2. In the year 1180 the archbishop of Sens went a tour through
his diocese, accompanied by seventy
attendants and forty horses, and compelled every one to board and lodge
them gratuitously. This and similar
extravagances led to the interference

of both kings and popes, and to numerous restrictions on the right.
Howard, *Coutumes Anglo-Normandes*,
tom. ii, p. 680.

[3] *Codex Diplom., Anglo-Sax.*, No.
216, A.D. 822, No. 257, A.D. 844, No.
258, A.D. 845. In Johnson's *Canons*
(vol. i, p. 126), is a grant by king
Wihtred (of very doubtful authenticity) relieving the clergy from the
obligations of hospitality.

[4] *Hist. Monast. Abingd.*, i, 26.

[5] *Codex Diplom., Anglo-Sax.*, No.
258, A.D. 845. The form of grants
freeing monasteries from liability to
furnish hospitality is given in Mar-
culfus, *Marculfi Formulæ*, 7 and 8.

tion of entertaining all envoys sent to the king from beyond sea, Wessex, or Northumbria. If they came before the middle of the day, they were to have a dinner and be passed on ; and if at a later hour, they were to have a supper and one night's lodging.[1] In a grant to the monks of Taunton (A.D. 904), releasing them from the obligation of hospitality, one night's entertainment for the king, with eight dogs and one dog keeper, and nine nights' lodging for his falconers, are stipulated for. Their hospitality to strangers was limited to an obligation to shew them the way to the nearest village,—a very cheap sort of entertainment. These privileges were sometimes conceded by the crown to the monks for the good of a monarch's soul, but much oftener for a certain number of valuable farms or mancusses of pure gold.[2]

As the monarchs and nobles relaxed their claims on the monks, or came to express agreements with them, so did the monks with their tenants; but always for a consideration, that the right to hospitality might not be waived. Lands were constantly let by them on lease, and one or two days' entertainment reserved as a portion of the rent. The value of a night's entertainment appears to have varied at different times. In the reign of king Offa it was valued at thirty shillings ; but in Edward the Confessor's time, three nights' entertainment were generally commuted for thirteen pounds, eight shillings, and four pence, of white money.

Even when the tenants did not expressly agree to entertain the abbot at fixed times, a right to some trifling

---

[1] *Cod. Diplom.*, No. 261, A.D. 848.

[2] *Ibid.*, No. 261, A.D. 848, in which the consideration money is stated. The monks gave Bertualfo, regi Merciorum, 180 mancusas in auro puro et terram quindecim manentium in duobus locis, æt Stanlege et æt Bellanforde. Kemble's *Codex*, vol. ii, p. 31. *Cyvreitheau Cymru*, b. xv; *Dimetian Code*, b. ii, c. 11 ; *Gwentian Code*, b. ii, c. 11, s. 8.

refreshment was reserved by their leases.[1] At the time of the Norman conquest, one Turkill held lands of the abbey of St. Mary, Thorney, subject to the payment of a "grace-cup" to the abbot whenever he chose to ask it. The commissioners of Domesday, who were required to value this obligation, gave up the task in despair, for the quaint and subtle reason that "how much the cup was (to hold) the men of the hundred knew not."

The right of entertainment was one of the points in dispute between the Saxons and the Normans. Edward the Confessor and his *Norman* nobles claimed the right of unlimited hospitality, not only from their tenants, but from the burghers and free towns, by whom the claim was strenuously resisted. An attempt was made to enforce it at Dover, which led to important political and social results.

Eustace, count of Boulogne, called from his long moustaches "Eustache aux grenons," had married a sister of king Edward, and came hither with a stately retinue to visit him. On his return he stopped at Canterbury for refreshment, and thence proceeded to Dover, where he proposed to remain a short time. A little distance from the town he and his knights halted and put on their armour, which led to a well-founded suspicion that they contemplated a course of conduct which might lead to conflict. On their arrival in the town they demanded gratuitous lodging and refreshment, and proceeded immediately to take possession of all the best houses and to expel the owners. In so doing, one of them wounded a householder, who killed him in self-defence. Upon this Eustace and his companions mounted their horses and made a general attack on the inhabitants. In the combat

---

[1] *Anglo-Saxon Chronicle,* A.D. 777; *Introduction to Domesday,* vol. i, p. *Domesday Book,* vi, fo. 1896 ; Ellis's 261.

that ensued, the householder above mentioned and about twenty others were killed. Many of the Frenchmen were also slain, and many more wounded; Eustace himself and a few of his companions escaped with difficulty, and fled to the king at Gloucester. Edward, who took part with his brother-in-law, ordered earl Godwin to punish the townsmen, but as the earl differed from the king as to the respective merits of the parties, he not only refused compliance, but demanded the punishment and expulsion of the foreigners.

The towns generally acted as the citizens of Dover did in this instance. They obstinately and successfully resisted the claim to enforced hospitality ; and there is, perhaps, no greater evidence of their power than the fact that, although the right was recognised by the law of Normandy, they obtained a formal abandonment of it from William the Conqueror. The citizens of London went further, and obtained express permission to slay any one who attempted to practise it.[1] The country districts were not equally fortunate, as they were compelled gratuitously to entertain the king, his ambassadors, and highest officers, till a much later period of history. The Norman bishops and earls claimed the same courtesy at the hands of their tenants, and the refusal of it was punished by them as an intolerable impertinence, but not as an illegality.

As a compensation to the nobles for the refusal to recognise their right to compulsory entertainment, the burghers established in every town a class of persons called "herbergeors," whose duty it was to provide lodging and refreshment for such travellers as were willing to pay liberally and were prevented by their rank from taking up their abode at common ale-houses. And it must be

---

[1] *Libertas Civitatum*, c. 2; *De Libertate Civium Lundonien.*, **and** *Carta Civibus Lundon.*, Thorpe, i, 502.

confessed that if in the earliest Anglo-Saxon era the townsmen suffered from being compelled to afford hospitality to the nobles, they were in the latest era most amply revenged by the extortions practised on the nobles by their official hosts.[1]

SECTION IV.—VALOUR.

Valour, in the eyes of the ancient Germans, was the greatest of all virtues. They knew that it afforded them protection and support in this world, and believed that it would secure them eternal happiness in that which is to come.[2]

It was by valour that they defended for so many years their native forests against the power of Rome ; and that, after many years of desperate warfare, they at last became masters of England. Their courage, though not greater, nor perhaps so great, as that of the Danes, was of a nobler kind, for it was unstained by that fiendish cruelty which rendered the very name of "Northman" terrible. That in their conquest of England many massacres took place, in which old and young, woman and child, layman and priest, were indiscriminately slaughtered, cannot be denied ; but we recollect no instance in which prisoners of war were deliberately tortured to death prior to the Danish era.

In the eighth century England enjoyed peace and prosperity such as she was not destined to know again for many ages. During this period the Anglo-Saxon nobles, as has been already stated, abandoned their warlike habits and sought in the repose of monasteries the calm and ease of peaceful life ;[3] and when in the ninth century

---

[1] Wright's *Domestic Manners and Sentiments of the Middle Ages*, p. 333.

[2] Tacitus, *Hist.*, lib. iv, c. 17.

[3] Bede, *Epist. Ecgbert., Opera Minora.*

they were called upon to protect their country by force of arms from the rage of the Northmen, they were found unequal to the duty.[1] To the fury of a nation of pirates, whose every occupation, passion, and religion, were summed up in the one word, "war," they opposed the drivelling superstitions of a century of cloistered life. They encountered the trained bands of the marauders with a procession of monks; the sword and double-edged axe with a new verse in the litany; and the torch that carried destruction everywhere, with the burning of sacred incense. Instead of defending their country by arms, they employed themselves in chanting day and night, "From the fury of the Northman, good Lord, deliver us!"[2]

Nor were they content with being personally superstitious and inactive. The Anglo-Saxon freemen were taught by them not to trust to their own right hands for the protection of their hearths, but to rely on the efficacy of relics and on the powerful intercession of the saints by whom they would be miraculously defended. To this end legend after legend was invented, of which an endless number might be quoted, but one will serve as a specimen of all.

When the Danes and Northmen besieged Chartres, in France, the pious townspeople, it is said, refused to arm in their own defence. They relied solely on the protection of the Virgin, to whom they prayed incessantly. In lieu of armed men they displayed on their walls the shift of the Holy Virgin, which Charles the Bald had brought as a relic from Constantinople. The invaders shouted with laughter at this novel banner, and scoffingly shot it full of arrows. Their impiety was miraculously punished. They were suddenly struck with blindness and cowardice,

[1] Pontopidan., tom. ii, p. 139.　　[2] Henry's *Hist. of Britain*, vol. ii, p. 336.

and allowed themselves to be quietly cut up, like a flock of lambs, by the unwarlike inhabitants.[1] This story was thus told and thus believed. The fact that an army under the command of the duke of Burgundy and the earl of Poitou came to the assistance of the Virgin's shift was studiously concealed, and the deluded Saxons were incited to rely on any safeguard rather than their own martial prowess. The Danes entertained the most profound contempt for the spiritual weapons with which they were opposed. "We sang them a mass in our turn," they said, "a mass of javelins which lasted from morning till night, and we lighted their abbey for a taper."

There were, happily, Anglo-Saxon freemen who shared the Danish contempt for the degeneracy of their nobles, and who did not hesitate forcibly to enter the monasteries, and dragging thence the recreant earls, to compel them, often reluctantly, to lead their followers against the common foe. Sigebert, king of East Anglia (the first royal monk), had been a popular king and a distinguished soldier, and at a moment of great peril was thus forced to leave his monastery and to assume the command of those whom he had often led to victory. He appeared at their head in the field of battle armed only with a wand, placed his arms on his breast in the form of a cross, and joyfully accepted the crown of martyrdom.[2] Such reluctant warriors were worse than useless in a conflict with the Northmen, a nation as warlike and ferocious as any the world ever knew. From their birth to their manhood they were trained with a single view to war and carnage. Their childhood and the dawn

---

[1] So this story is told by William of Malmesbury, who evidently believed it. (*De Gestis Regum Ang.*, lib. ii, c. 5.) Roger de Hovedon, A.D. 699. It may be observed that it is very doubtful whether Charles the Bald ever went to Constantinople.

[2] Bede's *Eccles. Hist.*, lib. iii, c. 18 and 19; William of Malmesbury, lib. i, c. 5.

of youth were wholly spent in running, leaping, climbing, swimming, wrestling, boxing, fighting, and such exercises as hardened both their souls and bodies, and fitted them for the toils of war. So soon as they could lisp, they were taught to sing the victories of their ancestors, their memories were stored with tales of war and piratical expeditions, of defeated enemies, burning cities and plundered provinces, and of wealth and honour earned by deeds of daring. With such an education it is not wonderful that the youngest hearts beat high with martial ardour, or that the first object of a boy's ambition was to grasp the spear and wield the sword, and to mingle with his elders in conflicts of blood and glory.

The manhood of the Danes was worthy of their youth. Their annals are crowded with tales of desperate daring performed by heroes. When surrounded in battle they laughed and sang, and thirsted only for the blood of their foes, and for the happy time when they should drink wine out of their skulls in the halls of Odin. A peaceful death was in their eyes a disgrace. They who were not killed in battle either induced their friends to kill them or committed suicide. Starcather, who had spent his life in war, finding that as age increased his strength and sight decayed, became miserable for fear he should die a peaceful death. To avoid this degrading calamity, he put a chain of gold about his neck, and offered it to any one who would cut off his head. Under similar circumstances, an illustrious warrior, Hadiger, the son of Gran, considering it a disgrace to die in his bed like an ox, "for the praise of the world and the glory of posterity, hung himself."

Neither the valour nor the ferocity of the Danes was diminished by their conversion to Christianity. They retained both these qualities in excess to the last moment of Anglo-Saxon history, and one of the three great earls in the time of Edward the Confessor was a remarkable instance of it. Siward, earl of Northumberland, was " a giant in stature and vigour of mind," who sent his son with a large army to war upon Macbeth and to place Malcolm on the throne of Scotland. At first the enterprise was unsuccessful, and his son was slain. When the old man heard the tidings of his death, he asked but one question—" Was his death-wound in front or behind ?" " In front," replied the messengers. " Then," said he, " I rejoice greatly. No other death was worthy of himself or of me."[1] It was in the same spirit, that, after a long life spent in warfare, being attacked by dysentery, he prepared for his own end. He was distressed, not at the prospect of dying, but of dying in peace. " Shame on me," he said, " that I did not fall in one of the many battles I have fought, but am reserved to die disgracefully the death of an old cow. At least put on me my armour of proof, gird my sword to my side, place my helmet on my head, my shield on my left hand, and my golden battle-axe in my right, that the bravest of soldiers may die in a soldier's garb." Thus he spoke ; and when armed as he desired, gave up the ghost.[2]

With such soldiers as these, the Saxon earls, dragged from the monasteries, could not hope to contend successfully. So inferior were they to the Danes at the beginning of the ninth century, that five Saxons, *it is said*, would run away at the sight of one of them.[3] During the latter half of the century, however, a state of incessant warfare had revived the military courage of the West Saxons; and there can be no doubt that the soldiers of Alfred, towards the end of his reign, rivalled in military

---

[1] *Anglo-Saxon Chron.*, A.D. 1054 ; Flor. Wigorn., A.D. 1054; Sim. Dunelm., A.D. 1054; Henry Huntingdon; Wm. Malmes., lib. ii, c. 13.
[2] Henry of Huntingdon, A.D. 1053.
[3] Hickes, *Dissert. Epist.*, p. 103.

merit any that could have been opposed to them. That a century later the Anglo-Saxons were not inferior to the best of the Danish troops was admitted by Cnut himself.

SECTION V.—CRUELTY.

The valour of the Danes was stained by a cruelty so ferocious as to be hardly credible. They were not content with plundering the countries they overran, nor even with the slaughter of the inhabitants, but with a horrible excess of cruelty they tortured them to death. The women they violated and then murdered, and the little children they tossed high into the air, and, as they fell, caught them on the points of their spears.[1]

Among them were a class of men called Bersirker, who endeavoured to resemble wolves or mad dogs, and were, or pretended to be, insane. They bit their shields, howled, and lashed themselves into fury, and prided themselves on nothing but the extreme atrocity of their cruelties. Long after they had passed away, the "*furor bursaticus*" was spoken of with horror and awe.[2]

Prior to the Danish invasion there is no instance of prisoners being tortured to death, but almost immediately afterwards we read of Eadbert, king of Kent, being taken prisoner by the Mercians, and being deprived of his eyes and hands. This, and many other horrible modes of treating prisoners, were common with the Danes, and with the Saxons after their amalgamation with them.

Two of these modes of torture are so remarkable for extreme barbarity as to deserve particular mention. One

[1] John of Wallingford, Gale, i, 536; Bartholinus, *Antiquitatum Danicarum, de causis contemptæ a Danis adhuc gentilibus mortis,* lib. ii, c. 9.

[2] Hook's *Archbishops of Canterbury,* vol. i, p. 304.

was called "behættie," and the other the spread-eagle ;
and there were few things on which their greatest warriors
prided themselves more than the skill with which they
performed them.

The first named (behættie) was a species of scalping.
The chief made one incision horizontallly round the
prisoner's head, and another perpendicularly, and then, if
a skilful operator, he could with a scalping knife twist off
the whole skin and hair of the head at a single wrench.[1]
The second of these diabolical performances was called by
the Northmen "at rista örn á bak einom"—"to describe an
eagle on the back of any one." The victim was placed
upon the ground naked, with his face downwards, and
with his arms and legs stretched out. The chief then
placed a broad axe between his spine and the left shoulder,
in a manner that enabled him at one blow to twist off and
spread out the ribs so as to look like the wing of an
eagle. He then wrenched out the right ribs in a similar
manner, stretching them out so as to represent the eagle's
other wing. In was in this mode that Ingvar (according
to the Danish historians), in the reign of Ethelred I, put
Ælle, the king of East Anglia, to death.[2]

These horrible cruelties were taught by the Danes to
the Saxons, and were too often practised in all their
ferocity by the English people down to the time of the
conquest. When earl Godwin had induced prince Alfred
(the brother of Edward the Confessor) to visit England,
he treacherously attacked him at Guildford, seized his
person, and made his guard of six hundred persons
prisoners. "Some of these he imprisoned, some he sold
for slaves, some he blinded by putting out their eyes,

[1] Thorpe's *Ancient Laws*, i, 395 ;
Johnson's *Canons*, vol. i, p. 200.
[2] *Hist. Reg. Norvag.*, vol. i, p. 108;
Harald's *Saga ens Harfagra*, cap. 31;
Saxo Grammaticus, *Hist. Dan.*, lib.
ix ; *Frag. Isl.* apud Langebek, tom.
ii, p. 278.

some he maimed by cutting off their hands and feet, and others he tortured by pulling the skin off their heads."[1]

The system of cruelty which the Danes introduced into England was not limited to the treatment of prisoners of war. It was carried into civil life, and permeated the whole of our criminal jurisprudence.

Prior to their invasion of Britain, there are only two punishments mentioned in our laws ; namely, death and scourging.[2] But no sooner was there a powerful Danish element in society, than a series of horrible punishments were introduced. Under Alfred the Great, cutting off the hand and tongue, castration, and mutilation, were sanctioned by law. Under Athelstan, casting from a height, drowning, stoning, and burning, became recognised punishments ; to which Cnut added cutting off feet, eyes, noses, and *scalping*. The opinion that we are indebted to the Danes for the introduction of a more barbarous system of punishment is supported by the persistence with which they struggled to have young children put to death for petty thefts, as has been mentioned in a previous chapter.

It was also during the era of the Danish wars that the horrible custom arose of blinding political opponents, *who were not belligerents,* by holding red-hot irons near the eye-ball ; and of shaving and castrating them that they might be deprived of the insignia of noble birth and manhood.[3] To such a terrible state of brutality had the country arrived, that the last ferocious system of mutila-

---

[1] This story appears to me supported by sufficient testimony, though it is disbelieved by Mr. St. John (*Four Conquests of England*) and other eulogists of the house of Godwin.

[2] *Ll. Withr.*, 22 and 23. I do not take into account the *Laws of Ina*, as we do not know to what extent the copy we have of them was altered by Alfred the Great. Nor do I notice archbishop Ecgbert's *Excerpt.*, as he merely quotes Irish Canons.

[3] *Ll. Alfredi*, c. 6, 25, 32, Thorpe, i, 67 and 79; *Athelst.*, iii, 6, v, 6–3, *Ll. Cnuti Sec.*, c. 30, Thorpe, vol. i, p. 395.

tion was sometimes employed as a *practical joke*, or to give point to a retort in a game of badinage ![1]

It is difficult to assign any reason for the greater cruelty of the English in the ninth and subsequent century. The only obvious one is the fact that all the tender feelings of domestic life were lost in the passions of perpetual warfare, and that by constant familiarity with human suffering the heart grows callous to misery. To this it may fairly be added that it was a very early era of criminal legislation, and that nearly all unenlightened legislatures have fancied that a *constant increase* in the ferocity of punishment is the only way of checking a *constant increase* of some particular crime.

SECTION VI.—CHASTITY.

It is generally supposed that no virtue was more universally admired or more severely practised among the Anglo-Saxons than that of chastity ; and this opinion, though in the main correct, must be held subject to some limitations as to times and persons.

In the earlier centuries the German women were models of female virtue. The slightest deviation from morality or propriety was looked upon with horror and punished with severity. If a married woman was guilty of misconduct, her husband assembled her relations, publicly cut off the long hair which was her proudest ornament, expelled her naked from his house, and drove her from the village.[2] At a later period, if a female, married or unmarried, was guilty of misconduct, she was required to strangle herself with her own hands ; and if she refused to do so, the women of the neighbourhood assembled, and cutting off her garments to the waist, attacked

---

[1] See Walter de Mapes, *Nug. Cur. Dist.*, iv, c. 15.   [2] Tacitus, *De Mor. Germ.*, c. xix.

her with whips and knives, and hunted her from village to village till death rescued her from further torture. They then seized her seducer and hanged him over her grave.[1]

However excellent may have been the character of the female sex among the continental Saxons, it must be admitted that the reputation of some classes of English women did not at certain periods command universal respect. In the eighth and ninth centuries, there were bitter denunciations of their conduct by bishops and chroniclers, whose knowledge, honesty, and zeal cannot be doubted.[2] Their censures, and the circumstances under which they were made, are worthy of careful consideration.

It may be premised, that when the Saxons commenced their system of forcible emigration into England, they rarely brought women with them; but when they had conquered the natives, they took from them their wives and daughters, and married or retained them as mistresses. To this it may be added, that when the Northmen came hither *direct* from their native land, they were unaccompanied by women ; but when, as was often the case, they arrived here at the termination of piratical voyages, they brought with them large numbers of women whom they had carried off from the shores of France, Spain, Italy, and even of Africa. A very small proportion of English women, therefore, were in the eighth century of Anglo-Saxon descent—at least, on the maternal side.

When we examine the imputations on the character of Englishwomen to which we have alluded, we shall find them so clearly limited as to persons and times, that it is easy to account for and explain them.

---

[1] Bonifacii *Opera*, i, 136 ; *Edict. Theod.*, lxi and xxxix; *Ll. Longobard.*, l. ccxii; *Ll. Burgund.*, tit. lxviii and lii; *Ll. Wisigoth.*, iii, iv. 14; Salvian, *De Guber. Dei*, vii.

[2] Bonifacii *Opera*, i, 133, 136, 137; Bedæ *Hist. Eccles.*, iv, 25 ; Theodor. *Pœnit.*, xvi, 17.

In the era which immediately preceded the Danish invasions, the complaints refer almost exclusively to the inhabitants of the convents. St. Boniface, in his letter reproving Ethelbald for immorality, accuses him of adultery with the nuns; and when he denounces the nobles of Mercia for the habitual practice of the same sin, he expressly states that nuns were the companions of their guilt.[1] The testimony of Gildas is to the same effect,[2] and the complaints as to the female pilgrims, of whom a large proportion were of the monastic order, tend to the same conclusion.[3] It may also be observed that, in stating the usual penances to be inflicted for the grossest excesses of refined debauchery, the Pœnitentials of that era mention them as the practices of nuns.[4] Hence it may be fairly inferred that the imputations thrown on the character of English women in the eighth century should be limited to the pseudo-nuns of that unhappy period.

The era which followed it, that of the Danish invasion, was not favourable to morality; nor is it marvellous that female character suffered in the universal misery and degradation of the times. The women whom the invaders brought with them were captives of the humblest rank, torn from their homes and exposed through long sea-voyages to all the license of their brutal captors. On their arrival here they were made slaves of the camp, and dragged at the rear of the army from place to place throughout the tedious marches of their owners. It is clear that by these unfortunate foreigners no small proportion of the reprobation bestowed upon the era was provoked.[5] But the Danes did not confine their cruel

---

[1] Bonifacii *Epis. Reg. Merciæ,* Will. Malmesb., l. i, p. 112.

[2] Gildas, *De excidio Britt.,* iii, 32.

[3] See *ante,* p. 251.

[4] *Pœnit.* Theod., xviii, 20; *Capit. Theod., De mulierum fornicatione Regim. inter.,* lib. ii, c. 250; *Pœnit.* Theod., xvi, 18.

[5] *Ll. Wihtr.,* c. 4 and 5; *Ll. Alfredi,* c. 50; *Ll. Edw. and Guth.,* s. ii; Johnson's *English Canons* (A.D. 878), pp. 334, 484, and 513.

treatment of women to foreign slaves. They no sooner obtained a footing in any part of England, than they seized the women of the district, treated them with the same brutality, and reduced them to the same degradation.

By this savage conduct they corrupted not only their victims but themselves, and when they settled down in the eastern districts, it was centuries before they learned to appreciate the dignity of women, or the obligations of morality. Such of the natives as were fair, with light hair and blue eyes, they accepted as demi-wives, and married them with a ceremony, which, though legal both here and on the continent, gave them an inferior position. Dark-haired and dark-eyed women they alleged to be "like slaves—black and bad"; and they accordingly reduced them to servitude.[1]

On the restoration of peace and tranquillity, and the amalgamation of the Danes and Saxons, the imputations on the character of English women ceased. Bishop Lupus (in the time of Cnut,) undoubtedly indulged in some vehement objurgation, but it forms part of a sermon in which, as some preachers occasionally do, he imputes total depravity to all whom he addresses, without any personal knowledge of individual character.[2]

This subject cannot be dismissed without remarking that gallantry, as it is termed, appears never to have existed in Anglo-Saxon times; and though there were bad men then as now, yet no man, as far as we can learn, boasted of vicious amours, or plumed himself on having misled an inexperienced maiden, or on overcoming the matrimonial fidelity of an unwise wife.

[1] *Oxford Essays* (1858), 170, Dasent; Palgrave's *Hist. of Norm.*, ii, p. 107.

[2] *Epist. Lupi Episcop.*, printed in Hickes's *Thesaurus*, p. 104.

Y

CHAPTER XIII.

POETRY.

SECTION I.—THE PRIMITIVE POETRY.

THE ordinary language of the Anglo-Saxons was of a figurative character, and when they were moved by strong passions or lofty sentiments it was highly poetic. We may readily quote an example.

The historian Bede has preserved the speech which is said to have been delivered by one of the nobles of king Edwin, when the missionary Paulinus was endeavouring to convert that king and his followers to the Christian faith. His topic was the transitory nature of human happiness, and he says : " Thou hast seen, O king, when the fire blazed and the hall was warm, and thou wast seated at feast among thy nobles, whilst the winter storm raged without, and snow fell, how some solitary sparrow has flown through and scarcely entered at one door before it disappeared at the other. Whilst in the hall it felt not the storm ; but, after a moment, it returned to whence it came, and thou beholdest it no longer ; nor knowest thou where or to what it might be exposed. Such, as it appears to me, is the life of man. A short moment of enjoyment, and then we know not whence we come or whither we go. If this new doctrine brings us any certainty of the future, I for one vote for its adoption."[1] This may be taken as a favourable example of the natural poetry of the youth of society.

The early poetry of every nation naturally divides itself into religious and secular ; and in the case of the Anglo-Saxons this division is peculiarly convenient, as the bulk of their religious poetry was written in Latin, while the secular was chanted in the national language. Of the religious poems written in Latin, which the laity were not learned enough to understand, and which, consequently, had no influence on domestic life, it is not proposed to say anything here.

The favourite topics of the *secular* poetry of most nations are history, love, and patriotic sentiment. Of these three, one appears to have been wanting to the Anglo-Saxons ; for whatever passionate devotion they may have entertained to the sex, it found, so far as we know, no utterance in songs. In as much of their poetry as has descended to us, there is not one single amatory verse, nor any one of those fantastic utterances of passion with which Norman poetry is crowded. There is possibly, in the opinion of some, a solitary exception in a poem of king Alfred, in which he describes the anxiety of a wife at the absence of her husband. He says, "Lives not thy wife also. She is prudent and very modest. She excels all others in purity ; for thee, for thee alone, she lives. She loves nought but thee. She has enough of the goods of this world, but for thee alone she despises all things. She despises all, because she has not thee—the one thing wanted. In thy absence she has nothing ; for thy love she is pining away. She is dying of sorrow and tears."[2]

Anglo-Saxon secular poetry, not being erotic, was

---

[1] Bede, *Histor. Eccles.*, lib. ii, c. 13.   [2] Alfred's Boethius, *Metres*, p. 17.

either narrative or patriotic. Among the most famous of the poems which have survived, is that of Beowulf. It is so called after its hero, a primæval chieftain, who distinguished himself by destroying monsters, natural and supernatural, nicors, grendels, dragons, and ferocious tyrants. There is also a fragment of the *Romance of Finn*, having for its subject the wars of two hostile tribes, continued till one of them was exterminated ; and (in a Latin prose version) the *Romance of Offa*, founded on the marriage of a king with a wood-nymph, and the hatred with which she is consequently regarded by his mother. There are also poems on the battle of Maldon against the Danes, on the death of Edgar, and on Athelstan's victory over the Danes at Brunaburgh, which are more historical, and to some, more pleasing compositions.[1]

[1] The following is a translation of the lines on the battle of Brunaburgh, taken from the *Anglo-Saxon Chronicle*.

Here Athelstan king,
the lord of earls,
the king-giver of warriors,
and his brother eke,
Eadmund the Atheling,
life-long glory
in battle won
with edges of swords
near Brunanburh.
The board-walls clave,
hewed the war-linden,
with the sword's hammering.
The offspring of Edward,
(such was their nature, noble
from their ancestors),
that they in battle oft
'gainst every foe
the land defended,
our hoards and homes.
The foe they crushed,
the Scottish people ;
and the ship-pirates
death-doomed, fell.
The field streamed
with warriors' blood,
from sun-rise
(at morning-tide),

till the mighty planet,
glided o'er lands,
(God's candle bright,
the eternal Lord's,
the noble creature),
sank to its sitting.
There lay many a warrior
by javelins strewed ;
northern men
o'er the shield shot ;
and the Scots eke,
weary, war-sated.
The West-Saxons onwards,
through the live long day,
in martial bands
pursued the footsteps
of the loathed nations.
They hewed the fugitives
behind, amain,
with swords mill-sharp.
The Mercians refused not
the hard hand-play
to any heroes
who with Anlaf,
over the ocean,
in the ship's bosom,
this land sought,
death doomed in fight.
Five lay
on the battle-stead,
youthful kings,

All of them are marked by the same peculiarities. There is in each the same constant repetition of nearly synonymous words or short phrases, which are often scarcely more than exclamations.

A poem might possibly begin thus :—" Edmund, bravest of chiefs, eagle of battle ;· lord of shields, helmet of nations, fiercest in war ;" and thence through a series of de-

by swords in slumber laid :
so seven eke
of Anlaf's earls;
and of the army countless,
shipmen and Scots.
There was made flee
the North-men's chieftain,
by need constrained,
to the ship's prow
with a little band.
The bark drove afloat :
the king fled
on the fallow flood,
and his life preserved.
So there eke the sage
Constantine,
hoary warrior,
came by flight
to his country north.
He had no cause to exult
in the meeting of swords.
He of his kinsmen bereft,
of his friends deprived
on the folk-stead,
in battle slain ;
and his son he left
on the slaughter-place,
mangled with wounds,
young in warfare.
The hero, grizzly-haired,
had no cause to boast
of the bill-clashing,
the old deceiver ;
nor Anlaf the more,
with the remnant of their armies ;
they had no cause to boast
that they in war's works
the better men were
in the battle-stead,
at the conflict of banners,
at the meeting of spears,
at the concourse of men,
at the traffic of weapons ;

when they on the slaughter-field
with Edward's
offspring played.
The North-men departed
(the gory leavings of darts)
in their nailed barks ;
on roaring ocean
o'er the deep water
Dublin to seek,
Ireland once more,
ashamed in mind.
Likewise the brothers,
both together,
king and etheling,
their country sought,
the West-Saxons' land,
in the war exulting.
They left behind them,
the swart raven with horned neb
to share the pale hued carcases,
and the white tailed eagle with
goodly plumage, the greedy war
hawk,
and that grey beast, the wolf of
the wood,
the carrion to devour.
Carnage greater has not been
in this island
ever yet
of people slain,
by edges of swords,
as books tell us,
(old writers,)
since from the east hither,
Angles and Saxons
came to land,
o'er the broad seas
Britain sought,
mighty war-smiths,
the Welsh o'ercame,
and earls, glory-greedy,
this land obtained.

scriptive phrases all meaning substantially the same thing. Sometimes these epithets are repeated every third or fourth line, breaking the narrative in a very unpleasant manner, and are apparently continued as long as the poet's power of inventing quasi-synonyms served him.

There is another peculiarity of Anglo-Saxon poetry which is an evidence of extreme antiquity. It is the omission of the "particles of speech;" those little abbreviations of language which convey the minutiæ of thought and give distinctness to our expressions. In the prattle of an infant, in the attempts of a traveller to express himself in a tongue of which he knows hardly anything, and in the infantile language of a barbarous people, particles are either unknown or unused. A dozen nouns, and one or two verbs expressive of transition—such as "give," "go," or "send," serve an infant to convey its wants to its mother, enable a cockney to obtain a dinner from a French waiter, or a savage to communicate his wishes to his friends.

Poetry is the *infantile* literature of every country, and is marked by all the peculiarities of the age to which it belongs. The language of the era dispenses with the use of particles, and poetry is consequently written without them. And when once a peculiar style of poetry (however defective it may be) becomes popular and national, it is retained unchanged for many years, though prose composition is habitually modified in accordance with every improvement or change of grammar. One of the reasons of this, probably, is that popular poetry is committed to memory in childhood, and men in advanced years willingly bear with the defects of compositions which were the delights of their infancy; though their maturer judgment, if honestly appealed to, would condemn the taste of their younger days.

Long after the form of composition which permitted the omission of particles in Anglo-Saxon prose was abandoned, it was continued in poetry. There are synonymous phrases expressed by Alfred the Great both in prose and verse. In the former the particles are used, while in the latter they are omitted. Writing in prose, he says, "*So* doth the moon, with *his* pale light, *that the* bright stars, *he* obscures *in heaven.*" In poetry, he says, "With pale light, moon obscures bright stars." Many instances of this difference between the prose and poetry of the period might be quoted from his works.[1]

The use of inversion (or the inverting of the natural order of words) is said to have been another *peculiarity* of *Anglo-Saxon* poetry ; but as at all times and in all languages poets have indulged in this license, it can hardly be considered a *peculiarity.*

It has been said that Anglo-Saxon poetry is remarkable for the total absence of similes and the redundancy of metaphor ; and to the latter part of the accusation its most enthusiastic advocates would be compelled to plead guilty. An unkind critic might say of some of their poems that they were little else than a collection of metaphors very inartistically strung together ; and that the metaphors themselves were not always beautiful or apt. It is difficult to offer any opinion with confidence on a matter which almost entirely depends upon taste ; but a few specimens, good and bad, selected from an enormous number, may assist the reader in forming his own judgment.

When it is wished to tell us that Beowulf slew the nicors at sea, and that their bodies were washed on shore, we read, "Amid the leavings of the ebbing

---

[1] Turner's *Anglo-Saxons*, b. ix, c. 1.

tide, in the morning, wounded with blades high on the beach they lay, put to sleep by swords ;" and when Beowulf's aged father died, it is said, " he abode many a year, ere he went on his way, old from his dwelling." When the hero is compelled to weigh anchor and put to sea, it is said, " he threw the reins on the neck of his war-horse, and went on the path of the swans."

These metaphors will be thought pleasing by many, because they add to the beauty or sublimity of the actions they represent, by the suggestion of associations more noble or beautiful than themselves. The "putting to sleep" brings to the painful idea of death a soothing sense of calmness ; and the "leavings of the waves" suggests the ebbing of the universal ocean ; while "the going on the way of the old man," calls to mind the long journey to eternal rest that all must one day travel.

But a metaphor that lowers the object it describes, will appear to most minds unhappy ; and the most frequent subjects of Anglo-Saxon metaphor were incapable of elevation. The favourite one was the Deity ; and from the simple sublimity of the idea of the God-head, fanciful allusions can only detract. The sun and the ocean, the most sublime of all created things, ranked next in favour, and involved difficulties that none but the greatest of poets have ever successfully encountered. The favourite metaphor for the sun was "the day's bright candle," a phrase which, when applied to "the glorious eye of day," adds nothing to sublimity, and seems "vain and ridiculous excess."[1]

The metaphors for the ocean were equally unhappy :—

[1] Other metaphors for the sun were rodores candel (the candle of the firmament), woruld-candel (the candle of the world), heofon-candel (the candle of heaven), and wyn-candel (the candle of joy).

"the bath of the whales," "the road of the swans," "the bath of the sea-fowl," and "the street of the sea," are comparisons which merely lower the grand idea of ocean's vast expanse. But where the poets were less ambitious, they were more successful. A tongue is called "the sword of speech;" night, "the veil of cares;" rocks, "the bones of the earth;" and arrows, "the hailstones of helmets." These are at least innocent; and one that is used for a woman is very pretty; she is called the "weaver of peace," in allusion to her ordinary domestic occupation, and one of her sweetest privileges. Had the metaphors been ever so beautiful, their number and iteration would have rendered them tedious in the extreme.[1]

Anglo-Saxon poetry was not modulated according to a foot measure like that of the Greeks and Romans, nor was it written in measured rhymes like that of modern languages. "It was modulated," says Bede, "not according to the laws of metre but by the judgment of the ear;"[2] nevertheless it may generally, by a certain amount of prosodaical audacity, be scanned as a species of iambic verse.[3]

But its chief peculiarity was its alliterative character. The versification was so arranged that in every couplet there were two principal words in the first line beginning with the same letter, which was also the initial letter of the first word in the following line on which the stress of the voice falls.

[1] Cædmon, in a very limited space, calls the ark—a ship, the sea house, the greatest of watery chambers, the great sea house, the high mansion, the holy wood, the house, the great sea chest, the greatest of treasure houses, the vehicle, the mansion, the house of the deep, the palace of ocean, the cave, the wooden fortress, the floor of the waves, the receptacle of Noah, the moving roof, the feasting house, the bosom of vessels, the nailed building, the vehicle of the ark, the happiest mansion, the building of the waves, the foaming ship, and the happy receptacle. Turner's *Anglo-Saxon Hist.*, b. ix, c. 1.

[2] Bedæ *Opera*, vol. i, p. 57.

[3] See Bosanquet's Preface to *Cædmon*.

This may be remarked in the following example taken from Beowulf.

*M*æton *m*ere-stræta,	Ye measured the lake paths,
*m*undum brugdon ;	with your arms ye whirled them;
*g*lidon ofer *g*ar-secg	Ye glided over the ocean ;
*g*eofon-ythura	With the waves of the sea
weól wintrys wylm.	the tide of winter boiled.

SECTION II.—DEVELOPMENT OF POETRY.

The introduction of writing had an important influence on Anglo-Saxon poetry. Before this art was generally known, the assistance that verse affords to the memory caused not only genealogies and histories, but many laws and legal forms, to be composed in it ; but the superior certainty and durability of written documents rapidly induced a universal custom of recording all matters of consequence in writing.

The narrative poem had also the disadvantage of having become inadequate to the ends for which it was required. While there were very few laws to be made public, and but a limited number of events to record, it was sufficient to express them in verse, and sing them from village to village; but when society demanded more extensive legislation, and history became crowded with events, it was difficult to include them in a poem. To meet the exigencies that pressed upon it, the length of the narrative poem was so increased, that its utility was destroyed. It included an immense mass of history, but it was so long that no one could remember it.

It is long before any popular and well established custom dies out ; and for centuries traditions, expressed in verse and conveyed orally, competed with written records as vehicles of history. It was to the historical songs of the vulgar that William of Malmesbury was indebted for all his knowledge of the private life of king Edgar, of whose irregularities the monkish historians were intentionally silent. But the inferiority of verbal tradition to written records, as historical evidence, was soon appreciated.

Social changes also demanded a modification of the endless historical poem. In the tenth century it was customary for every one who pretended to education to sing and recite poetry ; but no one who was not a professional bard would attempt to get by heart poems consisting of several thousand lines. A shorter style of poem had become a social necessity.

The audience to which the poet spoke had also changed. It was no longer exclusively his duty to pour into the ear of a great chief, as he sat hour after hour at the festive board entertaining successive crowds of hungry followers, an endless eulogium on his deeds, and a bombastic history of his imaginary ancestors. In addition to one great chief, he had now to please a multitude of minor nobles, private gentlemen, and even the attendants of the village ale-house, whence it became necessary to change such a subject as the genealogical descent of Cerdic from Odin for some topic of general interest, and to substitute for the declamatory and exaggerated style suitable to public meetings, the simple and unaffected language of private life. It was also necessary in the social circle (as both the best and the worst of story-tellers have found) to have some regard to brevity.

The period of transition was an inconvenient one for professional poets ; for however much the public approved the change, the great princes were not pleased at the substitution of short songs in their honour for the ancient lengthy outpourings. A minstrel named Thorarin Loftunga sang to the praise of Cnut at a feast given by that monarch, and in accordance with the new custom limited his performance to three or four verses. Cnut was greatly offended by the brevity of the song ; he said that no man had ever before dared to sing his deeds in so few verses ; that it was an insult to suppose they did not demand a longer song, and he concluded by ordering the minstrel to be hanged the following evening. As Loftunga was to live through the next day, he was permitted to be present at the king's early dinner, and availed himself of the opportunity to sing no less than thirty verses in his honour which he had composed in the night. With these the king was so pleased that he spared the minstrel's life, and presented him with thirty ounces of silver.[1]

It is probable that, during the tenth and eleventh centuries, the old poetic histories and the shorter and simpler poems were both in use.[2] We are told of St. Dunstan, that he *sang* the vainest poems (*carmina*) of the ancient heathen, and *studied* their historic chants. From this we may infer that the distinction between the two was then recognised.[3]

No example of the new class of poems has been preserved, unless we may class the *Battle of Brunanburgh* and the *Death of Edgar* among them. This is very much to be lamented ; as nothing could have been more interesting than to have compared these effusions of the feelings of the laity with the ecclesiastical annals which are at present the main fountains of history.

---

[1] Turner's *Anglo-Saxon Hist.*, vol. ii, p. 345 ; Wharton's *Hist. Engl. Poetry*, vol. i, p. 36.

[2] I should have called the shorter and simpler poems " ballads," had not that word obtained a technical signification in modern times. The old chroniclers call them "cantilenæ" and " trivia," terms which they do not apply to any histories in verse. The Danes called the shorter poem a " flok," and the longer a " drapa." Turner's *Anglo-Saxon Hist.*, b. vi, c. 11.

[3] Avitæ gentilitatis vanissima didicisse carmina et historiarum colere incantationes. (*MS. Cotton. Cleop.*, B. xiii, fo. 63.) Mr. Soames understood by the last three words, that St. Dunstan practised magic, which I cannot think the true meaning. Soames' *Anglo-Saxon Church*, p. 173.

The following verse is said to have been the first of a very popular ballad ascribed to Cnut, and is pretty enough to make us lament the loss of the remainder.

Merie sungen the muneches binnen Ely,	Merry sang the monks of Ely,
Tha Cnut ching reu therby :	As king Cnut was rowed along;
Roweth, cnites, noer the land,	Row, knights, row near the land,
And here we thes muneches sæng.	And let us hear these monks' song.[1]

Though no cantilenæ or ballads (if the phrase may be pardoned) have come down to us, we know what their chief attributes must have been. They must have been short enough to have been conveniently committed to memory by people in general, adapted to the few and simple airs then known, convenient for singing at popular entertainments, and composed on topics of general interest. Some of them, we know, were sarcastic or scurrilous, and aimed against those who persecuted the minstrels ; and some were, doubtless, in praise of their friends. The plot or story of many poems which might, perhaps, be called ballads has been handed down to us. The following is one which was popular through many ages.

There lived in a certain village a shepherd's daughter, a maiden of exquisite beauty, who had gained, through the gifts of nature, those graces which her birth denied. In a vision she beheld a wonder. The moon shone from her womb, and all England was illuminated by the light. She sportively related her dream to her companions, and was then inclined to forget it ; but they were far too earnest believers in dreams to regard it as lightly as she

---

[1] *Histor. Eliensis*, lib. ii, c. 23. These verses are written in the semi-Saxon of the twelfth century, when the language had been so entirely changed in its grammatical forms as well as in its orthography, that it could not possibly have been that used by Cnut, and at the same time the form of the verse and the rhyme belong to a later period. If there is any truth in the story, the verses *may* have been composed by Cnut, translated into Latin by the monks, in which language they appear in the chronicle, and afterwards re-translated into English.

did. They repeated the tale to the wise woman of the place, who had been the foster-mother of the king's son. The ancient matron recognised the dream's prophetic character. She sent for the young maiden and adopted her, reared her on delicate food, trained her to elegance of demeanour, and clothed her in costly attire. On some occasion, Edward, the son of Alfred the Great, passed through the village, and stopped to visit the scenes of his childhood ; " for, indeed, he would have thought it a stain on his character had he failed to pay his respects to his nurse." He fell in love with the adopted daughter, and had by her an illegitimate son, Athelstan, who succeeded him on the throne, and whose power and glory " spread a light over all England," and thus fulfilled the prophecy of his mother's dream.

There was another favourite ballad concerning Athelstan, of which the following is the story. He was persuaded by his cup-bearer to suspect his brother Edwin of treason and rebellion. Without any inquiry he caused him to be seized and placed in an old and crazy boat, without sail or oar, and with but one attendant, and to be then committed to the waves. At first the wind and tide appeared to pity him, and the boat seemed likely to be washed on shore ; but the gleam of hope soon vanished, and he floated far out to sea. Here the young man's courage failed him ; he threw himself overboard and was drowned. His attendant, with firmer nerves, recovered his master's body, and awaited his fate. He was rewarded for his courage by being ultimately washed ashore at Witsand in France. No sooner was Edwin dead than the king was overwhelmed with remorse for his crime, and with grief for his brother's loss. To appease his conscience and soothe his sorrow, he caused the cup-bearer, who had suggested his brother's infidelity, to be put to death ; and thus, by poetic justice, the last vengeance fell on the first author of the wrong.

This plot must have been very popular with ballad-mongers, for a similar tale is sung of Etheldrytha, the queen of Offa, and of Biörn, the murderer of the (famous) Danish king, Lod-brog. It is possible that the custom of putting a suspected criminal afloat in a boat without oar or rudder was looked on as a sort of ordeal, and as an appeal to the judicium Dei.[1]

[1] Lappenberg, *Anglo-Saxon Kings*, vol. i, p. 237, vol. ii, p. 32.

CHAPTER XIV.

MUSIC.

SECTION I.—ECCLESIASTIC MUSIC.

THE Teutonic nations have always been remarkable for their love of music. The Roman historians have borne testimony to its power in stimulating the German warriors in the day of battle, of consoling them in defeat, and of exciting their patriotic ardour when the defence of their native forests seemed a hopeless task.[1]

The love of song, which animated them in Germany, they brought with them to England ; and they brought it to a people as musical as themselves. It is, therefore, not marvellous that the early Saxon race should have been passionately given to music, or that one of the gravest of their philosophers and priests should have

---

[1] Mr. Chappell tells us that "the principal musical instruments of the Anglo-Saxons were the harp, the rote, the psaltery, the fiddle (which was of Anglo-Saxon origin), the cittern, and the organ. To these were added pipes, hornpipes, bagpipes, trumpets, cimbals, tabours, and drums." (Chappell's *Old English Ditties*, Preface.) The small harp was usually strung with wire, and the lyre or larger harp with gut, string, or leather. The former was played with the nails, and the latter either with the fingers or an instrument called a circulus. This instrument was possibly a short stick with a broad flat ring at the end, represented in some of the drawings published by Strutt, Chappell, Wright, and others. To be able to play with it was considered a superior accomplishment to playing with the fingers, and the penalty for injuring a harper who could so play was one-fourth more than for others. *Ll. Anglorum et Werin.*, tit. v, s. 20.

spoken of it in terms which appear exaggerated to modern ears. "Among all the sciences," says Bede, "music is most commendable, courtly, pleasing, mirthful, and lovely. It makes a man cheerful, liberal, courteous, glad, amiable ; it rouses him in battle, excites him to bear fatigue, comforts him in travail, refreshes him when disturbed, takes away weariness of the head and sorrow, and drives away depraved humours and desponding spirits."[1]

Anglo-Saxon music, like Anglo-Saxon poetry, may be considered under the two heads of ecclesiastical and lay. The music of the laity was traditional, learnt by ear and played from memory ; while the clergy were at a comparatively early period acquainted with a rough system of notation, by which they maintained a certain amount of uniformity in their chants and psalms.

There was also a difference between the lay and clerical musical instruments. The clergy early acquired the art of constructing a species of organ, while the laity were content with the simpler instruments, the harp, lyre, crowth, pipe, tabor, and cymbals.

Both clergy and laity appear to have regarded instrumental music as subsidiary to vocal. The clergy mainly used it as an accompaniment to their chants, and the laity at first to accompany their songs or choruses, and, also, at a late period, for the purpose of marking time to the pantomime of the gleemen, or to the performances of dancing bears and dogs.

The early church service was altogether musical. This was a great attraction to the Anglo-Saxon, who understood nothing of the Latin in which it was performed ; and a convenience to the Italian missionary, who could not have expressed it in the vulgar tongue. But its popularity produced some inconvenience. The uncon-

[1] Bedæ *Opera*, vol. viii, p. 417 ; Turner's *Anglo-Sax. Hist.*, b. ix, c. 9.

verted Anglo-Saxons had been accustomed to the idea that
every freeman had a right to take a part in the administration of religious rites ; and when converted they had
a strong notion of conducting divine service as pleased
them best. They insisted, in defiance of the clergy, in
bringing their dogs, hawks, and pigs to church ; and they
also claimed to accompany the choir on their crowths and
pipes, a claim which was then resolutely resisted ; though
it is permitted in certain villages at the present day.[1]

Prior to the time of Saint Augustine, the church had
divided the choir into two parts, each of which sang alternately and responsively in an appointed manner. It is
probable that the Anglo-Saxon peasant sang without any
regard to this arrangement, as we find a peremptory
order that they who could not sing in parts should hold
their tongues, and that they who sang out of time (or
tune) should be immediately turned out of church. If this
law was strictly enforced, it must have thinned congregations, and possibly might do so now.

Nothing could exceed the activity and earnestness of
the clergy in seeking musical instruction for their congregations. Teachers were obtained from Germany, France,
and all parts of Italy ; and the arrival of a great singing
master was as carefully entered in monastic records as
that of a great apostle. Each new arrival was scrambled
for with all the energy of a musical *furore:* and no remuneration was thought too great, and no dignity too
high, to bestow upon him.

Musical geniuses, however, did not always prove worthy
of the ecclesiastical honours heaped upon them. On the
death of Damian, bishop of Rochester, archbishop Theodore appointed as his successor Putta, " a simple minded

---

[1] *Canons under king Edgar*, 26,   *History of English Poetry*, vol. ii, p.
Thorpe, vol. ii, p. 251 ; Wharton's   221.

man in worldly matters, but well instructed in ecclesiastical discipline, and *"especially well seen in song and music."* What Putta knew of ecclesiastical discipline is not stated in detail; but he was evidently better suited for the occupation of a gleeman than that of a bishop. Shortly after his ordination his cathedral was burnt down by the Mercians. He made no effort to rebuild it, but, abandoning his episcopal duties, wandered about Mercia teaching music and singing at entertainments.

It is sometimes said that the system of church music first used in England was that of St. Ambrose; but early in the seventh century the Gregorian chant was introduced into the diocese of Canterbury. In A.D. 633, it was adopted in York, and thirty years later in Northumbria. By the end of the eighth century the Gregorian system was everywhere in use, and one of the great objects of the bishops—uniformity in church music—had been secured.

Among the many unpopular measures which followed the Norman conquest, was the attempted introduction of a new system of church music. At Glastonbury, abbot Thurstan introduced a new chant which he had brought from Feschamp, in Normandy. The monks resisted the innovation, on which their superiors insisted, and from words the disputants came to blows. The abbot, being defeated, called in the assistance of the Norman soldiery, by whom two of the monks were killed, fourteen wounded, and the rest expelled. The opposition of the monks, however, was ultimately successful. The abbot was expelled and died in exile. *After his death* he was, in consideration of the gifts of his relatives, restored to his honours, though, unless his posthumous restoration entitled his family to the emoluments of his office during the years of his deprivation, it is difficult to guess the object of it.

The clergy did not confine themselves to the musical

services of the church. Thomas, archbishop of York (A.D. 1070), anticipated the opinion of Luther and Whitfield, that the devil had no right to all the best tunes ; and whenever he heard any worldly air that pleased him, and was popular, he composed some hymn to be sung to it. Aldhelm's use of secular music for religious purposes was even bolder, and is a very curious proof of the fondness of the Anglo-Saxon for musical performances.

He found that his congregation were mainly attracted to church by the music and singing ; and that, on the conclusion of the musical portion of the service, they departed without waiting for the sermon.[1] On one occasion when the singing was over, he himself left the church, disguised himself as a gleeman, and stood harp in hand at the foot of the bridge over which his parishioners must pass. Here he sang short sportive songs, and between them delivered spiritual discourses. By the former he collected his congregation around him, and by the latter he so effectually aroused their consciences that they abandoned the practice of leaving church before the conclusion of the service. "Thus," says William of Malmesbury, "he attained an end to which, had he striven by severity and excommunication, verily he would have profited nothing."[2]

SECTION II.—SECULAR MUSIC.

It has already been said that the harp, crowth, and pipe were the favourite musical instruments of the laity; but it must not for a moment be supposed that they were of equal dignity or popularity.

The harp was, *par excellence*, the instrument of the gentleman, and the psaltery was constantly played on by ladies ; but there is not in all Anglo-Saxon history a

[1] Ecgb. *Excerp.*, 86, Thorpe, ii, 110.   [2] Will. Malmes., *De Pontif.*, lib. 5.

single instance of a man of rank carrying a crowth or pipe, save when he wished to disguise himself as a person of inferior station. The crowth, the tabor, and the pipe, were all used at Anglo-Saxon entertainments; but they were employed rarely; and the two last instruments merely, as drums and trumpets are used now, to heighten the effect when a powerful impression is to be made upon the ear.

The pipe was a favourite instrument with pantomimists, bear-leaders, and exhibitors of dancing dogs. It was employed then, as by the owners of Punch and Judy at the present day, to attract spectators, and to accompany the performance. The tabor was used for the same purpose.

Every noble child was taught to harp. In the orders given by the king of Westnesse for the education of Childe Horn, the only command repeated, is, " Teach him of harp and of song; teach him 'to tug o' the harp with his nails sharp;'" and of sir Tristram, one of the most famous of king Arthur's knights, we are told, that he applied himself so in his youth "to learn harping and instruments of music, that he learned to be a harper, passing all others, that there was none such called in any country."

The most famous monarchs and the most eminent saints gloried in their skill as harpers. Alfred and Cnut, our two greatest kings, and St. Aldhelm and St. Dunstan, two of our most celebrated saints and bishops, were re-nowned for this accomplishment. St. Dunstan's perform-ances, as might have been expected, were considered miraculous. If, when tired of playing, he hung his harp up in the hall, it continued to discourse as sweet music as when the saint handled it.

To be unable to play upon the harp was inconsistent

with the character of a gentleman, and was a practical exclusion from good society ; for, at the conclusion of a feast, the harp was always passed round, and every guest was required to sing or to leave the table.[1]

The celebrated Cædmon had been a Northumbrian herdsman, and had never been taught to harp or sing. After he had risen a little from his original position, he dined one day at a club or guild of gentlemen, who, after dinner, according to custom, passed round the harp that each might play and sing in turn. When the harp approached Cædmon, a sense of shame overcame him, and he rose and left the table. He retired to the bullock-pen, over which it was his turn to mount guard that night. Here he lay down, and overcome with vexation, fell asleep. While he slept, a stranger saluted him, and said, "Cædmon, sing me something." He replied, "I know nothing to sing ; my inability in this respect was the cause of my leaving the hall." "Nay!" said the stranger, "but thou *must* sing." "What must I sing ?" said Cædmon. "Sing the creation," was the reply ; and thereupon Cædmon began to sing. . When he awoke he not only remembered the verses he had composed in his sleep, but continued them in an admirable strain. The abbess Hilda and the learned men of Whitby recognised the miraculous character of his gift of song. They recited to him passages from Scripture, which, "like a clean animal ruminating, he turned into most sweet verse ;" and eventually composed a very long religious poem which is supposed to have survived to the present day in the poetry which has been edited under his name by Mr. Thorpe.

---

[1] Bede, *Hist. Eccles.*, lib. iv, c. 24. Numerous translations of Cædmon have appeared. The latest, with a very interesting introduction, is by Mr. Bosanquet. But there is no proof that the poem is Cædmon's.

What amount of musical knowledge was originally necessary to entitle a gentleman to be considered competent to play or sing to the harp, we cannot certainly tell; but it may fairly be presumed that a very humble amount was deemed sufficient.

The art of recitation had evidently been greatly studied at an early period. Ailred, abbot of Rievaulx, says, " Sometimes you may see a man with open mouth, not *sing*, but, as it were, breathe out his last gasp ; again, by a ridiculous interception of his voice, to seem to threaten silence ; then to imitate the agonies of a dying man, or the anguish of those who suffer ; in the meantime the whole body is stirred up and down with theatrical gestures, the lips are twisted and the eyes turned round, the shoulders play, and the bending of the fingers answers to every note."

Specimens of Anglo-Saxon music, of a very early date, are still extant, such as the music to *The Praise of Virginity*, and to other poems by St. Aldhelm, but, unfortunately, they are not intelligible to us, owing to the imperfect system of notation which then prevailed. Over the words were placed certain accents, stops, hooks, and crooks (like standing pothooks and hangers), and these were intended to guide the voice up and down to certain notes ; but as they were not written upon lines, it is impossible to decide with any certainty how far the voice should ascend or descend. As a tune must necessarily be learnt by ear where the length of the notes is undefined, this shews that Anglo-Saxon music, like Anglo-Saxon literature, was taught orally.

In the latter half of the tenth century some improvement took place in musical notation. A red line was used for F, and subsequently a yellow line for C (the singing marks or neumes being written between these lines), but still the time of all notes was as indefinite as before.[1]

It is difficult to understand how, under such disadvantages, any progress should have been made in harmony, yet the nation that used the harp and the organ could not have been without some practical knowledge of concordant sounds.

In the tenth century Wolstan published a work " *On the Harmony of Tones*," which for one hundred and fifty years was regarded as a great authority ; and Osbern of Canterbury, who lived about a hundred years later, was the author of several works on music.[2] That some progress had been made in music as early as the tenth century is proved by the terms used in teaching boys to sing, which include *Answege sang*—song in unison ; *Twegra sang*—duet ; *Hluddra sang*—chorus ; *Gethwære sang*—harmony ; and *Ungeswege sang*—discord.[3]

In the reign of Edward the Confessor part-music, or part-singing, was understood in the central counties, though it had not then found its way to the west. When Hereward went as a spy to a wedding in Cornwall, he astonished the guests not only by his skill as a harper, but by his singing *with his two companions*. " He sang with them in many ways, taking any of the voice parts. At one time he sang alone, and at another in harmony of three parts with his companions, after the manner of the Girvii," a mode of singing to which his hosts were evidently then unaccustomed, though it afterwards became common in Wales.[4]

---

[1] Chappell's *Old English Ditties*, Introd., p. 5.
[2] William of Malmesbury, l. ii, c. 8. Osbern was the author of a work, *De Re Musica*, and of another, *De Vocum Consonantiis*.
[3] *Alfric's Vocab.*, ed. Wright. p. 28.
[4] *De Gestis Herewardi Sax.*, c. 6 ; Giraldus Cambrensis, *Camb. Descrip.*, c. xiii.

It has been repeatedly said that Anglo-Saxon secular music was of a melancholy, or at least of a plaintive, character. The authority usually quoted is Giraldus Cambrensis, who says, speaking of the Irish, "their modulation is not slow and solemn, *as in the instruments of Britain* to which we are accustomed, but the sounds are rapid and precipitate, yet at the same time sweet and pleasing.[1]

A more correct view of the character of English music is, perhaps, given in an old French writer, who says, "the French *sing*, the English *carol*, the Spaniards *wail*, the Germans *howl*, and the Italians *caper*." In answer to the arguments in favour of the melancholy character of Anglo-Saxon music, it is sufficient to say that its professors were called glee-men, or men who make joy; that the music usually sung were "glees," or "joys;" that it was adapted as an accompaniment to drinking songs ; and that even the gravest of its professors, St. Dunstan, sang expressly to *enliven* the court. To this it may be added, that on occasions of sorrow or distress (funerals excepted), they abstained from music. "Then there was no joy of the harp—no pleasure of the musical wood;" but when happy days returned, "the poet again sang—serene in Heorot."[2]

---

[1] O'Brien's *Round Towers of Ireland*, p. 404. *Pictor. Hist. of England*, vol. i, p. 322. Giraldus, however, refers to the Welsh and not to the Anglo-Saxon when he speaks of Britain. The *Pict. Hist.* states, in reference to the first line of the ballad, "*Merry* sang the monks of Ely," that in old English *merry* signified *plaintive;* but gives no authority for such an interpretation.

[2] Beowulf, l. 987.

CHAPTER XV.

THE GLEEMAN.

AT a very early period of Anglo-Saxon history, a considerable number of persons adopted music and singing as a profession, and were known to their contemporaries by the names of scopes and gleemen. In modern times they have been commonly called minstrels, and to this inexact nomenclature we are possibly indebted for some erroneous opinions respecting them.

They are sometimes spoken of as the successors of the British bards, and as partaking in their dignity and learning ; and sometimes as the predecessors of the Norman minstrels, whose equals they are assumed to have been in birth, wealth, and genius. The descriptions of the British bards may be looked upon as not inapplicable to the early Teutonic bards, as both were characteristic of a similar condition of society.

The Celtic bard was inferior in rank to no man but the king. He was a priest of the sun, under a quasi-theocratic government. He was one of the three sacred orders of Druids, and, possibly, the most influential of them. He was the philosopher, historian, prophet, and poet of his age ; and often held, in addition to his theological and literary dignities, the civil government of provinces and important cities.

Such was the British bard at the time of Tacitus ; but the conversion of the country to Christianity, and the conquest of England by the Romans, were ruinous to his rank and power. The clergy abhorred him, as the priest of a false and idolatrous worship ; and the Roman detested him, as a popular agitator whose songs roused a conquered people to rebellion.

The bards, we are told by later writers, possessed unity and discipline. They had been originally an hereditary caste, with a right of adoption ; and they were to the last a self-electing body, with important rights and privileges. They were subdivided into three classes. The humblest were the pupil bards, next, simple bards, and then, chief bards. A few of the most eminent may have been, at the time of Hengist and Horsa, priests in idolatrous temples ; but the majority of the chief bards were attached to the court of some prince or chieftain. In time of war it was their duty to attend their patron in all his battles, that they might personally witness what it was their province to record, and that they who were to award the prizes of valour should know the merits of the candidates.

In time of peace, when there were no laurel crowns to distribute, their position was less influential. Their most important duty was to sing the praises of their patron, and to dilate on his noble descent, his wealth, and warlike deeds. They attended him at meals, and played whenever required by his wife, courtiers, or even servants. This tended to lower their dignity, and caused them to be, in the course of time, confounded with the other officers of the household. In this position, they struggled to maintain their influence by arts they would have once despised, and at last became obsequious dependents, flatterers, and parasites.

Some of them abandoned the courts of chieftains and became "*wandering bards*," who made a trade of straying from banquet to feast, and from wedding to wake, singing for money to all who would hire them, and repaying with exaggerated compliments the liberality of their hosts.

The *family* bard, even at a comparatively late period, possessed many privileges. He was free from military conscription, he had a right to a certain allowance of public lands, a high seat in the king's hall, fees, and numerous emoluments ; but the position of the *wandering* bard was very different. He was little better than a mendicant.

There is an anecdote of Leuern (the fox), prince of Avern, which illustrates his position. This chief gave a feast, to which he invited all the minstrels of the neighbourhood, and entertained them with profuse generosity. As he was driving home he met a bard who had not arrived in time, but who immediately ran after his chariot singing his praises, and lamenting the misfortunes of those who arrived at a feast just in time to see the guests departing. The chief was so pleased with his verses that he threw him some pieces of gold, and received for thanks the verse, "The fields that the wheels of thy chariot plough, O king! bear crops of gold and blessing."[1]

It was this inferior order of bard with whom the Anglo-Saxon mainly came in contact, and from whom the majority of gleemen differed but little.

In his best days it was the office of the Anglo-Saxon

---

[1] The reader who has been to Killarney, may probably have had applications and speeches addressed to him not dissimilar to those made to king Leuern. On this story M. Ampère observes, "l'attitude de ce barde courant après les roues du char de Louern, rappelle celle des mendiants qui suivent en chantant une chaise de poste, et elle atteste la dégradation où était tombés, sinon tous les bardes, au moins un certain nombre d'entre eux." *Les Bardes Bretons*, par le Vicomte H. de Villemarqué, p. 22.

scop, or gleeman, to sing to the harp songs composed by himself or others, on such topics as the peculiarities of his position demanded. Some of them were fortunate enough to be retained in the service of princes, and bore some resemblance to the British bards. It was the duty of the chieftain's gleeman to know the genealogy of his patron, the traditions of his house, the history of his family connections, and every fact or fable that could add to his dignity or flatter his pride. After dinner, when there was "song and music together, and the wood of joy was touched," he sang these topics to the assembled feasters. If his employer's deeds were not sufficiently famous, he sang those of his ancestors, or of any one from whom, by any reasonable perversion of facts, it might be alleged that he was descended.

Whenever the table was honoured by the presence of a distinguished guest, it was his duty to improvise verses in his honour. On Beowulf's return to Hrothgar, after the conquest of the terrible Grendel, the household bard sang his deeds. "The king's thane—a man laden with lofty themes—thoughtful of song (he who a great multitude of old traditions remembered), who invented new ones, fitly composed, this man now began Beowulf's expedition skilfully to relate."[1]

When no illustrious strangers were present, they sang the praises of some one of the king's companions, lauding him above the rest. This they called "the right of bestowing praise," and they wisely valued it, as giving them with a warlike and vain people enormous influence. Again and again, we are told in British and Saxon verse, that "he who conferreth praise hath, under the heavens, high established sway."[2] The spirit of Norman chivalry, which transferred this privilege from the bards to the

[1] Beowulf, v. 1728.　　　[2] *Codex Exoniensis*, p. 327.

ladies was a grave blow and great discouragement to them.

The office of the minstrel, however, was not confined to praise. If it was necessary that he should be eloquent in compliment to friends, he was required to be not less accomplished in abusing foes.[1] If there was any one to whom his chief desired to send an insulting retort, or an irritating defiance, it was the duty of the family minstrel to compose it, and after rehearsing it in a highly seasoned form to his own clan, to deliver it to the enemy.

In the earliest Saxon, and, also, in the Norman era, the gleeman possessed a privileged character, which was at first that of a licensed jester, and afterwards that of an humble order of ambassador. In both of these he was to a certain extent protected from the consequences of his vicarious impertinence. There is a curious instance of this in the *Morte d'Arthur*. Sir Launcelot had been offended by a letter from Mark, king of Cornwall, wherein he spake shame of the queen and Sir Launcelot. He was comforted by a knight named Sir Dinadan, who tells him "I will make a lay for him, and when it is made I shall make a harper for *to sing it before him :* and anon he went and made it, and taught it a harper, that hyght Elyot, and when he knew it by heart, he taught it to many harpers and so .... the harpers went straight into Wales and Cornwaile, to say the lay, which was the worst lay that ever harper sang with harp, or with any other instrument. And at a great feast that king Mark made for a victory that he had, came Elyott the harper; and because he was a curious harper, men heard him sing the same lay, that Sir Dinadan had made, the which spake the most vilanie of king Mark for his treason that ever man heard. When the harper had sung his song to the end,

[1] In this he was like the bards of whom we are told, "Ούs μεν ύμνουσι, ούs δε βλασφημουσι." *Diod. Sic.*, lib. 5.

king Marke was wondrous wrath with him ; and said, 'Thou harper! how durst thou be so bold as to sing this song before me ?' 'Sir,' said Elyott, 'wit you well, that I am a minstrel, and that I must do as I am commanded of the lord whose arms I bear. And sir king, wit you well, that Sir Dinadan, a knight of the Round Table, made this song, and caused me to sing it before you.' 'Thou saiest well,' said king Mark, 'but I charge thee thou hie thee fast out of my sight.' So the harper departed."

But all minstrels were not so fortunate as Sir Dinadan's deputy. A famous harper, Luke de Barré, had sung a multitude of facetiæ in ridicule of Henry the first; and in the Norman wars was most unfortunately taken prisoner by him. The king, who had been greatly annoyed by his witticisms, ordered his eyes to be immediately put out. The earl of Flanders pleaded for him, urging the license which custom accorded to minstrels ; but the king was inexorable. " This man," he said, " being a merry glee-man, composed many indecent songs against me, and sang them openly, and made me the laughing stock of my enemies ; and since it has pleased God to deliver him into my hands, I will punish him to deter others from doing likewise." He then ordered the cruel sentence of mutilation to be carried into effect. The unhappy satirist broke away from his executioners, as they were burning out his eyes, and, dashing his head against the dungeon wall, killed himself.[1]

The king's scop or gleeman was often an accomplished poet, and like all his household ministers held the rank of thane. It was, however, but a small number of gleemen who could find entertainment at the courts of princes ; the great majority had to rely on public patronage ; and to do so effectually, they were compelled to adapt them-

[1] *Ordericus Vitalis*, lib. xii, c. 39.

selves to the public taste. In this they were pre-eminently successful. They were passionately beloved by the laity, high and low, rich and poor; and not less so by the humbler order of the clergy, though the bishops and superior clergy regarded them as children of the devil, mockers, and vagabonds.

Their profession procured them whenever they chose free admission to the camp, the monastery, or the ale-house, and the assumption of the gleeman's garb, harp, and manners, often enabled spies to examine a foe's entrenchments, and sometimes to plan humbler attacks on a monastic larder, or on a convent's loveliness.

The stories of the adoption of a minstrel's disguise for the purpose of military espionage are so numerous that one must serve as a specimen of all. In the wars between Athelstan and the Danes, Anlaf, or Olaff (his name in Danish), desiring to obtain authentic information as to the number and position of the English forces, disguised himself as a gleeman, boldly entered the English camp, and sang to the king and his generals at dinner. He was liberally rewarded for his song, and after wandering about and ascertaining all he wished, he left the camp. As he did so, he flung away the money he had received. This act was noticed by a Danish soldier, who had formerly served under Anlaf. He at once guessed the pretended gleeman's object, and warned the king of the imposture and its probable consequences. Athelstan reproached him with not having sooner betrayed the hostile chieftain; to which the soldier replied, "King, the same oath that I have taken to you, I took to Anlaf; had I violated it you might have expected similar treachery towards yourself; but deign to listen to my counsel; move your tent to some other spot, and await reinforcements." Athelstan followed the soldier's advice.

In the evening the bishop of Sherborne arrived with additional forces, and established his quarters on the spot previously occupied by the king. During the night Anlaf and his followers forced their way into the entrenchments, surprised the bishop, and slew him and all his attendants. Following up their success, they attacked the king, and were only repulsed after a long and doubtful contest.[1]

Similar stories are told of Baldulph (in Geoffrey of Monmouth), and of Alfred the Great.[2]

If the camp was always open to the gleeman, the cathedral and the monastery were not less so. It is not probable that any but very lax abbots or abbesses would have sanctioned their performances in monasteries or convents; but the abbots and abbesses were not always strict, and sometimes enjoyed worldly amusements as much as their inferiors. In the middle of the tenth century the monasteries were said to have become a receptacle " for the sportive arts of poets, musicians, harpers, and buffoons;" "to be the brothels of prostitutes, and the rendezvous of actors." In them "there were dicing, leaping, and singing till the middle of the night," under the auspices of the gleemen ; and, when *they* were too tired to continue the sport, the younger monks and clergy adopted their costume, and sang, and leapt, and acted the gleeman.[3] The gleemen revenged the imitation, and, dressing themselves as ecclesiastics, gave faceti-

---

[1] Will. Malmes., *Hist. Reg. Angl.*, ii, c. 6; *De Gestis Pontif.*, lib. ii.

[2] Baldulph, when he disguised himself as a minstrel, *shaved himself* like a serf, which shews the ordinary rank of the wandering gleeman. The story as told of Alfred rests on the authority of William of Malmesbury and Ingulphus, the latter not possessing much weight with modern critics. Asser, in his life of Alfred,

does not mention it. It may be observed that Alfred is represented as having his harp carried behind him by a servant, which a Norman minstrel would have done, but which would have been fatal to his disguise as an Anglo-Saxon gleeman.

[3] Spelman's *Concilia*, vol. i, p. 97 and 159 ; Edgar's *Canons*, c. 58, Thorpe, ii, 57 ; Seldeni *Notæ et Spicilegium ad Eadmerum*, p. 161.

ous imitations of the superior clergy. The gleemaidens added their share to the riot, and more than their share to the scandal. When their male companions took their departure, they so often remained behind in the private houses of the priests, that at length a canon of the church absolutely forbad bishops and priests to keep gleemaidens in their dwellings.[1]   On the reformation under king Edgar, gleemen were expelled from the monasteries, but the monks and inferior clergy followed them to the village ale-houses, and there amused themselves with acting as "ale-poets" and gleemen, to the extreme annoyance of their superiors.

If the gleemen were popular with the laity and inferior clergy, they were the reverse with the superior ecclesiastics, who thought no name too bad for them. They are rarely spoken of in ecclesiastic chronicles as scopes or gleemen, poets or minstrels, but almost always as ale-poets, harpers, pantomimists, tumblers, saucy jesters, ribalds, players, jugglers, or mimics.[2]

At first it seems difficult to understand why the bishops should have detested them so vehemently as they did. That they were persons of very disorderly lives, cannot be doubted; but so were the kings and most of the nobles. It is probable that their habits of singing lampoons and squibs, of which the clergy were the butt, and of giving comic imitations of them and of their religious ceremonies, were the main causes of offence. The irritation must have been aggravated by the fact that the grand festivals of the church were chosen for these offensive performances ; and that they took place, sometimes in the church, commonly in the churchyard, and often

---

[1] Ecgb. *Excerp.*, s. 15, Thorpe, ii, 99; Spelman's *Concil.*, vol. i, p. 159; Gildas, *De Excid. Britt.*, s. 66, p. 73. (Edit. Hist. Soc.)
[2] Ludov. Imp. *Caput. Add.*, iii, 42, Lindenbrog, 1163 ; Archbish. Alfric's *Vocab.*, p. 39, in Wright's *Book of Vocab.;* Percy's *Reliques*, vol. i, p. 73 ; Warton's *Ancient Poetry*, vol. i, p. 240, note M.

during the performance of divine service.[1] Saint Dunstan indignantly forbad that the minstrels' "heathen songs and devil's games" should be celebrated on feast-days.[2]

The clergy revenged the lampoons of the gleemen by inventing numerous legends of their miraculous punishment, and by constantly holding them up to public execration. The following story we are solemnly assured is undoubtedly true.

In a public street leading to Rome, there lived two old witches, the most drunken and filthy creatures that can be conceived. On a certain night they took in a lad to lodge with them, who got his living by stage dancing, and turned him into an ass. In his new form the lad retained his talents and habits, though he had lost his power of speech ; and he went through his comicalities whenever the old women chose to exhibit him. After making much money by him, they sold him to a rich neighbour, who was warned that if he would retain him as a dancer, he must keep him from running water. For some time the ass amused his new master, till, through the negligence of a groom, he got loose, plunged into a stream, and by rolling in it a long time recovered his human form. Shortly afterwards the groom, who was looking for his lost charge, met him, and asked him if he had seen an ass ? The player replied, "that he had *not* seen one, but that he *had been* one." The groom heard his story, repeated it to his master, who reported it to the pope. The old women were seized, condemned, and executed ; and the history was narrated as shewing the results of stage playing in men, and witchcraft in old women.[3]

But being merely turned into an ass was a very insufficient punishment for gleemen who sang in church-

[1] Du Cange, *voce Choreare.*   [2] William of Malmesb., *Gest. Reg.*
[3] Edgar's *Canons*, c. 18, Thorpe, ii,   *Angl.*, lib. ii, c. 10. p. 282.
249.

yards in church time. What happened to such aggravated and aggravating offenders shall be told in the words of "one Ethelbert, a sinner," who (A.D. 1012) had been guilty of this offence. He says "we were on Christmas eve in a town in Saxony, where was a church sacred to St. Magnus, and in which a priest named Robert had begun to celebrate mass. I was in the churchyard with eighteen companions, fifteen men and three women, dancing and singing profane songs, so that we interrupted the priest, and our voices were heard above the sacred solemnity of the mass. Wherefore, having in vain commanded us to be silent, he cursed us in the following words : 'May it please God and St. Magnus that you may remain there singing for a whole year.' His words had their effect. The son of John the priest seized his sister, who was singing with us, by the arm and tore it from the body, but not a drop of blood flowed. She also remained a whole year with us dancing and singing. The rain fell not upon us, nor did cold, or heat, or hunger, or thirst, or fatigue, assail us ; but we kept on singing as if we had been insane. First we sank into the ground up to our knees, next to our thighs ; a covering was at last, by God's permission, built over us to keep out the rain. When a year had elapsed, Herbert, bishop of Cologne, released us from the tie by which we were bound, and reconciled us before the altar of St. Magnus. The daughter of the priest and the two other women died immediately, and the rest of us slept three whole days and nights ; some died afterwards, and are famed for miracles, and the remainder betrayed their punishment by the trembling of their limbs." The truth of this story was solemnly certified (A.D. 1013) by Peregrine, archbishop of Cologne.[1]

These stories may appear to us merely silly, but it

[1] Will. Malmes., *De Gestis Regum Anglorum*, lib. ii, c. 10, p. 285.

must be remembered that they were taught in those days as solemn truths, equal in veracity, if not in importance, to the doctrine of the incarnation, resurrection, or redemption, with which, in the eyes of the vulgar, they were amalgamated as a part of an indivisible and perfect scheme of Christianity. To shake their faith in any part of this teaching was to throw a doubt upon the whole ; and to ridicule these absurdities would have provoked a disbelief of fundamental truths. It was, therefore, the duty of the laity to believe all these tales against the gleemen, as a part of the Christian faith ; and to look upon them as outcasts from the communion of the church. But the clergy did not leave the question of the communion with gleemen a matter of inference. They formally excommunicated every gleeman, and refused him either baptism or absolution, even when *in articulo mortis*. This archbishop Theodore disapproved, and insisted that reconciliation to the church was not to be "*unconditionally* refused to actors, gleemen, and other persons of that sort."[1]

From the unpopularity of the gleemen with the clergy, and its possible causes, we will pass to the occupations by which the humbler members of the fraternity endeavoured to obtain their bread. The minstrels who could not obtain appointments at the courts of princes were obliged to live upon the general public. They at first gave a preference to the houses of powerful earls, and wandered from one to the other as long as they could obtain support. Even if they were not permanently retained, their visits were acceptable, as, in times when there were neither newspapers nor posts, they were the best, if not the only, medium of receiving and conveying intelligence.

---

[1] Theod. *Pœnit.*, xli, 6; Ecgb. *Excerpt.*, 83; *Concil. Carthag.*, iii, can. xxxv; Bingham's *Christ. Antiq.*, vol. iii, p. 492, 497, vol. vi, p. 19, 263.

As their living depended on the amusement their intelligence afforded, it is probable that their narrations of
what they heard were not always strictly accurate, and
that they sometimes spiced them to suit the taste of their
auditors.   This practice occasionally produced mischief.
At a feast, at which a minstrel was present, Kenneth,
king of the Scots, having drunk a little too freely, ridi-
culed king Edgar, marvelling how so many and great
provinces could be ruled by such a paltry little fellow.
The minstrel bore the amount of goodwill to Edgar, that
the harsh laws enacted in his name were likely to produce,
and he repeated Kenneth's satire in Edgar's presence
"with all the usual raillery of such people."   Edgar
shortly afterwards met Kenneth, and invited him to take
a walk in the woods.   When they reached a secluded
spot, he repeated the gleeman's tale, adding that it was
disgraceful to laugh at a man's prowess behind his back,
and to refuse to fight him when challenged.   Kenneth
understood the hint, declined the suggested combat, threw
himself at the king's feet, sued for, and obtained his
pardon.[1]

It is not likely that the gleeman's habit of tale-bearing
was confined to the king's court ; and it is probable that
the epithets of story-tellers and scandal-mongers bestowed
on them by the clergy were well deserved.

From the mansions of the wealthy the wandering gleeman betook himself to the village ale-house, which was,
after all, the place he loved most, and in which he was most
loved.   Here he had to suit his entertainment to the
taste of a number of half-drunken boors, who were
utterly incompetent to enjoy anything beyond the most
palpable and coarse fun.   "*Media inter carmina poscunt*

---

[1] Florence Wigorn. A.D. 975; Will.   vaulx tells a similar story of Mal-
Malmes., lib. ii, c. 8; Aildred of Rie-   colm, king of Scotland.

aut ursam aut pugiles ;" and for their amusement some-thing rougher than song and music was required.

The first addition to the gleeman's legitimate attractions was loud laughter and grimace. It has been the custom of clowns in all ages, when they cannot amuse by their wit, to go into violent fits of laughter at their own jokes, that by so doing they may set on some quantity of barren spec-tators to laugh also. When such laughter is accompanied by the charming distortions of countenance, which a coun-tryman puts on when grinning for a prize through a horse collar, it is generally successful with a vulgar audience, and "gratifies the most pitiful ambition of the fool who uses it." But the Anglo-Saxons were well aware that this was a degradation to a gleeman. It was told to the honour of one of them who played before Miro, that he created amusement by his wit, without having recourse to loud laughter, or any of the usual tricks of his craft.[1]

To the attraction of singing and buffoonery, the glee-man added the performance of a species of pantomimic tumbling, all kinds of mimicry, and, in his lowest state, the exhibition of bears, monkeys, and dancing dogs.

It is difficult to form an opinion of the influence which the introduction of Norman manners by queen Emma, and the subsequent conquest by William, had on the position of the gleeman. On the one hand it ought to have raised him, as the Norman gleemen were very superior in birth, wealth, and education to their Anglo-Saxon brothers, and were, consequently, in higher repute ; but on the other, the adoption of the Norman language by the Saxon nobles, tended to throw the household minstrel, who was the most honourable of their body, out of employment. It is probable that it at first contributed

---

[1] Gregor. Turon., *Miracula Sti. Martini*, lib. iv, c. 7. "Forbid their hea-then songs and loud cachinnations." Ælfric's *Canons*, Thorpe, ii, 358.

to the wealth of a few lucky members of the superior class, who obtained magnificent gifts from the later Anglo-Saxon kings, but to the debasement of the general body.

Edmund, the son of Ethelred II, gave a villa to Hitard, his gleeman, who, in the decline of life, gave it to the church of Canterbury, and went on a pilgrimage to Rome ; and, at the time of the Norman conquest, Berdic, the king's gleeman, owned three villages and five carrucates of land in Gloucestershire ; and Adelina, a gleemaiden, owned a village in Cladford (Surrey), which earl Roger had given her ; but these are the latest records of the possession of wealth or station by the Anglo-Saxon gleeman.[1]

From the Norman conquest to the period of his utter destruction in the seventeenth century, the Anglo-Saxon or *English* gleemen gradually sank in accomplishments, wealth, and rank.

[1] *Domesday Book,* tom. i, fo. 162, and fol. 38 b.

CHAPTER XVI.

SPORTS AND PASTIMES.

SECTION I.—HUNTING.

THE most common Anglo-Saxon amusements (in addition to drinking, harping, and singing, which have been already noticed), were hunting, hawking, occasionally fishing, keeping pet animals, bear-baiting, jumping and tumbling, and, above all, playing practical jokes on one another.

Of all these, hunting was not only the most common, but, at first, the most aristocratic. There was none (harping perhaps excepted) that could approach it in popularity or fashion.

The children of the nobility were trained to it from a very early age, and it was thought a lamentable innovation when Alfred the Great insisted on their learning to read before they were taught to hunt. The clergy aided the efforts of the king to postpone the period of the initiation of youth in the chase, declaring "that it was better children should acquire a knowledge of Scripture and learn to chant, than to dig up the burrows of foxes, or to follow the mazes of hares."[1] But though the clergy suc-

---

[1] Asser, *Vita Alfredi*, A.D. 834 ; Will. Malmes., l. i, c. 3.

cceeded in the tenth century in introducing many educational improvements, they did not succeed in checking the excessive love of hunting either in young or old.

If our Anglo-Saxon monarchs resembled one another in nothing else, they did so in their passion for the chase. Alfred the Great, Athelstan, and Edgar were all famous hunters ;[1] and to Cnut's excessive love of sport we are indebted for the introduction of those game-laws which caused so much bloodshed under our Norman kings, and have been a source of discontent ever since.[2]   Harold I, while the clergy filled the churches with solemn chants, awoke the echoes of the rocks with the barking of dogs and the loud ringing of his horn, and lured away their congregations.   And even Edward the Confessor, who allowed himself no occupation that savoured of this world, was an enthusiastic sportsman,[3] and after he had passed the early portion of the day at prayers, spent the rest of it in hunting.   The clergy under whose influence he was, were themselves zealous sportsmen,[4] though numerous laws, both in England and on the continent, idly prohibited their hunting.

England, in Anglo-Saxon times, offered every temptation to the hunter.   It was covered with forests, which abounded with animals of all sorts, from the most dangerous to the most timid, and afforded sport to every capacity and every taste.   They who did not care to

[1] Asser, *Vita Alfredi*, p. 16 (*XV Scriptores*, 256).

[2] *Cnut, Constit. de Foresta* (Thorpe, i, 428).

[3] Will. Malmes., l. ii, c. 13.

[4] Theod. *Pœnit.*, xxxii, 4, Thorpe, ii, 43; Ecg., iv, 215, Thorpe, ii, 215; Edgar's *Canons*, s. 62, Thorpe, ii, 259; Ludovici *Imper. Capitul. Add.*, iii, 43 ; Lindenb., p. 1163. Charlemagne (A.D. 788) forbad them to range the forests with dogs and hawks ; and as the prohibition was disregarded, repeated it in the following year in a more severe form. (*Caroli Magni Capit. Baluz.*, tom. i, 191, 369).   That these edicts were distasteful to the clergy, is proved by the ingenious excuses they made to evade them.   They applied for and obtained permission to hunt the hart and roe, not from any love of hunting, but simply *because* they required their skins to bind religious books. Lorenz, *Life of Alcuin*, p. 139; Mabillon, *De Re Diplom.*, 611.

encounter dangerous animals, pursued the hart, hind, and wild goat; the roebuck, fox, or hare; and if even these demanded too much exertion, they could worry beavers, martens, and rabbits, with ferrets and terriers. Professional hunters found their profit in chasing stags and wild boars; while the chiefs and daring spirits preferred to do battle with the bear, elk, buffalo, or wolf.

All these modes of hunting had their charms, but the last was by far the most beneficial to the public. The forests swarmed with wolves to an extent that rendered them terrible to all but armed and bold men; while the bears, though far less numerous, added to the traveller's danger. In the winter those animals became ravenous and reckless, and being unable to find sustenance at home, committed razzias on the cultivated country, and carried off the flocks and herds of a sparse population.

About the middle of the tenth century the Anglo-Saxons rapidly increased in numbers, and their monarchs obtained a short respite from the almost continuous invasions of Danish pirates. They devoted this transient leisure to the destruction of the multitude of wild beasts which could no longer be allowed to co-exist with the increasing population. Athelstan organised gigantic hunts for the capture of wolves; and he compelled the tributary Welsh to provide him annually with as many trained wolf-hounds as he chose to demand.[1] These were distributed throughout the country, and all the king's tenants and beneficiaries were forced to maintain them.[2] When king Edgar ascended the throne, he carried on the work of extermination with increased vigour. In addition to wolf-hounds, he compelled the Welsh to pay him annually a tribute of three hundred wolves. This they contrived to

---

[1] Will. Malmesb., l. ii, c. 6.   [2] Ellis, *Introd. Domesday*, vol. i, p. 261.

do for three years; but on the fourth neglected it, alleging, as an excuse, that there were no more wolves to be found.[1] Edgar's hostility was not·limited to full-grown wolves. He compelled the villagers to ascertain their haunts, and in breeding time to destroy their cubs as soon as born. By these energetic measures he considerably reduced their number, though he did not succeed in exterminating them, as he is commonly said to have done.[2]

With the wolves, the bears probably perished also; as we hear little or nothing of them after this time, except as kept for baiting or exhibition.

The modes of hunting were almost as numerous as the animals hunted. The earliest plan for catching the larger beasts was by pitfalls lightly covered with boughs and leaves, into which they fell, and when once in could not escape.[3] But the mode of hunting elks and wild boars adopted in the tenth century demanded a far greater amount of skill and courage than any in use either before or since.

These dangerous animals were not beset, as was the custom afterwards, with an unlimited number of dogs, and while encumbered with assailants killed by a large party of armed men; but the solitary hunter took his station in the forest in the usual track of wild beasts, and employed his slaves and dogs to rouse them from their lairs; when the animal approached, " he stood before him," and killed him in single combat.[4]

[1] Will. Malmesb., l. ii, c. 8; *Ancient Laws and Inst. of Wales*, vol. i, p. 234; *Chronicon Johannis Bromton, Decem Scrip.* col. 839.

[2] *Archæologia*, vol. x, p. 158 *et seq.*; *Cnuti Const. de Foresta*, s. 27. There are numerous grants or charters centuries later than those of Edgar, in which the duty of wolf-hunting is mentioned. Strutt's *Sports and Pastimes*, b. i, c. 1; *Chron. Monast. Abingdon.*, ii, 31.

[3] *Cæsar de Bello Gallico*, l. vi, c. 28.

[4] *Archb. Alfric's Colloq.*, p. 4; Gualteri Mapes, *De nugis Curialium*, distinc., iv, c. 15; *De Gestis Herewardi Saxonis*, p. 51.

The weapons generally used on these occasions were solely the hunting-spear and knife ; but both in solitary hunts, and in the collective charge, they who did not seek desperate encounters, availed themselves of bows and arrows. These were the weapons usually employed by the great bulk of sportsmen throughout the whole of the Anglo-Saxon period.

The system of awaiting the elk or wild boar, and way-laying him on his accustomed path, had grave disadvantages. The animal might be waited for in vain ; and, if he came, might possibly be victorious in the desperate conflict. In addition to this, it was only applicable to a very limited number of animals. The buffalo, bear, and wolf, were not worth the danger involved in this mode of encounter.

To aid the hunter in these desperate undertakings, strong nets supported by boughs were stretched across the tracks of wild beasts, towards which they were driven by dogs. When once entangled they were attacked at great advantage, and destroyed with comparative impunity.

When the Danish and Saxo-Norman monarchs organised hunts on a large scale, the system of netting was found inefficient, and a combination of materials, in which nets were subservient to hazels and underwood, was formed, whereby a larger number of beasts of a dangerous character could be entrapped.[1] These hedges, which the Saxons were probably taught by the Normans to construct, received the Norman appellation of *haiæ*, and soon grew to be strong enclosures for the reception of beasts . of the chase, with an entrance which could be closed with portable hurdles. When they were not required for the purposes of hunting, they were used as pens for wild animals.

[1] Du Cange, *v. Haia ;* Spelman's *Gloss. v. Haia.*

When the king made use of any of the haiæ constructed in the royal forests for the purpose of stag-hunting, every person in the neighbourhood was required to assist in the driving and stabling of the deer under a penalty of fifty shillings ; and any mischievous interference with the royal hunt involved the most severe penalties.[1] It is told, as shewing the incredibly mild and gentle disposition of Edward the Confessor, that, on one occasion when he was hunting, a countryman had overturned the hurdles by which the deer were retained in the haiæ ; in lieu of putting the man to death on the spot, he merely exclaimed, " with noble indignation," " By God and his mother ! I will serve you just such a turn if ever it come in my way."[2]

Not only were beasts driven into these enclosures on the occasion of great hunting parties, but in ordinary times decoy-does and other animals were employed to inveigle wild animals into them. These decoys were adorned with a collar and little bells, and heavy penalties were inflicted on any one who killed or injured them.[3]

But by far the most valuable ally and property of the huntsman were his hounds, and in these the Anglo-Saxons were particularly wealthy.

From a very early period England had been famous for its dogs. For centuries prior to the Anglo-Saxon era bloodhounds or mastiffs of a very large and fierce breed had been exported to various parts of the Roman empire for the purpose of hunting bears and buffaloes ;[4] and their strength and ferocity was such, that they are said to have been able " to pull down bulls and destroy lions."[5]

---

[1] *Domesday Book*, t. i, fo. 566, and fo. 252; *Ll. Edwardi Conf.*, s. 35.
[2] Will. Malmesb., l. ii, c. 13.
[3] *Ll. Salicæ*, tit. 36, s. 3; *Ll. Lon-* *gobard.*, lib. i, tit. 19 ; Du Cange, v. *Extellarius.*
[4] Strabo, l. iv, p. 192.
[5] Du Cange, v. *Canis Albaniæ.*

Under the later emperors they were valued for the desperate share they took in the cruel and disgusting exhibitions which disgraced the Roman amphitheatre.[1]

Another breed of dogs hardly less renowned was the wolf-hound, which added speed to ferocity and strength, and was competent to overtake and do battle with a stag, wolf, or bear.[2]

These dogs hunted by sight and not by scent; but there were several celebrated breeds of dogs that hunted by scent only. Foremost among these was a breed of hounds, which are described as being "warlike dogs, with eyes dropping and distorted, and lips and jowls so filthy and overhanging, that they seem to strangers sheer monsters; and the more deformed they are the more valuable they are thought, for the more their jowls overhang, the more certainly they catch the scent, and the more clearly they clarion forth the loud *howling* which marks a successful find, and from which they take their name of hounds."[3]

It is probable that these dogs were either bloodhounds or our modern stag-hounds, and that they are indebted for their reputation for "ferocity and monstrosity" to the superstitious wonderment with which, in all ages, foreigners have regarded British dogs.

They had also in use a smaller class of dogs, which the natives called "hare-hounds," and the monks "argutarii" or "canes loquaces," because they gave tongue when hunting; and a breed of hare-hounds about the same size called "canes taciti."[4]

But inferior in value to no breed of English dog

[1] Camden's *Brit.*, col. 139.

[2] Du Cange, *voce Veltris; Nemesian. Cyneget.*, 123.

[3] Du Cange, *v. Canis*. Clariorem ululatuun faventis vestigationis testem edunt.

[4] Du Cange, *v. Argutarii;* Spelman's *Gloss., v. Canis Argutarius.* Du Cange and Spelman differ as to the meaning of "Canis Argutarius" I have thought it safest to follow Du Cange.

(the bloodhound alone excepted) was the pure English veltris or greyhound, who, without the aid of scent or "breathing down," captured by dint of mere speed all the principal animals of venerie. There was also an inferior species of greyhound called "lang-lengeran" and "langeran" (possibly lurchers), kept by the poor, and held in great contempt by sportsmen.[1]

In addition to these they had "fen-hunds" or "rain-dogs" (probably a species of water-spaniel), which were used by falconers to find and put up herons, wild duck, teal, and other water fowl.[2] They had "befer-hunds" or "beaver-dogs," which, from their size, the Normans called "bigle" (little ones), afterwards corrupted into "beagles;" and they had also terriers or earth-dogs, so called, either from their burrowing into the holes of foxes or rabbits, or from their attending upon the ferrets which did so.[3] In addition to these they had a smaller breed of dog, seldom used in hunting, called by the Normans "brachs." These seem to have been generally ladies' lap-dogs, and were so exclusively feminine in their associations, that all female dogs of whatever breed were at a later time so called. They were a highly privileged class, and were allowed to nestle by the fire when all others were kicked into the yard. Like all favourites they gave themselves great airs, and were exceedingly unpopular ; and their unpopularity was soon extended, and their name sarcastically applied, to such of their fair owners as were of dainty and disdainful dispositions.[4]

These dogs differed materially in dignity and value. Among the Welsh (and probably among the Saxons at an early period) there were three *superior* orders of dogs. The first consisted of trackers, greyhounds and spaniels ;

[1] *Cnuti Constit. de Foresta*, s. 32, Thorpe, i, 430.
[2] Du Cange, *v. Canis*.
[3] Du Cange, *v. Bebar-hund*.
[4] Du Cange, *v. Canis ;* Spelman's *Gloss. v. Brach.;* Nares' *Gloss. v. Brach.*

what dogs composed the second class we are not informed; but the third consisted of watch-dogs or yard-dogs, whom the learned called " curiales," and the vulgar " curs." The trackers were divided into the three ranks of blood-hounds, covert-hounds, and harriers ; and the watch-dogs or curiales into mastiffs, sheep-dogs, and the cur proper, or yard-dog.[1]

The sum payable for killing or stealing a bloodhound was double that of a greyhound, and a greyhound was twice the price of a hare-hound, and twelve times that of a watch-dog.[2]

When Cnut and his successors introduced into England a system of game-laws, whereby the ancient and universal rights of hunting were greatly restricted, the huntsman's dog suffered with his master. No man under the rank of king's thane was allowed to keep greyhounds within ten miles of a king's forest unless they had been "lawed " in the presence of the king's forester.[3] The practice of lawing dogs, which was much extended by the Normans, con-sisted, in the time of Cnut, in cutting the knee of the right foreleg in a manner that prevented the dog running freely. At a later period the operation was performed by cutting off three claws, or taking out the ball of the right forefoot ; and when performed in this manner it was repeated triennially.[4]

In the earlier periods of their history the Anglo-Saxons usually hunted on foot, partly on account of the thick-ness of the forests, which rendered them difficult for

---

[1] *Ancient Laws and Institutes of Wales*, vol. i, p. 280.

[2] The comparative value of dogs would seem to have been rather dif-ferent on the continent. The hound that led the pack was worth six shil-lings, and the one that usually ran second was worth three. A cur or yard-dog was worth one shilling. A boar, bear, or bull-dog, a greyhound, or shepherd's dog, were worth three shillings each, but a laithund or staghound was worth twelve shillings. *Ll. Alam.*, tit. 82 (Lindenbrog,p.384).

[3] *Cnuti Const. de Foresta*, s. 31, Thorpe, i, 429.

[4] Du Cange, *v. Expeditare ;* Spel-man's *Gloss., v. Expeditatio.*

horsemen, and partly from a national dislike to horse exercise. "No man ever rides," says Alfred the Great, "for pleasure ; though some do so for health, some for exercise, and others for expedition."[1] Speed of foot was of course necessary to success in these expeditions, and was consequently a source of sporting distinction. Harold I, who was not remarkable for much that was wise or good, was so unusually swift in coursing, that he acquired the name of Harold Harefoot.

When the country had been partially cleared of forests, it is probable that the kings and earls adopted (at least to some extent) the Danish or Norman custom of hunting on horseback. Although riding on state occasions was in the Saxon-Danish period considered a mark of rank, yet riding *as an amusement* is rarely mentioned in the early Anglo-Saxon era, save in connection with an accident, a judgment on levity of conduct, or some other calamity.[2]

King Edmund (in a life of St. Dunstan of dubious veracity) is represented to have hunted on horseback at Ceoddri (Chedder, in Somersetshire). The chase was one of those collective hunts or battues which the Northmen had taught the Saxons. Edmund and his hounds selected a stag for themselves, and followed it regardless of the rest. The king *on horseback* chased it through the forest with great agility, his hounds *following* him. Near Ceoddri there are many lofty precipices and over-

---

[1] Alfred's *Boethius*, p. 20 ; Turner's *Anglo-Saxon Hist.*, vol. ii, p. 129. "Earl sceal on eos boge," "a chief shall ride on horseback." *Codex Exon.*, p. 337. Adhelm includes riding on horseback for amusement in a long category of crimes, "in quotidianis potationibus et conviviis ... in equitandi vagatione culpabili, seu in quibuslibet corporeæ delecta-tionis voluptatibus execrandis. *Vita Adhelmi, Anglia Sacra*, 116.

[2] Bede, *Eccles. Hist.*, l. v, c. 6. Among the presents sent by Hugh the Great (father of Hugh Capet) to Athelstan, when he proposed for the hand of his sister, were "equos cursores," which Strutt translates "race-horses," though "post-horses" is possibly the true meaning.

hanging deep declivities, and down one of these the stag dashed and was killed ; the hounds followed and shared his fate. The king, who was riding furiously, rushed onward to the precipice. At the last moment he perceived his danger, and strove energetically to stop his horse, but he laboured in vain ; he gave up all for lost, and recommended himself to God and the intercession of his patron saint. At the last moment, when the horse's feet trembled on the edge of the precipice, the power of the saint prevailed, and the king's life was saved.[1]

One of the consequences of hunting stags on foot was that the hunters were very rarely in at the death, and some arrangement was necessary for securing the game and taking care of the hounds. For this a British law provided, by declaring that if a hart was killed on any man's ground in the morning, he was to take care of it till mid-day ; if the huntsmen did not arrive by that time, he was to flay it, and to preserve the skin, liver, and hind-quarters, for the hunters, retaining the rest for himself. If they did not make their appearance by sunset, he might keep the stag, preserving the skin for the huntsmen, and taking care of the dogs.[2]

In the earlier times, there was no property in game. It was as plentiful as air and water, and no man cared to exclude another from the free use of it. Nor do we hear of any complaints of trespass in pursuit of it.[3]

The first limitations on freedom of hunting were introduced by Cnut. He allowed no man, save bishops, abbots, and barons, to hunt in the royal forests, and even

---

[1] *Vita Sti. Dunst., Cotton. MS. Cleop.,* B. 15.

[2] *Ancient Laws and Instit. of Wales,* vol. i, p. 286, etc.

[3] *Historia Monast. de Abingdon,* vol. i, p. 26. The monks of Abingdon obtained a charter (A.D. 821) which prohibited hunters and fal-coners from trespassing on their lands with hounds and hawks, and demanding entertainment for themselves and companions, dogs, and horses; but their objection was probably more to the compulsory hospitality which was claimed from them than to the sport.

these favoured nobles were forbidden to chase any royal beast. Every man, however, was to be permitted to hunt on his own land, outside the king's chase.[1]

The bishops, abbots, and superior nobles, were allowed to construct parks, a privilege of which, in Anglo-Saxon times, they did not very generally avail themselves. The number of parks in England at the time of the Norman conquest did not exceed twelve or fifteen; but after that event the passion for forming hunting forests became general, and led to much trouble and civil war.[2]

The social position of the huntsman rose with the passion for the chase. Originally he was a slave or serf who hunted for a master to whom he delivered the produce of his labours, and received in return food and clothing, with an occasional present of a horse or a few shillings to stimulate his exertions.[3] But in the time of Cnut the huntsmen became an organised body, varying very much from one another in rank and emolument.

This king entrusted the care of the royal forests to superior nobles, who were his chief huntsmen, and whom he empowered to exercise criminal jurisdiction in all matters affecting the property under their charge. Under these he appointed a certain number of middle men, who enjoyed the title of lesser thanes, and under these a number of minute-thanes, whom the English called "tine-men." The lesser thanes were a superior class of game-keepers, and their annual pay was a horse, a lance, a shield, and forty shillings in silver. The tine-men were under-keepers or night watchers, whose yearly wages were a horse, a cross-bow, and fifteen shillings in silver. The tine-men were often chosen from the serfs of the

[1] *Cnuti Const. de Foresta*, s. 30, Thorpe, i, 429; *Ll. Cnuti*, s. 81, Thorpe, i, 421.

[2] Ellis, *Introduct. to Domesday*, vol. i, p. 103.

[3] Alfric's *Colloquy* (Wright), p. 4.

estate, but were always manumitted on their appointment, and ranked as what our fathers called "very small nobles."[1] Under Edward the Confessor and William, the royal huntsmen rose rapidly in wealth and dignity. The names of many of them occur in Domesday book as owners of large estates ; and even the queen's huntsmen and those of minor barons seem to have been considerable landed proprietors.[2]

SECTION II.—HAWKING.

Hawking was also a popular amusement, particularly with the ladies, who preferred it to the rougher and more dangerous sport of hunting.[3] They probably were indebted for this taste to the Welsh, from whom they at first procured their hawks ; and the passion for it must have been increased by their communications with the Danes and Normans, who were enthusiastically fond of hawking.[4]

At the time of the Norman conquest, its popularity was at its height. No nobleman or gentleman travelled without his hawk, which he generally carried on his fist, and took with him even to church. So much interest did Edward the Confessor, who was a Norman in all his tastes and habits, take in this amusement, that he is said to have written an elaborate work on falconry, which for centuries bore a high reputation.[5]

The inferiority of the Anglo-Saxons as hawkers, at the earlier period of their history, arose from the fact that they hawked for food or profit, and not for sport, and

[1] *Cnuti Const. de Foresta,* s. 4, Thorpe, i, 426.

[2] Ellis, *Introduct. to Domesday,* vol. i, p. 110.

[3] Johan. Sarisbur., lib. i, c. 4.

[4] *Caroli Magni Capit.,* iv, tit. 21;

Ll. Burgund., add. 1, tit. 11; *Ll. Longobard.,* i, tit. 25, l. 37; *Ll. Boior.,* tit. 20, c. 1.

[5] This work is sometimes ascribed to Alfred the Great. (Lappenberg's *Anglo-Saxon Kings,* vol. ii, p. 72.)

consequently practised a too severe economy in the training and care of their hawks. They generally took them early in autumn, partially trained them, used them through the winter, and in the spring let them go.[1] "If a man has a hawk in the winter," they said, "it will feed itself and him, but if he keeps one in summer it eats off its own head and its owner's." When hawking was followed, not by the poor for profit, but by the rich for amusement, this careless mode of procedure was gradually abandoned. It was thought to be one of the most distinguished accomplishments of a gentleman to be able to train hawks, and to keep them in proper condition all the year round.

The English hawks must have been either of an inferior breed, or badly trained, as they were of poor reputation and low price. They were of two sorts, a large and a small breed, and were used by the general public for capturing teal, moor-hen, and small water fowl; but sportsmen of wealth, who desired to hunt cranes, herons, and other large birds, preferred to obtain their falcons from Wales and Norway.[2] As early as the seventh century, we read of a present of falcons from Boniface, archbishop of Mons, to Ethelbert, king of Kent, and of an application from the king of Mercia to the same archbishop for a similar gift;[3] and among the tributary gifts exacted by king Edgar from the Welsh were annual presents of trained hawks. At the time of the conquest, hawks had grown to be of immense value; and they who possessed valuable ones put on their legs silver rings on which their names were engraved, and armed them with small spurs like modern fighting cocks.[4] In Doomsday book we

---

[1] Archbishop Alfric's *Colloquy*, p. 5; and compare with it a document in Mr. Kemble's *Codex Diplom. Anglo-Sax.*, vol. ii, p. 380.

[2] Archbishop Alfric's *Colloquy*, p. 7; Du Cange, *v. Accipitres*.

[3] Bonifacii *Opera*, vol. i, p. 115.

[4] *Codex Exoniensis*, p. 332.

several times find a hawk valued at the incredible sum of ten pounds. It was probably in consequence of their extravagant price that aeries had been established in many counties, particularly in Cheshire, for the purpose of breeding them.[1] These aeries were of very great value, and could not after the conquest be established save under royal license.[2]

Nets, traps, and bird-lime were used, in addition to hawks, for the capture of water-fowl. The number of this species of game must have been prodigious, as the monks of Ely considered from one hundred to three hundred wild geese and ducks as the average result of a good day's sport.[3]

SECTION III.—FISHING.

It is curious that the Anglo-Saxons, who had so much taste for hunting and hawking, had none for fishing. Their lakes and rivers abounded with fish, yet at the earliest periods, though they were a nautical people, and constantly suffering from famine, they are alleged to have made no effort to catch them, until they were taught to fish towards the end of the seventh century by bishop Wilfrid.[4] It is said that finding them in a state of famine, he collected their eel-nets together, and constantly supplied them with what they considered miraculous draughts of fishes.

If this story be true, their ignorance possibly arose from the fact that the country was covered rather with meres and marshes, than with lakes and rivers ; and that eels,

---

[1] Ellis, *Introduction to Domesday,* vol. i, p. 340.
[2] Nash's *Observations on Domesday for Worcester,* p. 9.
[3] The wild fowl captured by the monks were innumerable, geese, thrushes, teal, moor hens, sea gulls, herons, and wild ducks. *Hist. Eliensis,* lib. ii, s. 105.
[4] Bede, *Eccles. Hist.,* l. iv, c. 13.

their favourite food, were so plentiful that they did not care for other fish. It is, probably, no exaggeration to say that (with the exception of the casual produce of the chase) the Anglo-Saxons in the early Saxon era lived mainly on hogs (fed on the mast or beech nuts of their interminable forests), eels caught in the marshes, and honey. Their agriculture was at first of the humblest and most precarious character; and the enormous number of bears, wolves, and other wild beasts, must have greatly diminished the produce of the hunting field.

The number of eels annually devoured considerably exceeded the consumption of the present day. The rent of mills was frequently paid in them; and one abbey (that of St. John of Beverley) received annually from a single tenant the large number of seven thousand eels.[1] The clergy had a particular passion for them; which may be probably accounted for by the enormous number of their fast-days, on which eels supplied the only rich food they were permitted to touch.[2]

Bede's rather improbable statement that the Saxons, prior to the end of the seventh century, never fished for anything but eels, is partly supported by the very limited number of fresh-water fish with which they were acquainted at the end of the tenth. Eels, eelpouts, pike, minnows, trout, and lampreys, are all that are mentioned; and most of these are to be caught in marshes and shallow streams more commonly than in lakes and deep rivers. The value attached to shallow-water fisheries is proved by the prominent position they occupy in various charters, and by the high price charged for them.

---

[1] See the *Introduct. to Domesday*, i, 123.
[2] Alfric's *Colloquy* (Wright), p. 6; *Historia Eliensis*, l. ii, p. 232. When boasting that their abbey possessed every known luxury, the monks of Ely give a list of the fish they took: eels, perch, jack, percidœ, roach, barbel, and lampreys. Occasionally they took salmon, *regales pisces*, and sturgeon.

In their deep-sea fisheries herrings were the favourite object of pursuit, particularly on the eastern and southern coasts. The canons of Canterbury received no less than forty thousand annually from Sandwich alone; and Lewes yielded not only three hundred and eighty-five thousand to the monks of Winchester, but sixteen thousand to William de Warenne. Yarmouth (or Beccles) paid thirty thousand annually to Edward the Confessor ; and as their bloaters were even then (unfortunately for the town's-men) of great reputation, William the Conqueror paid them the compliment of doubling their rent.[1]

Salmon were also in request, and were reserved as rent, though neither at so early a period nor so commonly as eels and herrings. The small number usually paid shew their scarcity and value. From two to sixteen appear to have been the usual number.[2] Eton in Cheshire, however, was an exception to this rule, as it yielded no less than a thousand salmon annually to earl Hugh.[3] According to a Welsh law, the legal value of a salmon was twopence, which was twice the value of a dish, sieve, comb, bowl, or baking board ;[4] and we read of a salmon-fishery in Wales which was worth the incredible sum of one hundred pounds of silver annually.[5] The sea fish which are mentioned as worthy of pursuit, were porpoises, sturgeons, oysters, crabs, mussels, periwinkles, cockles, plaice, soles, and lobsters. These the fishermen first offered for sale to the clergy and nobles, and, if any remained, the burghers were always ready purchasers. In addition to fishing for food and sport, the Anglo-Saxons, or more probably the Anglo-Danes, prose-

---

[1] *Domesday Book*, tom. ii, 370.
[2] Ellis, *Introduct. to Domesday*, vol. i, p. 142.
[3] *Domesday Book*, tom. i, fo. 1790.
[4] *Veneddion Code*, b. iii, c. 22.
[5] *Mabinogion* (Lady Charlotte Guest), vol. iii, p. 356 ; *Les Bardes Bretons* (Le Vicomte de la Villemarqué), vol. i, p. 40.

secuted the whale fishery with considerable success, and
dealt extensively in the teeth of the walrus, which they
used in place of ivory.[1]

Among a people so nautical as the English, even at
the earliest period of their history, swimming, skating,
and boating were sure to be favourite amusements.

To be a powerful swimmer was deemed by a Danish
warrior an almost indispensable accomplishment. Olaf
Frygesson, the famous king of the Northmen, was the
most powerful swimmer of his time ; and there are extant
several curious anecdotes of his swimming-matches, and
of the amusing tricks he played on less skilful antagonists. Beowulf, the Anglo-Saxon hero, also boasts of his
exploits in swimming. In the " brags " in which the
Danes indulged at their convivial meetings, wonderful,
and indeed impossible feats of swimming were told.
Two warriors are made to assert that they swam together
three days and three nights without intermission, and
were then only separated by a violent storm.

Skating was also a great accomplishment in the eyes
of the Danes, and the tales of the wonderful skill displayed in it are as incredible as their accounts of their
swimming. They not only, if we might believe them,
skated over lakes and frozen seas with the rapidity of the
flight of angels, but skated up to the summit of the
highest mountains, and came down again with the help
of an alpen-stock at a far greater pace.

As the Anglo-Saxons were constantly on the water,
they naturally put a high value on skill in boating.
The able use of an oar was a source of pride to men of

---

[1] Alfric's *Colloquy* (Wright), p. 6.

the highest rank. Eight kings condescended to row Edgar from West Chester to the church of St. John, while the fiery monarch sat in the stern and steered. One of the most celebrated of the vikings or pirate chiefs, boasted, that among his other numerous accomplishments, he could run or jump round a boat on the blades of the oars as the sailors pulled ; a statement which, if true, is equally creditable to *his* agility and to the steadiness of *their* stroke.

That all these " brags " were gross exaggerations no man can doubt ; but they teach us what accomplishments the people most admired, and their heroes desired most to display. Kolson, earl of the Orkneys, has left us a most amusing and valuable list of his acquirements. He says, " I am skilled in playing at tæfl, and I am hardened in nine exercises. I can explain magic signs (runes) ; am practiced in books and blacksmiths' work ; I can skate, hurl darts, and row elegantly. I know how to sing to the harp and compose poems." Kolson evidently considered himself, and was probably considered by others, the model of an accomplished chieftain, and by his enumeration of the talents on which he prided himself we may form a tolerably correct opinion as to the amusements and accomplishments most esteemed by his brother nobles.[1]

SECTION V.—DOMESTIC ANIMALS.

Such of the Anglo-Saxon clergy as paid any attention to the ecclesiastic prohibitions of secular amusements, and a considerable proportion of the nobility, appear to have been very fond of keeping domesticated animals— particularly small birds and dogs. To these they added

---

[1] Bartholinus, *Antiq. Danicæ*, lib. ii, c. 8.

deer, hawks, cranes, peacocks, and even weasels. We
have an account of an earl who kept tame ravens, which
were strongly suspected of being evil spirits in disguise ;
and of a crane kept by an archbishop, which had learnt
to bow its head and practise genuflexions when the
archbishop said grace or bestowed a benediction, thereby
earning for itself a character for gravity of demeanour,
and adding to its master's reputation.

There was no class more fond of pet animals than the
enthusiastic anchorites who had shut themselves up on
lonely rocks or barren isles from almost all communion
with their kind. Even in their solitude they retained a
spirit of humanity, and felt a yearning for something to
love, and the necessity of social intercourse, however
humble. There are numerous stories of their taming
birds to keep them company, of the marvellous intelligence
of their little pets, and of the miraculous punishment of
those who injured them.

We have a curious account of the manner in which
St. Cuthbert converted some rooks from a great annoyance into a source of pleasure. When he retired to the
island of Farne, and had exorcised all evil spirits, he constructed a little hut and covered it with fern ; but no
sooner had he done so, than a colony of rooks carried off
his thatch. The saint solemnly anathematised the thieves,
and forbad them to approach the place again. A few
days afterwards one of them flew to his feet, spread out
its wings pitiably, drooped its head, and with great
humility of manner asked pardon by the most expressive
signs. Saint Cuthbert granted it, and the bird departed.
A few days afterwards it returned, accompanied by a
companion, bearing in their beaks a huge piece of lard,
which they dropped as a peace-offering at the saint's feet.
He accepted the oblation, made the birds his companions

for many years, and tended them and their young. When noviciates came on certain festivals to visit the holy man, he pointed out to them how much they might learn even from thieving rooks, who repented, made restitution, and were received into favour.[1]

Long after Saint Cuthbert's death, his spirit was supposed to exercise a power over birds, and his name was a spell for their protection. A successor of his, at a later period, named Bartholomew, living on the same island, had a little bird whom he had taught to perch upon his table and eat out of his hand, and for a long time it had been his only companion. One day he left the island, and a hawk from the neighbouring shore pounced upon his pet, and killed and ate it. Satisfied with its repast, it attempted to return home, but it had " broken the peace of Saint Cuthbert," and the spell of the saint was upon it. The hawk flew round and round the islet the whole day, struggling to get away, but everywhere the heavens, heavy and angry, closing round it, forbad its escape. Its efforts to find a hole in which to hide its head were equally fruitless. Wearied and conscience-stricken, it at last flew for refuge to the church, and perched itself in a nook behind the altar. There, with drooping wings, ruffled plumage, and low bent head, it awaited the return of the monk. The feathers and bones strewed at the church door had apprised Bartholomew of the fate of his favourite, and the penitential appearance of the hawk pointed it out as the culprit. Appreciating its evident contrition, the monk took it in his hand, absolved it in the name of Saint Cuthbert, and, dissipating the enshrouding tempest, enabled it to fly to shore.[2]

But the tender conscience of the stricter anchorites

---

[1] Bede, *Vita S. Cuthberti*, c. xx.   [2] Regin. Dunelm. *Libellus*, c. cxi.

induced them to regard with anxiety even the trivial amount of fellowship with the world, which the possession of domestic animals suggested; and when they had more than a very limited number of such little favorites, they feared lest they should occupy too much of their time, and distract their minds from more important duties.[1]   At periods of ill-health, or approaching dissolution, these minute scruples often weighed heavily upon them.

When Robert Betun, bishop of Hereford, was seriously ill, he sent for his dear spiritual friends, Reginald the prior, and David the deacon.   On their arrival, he reproached them with faithlessness in having failed to admonish him of his sins, as they had promised to do. They positively denied the charge, asserting that they had done their duty to the utmost of their ability.   He persisted in his complaint, saying, "You know that I kept in my house a black dog with white feet, a cur, I admit, but a dog all the same; a tame stag, a four-horned ram, cranes, and peacocks, the delights of worldly vanity, which I fed with my own hands, giving them the bread which should have been given to the poor.   You knew that in so doing I was faithless, in that I took the children's bread and cast it to the dogs; and you were faithless, in that you did not reprove me."   Then, drawing out a rod and baring his shoulders, he said, "Take this and scourge me severely.   Remember to avenge my contempt of God, avenge the poor in Christ whose food I have thrown to dogs; avenge the faithful in the Lord whose souls I have endangered by my bad example." The prior did as the bishop bade him; but beat him very

---

[1] St. Boniface lays to the charge of bishop Gwielieb, as a very grave offence, that " propriis oculis se perspexisse illum cum canibus avibusque jocantem, quod episcopo nullatenus liceret."   *Vita Sti. Bonif.*, apud Bouquet, tom. iii, 668.

mildly; whereon bishop Betun snatched the scourge from his hand, and lashed himself until he had not only most grievously afflicted his sinful flesh, but his bones and his very marrow. Upon this he felt much more comfortable (as men do whose consciences are relieved from the weight of sin), and fell into a most sweet slumber. The end of the story is very sad; for the good bishop did not long survive his severe self-flagellation.[1]

The tenderness which some ecclesiastics displayed in the treatment of dumb animals formed a striking contrast to the customs of the laity. Bear-baiting, one of the most cruel of sports, was commonly practised; and in the Saxon-Norman era was highly popular. Edward the Confessor took particular delight in it, and required the city of Norwich to furnish him annually with a bear and six bear dogs, and in all probability exacted a similar tribute from other cities.[2] After the Norman conquest the kings and nobles compelled their vassals to lodge and feed their bears gratuitously, which they had long been required to do in the case of their hounds.

In the Saxon-Norman period, the bears were usually kept in bowers or out-houses; and from these they very often made their escape, to the great terror of the ladies of the family. Among the numerous adventures of Hereward the Saxon, there was one with a bear, which took place at the house of a northern thane called Gisebert of Ghent. This worthy had a passion for keeping wild beasts, which he let out at certain festivities to try the strength and courage of the young warriors who were his guests. Among other ferocious animals he kept a very large and fierce Norwegian bear; and one day it escaped from its den, and after killing everybody it

---

[1] *Anglia Sacra*, vol. ii, p. 218.   [2] Ellis, *Introd. to Domesday*, i, 206.

met in the courtyard, attempted to enter the women's apartments.   Hereward met it in the hall, encountered it single-handed, and killed it, whereby he acquired so great favour with the ladies of the establishment, that the men out of envy and jealousy conspired to murder him.

Bears were also commonly kept in England in the Saxon-Norman era, for the more innocent purpose of performing dances and tricks.   These animals would seem to have been the property of the wandering gleemen, who taught them to dance to the music of pipes and tambourines, and to make sham attacks on their owners.[1]

SECTION VI.—DANCING AND TUMBLING.

Among the amusements most esteemed by the humbler classes in Anglo-Saxon England, none ranked higher than jumping or tumbling ; but there is no sufficient reason for believing that any one but professional performers ever danced.   There is no word in the Anglo-Saxon language strictly equivalent to "dance;" nor have we any English word of Anglo-Saxon derivation for this amusement, save the vulgar one of a "hop."

The Anglo-Saxon for "to dance" was "tumbian" (to tumble), and for a dance, "hlyp" (leap) ; for a dancer, "tumbere" (a tumbler) ; hleapere and hleapestre (male and female leapers), or sometimes "hoppere and hoppestre" (male and female jumpers).[2]

In the translation of the gospels we are told that the daughter of Herodias *tumbled* before Herod ; and in two or three illuminated manuscripts she is represented as standing on her head, or rather in the act of throwing a

---

[1] Strutt's *Sports and Pastimes*, b. iii, c. 3.

[2] Archb. Alfric's *Vocabulary*, pp. 39, 66, 73, and 88.

somersault, with her head downwards.[1] There is a similar representation of her on the west door of Rouen
Cathedral, said to have been the work of English masons.[2]

The men had even less notion of dancing than the
women. They had in their German forests practised
what has been called a sword-dance — a performance
which would seem to have consisted in leaping from
space to space between the points of swords and javelins
stuck upright in the ground.[3] But in England the
sword-dance was a sort of sham-combat, not dissimilar to
the melodramatic combat which takes place at transpon-
tine theatres at the present day, and in which the cuts
and wards keep time to music.

Our ancestors also amused themselves with jumping
and hopping matches. If we may trust to the illuminations of manuscripts, the hopper held up his right foot in
his right hand, and jumped about on his left to the
music of a harp, pipe, or tabor.[4] They seem also to have
performed antics with dancing-dogs and bears, dodging
pretended attacks from these animals.

It is not improbable that Anglo-Saxon dancing was
slightly improved by intercourse with France, but at the
time of the conquest it still consisted of a rough species
of jumping, which the Norman jugglers loved to mimic
for the entertainment of their lords.[5]

---

[1] Strutt's *Sports and Pastimes*, b.
iii, c. 3.

[2] *Personal Observation.*

[3] Tacitus, *Germania*, c. 24.

[4] Strutt's *Sports and Pastimes*,
book iii, c. 3.

[5] Du Cange, *v. Bansatrices et Me-
nagium.* The opinion in the text as
to Anglo-Saxon dancing is at variance with that of Turner, Strutt,
Fosbroke, and others, who are properly considered as authorities on the
point. The following are the refer-

ences given by them in support of
their opinion. Robert de Graisstanes,
Hist. Dunelm., p. 740. His words are,
"Semper quando domi veniebat, pau-
peres villæ ante eum choreas duce-
bant." He is here speaking of Hugo,
prior of Durham, and of the year
1244, nearly two hundred years after
the Norman Conquest. It is then
stated, on the authority of William
of Malmesbury, that St. Aldhelm's
congregation used to dance before
him. Speaking of St. Aldhelm's re-

C C

The professional gleemen undoubtedly attitudinized and danced, as did the bansatrices or gipsies, who often accompanied them, and who were famed throughout Europe for their skill in dancing.

SECTION VII.—IN-DOOR AMUSEMENTS.

Of the in-door amusements of the Anglo-Saxons comparatively little is known. They probably consisted of drinking and singing, to which were added riddles and the games of throw-board, tæfl, and a species of chess. The first of these three games was preferred by the Welsh, the second by the Anglo-Saxons, and the third by the Anglo-Danes.

A very large number of their riddles have been preserved, but partly owing to their original obscurity, and partly from their having been copied and re-copied by persons evidently ignorant of the Anglo-Saxon language,

turn, he says, "Laicorum pars pedibus plaudunt choreas, pars diversas gestibus internas pandunt lætitias." "Pedibus plaudunt choreas," is probably intended as a quotation from Virgil, and does not seem to me any evidence of a custom of dancing. It is more probably an allusion to the custom of attitudinising when singing hymns or chanting : " Soliti cum plausu manuum et quadam saltatione hymnos concinere et multa simul tintinnabula funi appensa movere." (Baronii *Annal. Eccles.*, vol. i, p. 574 *et seq.; Concil. Laod.*, c. 59, Baronius, p. 571.) The other authorities commonly quoted are Fordun (*XV Script.*, 678) and Eadmer (Selden, p. 161). Both these set out king Edgar's letter to Dunstan, in which he complains of the irregularities in the monasteries, and says that there was in them dicing, leaping, and singing, till the middle of the night. We are then referred to *Ordericus Vitalis*, lib. ii, p. 872. But he does not say a word about *dancing*. His words are, " Dormitorium et crontochium et reliqua cœnobitarum abdita *scurris* et *meretricibus* patuerunt." It is probable that the two last uncomplimentary nouns should be translated " gleemen and gleemaidens," who, we know, attitudinized. I do not recollect to have seen any other authorities cited, save the illumination of certain manuscripts engraved by Strutt, Mr. Wright, and others. Setting aside all questions as to the value of these as evidence of customs, about which something might be said, it suffices to observe that in no instance are the *company* represented as dancing, but merely the gleemen and gleewomen who attend the feast.

and from our imperfect knowledge of it, the bulk of them are unintelligible to the best scholars.[1]

The following refers to Lot and his daughters, and has its counterpart in many languages.

> There sat a man at his wine,
> with his two wives and his two sons
> and his two daughters, sisters,
> and their two sons, comely first-born children,
> the father was there of each of the noble ones,
> with the uncle and the nephew (of each)
> (yet) there were (but) five in all
> sitting there.[2]

The next is easily guessed.

> A part of a field is fairly prepared
> with the hardest, with the sharpest,
> with the grimmest of man's produce,
> cut and rubbed, tied and dried,
> bound and wound, bleached and agitated,
> trimmed and poured out, and carried afar
> to the doors of the people.
> It is the joy of the inside of living creatures.
> It beats and slights those of whom when alive
> it obeyed the will.   After its death,
> it assumes to judge and to talk mixedly.
> For the wisest of men it is much to discover
> what this creature is.[3]

It need hardly be stated that it refers to the far-famed John Barleycorn.

Of the in-door games of the Anglo-Saxons the most

---

[1] Mr. Thorpe has published a considerable collection of them in the *Codex Exoniensis*, with translations of some.   In his preface he says, " From the natural obscurity to be looked for in such compositions, arising partly from inadequate knowledge of the tongue and partly from the manifest inaccuracies of the text, my translations, or rather attempts at translation, though the best I can offer, are frequently almost, and sometimes, I fear, quite as unintelligible as the originals."   There are also a considerable number of ancient riddles published in Wright's *Biographia Anglo-Saxonica*, but many of them are Latin riddles, and would not have formed the amusements of an Anglo-Saxon home.

[2] *Codex Exoniensis*, p. 431.

[3] *Codex Exoniensis*, p. 410.

ancient was the Welsh tawlbwrdd, or throw-board, the nature of which is not exactly known, but it probably bore some resemblance to draughts. It was played on a board with a king and eight black men against sixteen white ones. The king was as a piece in the game, and also in money value, equivalent to eight men, " because as much is played with him as with eight of the others." The best throw-boards were made of ivory, or the bone of the walrus ; and, like a harp, seem to have been regarded as a necessary piece of furniture by every gentleman. The Welsh princes presented one to each of their judges and superior courtiers, who were not permitted to part with it.[1]

This game was very popular in the Welsh districts, but the Anglo-Saxons appear to have preferred a game called tæfl. It was played with tæfl-stones, or dice, and tæfl-men, or table men, on a parti-coloured board, and probably resembled backgammon. It was generally played for money, and though strictly forbidden to the clergy, was a favourite amusement with them, and one by which they incurred some obloquy.[2] On one occasion a priest, who saw his bishop playing at it, shook his head at him in a scornful manner. The prelate, perceiving it, was very angry, and told the priest that if he did not shew him that what he was doing was forbidden by the canon law, he would immediately send him to goal. The priest, with an expression of terror, fell at his feet, and said, "Pardon me, my lord, I am so overwhelmed with fear that I could not repeat even the first verse of the first psalm, nor any one decree from the canons ; but I beseech you, most pious prelate, that you would recall to my mind what in my terror I have quite lost." On this, the bishop and the rest of the company began to laugh

---

[1] *Ancient Laws and Institutions of Wales*, vols. i and ii passim.

[2] *Ordericus Vitalis,* lib. v, c. 111.

and jest; but the priest being still urgent, the bishop yielded to his entreaties and repeated a couple of verses. "Blessed is the man that walketh not in the counsel of the ungodly, nor standeth in the way of sinners, nor sitteth in the seat of the scornful, but his delight is in . the law of the Lord, and in his law doth he meditate *day and night.*" "Very right, most holy father," cried the priest, "and then the *rest of your time* you may play at dice."[1]

To tæfl or dice the Anglo-Danes preferred chess, with which ‑they had probably become acquainted through their communications with the east. From the names of the men and the use of the words "check" and "mate," and the general descriptions we have of it, it was probably played much in the same manner as at present, though on a board and with men many times larger than the largest now in use. In the Saxon-Danish era it became very popular with all classes. Geoffrey Gaimar, in narrating the trick played upon king Edgar (A.D. 973) by Ethelwold when sent to report on the beauty of Ethelfrida, the daughter of Orgar, earl of Devonshire, describes her as playing at chess with her father, and adds that they had learnt to play at it from the Danes.[2] And when bishop Etheric went to the courtiers of Cnut to borrow the money with which he purchased the manor of Athelton, as mentioned in a previous chapter, he found the king and his officers playing chess at a very late hour of the night.[3]

The game was deemed a great trial of temper; and with the Danes it most undoubtedly was so. It is said that when an enamoured swain proposed to a Danish chief for the hand of his daughter, the cautious father,

[1] Maitland's *Dark Ages*, p. 34.
[2] Orgar jouoit à un echès,
Une giu qu'il aprist des Daneis;

Od lui jouout Elstruet la belle.
Wright's *Domestic Manners*, p. 46.
[3] *Ante*, p. 290.

after satisfying himself of the suitor's ability to maintain his lady-love, generally challenged him to play at chess. If he bore defeat patiently, it was concluded that he would make a good-tempered husband; but if he was out of humour at losing, he was at once rejected as unlikely to suffer amiably the petty trials of married life.

Among the most enthusiastic of chess-players was Cnut the Great, but he was by no means an agreeable antagonist. When he lost a game, or saw that he was on the eve of doing so, he very commonly took up the huge chess-board on which he played, and broke it on the head of his opponent. He was on one occasion playing with his brother-in-law, the earl Ulf, when the earl seeing that he had a forced mate, and knowing the king's weakness for knocking out the brains of successful antagonists, quietly left the table. Cnut, who guessed his motive, shouted after him; "Do you run away, you coward?" To which the other, who had lately rescued the king in an unfortunate engagement with the Swedes, replied, "You would have been glad to have run faster at the Helga, when I saved you from the Swedes who were cudgelling you." Cnut endeavoured to bear the retort patiently, but it was too irritating for his temper. On the following morning he commanded one of his thanes to go and murder Ulf; and though in anticipation of the vengeance he had taken sanctuary in the church of St. Lucius, the blood-thirsty order was carried into effect.[1]

Cnut, however, was not much worse than others. It seems to have been so common among the Anglo-Danes and Anglo-Normans for the losing player to apply the

---

[1] I tell this story as it is told by Dr. Lappenberg and Mr. St. John on the authority of Snorre, t. ii, p. 276, and Dahlmann, *Gest. v. Dänmen;* but at the same time it is right to state that Saxo Grammaticus, vol. i, p. 524, (Müller's edition), tells it rather differently.

chess-board to the head of the winner, that it is difficult
to conceive how any good player could be unwise enough
to play against a beginner. We have at least a score of
anecdotes of chess-matches, and a large proportion of
them end with the victor being struck on the head with
the board, or pelted with the heavy chess-men. In one
instance the defeated party knocked out his antagonist's
brains, and the spectators do not appear to have been
astonished or shocked. One famous player, at a somewhat later date, being asked to play a party of unskilled
players, expressly stipulated before he sat down, against
the usual misapplication of the chess-board. He beat the
youngsters to whom he was opposed, and then offered to
point out to them their blunders, and to teach them to
play better, which is a sufficient proof that he was himself
an inexperienced player or very indiscreet. In the course
of the lecture the pupils lost temper, drew their daggers,
and attempted to stab him ; but as HE was NOT bound to
abstain from the usual use of the chess-board, he caught
it up and with it brained three of them.

It is curious that a game at which no exhibition of
temper is now ever permitted, should have been then the
one that most commonly provoked it.

SECTION VIII.—FACETIÆ.

If we may judge the Anglo-Saxons by the sayings
which they have preserved as remarkable for their smart-
ness, they cannot have been a very witty people.

John Scotus Erigena was considered the great wit of
his day, but his jokes were not of a very brilliant character. He was one day sitting at table opposite Charles
the Bald, and conducted himself so rudely that the king

to rebuke him said, what is (*quid interest*) between a Scot and a sot (a fool)? Merely a table, retorted the scholar.[1] On another occasion when he was dining at the royal table, the servant presented a dish to the king which contained two large fish and one small one. He sent them to Scotus, and commanded him to divide them between himself and two clerks who were sitting opposite him. They were both persons of great stature, while he himself was a very small man. He immediately divided the small fish and passed it across the table to his huge friends, and allotted the two large ones to himself. On the king remarking on the inequality of the division, he maintained that it was perfectly even, "for here," he said, "is a small one," alluding to himself, "and here are two great ones," pointing to the fish; and then pointing to the clerks, he said, "there are two great ones," and touching the fish, "there is a small one, so there are two great ones and one small one on each side of the table."

Episcopal witticisms do not seem to have been much more brilliant than those of humbler persons. Wulfstan, bishop of Worcester, was reproved by Geoffrey, bishop of Constance, for wearing lamb's wool instead of the fur of sables, beavers, or foxes, as was the custom of ecclesiastics: he replied, "It is very well for you who are a politician and skilled in the tricks of the world to wear the skins of crafty animals, but I, who am an artless man, prefer that of the lamb." The other remarked, "If you object to these furs, you might at least wear cat's skin." "Believe me," replied Wulfstan, "my dear brother, *the lamb of God* is much oftener lauded in church than the *cat of God.*" This witty (?) answer, we are told, threw the whole company into a fit of laughter, and put bishop Geoffrey to silence.[2]

[1] Roger de Hoveden, A.D. 883.   [2] *Anglia Sacra*, tom. ii, p. 259.

Although the Anglo-Saxons cared little for verbal witticisms, they had (in common with all the cognate continental nations,) an intense passion for practical jokes, in which they indulged with the most reckless disregard of justice, humanity, and decency.

Numerous instances have already been given of the tricks they practised at feasts and weddings. On these occasions the quantity of beer and mead which was drunk formed some sort of excuse for the excessive roughness of their jokes. It must, however, be confessed, that this fault cannot be altogether charged to the account of honest John Barleycorn, for in their most sober moments they appear to have estimated the value of a practical joke, not by its ingenuity or novelty, but by the amount of insult or annoyance it caused the sufferer.

The only one of which we read that would be tolerated by the roughest jokers of modern times, was played off at the expense of Anglo-Saxon horsemen. They were in general bad and timid riders, and it was thought capital fun to tie thorns or prickles under their horses' tails, or to frighten them by shouting and jumping until the rider was thrown.[1] It was also very common to seize a man, tie his hands behind his back, and then putting a rope round his waist hang him up on the bough of a tree, and leave him in this situation till some passer-by cut him down.

We have already pointed out the almost incredible value that the Anglo-Saxons attached to long hair, as a sign of freedom and rank in men, and of rank and chastity in women; and how the want of it was the

---

[1] *Ll. Henrici Primi*, c. 903, Thorpe, 601. This joke was called by the Lombards " mer-worphin," from " mer," a mare, and " werphen," to throw down, and was forbidden by their laws. *Ll. Longob.*, tit. 36, c. 4. It was forbidden also by the Bavarians. *Ll. Boior.*, tit. iii, s. 33.

recognised mark of a slave, criminal, or prostitute.[1] Its
sanctity rendered it a favourite subject for practical
joking.   It was thought exceedingly facetious to bind a
man and shave off half his hair, and one moustache and
whisker ; and still more so to crop him in the fashion of
a criminal, who had stood in the pillory.   A milder
form of the joke, was to shave him like a slave, or
to hack his hair in a series of indentations like a
lunatic's, or to cut it so as to resemble a helmet, a
crown, or a harrow, as it was sometimes worn by professed fools.[2]

The following lines (of which the orthography is altered)
give an idea of this amusing process.

> Right unseemly, in quaint mannere,
> He him dight, as you shall hear.
> A barber he called, withouten more,
> And shove him both behind and before
> Quaintly indented out and in,
> And also he shove half his chin.
> He seemed a fool, that quaint sire,
> Both by head and by attire.[3]

The female sex were subjected to the same species of
fun as the male.   It was considered an excellent joke
to catch a young girl of good birth and character, and
crop her hair in the mode the law prescribed as a punishment for adultery.   The bitterness of the insult gave
piquancy to the joke, at least in the eyes of the jokers ;

---

[1] *Ante*, p. 175.

[2] A helmet was the favourite form
of facetious clipping. The operation
was called " Homolan." " In morem
morionis scindere." *Gloss., Anc. Laws
and Institutes, v. Homolan.* The king's
cooks attempted to play this joke on
Hereward the Saxon, when he was
disguised as a potter, but they paid
very dearly for their fun. (*De Gestis Herewardi Saxonis*, c. 24.) This

would seem to have been a favourite
amusement in the kitchen. When
Charlemagne accused Guenelon of
treason, and delivered him into the
care of his servants, the cooks immediately seized him, and entertained
themselves by pulling out all the
hairs in his beard. *Chanson de Roland*,
p. 71.

[3] Weber's *Metrical Romances*, vol.
ii, p. 340.

but the furious indignation that these facetiæ created, and the bloodshed to which they gave rise, caused them to be prohibited both in England and abroad.[1]

There was another style of joke, which, though now abandoned in England, is still practised in America, viz., that of tarring and feathering. When the bishop of Halverstadt captured a town in which there were two monasteries of nuns and friars, he caused an immense number of feather-beds to be ripped open and the feathers collected in a small space. He then stripped all the nuns and friars naked, and having first dipped them in hot pitch, rolled them in the feathers.

The jokes habitually practised on the female sex were numerous, and generally of a gross character. The customs of stealing their clothes when they were bathing, and of stopping them on the highway, and altogether or partially denuding them, are fair samples of a long list of brutalities, many of which are too coarse for description.[2]

Rough as the South Saxons were in their facetiousness, they were less so than the inhabitants of the eastern counties, who were mainly Danes.[3] One of *their* favourite pleasantries was to throw the bones of the huge joints of beef on which they dined at a companion's head. If a man took a higher seat in hall than the company thought his due, the first hint he received of their opinion was a shower of these missiles.[4] This system of bone-throwing, though very common, was not always taken in good part, particularly when, as often happened, the wrong man was

[1] *Ll. Burgund.*, c. vi, s. 4; *Ll. Alfredi*, c. 35, Thorpe, i, 84; *Ll. Burgund.*, addit. i, tit. 8; *Ll. Boior.*, tit. vii, c. 5 ; *Ll. Longobard.*, i, tit. 25 ; Du Cange, v. *Decalvare.*

[2] *Ll. Longobard.*, i, tit. 16, l. 6. Mulieri dum se lavat, si quis vestes sustulerit ut nuda permaneat. *Ll. Alaman.*, tit. 98. Mulierem in itinere vadentem, si quis denudaverit. *Ll. Longobard.*, i, tit. 16, s. 5. Mulierem ad necessitatem corporis sedentem si quis percusserit. *Ll. Alaman.*, tit. 95; *Capit. Caroli et Ludov. sup.*, c. 31.

[3] William Malmesb., lib. ii, c. 13.

[4] *Ll. Castr. Regis Cnuti* apud Bartholin. p. 538.

struck. In the reign of the Danish king Rolvo, a noble
named Anger was engaged to be married to Ruta, the king's
sister, and gave a grand feast to celebrate his wedding.
At this, a small number of persons was pleased to pelt a
certain Hjalton with bones. One of them, being clumsy
or tipsy, aimed badly, and struck a far-famed warrior, of
the name of Bjarc, who sat near Hjalton, a most violent
blow in the face. At this the jokers set up a loud shout
of laughter. Bjarc, enraged by the wound and ridicule,
having first sent the bone at the thrower's head, seized
him, and wrung his neck so artistically, that he wrenched
his chin round to his spine. On this a general riot
arose ; and, after a furious contest, the bone-throwers
were forced out of the hall. The matter did not end
here. Anger took mortal offence at the spoiling of his
wedding-feast, and the desecration of the sanctity of his
table. He challenged Bjarc to the " holm-gang."[1] The
challenge was accepted, and a most famous duel took
place between them, in which, after wonderful exhibitions
of prowess on both sides, Anger was killed.[2]

The murder of Elphege, archbishop of Canterbury, by
this same process of bone-throwing, is a very well-known
story.[3]

---

[1] The " holm-gang" was a peculiar
style of duel, so called from the small
" holm," or island, on which it was
fought. Each champion was armed
with a double-handed sword or heavy
battle-axe, and was accompanied by
his second who carried a shield. The
disputants struck at one another al-
ternate blows from above downwards,
the challenged, unless he was of inferior rank, striking first. It was the
duty of the second to interpose the
shield between his principal's head
and the descending battle-axe. The
great object of a duellist was either
by gigantic force to shiver both
shield and helmet and kill his antagonist, or so to strike the shield
that the sword glanced off and
wounded his enemy in the hip or
thigh.

[2] Saxo Gramm., *Hist. Dan.*, lib. ii.

[3] Will. Malmesb., *Gest. Reg. An-
glor.*, lib. ii, c. 10.

CHAPTER XVII.

BURIAL.

Burial is the last of the social duties connected with the home. In it the domestic relations closed in various ceremonies and superstitious practices, of which we obtain glimpses chiefly through the ecclesiastical canons against the continuance of pagan observances, but quite insufficient to enable us to treat this part of the subject otherwise than imperfectly. In the districts of England *first* occupied by the Angles, Saxons, and Jutes, numerous extensive cemeteries of the heathen period are met with, and many of them have been explored, and have furnished materials which throw much light on the conditions and manners of the people who were buried in them. In these cemeteries the graves were usually arranged in rows, and were dug exactly in the same manner and form as our modern churchyard graves, which are no doubt copied from them. After the burial a low mound was raised over the grave, also differing only in shape, for it was circular, from those in our churchyards.[1]

[1] On the subject of the primeval Anglo-Saxon cemeteries, the reader may consult Douglas's *Nenia Britannica;* Faussett's *Inventorium Sepulchrale;* Akerman's *Remains of Pagan Saxondom;* Wylie's *Fairford Graves;* the late lord Braybrooke's *Saxon Obsequies;* and a number of valuable papers in the later volumes of the *Archæologia,* Mr. C. R. Smith's *Collectanea Antiqua,* and other recent publications.

From the contents of these graves we learn that the body of the deceased was carried, no doubt in solemn procession, to the grave in the full dress worn when living, the men with their arms and military equipments, the women with their personal ornaments and jewelry. The body was, perhaps in the greater number of cases, laid on its back on the floor of the grave; but it was frequently enclosed in a wooden coffin. No instance, however, has been found of these early interments in a coffin of stone. The belief in a future life is shown by the care with which the relatives and friends of people of better condition placed in the grave, with the dead, objects which it was supposed would be necessary or useful in the next world; and even mere personal ornaments, or articles to which probably the deceased had been attached, or which can only have been placed there as tokens of affectionate remembrance. Frequent evidence, indeed, is found of the sentiments of tenderness which followed them to their last resting place. It was evidently believed that in their grave the dead were exposed to evil spirits, for amulets—especially beads of amber, which were believed to be protective against such bad influences—are usually found interred with them. The frequent occurrence, among the earth in the grave, of bones of animals which were commonly eaten by the Anglo-Saxons, would seem to show that there were both sacrifices, and feasting, at the burial; and in several instances human bones have been found in such a position as to justify us in supposing that a slave had been slain and thrown into the grave, perhaps in the belief that he would continue to serve his master in the spiritual world.

We have been speaking of the cemeteries in which the bodies were buried entire, which is almost always the case in the south and west of England; but in the districts which were occupied by the Angles, cremation, or the burning of the bodies before burial, appears to have been much more usual, and the interment consists of an urn filled with the burnt bones. It has therefore been supposed, and apparently with reason, that cremation was originally the mode of burial in use among the Angles; and that the Saxons and Jutes buried the body entire, or at least that they had adopted this mode of burial when they came into Britain.[1] It is curious that in *Beowulf*, which is supposed to be an Anglian poem, the body of the hero is described as being burnt. The poem has in this part unfortunately suffered from mutilation, but it appears that, after Beowulf's death, his fellow warrior, Wiglaf, kept watch over the body until the preparations for the funeral were made. The people wept loudly over their chief—their "tears bubbled forth," as they raised the funeral pile, which was made of Swedish pine, and was hung around with helmets, shields, and breastplates. While it was burning, the attendants seem to have raised a loud lament or wail. Afterwards, according to Beowulf's wish, they erected over him a great mound, or tumulus, round which a certain number of warriors paced, singing a song in praise of the departed chief.[2]

As it has already been stated more than once in the present volume, Christianity was established among the Anglo-Saxons much more slowly than is usually supposed, and it is probable that down to a very late period there

[1] The late Mr. Kemble, in a paper contributed to the *Archæological Journal*, No. 48, attempted to show that all the interments in these early Anglo-Saxon cemeteries where cremation was not practised were those of Christians, but he had evidently either not fully observed all the facts of the case, or not duly appreciated the evidence, which appears to show tolerably conclusively that he was wrong.

[2] Beowulf, ed. Thorpe, pp. 189, 211-214.

were people who still adhered to many of their ancient burial customs. Charlemagne, so late as the year 789, ordered his Christian Saxon subjects to bury their dead in the Christian cemeteries, and not in the tumuli of the pagans.[1] In England, the ordinary converts appear to have been drawn reluctantly from the burial places of their forefathers by the establishment of Christian cemeteries attached to the churches, and even there they seem long to have continued many of their old rites, which were certainly anything but Christian. A few of these ceremonies are alluded to in the Anglo-Saxon ecclesiastical laws and constitutions relating to funerals.

It appears from a rather curious regulation, which, though only preserved in the laws of Henry I, evidently belonged to the Anglo-Saxon period, that, as soon as any person was dead, the body was laid out, with the feet to the east and the head to the west.[2] This law enjoins any one who, either in revenging a feud or defending himself, should kill a man, not to take anything belonging to him, whether his horse, or his helmet, or his sword, or any money he may have, but to lay out his body in the manner usually observed with the dead, the head to the west and the feet to the east, upon his shield, if he have one, and to fix his lance, and place his arms round, and attach his horse by the reins ; and to go to the nearest town and give information to the first person he meets.

During the time that the dead body remained unburied, the relations and friends assembled to watch or wake over it, and this proceeding was evidently accompanied with feasting and drinking carried to an excess which will be best understood by any one who has seen an Irish

---

[1] *Capit. Carl. Mag.*, Walter, tom. ii, p. 107, Jubemus ut corpora Christianorum Saxonum ad cœmeteria ec-clesiæ deferantur, et non ad tumulos paganorum.
[2] *Ll. Hen. I*, lxxxiii, 6, Thorpe, i, 591.

"wake" at the present day. This ceremony appears to have been designedly one of merriment. So late as the end of the tenth century, archbishop Alfric addressed the following injunction to his clergy : "Ye shall not rejoice on account of men deceased, nor attend on the corpse, unless ye be thereto invited : when ye are thereto invited, then forbid ye the heathen songs of the laymen, and their loud cachinnations ; nor eat ye, nor drink, where the corpse lieth therein, lest ye be imitators of the heathenism which they there commit."[1] The clergy, however, appear to have paid little attention .to these injunctions, for they are elsewhere warned against being "hunters of funerals," and Alfric, in his pastoral epistle, tells us how some priests "rejoice when men depart hence, and unbidden gather about the corpse, like greedy ravens, wherever they see a dead carcase ; whereas it properly becomes them to bury those men who belong to their minster; and no one ought to go in another's following to any corpse unless he be invited."[2] From such allusions it is evident that the funeral feast was very numerously attended, and the guests afterwards accompanied the corpse to the grave, with loud howling (*ululatus*), at least such was the practice among the Saxons on the continent. There also, and probably at an early date among the Anglo-Saxons, they ate and drank again at the grave.[3] This last practice arose out of the older heathen custom of sacrificing certain animals for the dead, and then eating them. Saint Boniface complains that the Christian priests too often assisted in these ceremonies, in which they joined in eating the sacrifices of the dead, consisting of

---

[1] Alfric's *Canons*, 35, Thorpe, ii, 356.
[2] Alfric's *Pastoral* Epistle, 49, Thorpe, ii, 386.
[3] Et quandos eos ad sepulturam portaverint, illum ululatum excelsum non faciant...Et super eorum tumulos nec manducare nec bibere præsumant. *Capit. Caroli Mag. et Lud.*, vi, 197.

bulls and he-goats which had been offered to the gods of the pagans.[1]

We have no reason for supposing that people who were not rich were buried in coffins, but the body, having been wrapped up in its winding sheet, appears to have been merely laid in the grave, and then covered with earth. The first coffins used by the converted Anglo-Saxons were undoubtedly of wood, and it was the ecclesiastics who introduced the stone sarcophagi for eminent personages of their own order. St. Ceadda and St. Etheldritha were thus buried in wood; while St. Sexburga and Sebbi (the sainted king of the East Saxons), were buried in coffins of stone.[2] The superstitious belief that the dead were exposed in their graves to the influence of evil spirits prevailed among the Christian as among the heathen Saxons, and there are good reasons for believing that down to a very late period it was customary to place in the grave for protection a small vessel of holy water. This protection was also sought by enclosing and consecrating the cemeteries and attaching them to the churches and monasteries. The assistance of the clergy themselves was also obtained in a more direct manner, and the service of the priests was enlisted to conduct the departed soul in safety through the purgation which the church taught that it must undergo before it could attain to perfect bliss, and this was to be effected by the saying of prayers and masses. At every funeral, therefore, a payment called a soul-sceat was made to the church where the interment took place, and a legacy was also expected. A mancus of gold, or even a much higher sum, was usually paid in the case of a king or bishop, or of a person of high rank; and we read of a legacy or burial fee consisting of a bracelet, and two golden crosses, with garments and bed-

[1] Sti. Bonifacii *Epist.*, 71.   [2] Bede, *Hist. Eccl.*, iv, 3, 11, and 19.

clothes ; of another, which consisted of thirty marks of gold, twenty pounds of silver, two golden crosses, and two pieces of cloth set with gold and gems ; and another of a hundred swine, and a sum of money to be paid annually.[1] This of course was the origin of the obits of a later date.

The graves were no doubt arranged in what was now the "churchyard," in rows and covered with small mounds, as in the older pagan cemeteries, except that the mounds were elongated instead of being circular, and had head-stones. They seem at an early period to have been laid north and south, like many of those in the pagan ceme-tries, and not east and west ; such was the position of the bodies of the nuns of Hartlepool, buried towards the end of the seventh century, which were uncovered about twenty years ago.[2] It was probably considered a privilege to be buried near the church wall, and it was a still greater privilege, accorded at first only to the high ecclesiastics, to be buried within the church. This privilege seems, however, to have been in time greatly abused, so that the churches were encumbered with graves, and the terms used in the ecclesiastical canons in treating on this subject would lead us to suppose that graves were made on the floor of the church merely covered with mounds, like those in the cemetery outside. "It was an old custom in these lands," says the *Ecclesiastical Institutes*, a work of the tenth century, "often to bury departed men within the church, and the places which were hallowed to God's service, and blessed for offering to him, to make into cemeteries. Now we will not henceforth that any man be buried within a church, unless it be some man of the priesthood, or even so righteous a layman that it is known that he,

---

[1] Hooke, *Archb. of Cant.*, i, 241; Soames, *Anglo-Sax. Church*, 273.

[2] *Journal* of the Archæological Association, vol. i, p. 185.

living, by his life's deserts, merited such a place for his body to rest in. We will not, however, that the bodies which have previously been buried in the church be cast out, but the graves· which are there seen, that either they *be dug further in the earth,* or *covered over,* and the *church floor evenly* and decently wrought, so that no grave be there seen ; but if in any place there be so many graves that that be too difficult to do, then let the place be left as a cemetery, and the altar taken thence and set in a clean place, and a church be there raised, "where people may offer to God reverently and in purity".[1]

As at first severe ecclesiastical injunctions had been required to restrain the Christian converts from carrying their dead to be buried in the old cemeteries of their heathen forefathers ; so afterwards the converse took place, and, singularly enough, we find the pagans seeking interment in the Christian churches. Archbishop Theodore ordered that, when pagans, heretics, or Jews were buried in a church, the bodies should be torn up and thrown out, and the walls should be scraped and washed, and that then it should be sanctified or reconsecrated ; or, if there were any difficulty in removing the graves, that the church should be removed to another spot, and that a cross should be placed on the site of the altar.[2]

In earlier times, the tombs within the churches, as well as without, seem to have been buried under ground, and not always to have had any mark to distinguish them, and some at a later period, from motives of modesty, followed their example. The body of St. Cuthbert was buried under the pavement of the church of Lindisfarne, from whence it was raised eleven years afterwards to be deposited in a tomb above the pavement.[3] St. Swithun

---

[1] *Eccles. Inst.,* ix, Thorpe, ii, 408; *Ll. Athels.,* i, 25 ; *Ll. Edmundi Eccles.,* c. 1 and 4.

[2] Archb. Theodor. *Pœnitent.,* xlvii, Thorpe, ii, 56.

[3] Bede, *Hist. Eccl.,* lib. iv, c. 30.

was buried under the ground outside the church of Winchester, and it was not till long afterwards that his body was raised from it's grave and carried inside the church to be placed in a tomb above ground. The reason for these changes of position is easily explained. As soon as a cause or occasion was found for endowing the relics of certain individuals with the power of working miracles, it was useful to have them above ground to give more importance to their tombs. Some of the individuals thus sanctified would appear to have had no inscription externally on their original tombs, as they were only discovered by being revealed in dreams. Nevertheless, there can be no doubt that the relatives did endeavour to preserve the memory of the deceased by inscribing the name at least externally on the tomb, if it were the body of a person of any respectable family. Some years ago, the graves of some of the nuns of Hartlepool, where there was a very early nunnery, were accidentally discovered. Small flat stones, the largest less than a foot square, had been laid over the grave, each bearing a cross, and the name of the person it commemorated; some written in Anglo-Saxon runes, and some in the Roman letters of the seventh century, for to the latter end of that period they evidently belonged.[1]

The Anglo-Saxons had another subject of anxiety in regard to their graves—they appear to have been exposed to numerous depredators, for the violation and plunder of the graves of the dead is one of the branches of sacrilege to which great prominence is given in the early ecclesiastical laws. We can perfectly understand how the graves of the pagan Saxons, filled, as they frequently were, with gold and jewels, and other objects then of

[1] This curious discovery is described in detail in the *Journal* of the British Archæological Association, vol. i, pp. 185-196.

considerable value, offered no small temptation to plun-
derers, and some of them have been found in the course
of modern excavations, presenting appearances which
left no doubt of their having been opened and robbed at
a very early period.   Perhaps the graves in the Christian
cemeteries may have been opened to obtain portions of
the corpse for the purposes of witchcraft, which appears
to have been practised very extensively among the
Anglo-Saxons; but it is not at all improbable, also, that
among the Christian Anglo-Saxons the old practice, of
burying objects of some value with the dead, long continued to be preserved and cherished by many.   Archbishop Theodore, in the latter half of the seventh century,
ordered that any person who violated a sepulchre should
do seven years penitence, three of them on 'bread and
water; and the same injunction is repeated by archbishop
Ecgbert.[1]   The laws of the kindred tribes on the continent all contain enactments against the violation of
sepulchres, and state more precisely that the object was
plunder.   "Whoever digs up a dead man, and plunders
him," are the words of the Salic law of the Franks; and
another law fixes the fine which a man should pay who
had robbed a dead body before it was buried.[2]   The law
of the Burgundians enumerates, among the reasonable
causes for putting away a wife, the circumstance of her
being a "violater of sepulchres"; which, in this instance,
was perhaps intended to be synonymous with a witch.[3]

We have now traced the domestic life of the Anglo-
Saxon from the cradle to the grave; and it is for the
reader to judge whether the proposition which it is stated

---

[1] Theod. *Pœnitent.*, xxiii, 14,
Thorpe, ii, 28. Si quis sepulchrum
violaverit. Ecgb. *Excerpt.*, lxxv,
Thorpe, ii, 108.

[2] *Ll. Salic.*, lvii, 1, lxviii, 1.

[3] *Ll. Burgund.*, xxxiv, 3. Sepul-
chrorum violatrix.

in the introduction that we sought to prove has been established. Is it clear that the social state of England from the middle of the fifth to nearly the end of the eleventh century was one of marked, though irregular, progress ?

We have endeavoured to point out the gradual improvement in the social position of women and the growth of their legitimate influence ; to discover the mode in which children slowly lost the character of chattels and acquired the rights of humanity. We have also attempted *to shew* how the severity of personal servitude was diminished, and its conditions regulated ; the manner in which the rights of freemen varied from time to time, and how and when the basis of aristocratic rank was totally changed. The growth of the people in religious knowledge has not been discussed, as it is a subject exclusively theological ; but attention has been drawn to the influence of the clergy and the monks on the Anglo-Saxon Home ; and a humble attempt has been made to deal with a very difficult topic—the history of practical morality.

Inconclusive and unsatisfactory as all descriptions of manners and customs must be, which can only be discerned dimly through the mist of ages, yet enough has been probably stated to shew that the social history of Anglo-Saxon England exhibits a state of moral and domestic improvement, and that this advance may be mainly traced to the influence of the Christian religion and of Roman laws and literature, and to the adventurous self-reliant spirit of the Anglo-Saxon race.

GLOSSARY.

Acra, an instrument resembling a cobbler's knife, used for the punishment of children.

Amber, a measure, which, at the time of Edward the First, was four bushels.

Acolyth, the holder of the candle at the consecration of the eucharist and other rites.

Allodium, the allotted land of a family or proprietor held in absolute ownership and not by feudal tenure.

Bote, compensation, damages.

Carecloth, a cloth held over the bride and bridegroom during the matrimonial benediction.

Ceorl, a churl or freeman.

Ethel, hereditary—hereditary land or hereditary rank.

Fader-fioh, the father's fee, or gift made by the father to his daughter on her marriage.

Foster-lean, the amount paid by the husband to the father for the past nurture of the bride.

Fœtha, vendetta—the war of vengeance levied by the family of a murdered man on that of the murderer.

Frith, peace.

Frith-borg, a peace guarantee.

Gesith, comes—a companion—sizar, afterwards a thane.

Heulsfang, a punishment by flogging in a particular manner.

Hordere, a treasurer.

Mancus, equivalent to six shillings. It contained thirty pennies, five of which made a shilling.

Minnœ, toasts in honour of the dead—memory cups.

Morgen-gifu, a morning gift, presented by the husband to the bride on the morning after the wedding.

Morth, an attempt at *secret* assassination whether successful or not.

Morth-slayer, a secret assassin.

Mund, guardianship.

Nithing, a most offensive term of supreme contempt, for which we have no equivalent—a coward, liar, and blackguard combined—an utter reprobate.

Ora, the greater contained twenty peningas or fifty pence, and the less sixteen peningas or forty pence.

Scín-cræft, the art of raising phantoms.
Scín-lác, a ghost.
Scín-læca, a magician or wizard.
Thing, a meeting—business.
Tæfl, a game played with dice, similar to backgammon.
Theow, a slave ; "wite-theow," a convict slave, or "debt slave."
Thane, an official noble.
Viking, the captain and owner of a piratical ship.
Wed, security—pledge, whence, "wedding," a marriage.

Were,
Wer-geld, ⎰ The amount payable to the relations of a murdered man as com-
⎱ pensation for killing him, or payable by him to redeem his life
⎰ when forfeited.

Wite, a fine.
Witenagemote, a meeting of counsellors, a parliament.

ERRATA ET CORRIGENDA.

Page 60, line 9, for " staggered to" read "staggered on to."
  „   75, lines 21 and 30, for " Madame Guizot" read " M. Guizot."
  „ 110, „ 20, for " over the age" read "above the age."
  „ 118, „   7, for " men and children" read "women and children."
  „ 142, note 2nd col., line 2, for " without pressing" read " without ex-
            pressing."
  „ 183, line 4, for " any special interest" read "any special industry."
  „ 270, last line, for " previously flourished" read "previously been."
  „ 271, line 3, for " was sewed or worn" read " was sewn and were worn."
  „ 313, „ 15, for " desperate daring" read " desperate deeds of daring."

LONDON: T. RICHARDS, 37, GREAT QUEEN STREET.